THE MID STAF
NHS FOUNDATION TRUST
PUBLIC INQUIRY

Chaired by Robert Francis QC

Report of the Mid Staffordshire NHS Foundation Trust Public Inquiry

February 2013

Volume 3: Present and future

Annexes

Presented to Parliament pursuant to Section 26 of the Inquiries Act 2005

Ordered by the House of Commons to be printed on 6 February 2013

HC 898-III   London: The Stationery Office   £214.00

3 Volumes not to be sold separately

Any inquiries regarding this publication should be sent to us at www.midstaffspublicinquiry.com/contact

This publication is available for download at www.official-documents.gov.uk and from our website at www.midstaffspublicinquiry.com

ISBN: 9780102981469

Printed in the UK for The Stationery Office Limited

on behalf of the Controller of Her Majesty's Stationery Office

ID 2535330   01/13

Printed on paper containing 75% recycled fibre content minimum.

Volume 3: Contents

Annexes

Chapter 20
Culture

Key themes

- The challenge for the system is to identify a means of ensuring a common culture of positive values and methods prevailing over, and driving out, negative values and methods.

- The system requires a common positive safety culture. That is, one which aspires to cause no harm to patients and to provide adequate and where possible, excellent care and a common culture of caring, commitment and compassion.

- Aspects of a negative culture have emerged at all levels of the NHS system. These include: a lack of consideration of risks to patients, defensiveness, looking inwards not outwards, secrecy, misplaced assumptions of trust, acceptance of poor standards and, above all, a failure to put the patient first in everything done. The emergence of such attitudes in otherwise caring and conscientious people may be a mechanism to cope with immense difficulties and challenges thrown up by their working lives.

- A shared positive safety culture requires: shared values in which the patient is the priority of everything done; zero tolerance of substandard care; empowering front-line staff with the responsibility and freedom to deliver safe care; recognising them for their contribution; and that professional responsibility is accepted and pursued.

- Such a culture requires the support of strong and stable cultural leadership, mutual support in teams, organisational stability, useful comparable data on outcomes, and expectations of openness, candour and honesty.

- A positive safety culture at front-line level could be evidenced by thorough and thoughtful information provided to patients, clear identification of staff and their roles, open and receptive staff interaction with patients and visitors, meticulous attention to cleanliness, hygiene, nutrition and hydration of patients, production of and adherence to standard procedures, and insistence on proper discharge arrangements.

- Leaders of organisations must not only require others to adopt the shared culture, they must do so themselves and be seen to do so. This involves measures such as: open board meetings, personally listening to complaints, and an open and honest admission where there is an inability to offer a service. At a system level it has to be shown constantly how the well-being of patients is protected or improved by measures proposed.

Introduction

20.1   The Inquiry has heard a great deal about culture as the explanation for many of the deficiencies existing at the Trust and not found or acted on by others.

20.2   Many witnesses to the Inquiry have attributed the problems identified as due to culture. The first inquiry report identified various aspects of the culture in Stafford Hospital which played their part in the failure of service there. It is therefore important to consider what role culture played in the failures of the wider system. However, before considering the detail, we must define what we mean by culture in this context, as there are dangers in succumbing too easily to the temptation of attributing all ills to a "culture". Antony Sumara, former Chief Executive of the Trust, in a typically robust contribution to the seminar on organisational culture, quoted a telling observation of Professor John Glasby:

> *The trouble with culture is everyone blames it when things go wrong but no-one really knows what it is or how to change it.*[1]

20.3   The analysis in previous chapters has shown that in many cases there were more specific explanations for what went wrong. In that sense it is arguably too easy an excuse to attribute problems to an undesirable culture. It is an explanation which may unjustifiably offer a means of deflecting responsibility for what went wrong from organisations and their leaders. It is also a potential refuge from the task of looking for more difficult and unpalatable truths. Nonetheless, an understanding of the existing culture needs to be sought in order to consider the means by which the unacceptable behaviours identified by the inquiries relating to Stafford might be avoided in future.

What is meant by culture in a healthcare context?

20.4   Professor Charles Vincent points out that it is important to define what we mean by culture:

> *If our challenge is to change the culture, as so many commentators urge, then we need to understand what safety culture is, or at the very least decide what aspects to highlight, and bring as much precision to the definition as can be mustered.*[2]

20.5   Professor Vincent sums up culture as meaning "how we do things round here", "here" being anything from a small group or team, to a whole organisation, a profession or a health

1   *Mid Staffordshire NHS Foundation Trust Public Inquiry: Report from the forward look seminars*, November 2011, p26
2   Vincent, C, *Patient Safety* (2nd edition, 2010), BMJ Books, p271

system. More specifically, he adopts an analysis which defines organisational culture as having six formal characteristics:[3]

- Shared basic assumptions;
- Discovery, creation or development of those assumptions by a defined group;
- Group learning of how to cope with its problem of external adaptation and internal integration;
- Identification of ways that have worked well enough to be considered valid;
- Teaching new members of the group the correct way to perceive, think and feel in relation to any problems.

20.6 As Professor Vincent points out, an organisation may aspire to a common culture throughout, but in practice, in anything as complex and large as the NHS, culture can vary from organisation to organisation and from department to department. The challenge for the system as a whole is to identify a means of ensuring a positive and common culture throughout, ensuring that the positive values and ways of doing things, prevalent in much of the NHS front-line, chases out the negative which has been found in Stafford and elsewhere.

A safety culture

20.7 Within an overall culture in healthcare it might be hoped that a safety culture is an inherent component. A culture which aspires to cause no harm and to provide adequate, and, where possible, excellent care and treatment might be called a "safety culture", assuming that by safety we mean safety in a non-restrictive sense.

20.8 Emanuel, Berwick and others have defined "patient safety" as follows:

> *Patient safety is a discipline in the health care sector that applies safety science methods toward the goal of achieving a trustworthy system of health care delivery. Patient safety is also an attribute of health care systems; it minimizes the incidence and impact of, and maximizes recovery from, adverse events.*[4]

20.9 The authors remark that this definition sees patient safety as both a way of doing things and an emergent discipline. Patient safety, they say, is the "flip side of the therapeutic coin" from the risk that necessarily accompanies many therapeutic interventions.

---

3   Vincent, C, *Patient Safety* (2nd edition, 2010), BMJ Books, p272, citing Weick and Sutcliffe's analysis of the work of Schien
4   Linda Emanuel et al *What Exactly is Patient Safety?* (August 2008), Agency for Healthcare Research and Quality, p6; www.ahrq.gov/downloads/pub/advances2/vol1/Advances-Emanuel-Berwick_110.pdf; also quoted in Jarman WS0000042743, para 15

20.10   Various other definitions of safety culture have been offered. For example, the Health and Safety Executive (HSE) has used the following:

> *The safety culture is the product of the individual and group values, attitude, competencies and patterns of behaviour that determine the commitment to and the style and proficiency of an organisation's health and safety programmes. Organisations with a positive safety culture are characterised by communication founded on mutual trust, by shared perceptions of the importance of safety, and by confidence in the efficacy of preventative measures.[5]*

20.11   In the nuclear industry the International Atomic Energy Authority defines safety culture as:

> *That assembly of characteristics and attitudes in organisations and individuals which establishes that, as an overriding priority, nuclear plant safety issues receive the attention warranted by their significance.[6]*

A caring culture

20.12   In addition to safety, healthcare needs to have a culture of caring, commitment and compassion. It requires the hard lessons of a Stafford to realise that it cannot be assumed that such a culture is shared by all who provide healthcare services to patients. What are the essential ingredients of such a culture? They surely include:

- Acceptance that patients' needs come before one's own;
- Recognition of the need to empathise with patients and other service users;
- A willingness to provide patients and other service users with the assistance that one would want for oneself, or to refer them to a person with the ability to provide that help;
- A willingness to listen to patients and service users to discover what they want for themselves;
- A willingness to work together with others for the benefit of patients and other service users;
- A commitment to draw concerns about patient safety and welfare to the attention of those who can address those concerns.

Existing culture in the health service

The Trust

20.13   As in the first inquiry, the evidence has shown that an unhealthy and dangerous culture pervaded not only the Trust, as described in the first inquiry report, but the system of oversight and regulation as a whole and at every level.

---

5   Vincent, C, *Patient Safety* (2nd edition, 2010), BMJ Books, p275
6   *Safety Culture – a Report by the International Nuclear Safety Group*, (1991, Safety Series No. 75-INSAG-4), International Atomic Energy Agency, Vienna, p4; www-pub.iaea.org/MTCD/publications/PDF/Pub882_web.pdf (emphasis added)

20.14 The first inquiry report identified a number of cultural themes which were associated with the deficiencies that had been identified. They were summarised as:[7]

- Bullying;
- Target-driven priorities;
- Disengagement from management;
- Low staff morale;
- Isolation;
- Lack of candour;
- Acceptance of poor behaviours;
- Reliance on external assessments;
- Denial.

20.15 The evidence obtained at this Inquiry suggests that these negative aspects of culturally driven behaviours are not restricted to Stafford.

The wider NHS

20.16 Unfortunately, echoes of the cultural issues found in Stafford can be found throughout the NHS system. It is not possible to say that such deficiencies permeate to all organisations all of the time, but aspects of this negative culture have emerged throughout the system.

Lack of consideration of risks for patients

20.17 There was generally a lack of evidence of appreciation of the potential unintended consequences for individual patients of implementing policies, for instance, in relation to targets.

Defensiveness

20.18 For example, the treatment of Hospital Standardised Mortality Ratios (HSMR) and their implications generally started with a challenge to their reliability, rather than a consideration of what potential risks for patients were raised. Professor Sir Bruce Keogh, someone with a distinguished record in advancing the understanding of outcome data in his own specialty, described the prevalent instinctive reactions to data of this type:

---

7   *Independent Inquiry into care provided by Mid Staffordshire NHS Foundation Trust, January 2005–March 2009* (24 Feb 2010), vol 1, p152

One of the things I learnt through ten-plus years of dealing with people who didn't like what we were telling them about their heart surgery results is your first response is to say, "The data's wrong". Your second response is to say, "Okay, the data's right but your analysis is wrong". And your third response is to get your head down and try and sort out the problem. So when somebody comes along with an HSMR which is showing something that's uncomfortable, the first response is to say, "Well, there are problems with the HES data. There are problems with the coding". Then to say, "Well, this is a new kind of aggregate measure which has not been validated and all that kind of stuff". So you get a bunch of academics to argue about it. And that's what was going on the side. I think it would be fair to say that at the same time as allowing that argument to happen, it would be sensible to go in and look and see if there's a fire where there's some smoke.[8]

20.19   Nigel Ellis, Head of Investigations at the Healthcare Commission (HCC) and then Head of National Inspections and Investigations at the Care Quality Commission (CQC), thought there was a particular culture within the NHS which had been resistant to learning lessons from concerns raised, unless a full forensically based case was made for them:

I think there was something and there is something particular about the health service, being such a large – being such a complex organisation. And also, from my experience of most, if not in some cases all of the investigations that I was involved in, that what you would find after the investigation is that actually people knew all about this issue – on reflection, people who were working in this organisation knew all about this issue and had tried to raise their concerns and were unsuccessful. There's something about the culture – pervasive culture in organisations that prevented solutions, resolutions from being made, improvements from being made, which required an independent body to come in very, very thoroughly and forensically to identify, following on from the concerns, the evidence, findings of fact and reach our own conclusions, before these matters could really be properly dealt with.[9]

---

8   Keogh T123.38–39
9   Ellis T80.19–20

Looking inwards, not outwards

20.20 Ann Abraham, the then Parliamentary and Health Service Ombudsman (PHSO), suggested from her wide experience that the NHS was generally not responsive to external information or assistance:

My view is that the NHS is very good at a lot of things, but there are a number of things that in my experience, it's not good at. It's not good at capturing, using and sharing information. Lots of data, a lot less information and even less knowledge, and that's bad for patients and their families, it's bad for clinicians, bad for managers, bad for regulators and bad for policy-makers. It's not good at listening, and I've described the NHS, and I told David Nicholson and his management board this recently, it's self-referencing. It tends to measure itself against its own measures of success, by asking other people, especially users, about their experience. I suggested to a very senior doctor recently that he might ask his patients for feedback, and he wasn't unreceptive to the idea, but it was clearly a novel concept. And because the NHS is self-referencing, and it's a poor listener, it is very hard to make yourself heard. It's hard to make yourself heard even if you are the Health Service Ombudsman, and sometimes you have to make a lot of noise to make yourself heard. The other thing the NHS is not good at is partnership working, and I'm sure there's all kinds of internal partnerships, and there's lots of multi-disciplinary team-working, but I think the NHS is much less likely to see the value of collaboration beyond the NHS itself. And I think it's culturally disinclined to think of seeking information from other parts of the health system, or sharing information with them. I think it's even less inclined to work in partnership with patients and their families, but it's probably best not to get me started on that.[10]

20.21 Sir Hugh Taylor, former Permanent Secretary of the Department of Health (DH), largely accepted Ms Abraham's views:

Well, I think that's a powerful analysis. I'd find it hard to disagree with some of that. Obviously, she's speaking in generalities and there will be very honourable exceptions to that rule, but part of what I think lies behind that analysis is that she feels – felt that the NHS didn't listen hard enough to people who complained about its services. And overall I think those of us who have been proud to be associated with the successes of the NHS in recent years would acknowledge that one of the areas where we – where it needs to do better is in listening to its patients, and to the patients and to the users of services, and not just to patients, but to those who care for them as well.[11]

---

10   Abraham T108.67
11   Sir H. Taylor T126.96

Secrecy

20.22 The CQC's practice of requiring "gagging" clauses in termination agreements with staff and its reaction to the approach of CQC witnesses direct to the Inquiry has been described in *Chapter 11: Regulation: the Care Quality Commission*. This approach suggests an instinctive reluctance to face up to and react positively to challenge and a preference for suppressing that with which it does not agree.

20.23 NHS boards have had a widespread tendency to meet in private in spite of the public nature of their duties. Plausible reasons are put forward for this practice including commercial confidentiality, which fail to properly take into account the accountability that such boards owe to the public they serve.

20.24 An example of this was the episode whereby the Trust evinced reluctance to share its draft long term financial model and integrated business plan with the Primary Care Trust (PCT). The reason given by Mr Newsham, then Director of Finance at the Trust, was that a neighbouring PCT had "different resource assumptions" and was receiving more growth money than the other, and was reluctant for others to know about this.[12] It was unnecessary for the Inquiry to examine the detail of this episode, and such reluctance cannot be the subject of criticism when it would have been widely accepted as understandable at the time. In the end the documents were shared, with some provisos at the instance of the Strategic Health Authority, (SHA), but this is an example of an instinctive, and entirely unconstructive, minimisation of information disclosed, even within NHS management, encouraged no doubt by a supposed ethos of competition and commercial negotiation. The same instinct would promote reluctance to be open about quality issues and challenges.

Misplaced assumptions of trust

20.25 Much of the NHS system has appeared to operate from the premise that other bodies can be assumed to be fulfilling their responsibilities so satisfactorily that parallel duties need not be performed. An example of this can be seen in the West Midlands Strategic Health Authority's (WMSHA) closing submissions to this Inquiry:

> *... all supervisory bodies are entitled to work on the basis that the Management and Board of Trusts and the clinicians working there are persons of integrity, well qualified for their demanding jobs and carrying them out at least to a basic level of probity and competence unless and until the contrary is indicated. They are also entitled to assume that they are not being misinformed or led astray whether deliberately or through incompetence unless and until the contrary is indicated. Furthermore, they are entitled to assume that where concerns are identified they will be dealt with professionally and competently again, unless and until the contrary is indicated.*[13]

---

12   Newsham T60.187
13   CLO000000025, *WMSHA closing submissions*, p18, para 51

20.26 No organisation charged with a responsibility of supervision, oversight or regulation was entitled to assume others were fulfilling theirs. Were such a position to be considered valid it is open to question whether there was any purpose in having such a responsibility at all. It would be one devoid of any accountability, as, except in extreme circumstances, it could always be met by reliance on the assumption. However, the system appears to have operated on the basis of such an assumption. Sir Hugh Taylor said:

> I would want to emphasise that all systems do depend on levels of professionalism operating throughout them. And, of course, if people are, in a sense, deliberately or unconsciously misleading the system, or operating in ways that are outside the system, then that becomes quite a challenge.[14]

20.27 There have been numerous examples of misplaced trust exposed during the course of this Inquiry:

- Monitor's assumption that the HCC would tell it of any concerns and that the HCC knew the Trust was making an application for Foundation Trust (FT) status;
- The general reliance of the DH in its policy making and the HCC in its assessments of trusts that self-assessments of compliance were likely to be accurate;
- The assumption that the supposedly rigorous FT authorisation process would uncover deficiencies in applicant trusts leading to a less rigorous approach to the screening process;
- The SHA's acceptance of the Trust's assurances that its high HSMR was due to poor coding;
- Monitor's acceptance of the Trust's assurance it had no problems with mortality;
- The general reliance on "exception reporting" as assurance that all was well.

20.28 Organisations and individuals in the NHS all work under tremendous pressure and it is entirely understandable that they seek to identify what is their responsibility and what is not, in order to define the scope of the work to be done. Inevitably responsibilities overlap. This has led to a plethora of Memoranda of Understanding and similar policies which attempt to define the respective responsibilities of organisations with overlapping functions. Unhappily, these have not been sufficient to ensure the effective fulfilment of the tasks with which each organisation has been charged.

---

14   Sir Hugh Taylor T126.128

20.29 This phenomenon of misplaced trust appears to have been common in the period under review. Nigel Edwards and Ruth Lewis reported to the Inquiry:

> It is thought that one of the reasons for the loss of financial control in 2006 was a view that the Strategic Health Authority was working with individual Finance Directors on financial recovery plans. The idea that somebody else is taking responsibility for a complex and difficult area which is poorly understood or which creates a high level of organisational anxiety seems to be a common thread in previous failures. Implications of this are that Boards must pay attention to the whole agenda and not delegate critical issues to individuals.[15]

Acceptance of poor standards

20.30 An example of tolerance of poor standards comes from a surprising source, namely the peer review process for critically ill and injured children's services which revealed serious shortcomings at the Trust.[16] The standards by which these peer reviews were undertaken were said to represent "a minimum standard of care" and yet, in the same document the authors accepted in advance that the standards would not be met in their entirety:

> It is also clear that the Standards as published will not be currently met by institutions undertaking acute paediatric care in the entirety, but it is intended that they form a benchmark against which service configuration can be developed for the improvement of paediatric care overall.[17]

20.31 While neither the authors, nor the peer review team, can be criticised for pointing this out, rather the opposite, the SHA in particular should have ensured that steps were taken to require provider trusts to come up to minimum standards in such an important area. Instead, the SHA not only did not do so, but took no effective action even when peer review reports identified specific deficiencies at the Trust. Its failure to do so evidences a culture that tolerated substandard care and service provision in a particularly sensitive area, the care of children, a vulnerable group.

20.32 One constant refrain has been that matters of concern were thought to be ones that could have been found in other trusts. This observation was often offered as a reason why the Trust was not thought to be a cause for exceptional concern, but was also being presented as a reason why no specific action was taken.

---

15 *Balancing external requirements and a positive internal culture* (October 2011), Edwards and Lewis (King's Fund), p10; www.midstaffspublicinquiry.com/sites/default/files/uploads/Nigel_Edwards_-full_paper.pdf
16 See Chapter 4: Warning signs for an account of these reviews.
17 CJE/1 WS0000022947

20.33 An example of this was evidence given by Mrs Toni Brisby, former Chair of the Trust about her reaction to the patient stories in the first inquiry's report:

> A. One [set of reactions] is ... that it is really profoundly shocking, and I can absolutely see that. The other is a reaction that I've had from quite a lot of people within the NHS, which is actually that's the sort of thing that goes on in virtually all hospitals, and there but for the grace of God go we. Now, I'm not saying that to defend poor care, because I think poor care is indefensible, but I am saying that Stafford is not a peculiar hospital in spite of the shocking nature of part 2 of the report.

20.34 A response to a rule 13 notice of a criticism suggesting a lack of insight asserted that poor care existed in most other NHS trusts. It also referred to multiple reports from the National Confidential Enquiry into Patient Outcome and Death (NCEPOD), suggesting that, for instance, good care was only received by: 35% of patients commencing systemic anti-cancer therapy;[18] 50% of those receiving treatment for renal injury;[19] 37.5% of elderly patients undergoing surgery;[20] 48% of high risk surgical patients receiving perioperative care;[21] and 29% of patients given cardio-pulmonary resuscitation in hospital as a result of an in-hospital cardiorespiratory arrest.[22] Similarly, only 19% of those receiving parenteral nutrition had received care considered to be good practice.[23]

20.35 The knowledge or belief that matters are the same, or worse, elsewhere can lead to the comforting conclusion that more cannot be done. It is an attitude that leads to inaction and continued tolerance of unacceptable standards of service. Instead of provoking urgent and more general remedial action, a perception that a deficiency was common has led to a silent acceptance of it. The more common a problem, the less likely it has been that energy and resources would be expended in tackling it.

Failure to put the patient first in everything done

20.36 Many of the negative aspects of culture mentioned above derive from a failure to see things from the patient's perspective and to understand the effects of actions – or inaction – on them. In the maelstrom of discussions and efforts devoted to reorganisation, devising and implementing new systems and so on, the core purpose of healthcare services has all too often been overlooked. This Inquiry has seen evidence of many different examples of leaders, managers, regulators and others failing to have the interests and needs of patients at the forefront of their minds. Very few, if any, of the individuals involved have deliberately or consciously acted in this way. However, the pressures of their work and circumstances have led to this. Examples seen have included:

---

18 *For Better, For Worse* (2008), NCEPOD, p18; www.ncepod.org.uk/reports.htm
19 *Adding Insult to Injury* (2009), NCEPOD, p22; www.ncepod.org.uk/reports.htm
20 *An Age Old Problem* (2010), NCEPOD, p19; www.ncepod.org.uk/reports.htm
21 *Knowing the Risk* (2011), NCEPOD, p50; www.ncepod.org.uk/reports.htm
22 *Time to Intervene* (2012), NCEPOD, p97; www.ncepod.org.uk/reports.htm
23 *A Mixed Bag* (2010), NCEPOD, page 13; www.ncepod.org.uk/reports.htm

- Within the Trust, the reduction in staff numbers and dilution of skill mix without thorough assessment of the risks to patients;
- The general failure to act sufficiently quickly or robustly to address the patient safety implications of concerns raised about the Trust;
- The focus on coding, rather than patient care, when considering the implications of unfavourable HSMR results;
- The relentless drive to FT status;
- The loss of focus on safety and quality in assessing FT applications;
- The willingness to play down safety and quality deficiencies in public statements;
- The defensive reactions to suggestions of concerns;
- The failure of commissioners to use their powers to drive safety and quality improvements;
- The robust assertions of organisational independence at the expense of cooperation in the face of urgent safety concerns;
- The persistence in continuing with services known to be deficient;
- The absence of effective risk assessment or transitional arrangements for significant organisational changes;
- The priority given to confidentiality and support of colleagues and organisations over the duty to warn others of safety risks.

Underlying factors

20.37 The cultural tolerance of poor practice and continuing safety issues by caring people may in part be due to the difficulties people have in carrying on their daily working lives, with assessing and rationalising the seriousness of perceived harm, and perhaps subconsciously playing down the effects of such harm. This can be achieved by undervaluing the seriousness or the implications of the information before them, or by assuming that the problem is someone else's responsibility, or that it is being dealt with elsewhere in the system. The issue has been analysed compellingly by Professor Martin in the context of the direct care of patients, but what he says is equally applicable to managerial and leadership cultures:

> *To start with the most direct and intimate relationship we should consider staff views of patients. Human beings do not harm others callously unless they can justify this in some way. This is so in all walks of life, but in a hospital setting, so deliberately dedicated to the care of others, it is particularly necessary. Such rationalizations do not have to be consciously articulated, but somewhere or other in their minds some latent defence must be lurking ready to be voiced if callous behaviour is challenged. They are, as AM Rees has put it "a way of articulating the inacceptable".*

Rationalizations can be entirely false, they depend for their effectiveness on having at least a grain of truth in them. Sadists may indeed enjoy cruelty, but they are likely to justify it on the grounds of some form of utility – their duty to the Fuhrer, to the country, to regimental comrades, to the party, to fellow workers, or they may admit their wrongdoing but shift the blame to those in authority who expect results but give resources so inadequate that it is impossible to achieve them.

What have to be rationalized in a hospital setting are sins both of commission and omission. Being cruel or callous creates the most acute problem for the individual – he or she has to find a justification for a personal act contrary to all the tenets of professional conduct, and indeed contrary to everything the hospital stands for. By contrast sins of omission involve the lesser problem of turning blind eyes towards dubious acts and, unless the witness has a formal responsibility for supervision, it is often easier to do nothing than to act.[24]

20.38 Drawing on previous reports into medical scandals, he identified a number of ways in which unacceptable treatment becomes culturally permitted. These included:

- *Denial of injury* – where there is uncertainty as to whether a patient has been truly harmed by a perceived deficiency in care. Professor Martin thought this particularly likely to occur where the patients were elderly, confused and unable to communicate clearly for themselves.[25]
- *Denial of responsibility* – this includes situations where lack of resources make it difficult to provide appropriate care, "numbing" staff into believing nothing can ever be done and lapsing into "fatalistic acquiescence". It may also involve the excuse of acting on orders.[26]
- *Condemning the condemners* – Professor Martin cited a petition prepared by nurses at a much criticised mental hospital:

  We the nurses of Farleigh Hospital, feel strongly that we are now in a position which leaves us defenceless against, and wide open to, unfair criticism from people who are inexperienced in the care of subnormal people, and who are also hypersensitive and prone to exaggeration.[27]

20.39 Examples of these phenomena can be found in the evidence before this Inquiry.

---

24 Martin, JP, *Hospitals in Trouble* (1984), Basil Blackwell, Oxford, pp98–99
25 Martin, JP, *Hospitals in Trouble* (1984), Basil Blackwell, Oxford, pp99–101
26 Martin, JP, *Hospitals in Trouble* (1984), Basil Blackwell, Oxford, pp109–104
27 Martin, JP, *Hospitals in Trouble* (1984), Basil Blackwell, Oxford, pp104–105

Changing the culture

20.40 The culture will not be changed for the better unless the right attitude of mind is adopted at every level in the NHS and by all who work in it. Professor Sir Ian Kennedy told the Inquiry:

> I don't think putting the patient at the centre of what you do is a function of any particular structural approach. It's a function of culture, of what culture you'll be bringing to work every day. And that's the culture of professionals – of all ilk, whether nurses, physiotherapists, managers, and you can have as many structures as you like, and we've had pretty much all of them, but if you don't address the cultural challenge of "What are we going to work for today?", then it's going to be hit and miss whether it works.[28]

The need for a patient safety culture

20.41 Although it may now be difficult to quantify, there is no doubt that patients have suffered harm and detriment through the inadequacies of the service provided to them in Stafford. The culture found did not pay due regard to the need to protect patients from harm. "Safety" as a concept sometimes gets a bad press on the grounds that excessive avoidance of risk inhibits freedom or, in the case of healthcare, advances in means of treatment. Of course, virtually all forms of treatment carry some form of unavoidable risk, or risk which is worth taking given the potential benefits to the patient. The balance between taking and avoiding significant risks of that type is one to be drawn by the patient and not by omitting to offer useful treatment. However, this needs to be distinguished from the provision of a minimum standard of quality care. The cases of substandard care experienced at Stafford show on occasions an exposure of patients to risks of harm and detriment that they did not accept and would not have done so if asked. No patient should be expected to tolerate the neglect and assault on their dignity that some were exposed to.

20.42 The necessary observance of proper standards of safety and minimum quality has perhaps become assumed within the NHS. The emphasis has understandably been on the pursuit of excellence and general improvement. This has led to a lack of clarity about the foundation from which that quest is to start.

20.43 Healthcare has a high demand for safety given the serious consequences in death and injury that can follow from failure to observe the relevant precautions. Obvious examples are the requirements of hygiene to prevent infection, of nutrition and hydration to provide the means of sustenance to patients, and of the dignity and respect required for the minimally acceptable quality of life for patients. Maximising the prospects of all patients receiving such a service requires a culture of safety. No system, however theoretically perfect, will work unless the personnel responsible for it are fully committed to its objectives. Anna Walker emphasised the

---

28   Kennedy T77.160–161

role of leadership in maintaining a safety culture, in taking it seriously, and an avoidance of a blame culture:

> *My own view is that there are two things which are really, really important about a safety culture, and that is that the organisation takes it extremely seriously, and that needs to come from the top, in terms of real concern about safety issues. And, secondly, that where there is a safety incident, you at least start with a no blame culture, because the moment that there is a blame culture, and staff feel they're going to be blamed, these things will go underground.*[29]

How is a safety culture achieved?

20.44 The Inquiry received invaluable information about the nuclear industry, which, for obvious reasons, is highly sensitive about safety and keen to imbue all who work in it with a culture of safety. There are lessons that are of value for the health service.

20.45 The paper provided by the International Atomic Energy Agency, although now some 12 years old, contains a number of points which are as relevant to the healthcare sector today as they remain in the nuclear industry with regard to the necessary features of a healthy safety culture:[30]

Openness and fairness

> *Errors, when committed, are seen less as a matter of concern than as a source of experience from which benefit can be derived. Individuals are encouraged to identify, report and correct imperfections in their own work in order to help others as well as themselves to avert future problems. When necessary, they are assisted to improve their subsequent performance.*

> *Nevertheless, for repeated deficiency or gross negligence, managers accept their responsibility for taking disciplinary measures, since safety may otherwise be prejudiced. There is, however, a delicate balance. Sanctions are not applied in such a way as to encourage the concealment of errors.*[31]

29   A. Walker T83.131–132
30   *Safety Culture – a Report by the International Nuclear Safety Group* (1991, Safety Series No. 75-INSAG-4), International Atomic Energy Agency, Vienna; www-pub.iaea.org/MTCD/publications/PDF/Pub882_web.pdf
31   *Safety Culture – a Report by the International Nuclear Safety Group* (1991, Safety Series No. 75-INSAG-4), International Atomic Energy Agency, Vienna, paras 49–50; www-pub.iaea.org/MTCD/publications/PDF/Pub882_web.pdf

Commitment

> *The attitude of mind that produces satisfactory performance by people in groups or as individuals is fostered by demands for orderly work, by clarity of understanding of duties, by rewards and any necessary sanctions, and by the invitation of external scrutiny.*[32]

Individual responsibility

20.46 The paper suggests that the individual front-line worker contributes to safety by adopting:

- A questioning attitude;
- A rigorous and prudent approach;
- Communication.[33]

20.47 Questions it is suggested workers should ask themselves when conducting tasks include:

> *Do I understand the task?*
>
> *What are my responsibilities?*
>
> *How do they relate to safety?*
>
> *Do I have the necessary knowledge to proceed?*
>
> *What are the responsibilities of others?*
>
> *Are there any unusual circumstances?*
>
> *Do I need any assistance?*
>
> *What can go wrong?*
>
> *What could be the consequences of failure or error?*
>
> *What should be done to prevent failures?*
>
> *What do I do if a fault occurs?*

20.48 A rigorous and prudent approach involves:

> *Understanding the work procedures;*
>
> *Complying with the procedures;*

---

32 *Safety Culture – a Report by the International Nuclear Safety Group* (1991, Safety Series No. 75-INSAG-4), International Atomic Energy Agency, Vienna, para 55; www-pub.iaea.org/MTCD/publications/PDF/Pub882_web.pdf
33 *Safety Culture – a Report by the International Nuclear Safety Group* (1991, Safety Series No. 75-INSAG-4), International Atomic Energy Agency, Vienna, paras 58–63; www-pub.iaea.org/MTCD/publications/PDF/Pub882_web.pdf

Being alert for the unexpected;

Stopping and thinking if a problem arises;

Seeking help if necessary;

Devoting attention to orderliness, timeliness and housekeeping;

Proceeding with deliberate care;

Forgoing shortcuts.

20.49   Communication involves:

Obtaining useful information from others;

Transmitting information to others;

Reporting on and documenting results of work, both routine and unusual;

Suggesting new safety initiatives.

20.50   It might be thought that many of these precepts were missing from the wards of Stafford Hospital.

20.51   At the Inquiry seminar on regulation methods, Dr Andrew Spurr, EDF Managing Director for Nuclear Generation, was emphatic about the need for a completely open attitude in his workforce in order to ensure safety. For him "zero tolerance" of "defensive" behaviour was necessary. In order to foster oneness, it was necessary to avoid a "hire and fire" atmosphere as this inhibited reporting, particularly self-reporting. He sought to lead by example by welcoming reports or expressions of concern to him from anyone, including junior employees, on his frequent visits to plants. He always made a point of expressing thanks for such information and was committed to giving the informant his considered response, with reasons for any disagreement. Every incident is considered to be a "learning opportunity". This echoes what is said in the International Atomic Energy Agency paper:

Errors, when committed, are seen less as a matter of concern than as a source of experience from which benefit can be derived. Individuals are encouraged to identify, report and correct imperfections in their own work in order to help others as well as themselves to avert future problems. When necessary, they are assisted to improve their subsequent performance.[34]

---

34   *Safety Culture – a Report by the International Nuclear Safety Group* (1991, Safety Series No. 75-INSAG-4), International Atomic Energy Agency, Vienna, para 49; www-pub.iaea.org/MTCD/publications/PDF/Pub882_web.pdf

20.52 The opposite of that openness can be seen in the NHS. Dr Woodward of the National Patient Safety Agency (NPSA) told the Inquiry:

> ... what we have found is that in some organisations where the culture is one where an error or an incident occurs, the staff member is suspended or blamed and may be put on different duties associated with the incident outcome. What we tend to find is that the other staff members worry about what happened to their colleague, and consider that may happen to them. So ... there is some concern as to whether they would then report themselves if they were either party to or witness to an incident. So we do find that the blame culture that exists in the NHS means that some incidents are kept unreported.[35]

20.53 She said that this fear was one reason for a degree of reluctance to share information with the NPSA if it was going to pass it on to other organisations:

> They were very concerned about linking through to a new system that they were wary of, they didn't know quite what we would do with that information, and they were concerned that we would share it with regulators and performance managers, so that what they were concerned with was that they would be scrutinised in a way that wouldn't be helpful, and that that would lead to low reporting locally as well as nationally.[36]

20.54 Professor Charles Vincent would agree with this approach, emphasising that what is required is strong motivational leadership:

> Maintaining a safety culture, indeed any kind of culture, requires leadership and ongoing work and commitment from everyone concerned.[37]

20.55 Maintenance of safety and other minimum standards is not something to devolve to a safety officer, a safety inspectorate or a governance department but needs to be made the living responsibility of everyone in the system, each contributing their own input to this, and being rewarded and recognised for it.

20.56 Sir Adrian Montague, one of the Inquiry's assessors and someone with immense experience of leading complex organisations, advised the Inquiry that in his view, behaviour can be changed positively by leadership, but this can be best achieved by leaders having direct, personal and visible contact with their front-line staff in order to continually reinforce their message. Leadership by example is vital: if the board is continually asking about safety, the message will permeate the organisation. All have to learn that in a safety critical business, the prioritisation of safety is not only right but fundamental to an organisation's success.

---

35 Suzette Woodward T102.5
36 Suzette Woodward T102.32
37 Vincent, C, *Patient Safety* (2nd edition, 2010) BMJ Books, p285

20.57 Professor Sir Cyril Chantler, Chair of University College London Partners, at the Inquiry seminar on organisational culture, advocated a similar approach for doctors, again emphasising the importance of leadership, based on a strong set of values. He identified the roles doctors play, or should play, in the NHS as:

- *Diagnosis and treatment of patients;*
- *Caring for patients*
  this requires them to bring an understanding of humanity and good communication skills;

- *Management*
  taking responsibility for individual patients, for population health and for the way healthcare is delivered and organised;

- *Leadership*
  not all [doctors] would accept that doctors should be involved in management, I would argue that ... it is becoming essential that they do.[38]

20.58 Sir Cyril drew attention to the distinction Viscount Slim made between management and leadership:

> *Leadership is of the spirit, compounded by personality and vision – its practice is an art. Management is of the mind – a matter of calculation, of statistics, timetables and routine – its practice is a science. Managers are necessary, leaders are essential.*[39]

20.59 Many submissions and suggestions have been received on how the culture of providers in particular and in the NHS generally should be changed. It would be impractical to set out in this report all these immensely helpful contributions, but some common themes have emerged.

Patients must be the priority in everything done in the health service

20.60 Following his reflections on the Inquiry seminars, Sir Donald Irvine, Chair of the Picker Institute and former President of the General Medical Council (GMC), sent the Inquiry a note reporting on a recent visit he made to the Mayo Clinic, and the Amplatz Children's Hospital, Minneapolis. He found that the "overarching organisational principle" of the Mayo, that "the needs of the patient come first", has the effect of unifying all those who work there of whatever profession:

38 Chantler, *Doctors and Leadership*, presented to the Inquiry seminar on organisational culture, (25 October 2011), p1; www.midstaffspublicinquiry.com/sites/default/files/uploads/Doctors_and_Leadership_Cyril_Chantler.pdf
39 Chantler, *Doctors and Leadership*, presented to the Inquiry seminar on organisational culture, (25 October 2011), p1; www.midstaffspublicinquiry.com/sites/default/files/uploads/Doctors_and_Leadership_Cyril_Chantler.pdf

Wherever you go, you cannot escape it – in the hospital, the medical school and in research. What happens to patients matters from their point of first contact with Mayo to their last consultation. The effect, from the CEO and Board of Trustees down, is a relentless focus on clinical quality and on being sure that patients have the best experience.

A nice non-clinical example is the patient's main car park, which staff and consultants are not allowed to use, which is the nearest to the hospital entrance!

The contrast with even the best NHS hospitals, with their competing values and priorities imposed on them from on high, is quite stark.[40]

20.61 The spirit of this approach has recently been put forward by the NHS Confederation and others in their report *Delivering Dignity*, the first key recommendation of which was:

All hospital staff must take personal responsibility for putting the person receiving care first. Staff should be required to challenge practices they believe are not in the best interests of the people in their care.[41]

20.62 Such priority, including the necessary compassion to deliver it, cannot be assumed and needs to be the subject of training. As Professor Sir Liam Donaldson put it when asked if staff need training in this area:

Absolutely they do. Absolutely they do. Some people sometimes say that you're either a born communicator or you're not. That's absolute nonsense in my experience ... obviously, people come into the professions with compassion and interpersonal skills, but in the pressure of modern care environments I can remember it myself, when you're pulled out of bed at night two or three times to go down and see somebody who, you know, is lying, having had a stroke, and you've hardly had any sleep and you're being called to another part of the hospital, to keep in your mind that that person is somebody's mother, grandmother – it's vital that you do see that person as a person and not just as a diseased object to be processed, and that needs to be reinforced all the time. People instinctively know it when they come in, but when they're subjected to the pressures of a modern care environment they can become inured to suffering. And it may be shocking to people but in another way it is a human reaction to [a] high stress, high pressure job.[42]

40 OI00000000372, *A note to Robert Francis from Donald Irvine,* December 2011, para 4
41 *Delivering Dignity: Securing dignity in care for older people in hospitals and care homes. A Report for Consultation* (February 2010), Local government Association, NHS Confederation and Age UK, p5; www.nhsconfed.org/Documents/dignity.pdf
42 Donaldson T122.150–151

20.63 It is not only at the front-line that this principle needs reinforcement. Sir Liam spoke of the importance of those at the DH keeping patients firmly in mind:

> THE CHAIRMAN ... do you think it's perhaps too easy at the higher echelons, and I don't just mean secretaries of state but in the Civil Service and the NHS, for people to forget the effect of what is happening on real people?
>
> A. ... I absolutely agree with that, and ... that's why I ... tried to bring ... the experience of patient stories about patients into the ... equation. And ... I often said to people, "Think about your family, your friends, neighbours. Ask them about their experience of care". And most people's experience of care is fairly positive, but ... equally most will comment on some aspect of care that is negative, not necessarily of the whole episode of care. And I would say to my staff, "Well ... what are our policies doing to help this? Have we got the right policies? Are they being implemented properly?" So I absolutely agree that – ironically – although people are very cynical about politicians, ironically I think that the politicians are often the ones who do have the sharpest appreciation because they have their constituents and they have other MPs coming up to them in the lobby telling them about a constituent. So I think they often have a sharp appreciation of some of the realities.[43]

No tolerance for substandard care

20.64 It is axiomatic that a culture of safe care does not tolerate lapses in standards below a recognised minimum level. The attitude that errors are unavoidable should not lead to error causing harm being acceptable. Cynthia Bower, former Chief Executive of the WMSHA and then of the CQC, offered the Inquiry an insight into the need for clear action to be taken when lapses in acceptable standards were found and for undue weight not to be given to assurances that improvements are in hand:

> THE CHAIRMAN. Do you think there needs to be less tolerance afforded, not only in trust management but also by the regulator to instances of substandard care when they are found?
>
> A. I think we all have to be less tolerant, really ... I think an issue with regulating something like the NHS is that there's always something that a big organisation like the NHS can do. So ... if you find a problem with an NHS organisation, there's always some clinical audit that the chief exec could do, or there's a Royal college that might come along and help them, or there might be some peer review work. There's an entire industry, if you like, around the NHS, saying "Yes, we know that's a problem but somebody from down the road is just about to come and help us with that". Or "We've clocked it and we're doing some training".

---

43 Donaldson T122.23–24

Now, if you go to a small care home provider, ... you've either found them out, for want of a better way of expressing it, or you haven't ... And I think what we have to learn as a regulator is to say ... "That may be so, but actually this day we came in, you weren't compliant, and we're now going to take action off the back of that" ... you can always give a reason, but the fact remains, again, for want of a better analogy, the point you went past the speed camera you were going at 40 miles an hour; there's no point in saying for the rest of the journey you were only doing 30. It's how you push on to take enforcement when you know the NHS can often bring in other sources of support to help them improve the quality of the care ... It's getting that tension right that I think is sometimes a difficulty that makes it look like we may be more tolerant than we should be.[44]

20.65   This suggests, correctly, that lapses below the required minimum standards should not be tolerated and should be seen not to be tolerated by a regulator when they are found. Improvements and remedial action are of course important and essential, but recognition must be given to the fact that the lapse should not have occurred in the first place. It will have impacted on one or more patients, and it should not have happened. Clarity of response of this type requires the standards also to be clear, and for genuine minimum requirements to be distinguished from more discretionary or aspirational matters. In other words, the system needs to be clear about what cannot be tolerated.

20.66   There is a risk that tougher responses to findings of substandard service will result in less openness. A regulator will want to encourage provider trusts to inform it of problems rather than hope they will remain undiscovered. However, a trust that is found to have concealed lapses in standards would soon lose the public's confidence, and the consequences of non-disclosure should be expected to be at least as serious as that for non-compliance in provision, if not more so.

Front line staff must be empowered with responsibility and freedom to deliver safe care

20.67   The Rt Hon Andy Burnham MP, speaking of his time as a junior Health Minister, found that the system was not good at empowering staff:

I came to the conclusion that the NHS is not good at giving its front-line staff a sense of empowerment. People with good ideas do not feel that they can easily put them into action, there is a prevailing sense that those decisions are taken by somebody else.[45]

20.68   It was because of this perception that he had made it his business to undertake semi–private visits to various NHS organisations to work with staff so he could understand their perspective

---

44   Bower T87.130–131
45   Burnham T115.51

and use this to inform his report to the Secretary of State.[46] He considered that there was, at least at that time:

> ... this whole sense of a disconnect between what happens at national level and then how it's felt and interpreted on the ground.[47]

20.69 On behalf of the NHS Confederation, Mike Farrar, its Chief Executive, said:

> It is my abiding belief that primary responsibility for the delivery of high-quality patient care rests with the front-line staff responsible for delivering that care (be they clinicians or managers) and the board and senior management of the organisation in which they work.[48]

20.70 Nigel Edwards and Ruth Lewis of the King's Fund pointed to research indicating the importance of developing a culture of improvement through encouraging "discretionary effort (that which we do willingly because we want to)", through promoting the engagement of staff and exploiting their passion.[49] This is the exact opposite of the attitude reported to these researchers by one chief executive:

> I find a lack of anger in clinicians at the moment; previously they would tell you it's wrong, doesn't seem to happen now, people's heads are down and they are getting on with it.[50]

20.71 The Inquiry has certainly seen examples of that having occurred at Stafford.

20.72 At a more corporate level these contributors observed that:

> A key feature of hospital management over the last 20 years has been increased devolution of power to clinical divisions, increasingly run by doctors taking full managerial responsibility and supported by their own management team including finance and HR support. Chief executives are convinced that engaging their clinical leaders in this way is a highly effective method for managing increasingly complex organisations.[51]

---

46 Burnham WS0000063407–409, paras 23–32; AB/1 WS0000063445
47 Burnham T115.53
48 NHSCONF000000022, *Submission of Mike Farrar* (1 December 2011), p2
49 *Balancing external requirements and a positive internal culture* (25 October 2011), Edwards and Lewis (the King's Fund), pp 7–8;
    www.midstaffspublicinquiry.com/sites/default/files/uploads/Nigel_Edwards_-_full_paper.pdf
50 *Balancing external requirements and a positive internal culture*, Edwards and Lewis (the King's Fund), p9,
    www.midstaffspublicinquiry.com/sites/default/files/uploads/Nigel_Edwards_-_full_paper.pdf
51 *Balancing external requirements and a positive internal culture*, (25 October 2011), Edwards and Lewis (the King's Fund), A paper
    produced for the Inquiry seminar on organisational culture, p10,
    www.midstaffspublicinquiry.com/sites/default/files/uploads/Nigel_Edwards_-_full_paper.pdf

20.73 In *Delivering Dignity* one of the key recommendations was:

> *Hospital boards need to embrace a devolved style of leadership that values and encourages staff and respects their judgement when they are the people working closest with older people and their families. Hospitals must enable staff to 'do the right thing' for patients.*[52]

20.74 "Doing the right thing" should perhaps be regarded as shorthand for Cure the NHS's suggested principle that it should be done "right first time, every time".[53]

Staff must be valued

20.75 At the seminars, the "John Lewis model" was described. In a large and successful retail business, the top priority is its partners' happiness. While that would seem a strange approach from a healthcare perspective, or even a retail one, this priority is part of a virtuous circle in which the other stages were customer satisfaction, leading to maintenance of profitability, leading to the bonuses for the partners and thus staff well-being:[54]

Figure 20.1: The John Lewis model

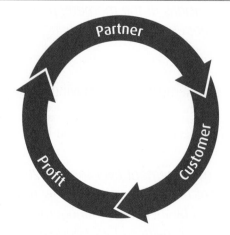

20.76 Victoria Simpson, from the John Lewis Partnership, told the seminar of the importance attributed to enabling staff partners to deal with complaints and concerns from customers as they arose on the shop floor rather than relying on some remote system to undertake this task. This required staff to be trusted with exercising their discretion with regard to offering what was required, even if it fell outside what was normal.[55]

---

52   *Delivering Dignity: Securing dignity in care for older people in hospitals and care homes. A Report for Consultation* (Feb 2010), Local government Association, NHS Confederation and Age UK, p5; www.nhsconfed.org/Documents/dignity.pdf
53   CURE0026000065 *Turning the NHS the Right Way Up Again – Starting with Stafford Hospital* (4 Sept 2009), Cure the NHS
54   Victoria Simpson, *Customer Service: a John Lewis Perspective*, presentation to the Inquiry seminar on organisational culture, 25 October 2011, p3; www.midstaffspublicinquiry.com/inquiry-seminars/patient-experience
55   Victoria Simpson *Customer Service: a John Lewis Perspective*, presentation to the Inquiry seminar on organisational culture, (25 October 2011); www.midstaffspublicinquiry.com/inquiry-seminars/patient-experience

20.77 During the Inquiry's visits to hospitals, examples were seen of wards where the ward leaders were able to ensure patient safety and good quality care by making their own decisions about the criteria for the recruitment of staff and to influence the budgetary framework set by more senior management, by making an evidence-based case that more staff were needed. There were examples of ward staff taking ownership of the results on quality indicators for their ward, and taking pride in their achievements in eliminating pressure sores, reducing falls and so on. In one case, staff were content to have the daily and monthly results on public display.

20.78 Clearly, there are a number of approaches that can result in this sort of healthy autonomy at a level which allows staff to:

- Identify positively with the team in which they work and feel pride where this is due;
- Believe they can contribute to patient well-being and to high standards by their own expertise and experience from their own professional perspective;
- Enable themselves to put right matters of concern and to see that others in the organisation will assist in that process;
- Receive the moral rewards of doing a good job and being recognised as doing so.

20.79 A poorly performing organisation has a negative effect on all staff, however good they were at the outset of any problems. Morale drops, sickness absences rise, and more stress is placed on the diminishing number of well-motivated staff. The overwhelming majority of people respond positively to being appreciated for what they do. The work done by everyone in the NHS is of immense social and human value when done properly – that is why most staff wanted to work there in the first place. The motivation to do good for others is surely a basic characteristic that should be looked for in all who seek any job in the service. However, such altruistic motivation can be crushed out of all but the most determined individuals if it is not reinforced by positive indications to them of the value placed on their work. This need not take the form of financial recompense, but does require the leadership of organisations to ensure that their workforce do not feel taken for granted.

20.80 At the Inquiry visit to Gateshead Hospital NHS Foundation Trust it was observed that efforts were made to ensure that all staff, even those working in back-office functions, were included in information about the effect they had on safety and improvements in patient care.

20.81 Sir Donald Irvine said that at the Mayo Clinic the strongly motivated nursing workforce was encouraged by the hospital's achievement of Magnet status, a difficult to achieve seal of quality awarded by the American Nursing Credential Center, an affiliate of the American Nursing Association.[56] The scheme has simple and clear aims:

The Magnet Recognition Program® advances three goals within health care organizations:

---

56   OI00000000374, *A note to Robert Francis from Sir Donald Irvine* (December 2011), para 8

Promote quality in a setting that supports professional practice

Identify excellence in the delivery of nursing services to patients/residents

Disseminate best practices in nursing services.[57]

Acceptance and pursuit of professional responsibility

20.82 Sir Donald Irvine observed a professional culture at the Mayo Clinic, which was:

> *... patient centred and driven by the pursuit of excellence. It is professionalism which encourages maximum performance, rather than reliance only on regulatory compliance ... At Mayo, if a doctor or nurse does not embrace the culture, and reflect it in their practice, sooner than later they will go. Persistent underperformance has direct consequences for the individual.*

> *Contrast this with the culture in the NHS where too often poor practice is tolerated, something patients are expected to put up with. The consequences for such practice are exceptional – with a heavily unionised workforce jobs tend to be protected.*[58]

20.83 As Sir Donald also points out, much evidence has been seen of the tolerance of poor practice in the history of events at Stafford. This is not, however, due to membership of unions as he suggested. As has been seen in the consideration of the involvement of the unions at Stafford, they were not an active force in seeking to protect patients or drive up standards; they did not have active involvement of their members to any great degree. The worst that can be said of them is that the unions had no influence, positive or negative, on the standards of performance of their members.

20.84 The culture of not raising concerns about colleagues' standards had been embedded in the medical profession, although there is every sign that this is now changing. Niall Dickson commented:

---

57 For an overview of this scheme see: www.nursecredentialing.org/Magnet/ProgramOverview.aspx.
58 OI00000000373, *A note to Robert Francis from Donald Irvine* (December 2011), para 6

I spoke to a medical director a couple of months ago, who said when he was training he can remember two surgeons who nobody would ever have sent ... their family – and no doctor, nurse in the hospital would have gone anywhere near, and nobody did anything about it. He said, "In my time as a medical director, I have had two surgeons in my office and stopped them practising that afternoon" ... I accept, there's quite a lot more still to do, and I don't deny the difficulty of being a responsible officer, particularly if you've known these people over a long period of time. But you do have a duty, as a medical director, to put patient interests first ... And I do think ... the culture within medicine is changing and that people ... are more willing to be their brothers or their sisters' keeper and to recognise, as we say, that this is one of the most important aspects of patient safety, is having the ability to say somebody's not up to scratch, to do something about it.[59]

20.85 What is clear is that all staff in the NHS, but particularly the professionally qualified staff, have a vital role to play in maintaining appropriate standards for their patients, not only in their treatment of individual cases but in exercising a collective responsibility for the patients of their organisation in general. This requires them all not only to deal effectively with their own caseload, but to participate in the maintenance of standards by colleagues and their teams, and in the management of the teams, departments and organisations of which they are part. It should not be possible for any member of the NHS community to justify inaction inimical to the safety or well-being of patients by saying it was someone else's responsibility.

Strong and stable leadership

20.86 Marcia Fry, previously Head of Operational Development of the HCC, told the Inquiry of the importance, in her view, of cultural leadership in relation to the adoption of a willingness to learn openly from mistakes:

I think you've got to recognise the reality that in human nature people don't like to be criticised. So it's trying to find some way beyond that in the culture of an organisation that allows mistakes to be recognised and learning to be acted on. And it can only come from the leadership and the tone that's set at the organisations' highest levels.[60]

20.87 Katherine Fenton, Chief Nurse at University College London Hospitals NHS Foundation Trust, in an interview for the Inquiry's nursing seminar, pointed out that an organisation's culture is led by the style and values promoted by its Chief Executive, and that sometimes to change the culture it was necessary to change the person in that post.[61] Mike Farrar, Chief Executive of

59   Dickson T105.39–40
60   Fry T79.192
61   Katherine Fenton, interview given as part of the Inquiry's nursing seminar on 31 October 2011;
     www.midstaffspublicinquiry.com/inquiry-seminars/nursing

the NHS Confederation, referred in his submission to the need for "strong, visionary leadership."[62]

20.88 Edwards and Lewis observed that:

> *A stable leadership cadre seems to be a very important aspect of creating and sustaining a positive culture. One of the most undesirable aspects of the top down performance management style of the NHS in the last 15 to 20 years has been the effect this has had on the longevity of Chief Executives.*[63]

20.89 The experience of this Inquiry is that chief executives do not stay in post for long enough. It was suggested that the average tenure in post at this level has been less than two years.[64] Dr Judith Smith has undertaken research which indicated that the average tenure was less than three years in the period between 2003 and 2006.[65]

20.90 While regard must be had for the particular immediate needs of failing organisations, stability under strong and competent leadership is clearly important, and something which is difficult currently to find with consistency in the NHS. Dr Smith pointed to research indicating a correlation between consistency and longevity of senior managers and clinical leaders with the success of organisations.[66] In her joint report with Professor Christopher Newdick, one of the themes identified by them was:

> *... evidence on high-performing health organisations points to the importance of long-term, sustained clinical and general managerial leadership with senior teams amongst whom there is trust and expertise developed over many years.*[67]

20.91 Mr Sumara agreed:

> *THE CHAIRMAN: ... [There] must be horses for courses. But if it is true that the average tenure is two years or less, that would suggest, wouldn't it, that something's wrong about the process of appointment and choice?*
>
> *A. I've no doubt, actually, that there's a ... problem with the numbers and the quality of leaders in the NHS and that's an accepted fact. I think it's seen as a problem for the future.*[68]

---

62 NHSCONF000000022, *Submission of Mike Farrar* (1 December 2011), p2
63 *Balancing external requirements and a positive internal culture* (25 October 2011), Edwards and Lewis (the King's Fund), p11; www.midstaffspublicinquiry.com/sites/default/files/uploads/Nigel_Edwards_-_full_paper.pdf
64 Sumara T58.123
65 Smith T6.46–47
66 Smith T6.47
67 EXP0000000047–48 Newdick and Smith, *The Structure and Organisation of the NHS,* Newdick, para 114
68 Sumara T50.124

Organisational stability

20.92 The best healthcare organisations and staff should welcome and embrace change which results in better services for patients, but generally this should be evolutionary and risk-based. During the period under review by the Inquiry, the NHS has been subjected to almost constant fundamental reorganisations, at every level. Just as successful organisations are likely to have stable and long-serving leadership, they are also likely to be given a reasonable opportunity to achieve the objectives for which they were created. Large and visible changes are sometimes necessary but they are often attempted when perhaps a less radical solution could have achieved the same ends. The Inquiry has seen many examples of reorganisations which have resulted in loss of corporate memory, diversion of resources away from core tasks, lack of time to allow effective implantation of the chosen objectives, and disengagement of staff whose focus inevitably has turned to their career interests rather than the work of the organisation.[69]

Quality care for patients has to be driven by quality information

20.93 Sir Donald Irvine noted that the Mayo Clinic publishes a range of comparative data on outcomes, compliance with guidelines, patient experience and satisfaction. These are accessible to all via its website. He considers that it is vital that information of this type is shared widely and comprehensibly with the public.[70]

20.94 It is clear that there is a long journey to be undertaken to ensure that the stream of information between patients, staff, organisations and the public is uniformly useful, reliable, and transparent.

Openness, candour and honesty

20.95 The evidence before this Inquiry has shown on occasion a regrettable absence of regulators, the public and patients access to the full facts which would enable them to make necessary judgements. Dr Bill Moyes offered a telling description of what he saw as the prevailing culture within the NHS among trusts which were not FTs:

> *The culture of the NHS, particularly the hospital sector, I would say, is not to embarrass the Minister ... that's a big pressure and has been on managers in the NHS almost since its creation. Don't do anything to embarrass the Minister. And what Monitor was saying, which was a completely different approach, was, "Be honest, acknowledge where things are going wrong, or might go wrong, and give us some comfort that you're doing something about it". And every so often, we had to take steps to remind people that we would rather have honesty, than good spin, if I can put it that way.[71]*

69 EXP0000000047, Newdick and Smith, *The Structure and Organisation of the NHS*
70 OI00000000374, *A note to Robert Francis from Donald Irvine* (December 2011), para 7
71 Moyes T93.11–12

20.96   The subject of openness and candour is addressed in more detail in *Chapter 22: Openness, transparency and candour*, but the culture of the NHS must embrace principles and practices that require the full truth to be told about the standard of care being provided in particular organisations and, where possible, individual specialties. Patients ought to be able to know about the performance record of a surgeon into whose hands they are about to commit their lives. Regulators need to know about causes of concern. Ministers can make it clear that they are more likely to be "embarrassed", to use Dr Moyes's expression, by concerns not being brought into the open and discovered later, than by openness. The public interest requires openness and honesty in relation to the maintenance of standards of service. Without this, public confidence in the system will drain away.

20.97   The requirement for honesty includes the need for providers to acknowledge openly when they are unable, for whatever reason, to meet fundamental safety or quality standards, and if that deficiency cannot be corrected to take rigorous decisions including the suspension of services, where this is necessary, to protect patients. The evidence points overwhelmingly to the conclusion that this is more likely to occur if the honest disclosure of error does not lead to disciplinary consequences for the individual unless there is evidence of wilful disregard of standards or recklessness or other forms of serious misconduct such as a persistent failure to remedy deficiencies of practice. Professor Sir Liam Donaldson, a consistent advocate of the need to do away with such a culture of blame, said the following:

> Honest failure is something that needs to be protected otherwise people will continue to live in fear, will not admit their mistakes and the knowledge to prevent serious harm will be buried with the patient.[72]

20.98   Sir Liam suggested to the Inquiry that such a culture of fear and blame had yet to be banished:

> ... if we leave to one side as, if you like, extreme and unusual cases where someone has disregarded an instruction and gone ahead, or a – totally ignored good practice and – and – and harmed somebody, that the majority of cases are cases where a genuine mistake has been made, that the person regretted that they were driven to it almost by the circumstances that they were in.
>
> ... But there's a very inconsistent approach to that, to dealing with that ... in some cases there are organisations that genuinely will deal with it neutrally, and not ... blame the individual. The individual and, indeed, in the best places the ... victim's family, or the victim if they've survived, will also be part of the process for learning and making sure it doesn't happen again.

---

72   Donaldson WS0000070116, para 39

But in other places ... they're immediately suspended. A nurse is more likely to be suspended than a doctor. Sometimes the police are called, and when that happens ... it's inevitable that the thing will drag on for sometimes years, and people are prosecuted.

And it's unsatisfactory that ... there can't be a consistent approach everywhere. The media have a part to play, because they're usually very hostile and do seize on the individual quickly, but over time I think we've improved the situation a little bit, but not a lot.[73]

20.99 He pointed to "spectacular" successes in other parts of the world, for example:

I've talked at length to one team in – in North America ... who had a policy of immediately going to the family and telling them what happened, apologising, and then staying with them through the whole period of bereavement, telling them they would understand their anger ... but working it through, making it clear it was an honest mistake, and then asking that family to be part of the planning to ensure that the incident's being properly understood and that policies have been put in place to prevent it happening again.[74]

20.100 Professor Sir Ian Kennedy pointed to another aspect of honesty which was difficult to maintain in the NHS: the ability to admit that it is not possible within current constraints to provide a service to acceptable standards:

... in Bristol an additional factor [was] that it had aspirations to move on and be highly regarded to have even a transplant unit in time, so they – they had a vision and an ambition which didn't – which I think went beyond their current and future capacity.

Q. Is that, do you think, because the wants and needs of clinicians are sometimes overborne by the manager who will say, "You can't do that, you're not going to stop that service or close the door"?

A. Well, in the ideal world it should be a proper conversation and people should stay within their area of competence, and the courageous clinician say, "Well, we can't deliver that services [sic] under those circumstances", and not deliver it. But you're absolute rightly [sic], if I may say so, that there is the tendency that, "If we stop providing this service, this will be seen as a failure", and of course in part, given that members of the public look to that institution to provide that service, all things being equal, it would be good if it could continue. But if it can only continue in circumstances where the service is below par, then clearly it shouldn't be offering that service.[75]

---

73   Donaldson T122.35–36
74   Donaldson T122.38
75   Kennedy T77.21–22

What would a common culture look like?

20.101 There is no one way in which a satisfactory common culture could be displayed, and if the culture is to be "owned" by those who are part of it, it is necessary for the local ingredients to be devised locally. A common culture is not the same as a monolith of entirely uniform practices. What is important is that the measures taken, whether locally or more globally, result in behaviour in the provision of the service which shares the necessary common characteristics. What follows are, therefore, merely suggestions, mainly derived from the seminars and observation at hospital visits, which would appear to present at least some of the desired cultural outcomes. Some of this may be thought to be statements of the very obvious, but the obviously required does not always happen unless it is made to happen, and consistency may well not be achieved unless the need is constantly repeated.

Ward level

20.102 What is it that patients and their visitors would be reassured by experiencing during a stay in an acute admission ward?

On arrival

20.103 Whenever a patient is admitted to a ward he/she needs to be made aware of a lot of information, some specific to the individual, some more general:

- The specific information which should be available to the patient includes:
  - The reason for the admission, and whether the staff's understanding of that reason accords with that of the patient;
  - The plan for treatment and care in terms of what, to the extent that this is known, the patient can expect to happen, and, approximately, when it is going to happen;
  - Who is responsible for the treatment and care of the patient while in that ward, including the name of a consultant or other leader of the relevant team, and the name of a nurse or nurses who have prime responsibility for coordinating the patient's nursing care;
  - A list of contact details for patients to contact the identified leaders of their care;
  - What approach to sharing information about the patient with visitors or family is to be taken, including a list of those authorised by (or where appropriate, on behalf of) the patient to receive such information and how that list may be changed.

- The generic information available for patients and visitors should include:
  - Some description of the physical layout of the ward, including where toilets and other patient facilities are, and its position within the hospital;
  - A list of the standards patients can expect to experience on the ward such as those in relation to cleanliness, hygiene, response to calls for help, courtesy, privacy and dignity;

- How help can be summoned including what to do if a buzzer is not answered within an expected time;
- The ward routine timetable including visiting hours if any;
- Any restrictions on visiting together with the reasons for these;
- Arrangements for secure storage of personal property;
- A list of the ward staff, including not only nurses and support workers but household staff, whom patients and visitors may encounter on the ward, or reference to a point where a daily list of such information can be found;
- An explanation of the meaning of any different staff uniforms that are commonly seen on the ward;
- Information about the catering provided, mealtimes and the system for ordering food and drink, including information about the ward policy towards assistance being provided by visitors and what access visitors have to catering facilities;
- Information about any discretionary or chargeable facilities available to patients, such as telephones, TV and libraries;
- How patients may obtain further information about their planned treatment or any other matter;
- How patients or visitors can raise concerns, together with a commitment that these will be listened to and, where appropriate, acted on. Patients and visitors need to understand that the raising of concerns and complaints is welcome and will be acted on.

20.104 Much of this information could be provided in written form at the bedside, but many, if not all, patients would benefit from an oral induction by a senior ward nurse, tailored to the individual patient's needs.

Staff identity

20.105 Patients and visitors need to know who they are talking to or observing and what their role is. Patients need to know who is responsible for looking after them. Productive personal interaction requires knowledge of staff names and their post and seniority. While identity badges are nearly universal in hospitals, legibility and visibility are not. Doctors in particular have been seen with their badges positioned where they cannot easily be seen. Elderly patients and all with sight difficulties will have a problem reading names if they are not in large, easily read print. Name recognition needs to be reinforced by individuals introducing themselves and continuing to do so, unless it is obvious the patient knows who they are.

20.106 Patients may not understand what the role is of the various members of staff that come to their bedside. A rushed introduction does not achieve this. Patients cannot always be expected to remember from one day to the next what are the various roles of staff in their care. It should, for example, be made easy for patients and visitors to tell the difference between a registered nurse and a healthcare support worker. If these roles are differentiated by uniforms, this can be explained in the information suggested above. Some hospitals have adopted a system whereby a common uniform is used, with the roles written on them in large letters.

20.107 It is just as important for patients and visitors to be able to identify the ancillary staff such as cleaners, maintenance personnel, therapists and so on.

Staff interaction with patients and visitors

20.108 In a well-run ward, staff, whether nurses or maintenance personnel, will have time and make time when appropriate to talk in a friendly fashion with patients, asking after them, finding out if they need anything, and offering either to help or get help when it is asked for. Job boundaries should not hinder staff of all grades and types offering to help or find help where it is needed. Inevitably, there will be times when workloads make this difficult, in which case, the least that can be expected is a courteous explanation of when help or other intervention will be available. Underlying this form of interaction may be a system of policies and guidance, but the priority should be ensuring that the patient's safety and minimum care requirements (at least) are being met, rather than standing by some procedural requirement that prevents it. Staff should be encouraged to exercise their judgement in favour of providing for a patient's reasonable needs.

20.109 Staff on well-run wards for the elderly in particular, will do what is necessary to ensure that patients are eating and drinking sufficiently, and do not have to wait more than a minimal time for toileting assistance.

20.110 Staff should also freely interact with visitors, provided that the patient has consented to them doing so. Much anxiety can be allayed by provision of up-to-date, accurate information about a patient's progress, needs and care plans when this is asked for. This, of course, requires staff to be familiar with a patient's status, or at the very least to be able to refer an inquirer to a member of staff who can provide that information.

20.111 There appears to be a common problem of staff on night shifts (and indeed on shifts at other times of the day), either not having adequate knowledge of the patients in their care, or not being prepared to share their knowledge, sometimes taking the attitude that interaction with patients and family is a matter for day staff. This should not be acceptable.

20.112 Visitors, particularly close relatives, can be an invaluable source of information and help. It is counterproductive to make them feel excluded from the care of their loved one. Where appropriate they can, if willing, able and available, be involved in providing direct care, whether it be assistance with feeding, support to the toilet, or providing moral encouragement. Such involvement is not a matter the ward can or should expect, or rely on, but where it is obvious that family members want to help, that should, if the patient agrees and it is in her/his best interests, be encouraged.

Cleanliness and hygiene

20.113   A well-run ward has very high standards of cleanliness and hygiene. Not only is a clean ward more likely to be a healthy one, it is an environment which will improve morale and confidence. Spillages and litter should not be allowed to remain untackled for more than a minimum time. Cleaning is organised in different ways in different trusts. However, it is not just the responsibility of cleaning staff to keep the ward spotlessly clean, but of all staff. Consultants and senior executives should be just as alert to picking up and disposing of waste on the floor as cleaning staff. All who detect something that needs cleaning should alert those responsible for taking action immediately.

20.114   Hygiene needs to be observed by all in a ward, including doctors and visitors. Both the latter groups may, unfortunately, need to be reminded of the need to use hand washes. Any member of staff, however junior, should feel free to remind others of the requirements. Senior staff need to be role models for all in their observance of hygiene requirements.

Nutrition and hydration

20.115   Many different schemes are being developed to ensure that those incapable of feeding or hydrating themselves adequately receive the necessary assistance. This is not the place to evaluate these schemes, but what is essential is that nutrition and hydration is regarded as part of the responsibility of all staff. Not all will be able to offer direct assistance but all can observe whether particular patients appear to be in difficulties, and draw that to the attention of someone who can provide help. Medical and ancillary staff need to recognise the importance of this function of a ward and do their best not to hinder it with their own work. A patient taken away for physiotherapy in the middle of her lunch is likely to be an underfed patient. The patient who returns from an X-ray to find their food is cold is one of whom insufficient care is being taken.

20.116   This is an area where hospitals are exploring the use of volunteers to assist.

Standard procedures

20.117   Many areas of healthcare provision are now generally subject to standardisation. Care pathways indicate the steps that should generally be taken in the treatment of particular conditions; surgical checklists are becoming increasingly used. Evidence-based standard procedures reduce the scope for error, and enable those familiar with them to work in new environments with the minimum of induction and retraining. They promote safety and adherence to acceptable standards by eliminating methods which may be unfamiliar to some and avoid unnecessary duplication of effort in preparing and executing different procedures for the same treatment.

20.118   Some professionals object to, what they see as, a restriction of their professional freedom to act as they judge best for their patients. Such objections are likely to be borne out of a failure of communication or a failure of colleagues and teams to agree on the best approach. A professional who refuses to comply with a standard procedure either knows or believes he/she knows a safer method and has not persuaded colleagues of this point of view or is unprepared to work effectively as a member of a team. Either way patient care is likely to be compromised and it is incumbent on the managers and leaders of the organisation to resolve the impasse. Healthcare professionals should be prepared to comply with and contribute to the development of standard procedures in the areas in which they work. Their managers need to ensure that their employees comply with these requirements. Staff members affected by professional disagreements about procedures must be required to take the necessary corrective action.

20.119 Professional bodies should work on devising evidence-based standard procedures for as many therapeutic activities as possible.

Discharge arrangements

20.120 It is commonplace in the NHS that beds are being made unavailable to those who need treatment because of difficulties in discharging patients. This is often due to a lack of appropriate resources in the community to support patients who cannot look after themselves or relatives refusing to care for them. Whatever the reasons, there is no excuse either for the discharge of patients without appropriate support or retaining them in hospital with less than adequate care. If it be the case, as recently reported, that elderly patients are transferred between wards without adequate handover or consideration of their needs, or even discharged without support in the middle of the night, this would not be allowed to occur in a hospital with a healthy culture of putting the patient first.[76] Whatever the pressures, a ward's first responsibility is to the patients accepted into its care. Any professional who fears that an inappropriate or unsafely managed transfer or discharge is about to take place needs to be empowered to take appropriate protective action.

Incident reporting and learning

20.121 Reporting of incidents needs not only to be encouraged but insisted upon. Staff need to feel free to report something even if in doubt as to whether it fits in the definition of the relevant policy. The sole criterion for reporting should be whether they consider there is a concern relevant to patient safety or compliance with fundamental standards or some high requirement of their employer. Staff must invariably receive feedback in relation to any report they have made, including information about the action, if any, taken as a result. If no action has been taken, the informant should be given the reasons for this.

---

76   *Hospitals on the edge? The time for action. A report by the Royal College of Physicians* (13 September 2012), Royal College of Physicians; www.rcplondon.ac.uk/sites/default/files/documents/hospitals-on-the-edge-report.pdf

Chapter 20 Culture

Measures of performance

20.122 Staff in all wards or other units within a provider organisation should be enabled to measure their collective performance against other wards and units. Many measures may be chosen by management but ward staff should be able to produce and maintain their own indicators. Many wards visited disclosed their results openly in public spaces. This welcome acknowledgement of the requirement of openness should be encouraged.

20.123 More generally, there is an urgent need in many areas for measures to be developed to allow the effectiveness of a service to be understood. In some areas, such as cardiac surgery, this is better developed than in others. It should be considered the duty of all specialty professional bodies to develop measures of outcome in relation to their work. While this will be more difficult in some areas than others, it should be possible in all. It should no longer be acceptable for treatment to be offered to patients without information being available on how effective it is and what it is reasonable to expect as an outcome. The rate at which such outcomes are in fact achieved by units and individuals can then be better understood, and, where necessary, corrective measures taken. The more such information is available to the staff providing treatment, the more likely is a culture of striving for evidence-based excellence to be adopted.

Appraisals and other professional development support

20.124 Any number of reports have pointed to the importance of proper professional appraisals, and the provision of this is now measured and monitored. It remains to be seen whether appraisals are truly accepted and used by staff and management as a worthwhile tool to spread best practice and to allow reflection on what improvements could be made, as opposed to a burdensome chore to be observed as a formality.

20.125 Revalidation of doctors could, and should, become a valuable focus for appraisal and evidence gathering about their performance, but it requires a real commitment by employers, specialties and individuals to identify truly informative means of objectively measuring performance and identifying areas for improvement.

20.126 There is no reason why other professional staff, including nurses, should not welcome equally incisive appraisal. Again, it must be constructed so as not to become a bureaucratic burden, as opposed to a genuinely helpful tool for professional development.

20.127 Appraisals need to include participation by all colleagues. This requires an abandonment of reluctance to offer constructive comment on colleagues, and for those receiving the comments to welcome them, even if they are critical. This form of support can perhaps best be built up from group meetings in which the contribution of all to cases under review can be considered.

Teamwork and leadership

20.128 Most service provision in an acute hospital setting is the result of teamwork and often the work of more than one team. The core team in most inpatient wards is usually the nursing team led by a ward sister. It is they who have the most contact with patients and are responsible for their minute-to-minute care. The medical or surgical team will regard themselves as separate, often being seen as visitors to the ward for the purpose of examining the patient and issuing instructions about future treatment and care. Greater efforts may need to be made to bring teams like this closer together. They need to recognise that their joint efforts are required for the benefit of the patient, properly coordinated and with a free flow of information between all concerned. In an era where the doctor who attends a patient is likely to change almost daily and nurses come and go, ensuring continuity is key to the patient's welfare. Absolute clarity is required about who at any given time is responsible for the care of the patient; to whom referral should be made for further assistance or advice, and how coordination of effort is to be achieved. A sense of there being one team for the patient should be fostered where possible. One way to help in this might be to involve staff of all backgrounds in case reviews, clinical audit, and in overall team meetings.

20.129 One method whereby this has been achieved has been by Schwartz rounds. These are a "multidisciplinary forum designed for staff from across the hospital to come together once a month to discuss the non-clinical aspect of caring for patients – that is, the emotional and social challenges associated with their jobs."[77]

20.130 The Royal College of Physicians (RCP) and the Royal College of Nursing (RCN) have also recently published some principles for best practice in ward rounds, emphasising their role as a means of multidisciplinary team-working:

> [Medical ward rounds] *provide an opportunity for the multidisciplinary team to come together to review a patient's condition and develop a coordinated plan of care, while facilitating full engagement of the patient and/or carers in making shared decisions about care. Additionally, ward rounds offer great opportunities for effective communication, information sharing and joint learning through active participation of all members of the multidisciplinary team.*[78]

Provider level

20.131 For a common culture to flourish it must be evident not only at ward level but throughout the provider organisation. It is not enough for provider boards and their management teams to formulate policies and require others to behave in a specified way. They must behave in the

77   *The Contribution of Schwartz Center Rounds® to Hospital Culture,* Goodrich and Cornwell, paper produced for the Inquiry seminar on organisational culture, (25 October 2011), p1; www.midstaffspublicinquiry.com/sites/default/files/uploads/Jocelyn_Cornwell_-_paper.pdf

78   *Ward rounds in medicine: principles for best practice* (October 2012), a joint publication of the Royal College of Physicians and the Royal College of Nursing, p1; www.rcplondon.ac.uk/resources/ward-rounds-medicine-principles-best-practice

required way themselves and be seen to do so. If front-line staff see their leaders acting in conformity with a positive common culture and its values, they will be empowered to do so themselves, even when this may be challenging. Among the manifestations of a board acting as a role model for a positive common culture would be:

- Open board meetings;
- Setting a strategy in which the patient is given priority throughout;
- Priority given to safety and quality issues in the agenda;
- Frequent and regular direct personal contact with patients and staff;
- Directors personally listening to complaints, concerns and suggestions of patients and staff, and being seen to act on them, including visible support for *bona fide* whistleblowers;
- Swift recognition of any failure to comply with necessary standards, whether they be corporate or internal to the board, and implementation of the necessary corrective action;
- Open and honest admission where the organisation is unable to deliver a service or part of a service to the required standard with a full explanation of the reasons for this;
- Visible and proactive involvement of patients, staff and the public in the formulation of plans;
- Zero tolerance of staff not committed to the common culture and maintenance of necessary standards;
- Wherever possible leading by example.

System level

20.132 The culture must be shared by all who work in the system whether they be commissioners, performance managers, regulators or in support functions. The more remote from the front-line individuals and the organisations for which they work are, the more difficult this is likely to be. A key to overcoming this challenge may be to increase the personal contact between those who work in these positions and individual patients and staff and expose them to experience of the impact on them of poor standards of service or support. Just as many provider boards now include consideration of particular examples of patient experience in their meetings, similar activity in more remote organisations could be particularly beneficial. Decisions and the reasons for them should be referenced to the way in which they support and further the common values of the healthcare system.

20.133 An example of such an attitude is the realisation in the DH that staff receiving complaints needed training to understand their significance and the need to ensure that someone was taking appropriate action about them, even if strictly speaking that was not part of the DH's "job".[79] In reflective evidence, Una O'Brien, the DH's Permanent Secretary, acknowledged the importance of demonstrating better how policies will result in good quality healthcare. Referring to a conclusion of the Health Select Committee that Government policy has often

---

79   O'Brien T125.121–2

given the impression of prioritising attainment of targets, financial balance and FT status over patient safety,[80] she said:

> ... I think the important challenge that it's making, which I do accept, is that the major initiatives that were undertaken on those matters we've been talking about have not been sufficiently grounded in a broader purpose in relation to quality and safety that they should have been.
>
> That said, I think I would want to add that the truth is that many aspects of those changes that are referred to there, for example achieving financial balance and attaining foundation trust status, are not ends in themselves, or were certainly never intended as such. They are not sort of initiatives that are pursued as off to one side.
>
> What we've probably failed to do is to sufficiently articulate them as being connected to improvements for patients and the public ... the idea that somehow achieving financial balance is not a good thing, that sometimes I know the impression is given that it's ... shouldn't get the attention it receives, actually it's in nobody's interests to have organisations that are in financial crisis. That's not good for patients and it's not good for the taxpayer.
>
> So the question really for me is, how do we balance these things off in a way that they're all given their right space and proper respect? To suggest that there's a hierarchy or that we should disdain, for example, financial balance or waiting times and that they're not part of quality, I think would be quite wrong.
>
> So we've got clearly much more to do to keep quality at the absolute centre stage and then to be able to demonstrate where – issues to do with, for example access, issues to do with maintaining good governance, issues to do with financial balance, to demonstrate how they are properly part of a good quality healthcare system, and so to that extent I think there is a lot in what the Health Select Committee are saying.[81]

Summary

20.134 The NHS needs to reinforce a positive and all-embracing culture shared by all front-line, managerial, regulatory, and governmental staff. It is a culture which demands that patients are put before other considerations, fundamental standards are observed, non-compliance is not tolerated, and all commit to full personal engagement in the organisations to which they belong to achieve these ends.

20.135 There are many areas in the NHS where a positive culture already exists, but the evidence before this Inquiry suggests that for all the emphasis on a universal system, individual units

---

80   KM/13 PA0002000172, *Patient Safety, Sixth Report of Session 2008–09* (June 2009), Health Select Committee
81   O'Brien T125.134–135

and organisations display a wide range of cultures, some very positive, but in some, as in many of the wards of Stafford Hospital during the period under review, an unhealthy culture is able to persist.

20.136 As the NHS as a system evolves from a command and control or "top-down" structure to a network of increasingly autonomous units, it is the overall culture – "the way we do things in the NHS" – which will define what the NHS means and does, and will be the principal means of seeking to ensure uniformity of the standard of care and treatment.

20.137 A positive culture as described does not just emerge through the good intentions of those working in the system. It needs to be defined, accepted by those who are to be part of it, and continually reinforced by leadership, training, personal engagement and commitment.

20.138 Quite how the required common culture is delivered is less than easy to discern, given the mixed success met with by previous attempts at cultural change, but it is clearly a coordinated combination of factors that must be looked for, rather than some simplistic solution. Asked how cultural change could be brought about, Dame Christine Beasley, the former Chief Nursing Officer for England, wisely said:

> I'd be very famous and rich, I suspect, if I had all the answers to that ... I mean, [in relation to changing attitudes about hospital infections] it's all the things we know. It was processes. It was performance management. It was how you trained and educated people. It's how you publish the data. All of that, I think, begins to drive the cultural shift that you need to make this sustainable across a whole organisation.[82]

20.139 From the evidence at the Inquiry hearings, the discussions at the seminars, and our visits to various hospitals, the important drivers towards a positive and universal culture would appear to be:

- A common set of core values and standards shared throughout the system;
- Leadership at all levels, from ward to the top of the DH, committed to, and capable of, imbuing all staff with those values and standards;
- A system which recognises and applies the values of transparency, honesty and candour;
- Freely available useful, reliable and full information on attainment of the values and standards;
- The use of a tool or methodology, such as a cultural barometer to measure the cultural health of all parts of the system.

20.140 These topics are considered in the chapters which follow.

---

82   Beasley T117.101

Summary of recommendations

Recommendation 2

The NHS and all who work for it must adopt and demonstrate a shared culture in which the patient is the priority in everything done. This requires:

- A common set of core values and standards shared throughout the system;
- Leadership at all levels from ward to the top of the Department of Health, committed to and capable of involving all staff with those values and standards;
- A system which recognises and applies the values of transparency, honesty and candour;
- Freely available, useful, reliable and full information on attainment of the values and standards;
- A tool or methodology such as a cultural barometer to measure the cultural health of all parts of the system.

Recommendation 11

Healthcare professionals should be prepared to contribute to the development of, and comply with, standard procedures in the areas in which they work. Their managers need to ensure that their employees comply with these requirements. Staff members affected by professional disagreements about procedures must be required to take the necessary corrective action, working with their medical or nursing director or line manager within the trust, with external support where necessary. Professional bodies should work on devising evidence-based standard procedures for as many interventions and pathways as possible.

Chapter 21
Values and standards

Key themes

- There are many statements of values in the healthcare system addressed to separate groups within it, but there needs to be a common statement of values to which all can commit together.

- The NHS Constitution is intended to be a common source of values and principles by which the NHS works, but it has not as yet had the impact it should. It should become the common reference point for all staff. Priority needs to be given in it to requirement of putting patients first in everything done and the values associated with this. All staff should be required to commit to abiding by its values and principles.

- The system of standards in the NHS is in a state of evolution but there is evidence that essential standards are not yet effectively adopted on a universal basis.

- The structure of standards should be provided with improved clarity of status and purpose by distinguishing between fundamental safety and essential care standards formulated by regulation, enhanced standards of quality formulated by the NHS Commissioning Board, and discretionary developmental standards formulated by commissioners and providers. Persistent non compliance with fundamental standards should not be permitted and individual cases of non-compliance leading to serious harm should have serious consequences.

- Indicators of compliance with fundamental standards should be set by CQC and NICE should be commissioned to formulate standard procedures and guidance designed to provide practical means of compliance.

- Formulation of any standard needs to be "owned" by patients and front line professionals: full involvement of patient groups and professional bodies in the formulation of all standards as well as the methods and measurement of compliance is vital. Accurate information about compliance and non-compliance, capable of comparing individuals, services and providers, must be readily accessible to all.

- Policing of compliance with fundamental standards should remain the responsibility of the CQC but it needs to be recognised that while information gathering and analysis is important the most effective means of monitoring involves direct observation, contact with patients, carers and staff, and inspection of records. Where extensive investigations are required these should not inhibit the use of protective interim measures.

- Peer review is an invaluable means of spreading and maintaining a positive common culture in which good practice is encouraged to flourish and bad practice can be identified and remedied. It should be an intrinsic part of the practice of all professional, managerial and leadership activity in NHS provider organisations.

Introduction

21.1 A consistent culture producing the best chance for all patients to be treated in accordance with acceptable fundamental standards of safety and quality requires the NHS and all who work in it to develop and adhere to a common set of standards and values. There are many sources from which such values can be drawn and defined already, but they have been developed from the perspective of individual professions or groups of staff. Many of them derive from professional regulators and have disciplinary connotations. While this may be inevitable, it does mean that they are not sufficient to produce an overall culture shared by all in the healthcare community. Disciplinary codes are necessary but are more likely to be regarded as something to comply with rather than something to be owned and lived by.

21.2 It is not suggested that these individual codes are done away with, but they do lead to a separation of cultural identity between different groups. Doctors will properly regard themselves as members of a proud and distinguished profession, as will nurses and others. Other staff may have no such tradition, and find it difficult to see themselves as part of the same great endeavour of healing the sick and promoting health. In order for the NHS to deliver uniformly safe and good-quality care to those it serves, all who work in the system, regardless of their qualifications or role, must recognise that they are part of a very large team who all have but one objective, the proper care and treatment of their patients. For example, it needs to be recognised that all staff have a role to play in ensuring dignity and respect for patients. The maintenance man repairing a ward window can pick something up for an elderly patient or ignore them; the cleaner can make all the difference by drawing a nurse's attention to a distressed patient as opposed to assuming the patient's welfare is someone else's job. They are just as much part of the team working for the patient's benefit as are the nursing and medical staff. Therefore in addition to their identification through their individual roles, all staff need to be made part of an overall NHS culture of which they can be proud and identify with. The challenge is to work out how to achieve this.

Values

21.3 A shared common culture requires a commitment to shared values. It does not encourage such commonalty that currently there are many different value statements, most of which are addressed to distinct groups of healthcare staff. They may have common themes but these are all expressed in different ways. Some groups do not have the benefit of their own set of values, and statements of general application are not always very prevalent or "owned" by those who are intended to adopt them.

Current sources of values and standards

21.4 There are many statements of the standards of behaviour expected of those who work in the NHS. Each sector – doctors, nurses, managers and so on has its own codes and definitions, but they can be seen to have a common core.

Nolan principles

21.5 The Committee on Standards in Public Life set out seven well-known principles all in public life should follow, known as the Nolan principles:

- Selflessness;
- Integrity;
- Objectivity;
- Accountability;
- Openness;
- Honesty;
- Leadership.

21.6 These clearly should apply to all who work in the NHS, and, it may be argued, to all who work in any capacity serving the public in healthcare, including the independent sector.

Medical practitioners

21.7 The General Medical Council (GMC) promulgates a code of conduct for registered medical practitioners which starts with a short list of duties (see box below).

The duties of a doctor registered with the General Medical Council

Patients must be able to trust doctors with their lives and health. To justify that trust you must show respect for human life and you must:

- Make the care of your patient your first concern
- Protect and promote the health of patients and the public
- Provide a good standard of practice and care
  - Keep your professional knowledge and skills up to date
  - Recognise and work within the limits of your competence
  - Work with colleagues in the ways that best serve patients' interests
- Treat patients as individuals and respect their dignity
  - Treat patients politely and considerately
  - Respect patients' right to confidentiality
- Work in partnership with patients
  - Listen to patients and respond to their concerns and preferences
  - Give patients the information they want or need in a way they can understand
  - Respect patients' right to reach decisions with you about their treatment and care
  - Support patients in caring for themselves to improve and maintain their health
- Be honest and open and act with integrity
  - Act without delay if you have good reason to believe that you or a colleague may be putting patients at risk
  - Never discriminate unfairly against patients or colleagues
  - Never abuse your patients' trust in you or the public's trust in the profession.

You are personally accountable for your professional practice and must always be prepared to justify your decisions and actions.

Good Medical Practice (2006) GMC

21.8   This is accompanied by a 52-page book of guidance, which identifies non-exhaustively actions that might be expected or should be avoided by a practitioner. There is also a series of other guides dealing with particular aspects of a doctor's duty, such as safety in good practice in prescribing, and acting as an expert witness.[1]

---

1   See www.gmc-uk.org/guidance/ethical_guidance.asp

21.9 The guidance recognises that doctors have a role to play in management of the organisations for which they work. A guide on management includes the following requirements:

- Doctors have to recognise that they have a role to play in management of healthcare as well as the treatment and care of individual patients:[2]

  All practising doctors are responsible for the use of resources; many will also lead teams or be involved in the supervision of colleagues; and most will work in managed systems, whether in the NHS or in the independent, military, prison or other sectors. Doctors have responsibilities to their patients, employers and those who contract their services. This means that doctors are both managers and are managed.

  Doctors make an important contribution to the management and leadership of health services and the delivery of healthcare across the UK as part of a multidisciplinary team. All doctors have some responsibilities for using resources; many will also lead teams or be involved in supervising colleagues.

- Their duty of safety as doctors continues in their managerial role:[3]
  You continue to have a duty of care for the safety and well-being of patients when you work as a manager.

- Doctors must still make patients their first priority even if they have a managerial role, but they also have a duty to the health of colleagues and their organisation:[4]
  Whether you have a management role or not, your primary duty is to your patients. Their care and safety must be your first concern. You also have a duty to the health of the wider community, your profession, your colleagues, and the organisation in which you work.

- Importantly, it is recognised that the execution of the duty to individual patients has to be informed by the resources available, subject to an obligation to raise and address any consequent concerns about safety:[5]
  Management involves making judgements about competing demands on available resources. If managerial concerns conflict with your primary duty to the extent that you are concerned for the safety or well-being of your patients, you should declare the conflict, seek colleagues' advice, and raise your concerns formally with senior management and external professional bodies as appropriate.

---

2   *Management for Doctors* (2006), General Medical Council, p4 para 1;
    www.gmc-uk.org/Managment_0510.pdf_32611806.pdf
3   *Management for Doctors* (2006), General Medical Council, p4 para 4;
    www.gmc-uk.org/Managment_0510.pdf_32611806.pdf
4   *Management for Doctors* (2006), General Medical Council, p11 para 20;
    www.gmc-uk.org/Managment_0510.pdf_32611806.pdf
5   *Management for Doctors* (2006), General Medical Council, p11 paras 21–23;
    www.gmc-uk.org/Managment_0510.pdf_32611806.pdf

22 At times you may not have the resources to provide the best treatment or care that all your patients need. At such times your decisions should be based on sound research information on efficiency and efficacy, and in line with your duties to protect life and health, to respect patients' autonomy and to treat justly.

23 You should take into account the priorities set by Government and the NHS or your employing or funding body. You should discuss the issues within the healthcare team, with senior management and, when appropriate, with patients.

21.10   Other requirements are shown in the box below.[6]

Providing a good standard of management practice

... you should do your best to make sure that:

- systems are in place to enable high quality medical services to be provided

- care is provided and supervised only by staff who have the appropriate skills (including communication skills), experience, training and qualifications

- significant risks to patients, staff and the health of the wider community are identified, assessed and addressed to minimise risk, and that they are reported in line with local and national procedures

- the people you manage (both doctors and other professionals) are aware of and follow the guidance issued by relevant professional and regulatory bodies, and that they are able to fulfil their professional duties so that standards of practice and care are maintained and improved

- systems are in place to identify the educational and training needs of students and staff, including locums, so that the best use is made of the time and resources available for keeping knowledge and skills up to date

- all decisions, working practices and the working environment are lawful, with particular regard to the law on employment, equal opportunities and health and safety

- information and policies on clinical effectiveness and clinical governance are publicised and implemented effectively.

---

6   *Management for Doctors* (2006), GMC, p7 para 12

21.11 Requirements are set out for raising and recording concerns where a practitioner believes that safety issues are not being addressed by boards, NHS bodies or the Government, although he/she is advised to take advice from a medical defence organisation before making concerns public.[7]

21.12 The GMC also publishes supplementary guidance on raising concerns and whistleblowing.[8]

Nurses

21.13 The Nursing and Midwifery Council (NMC) has a code of conduct for registered nurses, which runs to eight pages and covers 61 requirements.[9] The code starts with some overarching principles about trust:[10]

The people in your care must be able to trust you with their health and well-being

To justify that trust, you must:

- make the care of people your first concern, treating them as individuals and respecting their dignity
- work with others to protect and promote the health and well-being of those in your care, their families and carers, and the wider community
- provide a high standard of practice and care at all times
- be open and honest, act with integrity and uphold the reputation of your profession.

As a professional, you are personally accountable for actions and omissions in your practice, and must always be able to justify your decisions.

You must always act lawfully, whether those laws relate to your professional practice or personal life.

---

7   *Management for Doctors* (2006), General Medical Council, pp11–12 paras 24–25;
    www.gmc-uk.org/Managment_0510.pdf_32611806.pdf
8   Raising and Acting on Concerns About Patient Safety (2012), General Medical Council;
    www.gmc-uk.org/guidance/ethical_guidance/11860.asp
9   *The Code: Standards of conduct, performance and ethics for nurses and midwives* (2008), NMC
10 *The Code: Standards of conduct, performance and ethics for nurses and midwives* (2008), NMC, p3

21.14 The requirements developed from these principles include:

You must treat people as individuals and respect their dignity.

You must treat people kindly and considerately.

You must disclose information if you believe someone may be at risk of harm, in line with the law of the country in which you are practising.

You must work with colleagues to monitor the quality of your work and maintain the safety of those in your care.

You must work cooperatively within teams and respect the skills, expertise and contributions of your colleagues.

You must act without delay if you believe that you, a colleague or anyone else may be putting someone at risk.

You must inform someone in authority if you experience problems that prevent you working within this code or other nationally agreed standards.

You must not tamper with original records in any way.

21.15 Detailed guidance is given on subjects such as professional development, medicines management and the care of older people.

Other healthcare professionals

21.16 In its provisional statement to the Inquiry, the Health Professions Council explained that it regulated 15 professions, including physiotherapists, radiographers, paramedics, operating department practitioners, dieticians, and chiropodists.[11] In the Health and Social Care Act 2012, the council's remit was extended to also include the regulation of social workers, and its name changed to the Health and Care Professions Council (HCPC). The HCPC has a short document setting out the standards of conduct, performance and ethics applicable to all professions regulated by it:[12,13]

---

11 HPC Provisional Statement; Health Professions Order 2001 Schedule 3 [SI 2002/254] as amended.
    see www.hpc-uk.org/Assets/documents/10002D20HPORDER-2010CONSOLIDATION.pdf for consolidated version
12 *Standards of conduct, performance and ethics* (2012), HCPC, p3;
    www.hpc-uk.org/publications/standards/index.asp?id=38
13 *Standards of Conduct, Performance and Ethics,* (2008), HPC

Chapter 21 Values and standards

Your duties as a registrant

The standards of conduct, performance and ethics you must keep to

1   You must act in the best interests of service users.

2   You must respect the confidentiality of service users.

3   You must keep high standards of personal conduct.

4   You must provide (to us and any other relevant regulators) any important information about your conduct and competence.

5   You must keep your professional knowledge and skills up to date.

6   You must act within the limits of your knowledge, skills and experience and, if necessary, refer the matter to another practitioner.

7   You must communicate properly and effectively with service users and other practitioners.

8   You must effectively supervise tasks that you have asked other people to carry out.

9   You must get informed consent to provide care or services (so far as possible).

10 You must keep accurate records.

11 You must deal fairly and safely with the risks of infection.

12 You must limit your work or stop practising if your performance or judgement is affected by your health.

13 You must behave with honesty and integrity and make sure that your behaviour does not damage the public's confidence in you or your profession.

14 You must make sure that any advertising you do is accurate.

21.17   The standards are drawn deliberately broadly, and it is recognised that not all standards may apply to all professions. For example, standard 11 with regard to infection is unlikely to apply to them all. Explanation and amplification of each standard is given in the document. The guidance so given includes requirements:

- To treat service users with dignity and respect;
- To work in partnership with service users;
- Not to do anything there is reason to believe may put the service user's health and safety in danger;
- The health and safety of service users must come before any personal or professional loyalties at all times.

Healthcare support workers

21.18   Members of unqualified nursing staff, the support workers who now undertake so much of the hands-on care of patients, have no individual statement of values or code of conduct. They are expected to adopt the varying statements issued by their different employers and the general principles of the NHS Constitution.

Health service managers

21.19   There is a code of conduct for NHS managers. This applies to all NHS managers within the NHS structure. It continued to apply to NHS managers whose employers became NHS foundation trusts (FTs) as their contracts of employment in which the code was incorporated would have continued to be in force. It is a matter for FTs whether they incorporate it into new contracts.[14]

21.20   The code requires managers to observe a number of principles including the following:[15]

- Make care and safety of patients their first concern and to protect them from risk;
- Respect the public, patients, relatives, carers, NHS staff and partners in other agencies
- Be honest and act with integrity;
- Accept responsibility for their own work and the proper performance of the people they mange;
- Show commitment to working as a team member by working with all of their colleagues in the NHS and the wider community;
- Take responsibility for their own learning and development

21.21   The information available to the Inquiry suggests that the adoption of the Code of Practice in the contracts of managers is not universal. It does not, for instance, apply to in-house solicitors working for trusts.[16] Unlike the codes for doctors and nurses, there is no system of accountability directly attached to the manager's code.

The Institute of Healthcare Management code[17]

21.22   The Institute of Healthcare Management has produced a management code, aimed at building and sustaining workplaces with a positive work culture assured by a high quality of management in health and social care. A patient-centred approach is implicit in the code, which focuses on four areas:

---

14   Cumming WS0000016672–3, paras 59–62
15   Cumming WS0000016673, para 61
16   Knowles WS0000074634, para 6, T133.12
17   *The Management Code* (2012),The Institute of Healthcare Management; www.ihm.org.uk/documents/about_us/About_us_code_of_conduct_4ihmmanagement_code

- Managing self. To ensure a consistent and authentic approach to the provision of healthcare, managers of any NHS organisation are expected to exemplify the highest standards of professional behaviour and performance, remaining accountable for their actions and keeping up to date with best practice. They are required to disclose any personal interests and to safeguard confidential information, not seeking personal advantage from it.

- Managing the organisation. Providing a framework within which excellence can be delivered and patients/clients will be safe, managers should provide "clarity of purpose", ensuring that the organisation upholds its organisational objectives and that staff and the public can understand and relate to the way in which the organisation is run. This includes providing clear and unambiguous guidelines on recruitment, training and development, as well as ensuring a secure work environment with a high level of communication between staff and managers with regular appraisals.

- Managing people. To build and sustain trust, commitment and engagement between managers and those they manage, managers are expected to demonstrate a variety of qualities, including honesty and trustworthiness, politeness and fairness, as well as excellent communication skills. Furthermore, they should endeavour to support those they manage, listening and responding appropriately.

- Managing the service. To build, sustain and deliver high-quality health and care services, effective managers are expected to demonstrate an awareness of the impact of the NHS provider on society and of how to moderate that impact to society's benefit. They must also promote health and well-being within the service and prevent harm by taking appropriate actions to prevent or limit risks of harm to society that arise from any health and care activity of the organisation.

Foundation trust governors

21.23 Monitor issues a guide for governors of NHS foundation trusts. The guide does not contain a statement of values they are expected to adopt, but cross-refers to Monitor's code of governance for NHS governors,[18] which expects governors to act in the FT's best interests and adhere to its values and code of conduct.[19]

---

18 *Your Statutory Duties: A reference guide for NHS foundation trust governors,* (October 2009) Monitor, p17; www.monitornhsft.gov.uk/sites/default/files/Monitor_Governors_Guide%2011.08.2010.pdf

19 *The NHS Foundation Trust: Code of Governance,* (March 2010), Monitor, p14; www.monitornhsft.gov.uk/sites/default/files/Code%20of%20Governance_WEB%20%282%29.pdf

Foundation Trust Board directors

21.24 Monitor's corporate governance code requires that FT directors:

> *... should set the NHS foundation trust's vision, values and standards of conduct and ensure that its obligations to its members, patients and other stakeholders are understood, clearly communicated and met.*[20]

21.25 Directors should take decisions objectively in the interests of the FT. They are also required to:

> *... establish the values and standards of conduct for the NHS foundation trust and its staff in accordance with NHS values and accepted standards of behaviour in public life, which include the principles of selflessness, integrity, objectivity, accountability, openness, honesty and leadership (The Nolan Principles) ...*[21]

and

> *... operate a code of conduct that builds on the values of the NHS foundation trust and reflect high standards of probity and responsibility. The board of directors should follow a policy of openness and transparency in its proceedings and decision-making unless this conflicts with a need to protect the wider interests of the public or the NHS foundation trust (including commercial-in-confidence matters) and make clear how potential conflicts of interest are dealt with.*[22]

NHS directors

21.26 The Department of Health (DH) published a code of conduct and accountability for NHS boards in 1994, which was last revised in 2004. This sets out three public service values of accountability, probity and openness:

> *Accountability – everything done by those who work in the NHS must be able to stand the test of parliamentary scrutiny, public judgements on propriety and professional codes of conduct.*

> *Probity – there should be an absolute standard of honesty in dealing with the assets of the NHS: integrity should be the hallmark of all personal conduct in decisions affecting patients, staff and suppliers, and in the use of information acquired in the course of NHS duties.*

---

20 *Code of Governance* (March 2010), Monitor, p9;
     www.monitor-nhsft.gov.uk/sites/default/files/Code%20of%20Governance_WEB%20%282%29.pdf
21 *Code of Governance* (March 2010), Monitor, p11;
     www.monitor-nhsft.gov.uk/sites/default/files/Code%20of%20Governance_WEB%20%282%29.pdf
22 *Code of Governance* (March 2010), Monitor, p11;
     www.monitor-nhsft.gov.uk/sites/default/files/Code%20of%20Governance_WEB%20%282%29.pdf

Openness – there should be sufficient transparency about NHS activities to promote confidence between the NHS organisation and its staff, patients and the public.[23]

21.27 Among general principles outlined is that those who work in the NHS:

... have a responsibility to respond to staff, patients and suppliers impartially, to achieve value for money from the public funds with which they are entrusted and to demonstrate high ethical standards of personal conduct.[24]

21.28 Breaches of the code by a chair or non-executive director of a board were required to be reported to a Regional Commissioner of the NHS Appointments Commission.[25]

21.29 Boards are informed that they had a duty to:

... add value to the organisation[26]*, enabling it to deliver healthcare and health improvement within the law and without causing harm. It does this by providing a framework of good governance within which the organisation can thrive and grow ...*

21.30 While this document places an understandable emphasis on probity and governance, it would be difficult to discern from it the priority to be given to protecting patients and ensuring the maintenance of minimum standards. In any event, it predates the many changes that have been made to the system since 2004.

CHRE Consultation on standards for NHS board members

21.31 Between January and April 2012, the Council for Healthcare Regulatory Excellence (CHRE) ran a draft consultation on high-level ethical standards it had developed for members of NHS boards and governing bodies in England. These standards covered three distinct areas: personal behaviours, technical competence and business practices, and were intended to apply to members of the boards and governing bodies in NHS organisations, including chief executives, executive and non-executive directors and members of governing bodies of clinical commissioning groups. It was anticipated by the CHRE that the standards would apply to the boards and governing bodies of all existing, remaining and/or outgoing NHS trusts, clinical commissioning groups, NHS foundation trusts and the NHS Commissioning Board.

---

23 *Code of Conduct for NHS Boards; Code of Accountability for NHS Boards* (2nd ed 2004) Department of Health and NHS Appointments Commission, p2; www.dh.gov.uk/prod_consum_dh/groups/dh_digitalassets/@dh/@en/documents/digitalasset/dh_4116282.pdf
24 *Code of Conduct; Code of Accountability in the NHS* (2nd ed 2004) Department of Health and NHS Appointments Commission, p2; www.dh.gov.uk/prod_consum_dh/groups/dh_digitalassets/@dh/@en/documents/digitalasset/dh_4116282.pdf
25 *Code of Conduct; Code of Accountability in the NHS* (2nd ed 2004) Department of Health and NHS Appointments Commission, p4; www.dh.gov.uk/prod_consum_dh/groups/dh_digitalassets/@dh/@en/documents/digitalasset/dh_4116282.pdf
26 *Code of Conduct; Code of Accountability in the NHS* (2nd ed 2004) Department of Health and NHS Appointments Commission, p5; www.dh.gov.uk/prod_consum_dh/groups/dh_digitalassets/@dh/@en/documents/digitalasset/dh_4116282.pdf

21.32   Under the heading of personal behaviours, members were asked to commit to the values of the NHS Constitution and to promote equality, diversity and human rights in the treatment of staff, patients, their families and carers, and the wider community in the design and delivery of services for which they are responsible. In doing so, they should apply the values of accountability, honesty, openness, respect, professionalism and integrity.

21.33   In terms of technical competence, members should seek to make sound decisions in order to ensure excellence in the safety and quality of care as well as long-term financial sustainability and value for money. They should do this by, among other things, engaging in training and professional development, ensuring that performance is measured and by focusing on the safety of patients, the quality of care and patient experience.

21.34   In terms of business practices, members should demonstrate honesty, probity and integrity in their conduct, decisions and financial and commercial relationships. They should manage public money wisely and seek best value in the interests of the community they serve. Ultimately, they should be transparent in decision-making, providing evidence, reasoning and reasons behind decisions about budget and resource allocation.

NHS Constitution

21.35   The closest the NHS appears to have to a set of common values is the NHS Constitution. This is given statutory authority as a document to which all NHS bodies, including foundation trusts, must have regard in performing their functions.[27] It contains seven "guiding principles" which may not be changed in the course of the statutorily required 10-yearly review of its provisions.[28] A handbook of guidance which accompanies the Constitution must be reviewed every three years, and the Secretary of State is also required to publish a report on the effect of the Constitution in the same period.

---

27   Health Act 2009, section 2; www.legislation.gov.uk/ukpga/2009/21/contents
28   Health Act 2009, section 3; www.legislation.gov.uk/ukpga/2009/21/contents

21.36 The latest edition of the Constitution was published in March 2012.[29] The seven principles, each of which is developed in more detail in the text, are:

1. The NHS provides a comprehensive service to all

2. Access to NHS services is based on clinical need, not an individual's ability to pay

3. The NHS aspires to the highest standards of excellence and professionalism

4. NHS services must reflect the needs and preferences of patients, their families and their carers

5. The NHS works across organisational boundaries and in partnership with other organisations in the interest of patients, local communities and the wider population

6. The NHS is committed to providing best value for taxpayers' money and the most effective use of finite resources

7. The NHS is accountable to the public, communities and patients that it serves.

21.37 The Constitution includes, perhaps somewhat unfortunately at the back of the document rather than prominently at the front, a set of core "NHS values" which are said to underpin the principles and to be derived from extensive discussions with patients, staff and the public. These are shown in the box which follows:[30]

29 *The NHS Constitution* (8 March 2012), Department of Health; www.dh.gov.uk/prod_consum_dh/groups/dh_digitalassets/@dh/@en/documents/digitalasset/dh_132958.pdf. The Government also launched an exercise on 3 September 2012 through the NHS Future Forum to consider how the Constitution might be strengthened. This was intended to be followed by a formal public consultation later the same year. See: www.dh.gov.uk/health/2012/09/constitution-blog/

30 *NHS Constitution,* March 2012 edition, p14

Respect and dignity. We value each person as an individual, respect their aspirations and commitments in life, and seek to understand their priorities, needs, abilities and limits. We take what others have to say seriously. We are honest about our point of view and what we can and cannot do.

Commitment to quality of care. We earn the trust placed in us by insisting on quality and striving to get the basics right every time: safety, confidentiality, professional and managerial integrity, accountability, dependable service and good communication. We welcome feedback, learn from our mistakes and build on our successes.

Compassion. We respond with humanity and kindness to each person's pain, distress, anxiety or need. We search for the things we can do, however small, to give comfort and relieve suffering. We find time for those we serve and work alongside. We do not wait to be asked, because we care.

Improving lives. We strive to improve health and well-being and people's experiences of the NHS. We value excellence and professionalism wherever we find it – in the everyday things that make people's lives better as much as in clinical practice, service improvements and innovation.

Working together for patients. We put patients first in everything we do, by reaching out to staff, patients, carers, families, communities, and professionals outside the NHS. We put the needs of patients and communities before organisational boundaries.

Everyone counts. We use our resources for the benefit of the whole community, and make sure nobody is excluded or left behind. We accept that some people need more help, that difficult decisions have to be taken – and that when we waste resources we waste others' opportunities. We recognise that we all have a part to play in making ourselves and our communities healthier.

21.38   In between the principles and the values is a list of rights, responsibilities and pledges owed by and to patients and staff. The rights described are derived from a range of other legal sources and the Constitution provides a convenient means to bring them together. The responsibilities of staff are recited in the following box:[31]

---

31   NHS Constitution, March 2012 edition, pp12–13

You have a duty to accept professional accountability and maintain the standards of professional practice as set by the appropriate regulatory body applicable to your profession or role.

You have a duty to take reasonable care of health and safety at work for you, your team and others, and to cooperate with employers to ensure compliance with health and safety requirements.

You have a duty to act in accordance with the express and implied terms of your contract of employment.

You have a duty not to discriminate against patients or staff and to adhere to equal opportunities and equality and human rights legislation.

You have a duty to protect the confidentiality of personal information that you hold unless to do so would put anyone at risk of significant harm.

You have a duty to be honest and truthful in applying for a job and in carrying out that job.

The Constitution also includes **expectations** that reflect how staff should play their part in ensuring the success of the NHS and delivering high-quality care.

You should aim:

- to maintain the highest standards of care and service, taking responsibility not only for the care you personally provide, but also for your wider contribution to the aims of your team and the NHS as a whole;

- to take up training and development opportunities provided over and above those legally required of your post;

- to play your part in sustainably improving services by working in partnership with patients, the public and communities;

- to raise any genuine concern you may have about a risk, malpractice or wrongdoing at work (such as a risk to patient safety, fraud or breaches of patient confidentiality), which may affect patients, the public, other staff or the organisation itself, at the earliest reasonable opportunity;

- to be open with patients, their families, carers or representatives, including if anything goes wrong; welcoming and listening to feedback and addressing concerns promptly and in a spirit of cooperation. You should contribute to a climate where the truth can be heard and the reporting of, and learning from, errors is encouraged; and

- to view the services you provide from the standpoint of a patient, and involve patients, their families and carers in the services you provide, working with them, their communities and other organisations, and making it clear who is responsible for their care.

21.39 The associated handbook runs to 150 pages.[32] Of those 64 explain the rights of and commitments to patients and the public, 46 address the rights of, commitments to and responsibilities of staff, and none refer to the NHS core values.

21.40 There are obviously different ways in which these principles, values, rights, duties and expectations could be expressed, but it can be accepted that the Constitution appears to capture most of the matters many people would consider to be essential to a healthy NHS culture. There are a number of points to be made which go beyond mere drafting:

- The collection of values headed "working together for patients" should be given greater prominence or priority.
- The *overriding* value of the NHS should be that patients are put first in everything done by the NHS and everyone associated with it within their respective abilities to do so. This should ideally be a principle of the Constitution, but as legislation would be required to make it one, it should at least be promoted to being the overarching core value.
- While the usefulness of the handbook must be in doubt bearing in mind the quantity of NHS guidance and literature competing for the attention of patients, public and staff, it should be revised to include a much more prominent reference to the values and their significance.

21.41 Clearly any change to the Constitution can only be made in accordance with the Health Act 2009, but it is suggested that consideration is given to a change of the heading "Working together for patients" to include the following ingredients:

- The theme or heading of this group of values should be "Putting the patient first in everything we do".
- The ways in which this is achieved should not be limited to "reaching out", which in any event is a term lacking clarity in this context. Consideration should be given to including expectations that:
  - Staff put patients before themselves;
  - They will do everything in their power to protect patients from avoidable harm;
  - They will be honest and open with patients regardless of the consequences for themselves;
  - Where they are unable to provide the assistance a patient needs they will direct them where possible to those who can do so;
  - They will apply the NHS values in all their work.
- It would be helpful for the Constitution to include reference to, but obviously not recite, all the relevant professional and managerial codes mentioned above by which its staff are bound, including the code of conduct for NHS managers. As can be seen, they embrace

---

32   *The Handbook for the NHS Constitution for England* (8 March 2012), Department of Health;
     www.dh.gov.uk/prod_consum_dh/groups/dh_digitalassets/@dh/@en/documents/digitalasset/dh_132959.pdf

most if not all of the values summarised in the Constitution, and expand them in order to be relevant to the professions concerned. It should also incorporate an expectation that staff will follow guidance and comply with standards relevant to their work, such as those produced by the National Institute for Health and Clinical Excellence (NICE) and, where relevant, the Care Quality Commission (CQC), subject to any more specific requirements of their employers.

- The Rt Hon Andy Burnham MP, a former junior health Minister who proposed the development of an NHS constitution and who was later Secretary of State for Health, explained the genesis and purpose, as he saw it, of the Constitution. He told the Inquiry:

It was an idea that I first recall reading about in an article by Will Hutton, the writer and journalist, saying that some of the reform journey was creating a sense that the NHS was fragmenting, it was losing its sense of its – its core purpose. And as I went round ... I was thinking about how do you give people on the ground kind of certainty about what they value? And what they value is the NHS values. Thos are the things that get them out of bed in the morning, that's what matters to them, that's why they [sic] working for the NHS ... so I picked up the idea from there, but then thought one of the ways in which you give people the confidence to face a changing NHS was by putting the values very clearly into a – into a constitution. And I'm pleased that that was accepted as a recommendation and then it came into force.[33]

21.42 There is evidence that this objective has not yet been fulfilled. In an Inquiry which went to the heart of a breach of patients' rights and expectations, as well as those of staff, the Constitution was mentioned surprisingly infrequently by witnesses, except by way of apparent afterthought. Peter Walsh, Chief Executive of Action Against Medical Accidents (AvMA), told the Inquiry of information obtained as a result of a Freedom of Information Act request which suggested that there had been no case of DH contact or intervention in relation to a non-compliance of an NHS organisation with the Constitution.[34]

21.43 This suggests that it lacks the prominence and the acceptance it requires to be effective for the purpose for which Mr Burnham and no doubt Lord Darzi, who made the case for an NHS constitution in *High Quality Care*, for the HCC the final report of his NHS Next Stage Review; envisaged it. This requires correction, as the benefit of the Constitution may otherwise be reduced. The NHS Future Forum under the chairmanship of Professor Steve Field recently advised the Secretary of State in relation to the effect of the Constitution that:

---

33 Burnham T115.64–5
34 Walsh T23.143–4

We take heart from the fact that staff who are most informed about the NHS Constitution are also the most likely to value and champion it; and from the extent to which people in the East of England have become aware of the Constitution, showing the effectiveness of efforts made there. It is also clear that, when shared with different groups, the Constitution has the power to enthuse and galvanise people.[35]

21.44 However it was noted that:

In general, patients do not use the NHS Constitution as a benchmark for challenge and this suggests that the Constitution is not yet having the effect originally intended. For the Constitution to have real effect, it will be vital to raise awareness and embed it at every level in the NHS.[36]

21.45 In the letter accompanying the report Professor Field said:

It is not surprising but neither is it satisfactory that the Constitution is so little known – and rarely used – by staff and even less so by patients and the public. Just 3% of NHS staff say they have encountered a patient using the Constitution in this way. Plans to raise awareness of the Constitution among NHS staff were not consistently carried out, and plans to raise awareness among the general public were not implemented as intended. There is a big task ahead not only to raise awareness, but also to help people understand how to use the Constitution. Far from being the 'lawyer's charter' that some feared, the Constitution so far seems to have been very little used as a means of securing particular rights and pledges for people or of challenging poor service.[37]

21.46 The NHS Constitution should be made the point of first reference common to all NHS patients and staff in respect of the system's values and their respective rights, obligations and legitimate expectations. It should be kept as simple and concise as possible, but offering direction to more detailed provisions and guidance in relation to particular matters. If it could become the true gateway to information about such matters, the principles and core values would also be more widely disseminated and absorbed.

21.47 The values in the Constitution are deprived of meaning if staff are not obliged to act on them. All staff should be required to enter into an express commitment to abide by the NHS values and the Constitution, both of which should be incorporated into the contracts of employment to a greater extent than this is done at the moment. Contractors providing outsourced services should also be required to abide by these requirements and to ensure that staff employed by

---

35 *Report on the Effect of the NHS Constitution* (July 2012), Department of Health, p44; www.dh.gov.uk/health/2012/07/nhs-constitution/

36 *Report on the Effect of the NHS Constitution* (July 2012), Department of Health, p5; www.dh.gov.uk/health/2012/07/nhs-constitution/

37 *Letter to the Secretary of State from the NHS Future Forum working group on the Constiution* (26 June 2012), Department of Health, page 1; available at: www.dh.gov.uk/health/2012/07/nhs-constitution/

them for these purposes do so as well. These requirements could be included in the terms on which providers were commissioned to provide services.

Standards

What are standards for?

21.48   The standards which are the subject of professional regulation are set not to found a regime of punishment for wrongdoers, or the identification of liability, but for three distinct purposes:

- Protection of patients;
- Maintenance of confidence in the profession;
- Declaration and maintenance of proper standards of conduct and behaviour.[38]

21.49   In the setting of a healthcare system, standards can be set for a number of purposes including driving improvement and setting aspirations. However, the principal purpose of a system of standards in the healthcare system overseen by systems regulators can best be described by adapting these simple objectives from the professional sphere:

- Protection of patients and other users of the service;
- Maintenance of confidence in the healthcare system;
- Declaration and maintenance of proper standards of service.

21.50   It would be helpful if the standards which are set both for the healthcare professions and the healthcare system could be aligned in this way. It provides a degree of simplicity, and clarity of purpose.

Definition of standards

21.51   In healthcare there are multiple ways in which the quality of practice is influenced, but not all involve the formal setting of standards by an external body, whether it be Government or a regulator. The available methods include:

- Academic learning, teaching and training. Much of what healthcare professionals do and how they do it is led by what they learn not only at the beginning of their careers, but through subsequent professional training and development throughout. The messages transmitted in this way range from the near mandatory, where there is no room for controversy, to the completely discretionary, where there are many "schools of thought" and little evidence base.

---

38   *Report of the Committee of Inquiry into the Regulation of the Medical Profession* (1975), HM Stationery Office; *Raschid and Fatnani v The General Medical Council* (2007) 1 WLR 1460; *Bolton v Law Society* (1994) 1 WLR 512

- Clinical guidance. These range from published conclusions drawn from experience and anecdote to the more rigorous evidence-based methodology of the Cochrane Collaboration.[39] Guidance using the latter method brings together and reviews the existing published research evidence, often using the combined power of multiple research studies, and clarifies the conclusions to be drawn in favour of or against particular treatment and disease management methods. Clinical guidance by definition always admits room for clinical discretion and variation in relation to individual treatment decisions as it is rare for a recommended course of management to be invariably the right answer in every case. The necessary allowance for individual discretion carries with it the almost inevitable consequence that new guidance can take a long time to be commonly accepted. There is some evidence that the take-up of guidance is generally low.[40]
- Local protocols. All hospitals will have locally generated protocols for specific treatments or areas of treatment which junior doctors and nurses in particular are expected to follow. These are usually created by the relevant consultants acting collaboratively, but can sometimes be individual to particular consultants.
- Professional guidelines. Professional bodies and groups produce consensus statements and guidance on a range of treatment and ethical issues, the effect of which ranges from descriptive to near mandatory, such as surgical checklists.
- Public authorities' guidance. Guidance emanates from various public bodies such as NICE.
- Governmental and regulatory standards. Standards tend not to be specific to particular areas of clinical activity but generic.

21.52 Two consequences can flow from guidance for individual practitioners. It can justify a course of treatment against criticism of it. It may also expose practitioners and the organisations they work for to the risk of civil liability or disciplinary sanction in the event of non-compliance.[41] However, the more rigorous the evidence base used to produce guidance, the wider the professional consensus shown to be in agreement with it, and the clearer the logical justification for it, the greater the chance that it will have such consequences for those who elect not to follow it.

Different types of standards

21.53 Standards may be of general application to all healthcare, or specific to particular types of diagnosis, treatment or pathway. They can be of one of two types: they can set a minimum threshold below which practice must not fall, or they can define an aspiration to be achieved of excellence. In its work for Lord Darzi in 2008, Rand Health reviewed the standards being used in the NHS at the time.[42] They identified a crucial difference between the use, up to that

---

39 See www.cochrane.org for its methodology
40 Samanta, Samanta and Gunn (March 2004) "Legal consideration of clinical guidelines: Will NICE make a difference?", *Journal of the Royal Society of Medicine 133*, Vol. 96
41 Tingle, Foster (2002) "Clinical Guidelines, Law Policy and Practice", London Cavendish, pp101–et seq.
42 KM/12 PA0002000001

time, of the concept of standards by the DH as aspirations, and the practical use of standards as a means to define a level to be complied with:

The Department of Health (DH) defines standards as "a means of describing the level of quality that healthcare organisations are expected to meet or aspire to." We are more familiar with the use of standards as a level an organisation is expected to meet; aspirations would seem to be more consistent with goals than with standards.[43]

21.54 The review found that there were many bodies setting and implementing and monitoring standards, but that there was no overarching framework for quality within which they could operate.[44]

21.55 The report included a helpful table of the types of standard in use:[45]

Table 21.1: Types of standards

Type of Standard?	Purpose?	Who uses?	Nature of evidence?
Clinical performance	Improve outcomes of care	Physicians, patients, managers	Scientific, professional consensus
Safety: • Patient • Staff	Reduce the likelihood of harm	Managers, clinicians, regulators	Epidemiology (either from literature of [sic] from reporting systems)
Access (e.g., waiting times)	Reduce barriers to needed care; improve patient experience	Patients, managers	Patient preference, clinical evidence (delays that affect outcomes)
Service (e.g., patient experience)	Improve patient experience	Patients, managers, clinicians	Patient preferences
Regulatory	Ensure minimal acceptable levels of quality	Regulators, managers	Consensus
Professional	Ensure fitness for practice	Licensing bodies, regulators	Professional consensus
Population health	Motivate action to improve health	Public health professionals	Epidemiology
Financial	Increase value of health care product	Purchasers, regulators	Comparative performance
Data	Enhance utility	Standards setting bodies, vendors	Consensus

---

43   KM/12 PA0002000008, p8
44   KM/12 PA0002000024, p24
45   KM/12 PA0002000008-9, p8-9

21.56 The authors observed that:

The development of clinical standards is most mature and benefits from a scientific research tradition that allows the strength of the evidence to be accounted for. Standards in other areas have less sophisticated or well developed evidence bases to draw on and the process for developing standards is not as systematised.[46]

21.57 The aspiration for excellence is healthily embedded in the healthcare system. It is a principle eloquently described by Professor Sir John Tooke in his damning report on the Modernising Medical Careers/Medical Training Application Service (MMC/MTAS) disaster in 2007:

In reflecting on the evidence it received and formulating its Recommendations, the Independent Inquiry Panel was clear: mechanisms that smacked of an aspiration to mediocrity were inadmissible. Put simply 'good enough' is not good enough. Rather, in the interests of the health and wealth of the nation, we should aspire to excellence.[47]

21.58 Regulatory standards in healthcare, since Lord Darzi's report, *High Quality Care for All* have increasingly been in relation to the quality of care. This, in Lord Darzi's terminology is a concept which includes safety. In this report in Lord Darzi said:

High quality care should be as safe and effective as possible, with patients treated with compassion, dignity and respect. As well as clinical quality and safety, quality means care that is personal to each individual.[48]

High quality care is care where patients are in control, have effective access to treatment, are safe and where illnesses are not just treated, but prevented. These are manifestations of high quality care.[49]

21.59 First and foremost among the objectives was:

Getting the basics right, first time, every time.[50]

---

46 KM/12 PA0002000009, p9

47 *Aspiring to Excellence: Findings and Final Recommendations of the Independent Inquiry into Modernising Medical Careers* (Jan 2008), Professor Sir John Tooke, p5; www.mmcinquiry.org.uk/Final_8_Jan_08_MMC_all.pdf

48 *High Quality Care for All: NHS Next Stage Review Report* (June 2008), Department of Health, Cm 7432, p11; www.dh.gov.uk/en/Publicationsandstatistics/Publications/PublicationsPolicyAndGuidance/DH_085825

49 *High Quality Care for All: NHS Next Stage Review Report* (June 2008), Department of Health, Cm 7432, p45, para 57; www.dh.gov.uk/en/Publicationsandstatistics/Publications/PublicationsPolicyAndGuidance/DH_085825

50 *High Quality Care for All: NHS Next Stage Review Report* (June 2008), Department of Health, Cm 7432, p11; www.dh.gov.uk/en/Publicationsandstatistics/Publications/PublicationsPolicyAndGuidance/DH_085825

21.60 In connection with safety Lord Darzi said:

Continuously improving patient safety should be at the top of the healthcare agenda for the 21ˢᵗ century. The injunction to 'do no harm' is one of the defining principles of the clinical professions, and as my Interim Report made clear, safety must be paramount for the NHS. Public trust in the NHS is conditional on our ability to keep patients safe when they are in our care.[51]

21.61 His concept was that high-quality care should combine improvements in safety with empowerment of patients, increasing effectiveness of treatment and care, analysis and understanding of the patient experience, including the dignity and respect afforded to them.

21.62 To do this he argued that seven steps were required:

Bring clarity to quality. This means being clear about what high-quality care looks like in all specialities and reflecting this in a coherent approach to standards.

Measure quality: In order to work out how to improve we need to measure and understand exactly what we do. The NHS needs a quality measurement framework at every level.

Publish quality information. Making data on how well we are doing widely available to staff, patients and the public will help us understand variation and best practice so we can focus on improvement.

Recognise and reward quality. The system should recognise and reward improvement in the quality of care and service. This means ensuring that the right incentives are in place to support quality improvement.

Raise standards. Quality is improved by empowered patients and empowered professionals. There must be a stronger role for clinical leadership and management throughout the NHS.

Safeguard quality. Patients and the public need to be reassured that the NHS everywhere is providing high quality care. Regulation – of professions and services – has a key role to play in ensuring this is the case.

Stay ahead. New treatments are constantly redefining what high quality care looks like. We must support innovation to foster a pioneering NHS.[52]

---

51   *High Quality Care for All: NHS Next Stage Review Report* (June 2008), Department of Health, Cm 7432, p44, para 52; www.dh.gov.uk/en/Publicationsandstatistics/Publications/PublicationsPolicyAndGuidance/DH_085825
52   *High Quality Care for All: NHS Next Stage Review Report* (June 2008), Department of Health, Cm 7432, pp48–9; www.dh.gov.uk/en/Publicationsandstatistics/Publications/PublicationsPolicyAndGuidance/DH_085825

21.63 It was proposed that greater clarity would be brought to the definition of quality by commissioning NICE to "expand the number and reach" of quality standards, a process which is now under way. To measure quality a national quality framework was required, enabling the publication of comparable data on a national basis. Such national metrics needed to be supplemented by providers producing and using their own metrics adapted for their own circumstances, and expertise. The concept of "Quality Accounts" was introduced to require providers to publish information on their performance on quality.[53]

Effectiveness of standards

21.64 The Rand Health review referred to above surveyed perceptions of the effectiveness of the standards then in use. In considering *Standards for Better Health*, the core and developmental standards first published by the DH in July 2004 and updated in April 2006, the report discerned from respondents significant dissatisfaction. In summary:[54]

- The standards were not linked to a clear set of aims or goals;
- Although linked to domains such as patient safety, the effect of compliance on patient outcomes was not explained;
- The distinction between core and developmental standards was unclear;
- The standards were written at a high level making assessment of performance difficult;
- Self declaration was viewed with suspicion by outside observers;
- The Healthcare Commission (HCC) metrics were viewed as micro-management;
- There was no clear linkage between the standards and National Service Framework and NICE standards;
- The standards were viewed as being imposed by a "top-down" process and had not engaged providers and patients in their development.

21.65 The review found much support for the methodology of the National Service Frameworks (NSFs), noting that:[55]

- Each standard was set within the context of an aim (what result is being sought) and a rationale for the standard;
- Markers of good practice were clearly articulated with targets related to the strength of the evidence that supported the standard;
- National clinical audits were used to identify gaps and areas for prioritisation;
- NICE clinical guidelines were used where possible to inform the markers of good practice;
- The NSFs were developed by external groups representing the range of stakeholders;
- A well-respected, named clinical leader was responsible for overseeing implementation;

---

53 *High Quality Care for All: NHS Next Stage Review Report* (June 2008) Department of Health, Cmnd 7432, page 49–51; available at: www.dh.gov.uk/en/Publicationsandstatistics/Publications/PublicationsPolicyAndGuidance/DH_085825
54 KM/12 PA0002000014–5
55 KM/12 PA0002000011–2

Chapter 21 Values and standards

- While frameworks had a long-term focus, shorter-term actions were also included and they were updated to reflect progress made and/or new scientific developments.

21.66   One telling comment was made:

> *In general we found there was a gap in many other types of standards between the design of the standard and the approach to implementation. Often a different organization is tasked with either implementing or evaluating the implementation of a standard which can either result in disconnects or in failure to follow through.*[56]

21.67   The review considered NICE. It found that internationally NICE was regarded as "best in class" for its evidence-based products, and that it was well respected in the UK. There were concerns that it was too slow and too focused on fiscal issues, but it was thought to be responsive to criticism. The report recommended that it was unlikely that a new organisation could do better.[57]

21.68   It remarked that NICE guidance and the NSFs had been more effective:

> *... in part because of the clear link between the overall aims and the specific actions required to achieve those aims.*[58]

21.69   It considered that the aims articulated by Lord Darzi ("fair", "personalised", "effective" and "safe") were too high a level to be actionable, although they could be used to organise more specific goals related to specific clinical or service areas. It recommended that systematic approaches to integrating clinical guidelines with measures of quality should be developed, as there did not appear to be consistent links between standards and measures used to assess compliance.[59]

21.70   The aspiration to be "world class" was laudable, but as the report commented:

> *We would argue that being world class starts with getting the fundamentals right. From a clinical perspective, this might mean delivering care consistent with NICE Clinical Guidelines and the National Service Frameworks 95% of the time. Given that these cover the leading causes of death and disability, one imagines that this might contribute to substantial improvements in the health and well-being of the people of England. No other country has achieved this which would truly make England world class.*[60]

---

56   KM/12 PA0002000012
57   KM/12 PA0002000017–8
58   KM/12 PA0002000040
59   KM/12 PA0002000040–1
60   KM/12 PA0002000046–7

21.71 In a report for Lord Darzi prepared at the same time, *Achieving the Vision for Excellence in Quality*, the Institute for Healthcare Improvement (ICI) summarised its responses as showing

> *Most targets and standards appear to be defined in professional, organisational, and political terms, not in terms of patients' experiences of care ... Interviewees thought that the measurement of waiting times was a good start, but that this process measure needs to be set within a widely adopted, regularly used, larger set of measures of personalised care ... For example, measurement of patient satisfaction with waiting times would demonstrate a more personalised approach.* [61]

21.72 We have seen multiple examples of the Trust succeeding in evidencing "compliance" with standards and thereby giving false assurance that all was well. A key example is the Trust's approach to the HCC self declaration process and its reliance on external assessments, such as that produced by the NHS Litigation Authority. This is described in *Chapter 2: The Trust*.

21.73 Therefore, on the evidence of that experience alone it has to be concluded that the various approaches to regulation through standards compliance have failed to uncover the deficiencies which matter to patients. That there is a disconnect between "compliance" and reality has been demonstrated graphically by the National Audit of Dementia Care in Hospitals 2011. [62] That revealed that:

- None of the hospitals audited met all the standards considered to be essential; [63]
- There was little correlation between the results of the organisational checklist (ie compliance with standards relating to policies) and the case note audit (in which compliance with standards in practice was examined):

> *... at hospital level the percentage of casenotes showing that a mental state assessment had been carried out was not significantly different between those hospitals that had a policy specifying the assessment and those that did not.* [64]

> *Hospital guidelines and procedures often set out the range of assessments that should be expected. The results of the casenote audit showed that important elements of the assessment were not routinely carried out.* [65]

61 KM/12 PA00020000096
62 *Report of the National Audit of Dementia Care in General Hospitals 2011* (December 2011), Royal College of Psychiatrists, London, www.rcpsych.ac.uk/workinpsychiatry/quality/nationalclinicalaudits/dementia/nationalauditofdementia.aspx
63 *Report of the National Audit of Dementia Care in General Hospitals 2011* (December 2011), Royal College of Psychiatrists, London, p11; www.rcpsych.ac.uk/workinpsychiatry/quality/nationalclinicalaudits/dementia/nationalauditofdementia.aspx
64 *Report of the National Audit of Dementia Care in General Hospitals 2011* (December 2011), Royal College of Psychiatrists, London, p11; www.rcpsych.ac.uk/workinpsychiatry/quality/nationalclinicalaudits/dementia/nationalauditofdementia.aspx
65 *Report of the National Audit of Dementia Care in General Hospitals 2011* (December 2011), Royal College of Psychiatrists, London, p12; www.rcpsych.ac.uk/workinpsychiatry/quality/nationalclinicalaudits/dementia/nationalauditofdementia.aspx

21.74 The results for the individual themes set out in the standards were striking:[66]

Table 21.2: Assessment of individual themes

Area for assessment	% of hospital assessment procedures including this area	% of assessments recorded as carried out in casenotes
Assessment of functioning	84	26
Nutritional status	96	70
Social assessment	96	72
Environmental assessment	91	65
Pressure sore risk assessment	–	87 [= 13% not carried out]
Inquiry about pain	–	76 [= 24% patients not asked about pain]
Measurement of cognitive impairment of dementia patients on admission and discharge	–	6
Multi-disciplinary nutritional assessment	96	70 [63% of which included recording of weight]
Record in casenote of factors that might cause distress to the person with dementia	–	24
Planning for discharge within 24 hours of admission	94	+/- 50%

21.75 In addition, only 5% of hospitals had mandatory training in awareness of dementia for all staff.[67]

21.76 That means that even if there were no other evidence to suggest that Stafford was not a unique case, it would not be possible to be assured by the present system that there were no other such cases.

How can the standards system be improved?

An integrated hierarchy of standards

21.77 The standards bequeathed to the HCC were criticised, at least with the benefit of hindsight, for being referable to processes rather than outcomes, whereas the CQC has replaced the HCC's 44 standards with 16 key outcomes.[68] However, it needs to be emphasised that this was an early attempt to produce system-wide standards where effectively there had been none before. It would be wrong to dismiss assessments of systems as having no value. There is no

---

66 *Report of the National Audit of Dementia Care in General Hospitals 2011* (December 2011), Royal College of Psychiatrists, London, pp13–16 and p19; www.rcpsych.ac.uk/workinpsychiatry/quality/nationalclinicalaudits/dementia/nationalauditofdementia.aspx

67 *Report of the National Audit of Dementia Care in General Hospitals 2011* (December 2011), Royal College of Psychiatrists, London, p17; www.rcpsych.ac.uk/workinpsychiatry/quality/nationalclinicalaudits/dementia/nationalauditofdementia.aspx

68 Burnham T115.43–5; Keogh T123.26–7; Hamblin WS0000031009, para 15

doubt that the formulation of such standards was an advance on what had gone before, and it may well have been easier as a first step to produce process rather than outcome-based standards. It was then believed that a well run system could be used as a proxy indicator of a good standard of care. The danger has turned out to be that the demonstration of a system on paper can become an end in itself, with insufficient attention being paid to whether it actually delivered good care.

21.78   Another criticism, made by Mr Burnham, was that the HCC standards, the compliance with which was combined into a rating given in the Annual Healthcheck, produced one result, which pre-supposed that the same standard was being reached throughout an organisation.

> *I felt, even at that time as a Minister, that the – the placing of one label on an organisation when it came to quality of service, be that poor, acceptable, fair or good, or whatever the system was used at the time, would never capture the full range of what went on within a hospital, and that was something that I became more and more clear about the longer I was a health Minister. It seems to me that the Health Service is not – or hospitals are not uniformly good or bad. There will always be a mixture of quality within any organisation. And the troubling things about the health check, as was then, is it would place one label on an organisation and not actually capture the full range of what was taking place within it.[69]*

21.79   Again, it is understandable that an attempt was made at reducing the results of compliance assessment to information thought to be more easily understood by the public. However, experience has shown it to be important that the system of standards is capable of requiring compliance in all relevant services, and that the system of regulation is capable of detecting poor practice in parts of organisations which may otherwise be functioning successfully.

21.80   In *Chapter 11: Regulation: the Care Quality Commission*, the difficulties posed by the current format of the core outcomes are considered. It is concluded that, while it is acceptable that universally accepted minimum standards can properly be set at a high level, there needs to be greater clarity about what is a fundamental standard below which service provision is simply unacceptable, and what is a more discretionary standard of performance, or enhanced standard, which may be dependent on factors other than the interests of the individual patient.

21.81   Beneath these overarching outcomes there needs to be a set of practical standards by which the overarching outcomes can be achieved in the clinical setting. These, it has been recommended, should not be within the province of the Government or the regulator but NICE, or pending its production of a relevant standard, with other established professional organisations such as the Royal Colleges, using well respected methodologies for identifying

---

69   Burnham T115.13

best practice. These practical standards would be required to be followed by providers unless they could demonstrate that they had an equally safe way of providing the same service.

Clarity of status and purpose

21.82 Standards/outcomes should be classified to make their status and purpose clear; the following categories should be developed:

- Fundamental standards or outcomes of safety (fundamental safety standards) and of care (fundamental essential care standards) should be set, which are designed to protect patients from avoidable harm and treatment and care of a quality below that which is acceptable. These are standards in respect of which non-compliance should not be tolerated. These could include requirements with regard to consent, nutrition and hydration, hygiene, infection control, and operating theatre safety procedures. Examples of what these might look like are described in *Chapter 11: Regulation: the Care Quality Commission*.
- In *Chapter 11: Regulation: the Care Quality Commission* it is suggested that there be a defined set of duties to maintain and operate an effective system, which avoids unacceptable outcomes, or, put in another way, complies with fundamental safety and essential care standards. A service which persistently failed to comply with these standards should not be permitted to continue. Individual cases of non-compliance leading to serious harm or the exposure of risk of such harm which are not shown to be exclusively due to an individual's failure in performing their duty, and which could have been prevented by the organisation's system, should be taken seriously, and should expose the organisation to potentially serious consequences. Currently, breach of this sort of requirement leaves an organisation open to regulatory interventions and in the last resort prosecution for regulatory offences. Systemic failures leading to unacceptable outcomes should remain offences for which prosecutions can be brought against organisations in serious cases.
- Standards of quality (enhanced standards), which do not concern risks of unacceptable harm but rather desirable quality, might include access standards (in relation, for example, to waiting periods falling short of those causing an unacceptable risk of harm) or more efficient methods of treatment. Such standards could still set minimum requirements but these could be more discretionary and subject to availability of resources.
- Developmental standards encouraging the pursuit of excellence. These would be more by way of guidance to ambitious organisations wishing to provide a standard of care over and above the minimum.

21.83 All such standards would of course require regular review and modification. Today's enhanced standard could become tomorrow's fundamental requirement.

A coherent system

21.84 It would assist if there was some form of structure for the standards that providers and their staff are required to work to, rather than the existing state of affairs in which standards come from multiple sources, often without reference to other standards addressing overlapping issues, and for which there is accountability to different organisations. Efforts need to be made to remove duplication and overlap as far as possible and to work towards a cohesive structure of:

- Overarching standards; and
- Operational and procedural standards.

21.85 The system of standards requires clarity and consensus as to where the responsibility lies for the creation, review and promulgation of each standard.

21.86 Standards need to be formulated as far as possible so that:

- They promote the likelihood of the service required by patients being delivered safely and effectively;
- It is clear what has to be done to comply with it;
- There is accessible reference to the evidence base informing the standard;
- Measurable indicators of compliance and non-compliance are defined.

Who should set the standards?

21.87 Historically, standards in healthcare have been set and defined by governments, interpreted by regulators and performance managers, and applied by those who are regulated. As can be seen in *Chapter 9: Regulation: the Healthcare Commission* and *Chapter 11: Regulation: the Care Quality Commission*, there have been challenges in establishing an effective system for assuring that proper care is delivered by this means. There have been issues about the nature of the standards, also whether they should be process or outcome based.

21.88 As recommended in *Chapter 11: Regulation: the Care Quality Commission*, responsibility for standard setting should be allocated as follows:

- Government: through regulation should define in fundamental standards outcomes which must be avoided. These should be limited to those matters it is universally accepted should be avoided for individual patients accepted for treatment by a healthcare provider. Of necessity, most of these are likely to be high level generic requirements.

- Either by itself or through other bodies, the NHS Commissioning Board (NCB) should be free to devise enhanced standards designed to drive improvement in the health service. Failure to comply with such standards should be a matter for performance management by commissioners rather than the regulator, although the latter could be charged with enforcing the provision by providers of accurate information about compliance to the public.
- NICE should be commissioned to formulate standard procedures and practice designed to provide the practical means of compliance, and indicators by which compliance with both fundamental and enhanced standards can be measured.
- The CQC should set down the indicators by which it intends to monitor the accuracy of information in relation to compliance with fundamental standards, using wherever possible the tools offered by NICE
- Individual organisations: in an innovative health service culture where excellent quality is the priority, it is hoped that cutting-edge organisations would also push themselves to work beyond NICE in developing advances in healthcare, by setting their own, higher standards.

21.89   In every case, it is important that those who have to apply the standards, mainly doctors and nurses, are able to understand their purpose, to accept their significance for patients, and agree that measurement of compliance is fair and reliable. It was a criticism made by David Haslam, a clinical adviser of the HCC, in an email exchange with Dr Heather Wood, who led the HCC; investigation into the Trust that clinicians were insufficiently engaged in the then prevalent standards:

> *There are many reasons for this – partly to do with the fact that it isn't seen to measure the things that really matter to clinicians and their patients, partly because of overt gaming, and partly because few clinicians actually identify personally with their trust anyway – they identify more with their service and their specialty.*[70]

21.90   For these reasons, it is essential that patient groups, as well as professional bodies in whom doctors and nurses have confidence, are fully involved in the formulation of standards, and in the means of measuring compliance. A standard which is not seen as relevant and helpful by both healthcare professionals and their patients is unlikely to be a standard worth maintaining.

Information about compliance

21.91   In order for the public and commissioners to make informed decisions about treatment, it is necessary for full and accurate information about compliance with all standards to be available to them.

---

70   HCC0000000187, Email exchange between Heather Wood, David Haslam and Nick Bishop (29 October 2008)

21.92 Trust Boards must be made responsible for providing, through their quality accounts, full and accurate information about their compliance with each standard which applies to them. To the extent that it is not practical in a written report to set out detail, this should be made available via each trust's website. Reports should no longer be confined, as is the case with some organisations, to reports on their achievements as opposed to a fair representation of areas where compliance has not been achieved. A full account should be given as to the methods used to produce the information.

21.93 Any false information should be outlawed. To make or be party to a wilfully or recklessly false statement as to compliance with fundamental standards in the required quality account should be made a criminal offence.

Policing of compliance with standards

21.94 The means of monitoring compliance by the CQC is considered in *Chapter 11: Regulation: the Care Quality Commission*. It is concluded that while gathering and analysis of information about risk-related matters is an important aid to the regulator's task, the most effective means of protecting patients is to police compliance by direct observation of practice, direct interaction with patients, carers and staff, and audit of records. All this may be supported by collection and analysis of intelligence. Such activities should take priority over monitoring and audit of policies and protocols.

21.95 The regulatory system should retain the capacity to undertake in-depth investigations where these appear to be required. The interests of patients and the public require that where a serious deficiency is found or suspected, and there is a risk that the local management have not or cannot correct it, regulators can undertake an organisation-wide inquiry. It is not always sufficient to identify a particular cause for concern and see that it is corrected. Such symptomatic treatment may overlook the cause of a more widespread disease. Where such investigations are necessary they may, as in the case of the Trust, take some time. Such interventions can be complicated and require time to perform properly. The need for time should not, however, inhibit the taking of whatever precautionary measures are needed to protect the public. Just as the GMC, for example, exercises readily a power to suspend practitioners from the register on an interim basis if this is deemed necessary to protect the public while investigations are concluded, a healthcare regulator must be free to require or recommend immediate protective steps even if it has yet to reach a concluded view or acquired all the evidence. The test should be whether it has reasonable grounds to make the interim requirement or recommendation.

Peer review

21.96 It is clear from the evidence before the Inquiry that a large number of staff, and indeed departments at the Trust, became isolated from their peers in both other organisations and their professional bodies.

21.97 A common culture, and the adoption of an honest and transparent approach to service provision, demands that all those engaged in healthcare provision are aware of how common problems and issues are faced and met by peers, either working within the same organisation, or in other organisations. This may be achieved, on occasion, by short periods of secondment on an inter-departmental, or inter-organisational basis. Peer review is therefore a key issue in the formulation of the common culture and openness and transparency that is needed by all those working in healthcare provision.

21.98 The Inquiry heard from witnesses, attendees at the Inquiry Seminars and from the hospital visits undertaken how important it is that organisations do not become isolated and how vitally important it is that they constantly benchmark themselves with other organisations and against best practice. There is not one of us who cannot learn from observing how others engaged in similar work meet the challenges that they face – even if only to gain reassurance on occasions that others do not do things differently, or better. Keeping up-to-date in one's everyday practice, and providing modern and up-to-date care should be at the forefront of all practitioners' minds, whether clinicians, registered nurses or healthcare workers. Leaders of healthcare provision, or managers of organisations are often in lonely places, and may feel that problems are for them alone to solve, even though peers may well have faced down, and resolved, very similar issues. It may well be that, had the Trust not been an isolated organisation, its board could have learned to manage better the implementation of cost improvement plans had they had detailed discussions with others who had done so effectively, and safely. The benefit of peer review should therefore permeate any organisation, from the top to the bottom.

21.99 There is much literature written about peer review and it is not the place of this Inquiry to give a critique of how individuals and organisations should best and most effectively approach this. However, peer review can and should play a fundamental and key role in ensuring that organisations are delivering against the fundamental standards to be regulated by the CQC, and the enhanced standards contracted by commissioners of services. Professional regulators should be concerned with evidence of peer review in considering issues of revalidation. Managers and executives should be able to evidence peer review to their boards, which themselves should be able to demonstrate to the public their own learning from benchmarking with other providers. Learning from peer review should be a topic for consideration at any individual appraisal of performance.

21.100 Whilst peer review will also have specific relevance in cases of practitioners where there may be concerns about substandard performance, its role is far more fundamental in changing behaviours and ensuring a consistent and caring culture throughout the provision of healthcare services. Peer review should therefore form an essential part of practice across all providers of NHS-funded care and be an important contribution to both internal and external governance, oversight and regulation, and participants should engage in such review publicly and enthusiastically.

21.101 It should be regarded both by employers of healthcare professionals and the professionals themselves as an intrinsic part of their employment to participate in peer review of this nature. It should become the norm as a primary means of spreading good practice, guarding against poor standards, and protecting patients in a spirit of mutual cooperation. Whatever may be said about patient choice and competition, there should be no competition over compliance with fundamental standards, only a mutual determination to assist each other to maintain compliance and to develop ever-improving practice above those standards.

21.102 Therefore all healthcare organisations, whether providers, commissioners and regulators, or professional representative bodies, should consider how best to build on existing peer review networks and to develop new ones for these purposes.

Summary

21.103 A common culture needs a set of common values. There are many sources from which the values essential to patient-centred healthcare can be derived and these are currently found mainly in relation to different parts of the workforce. The NHS Constitution is a laudable start at identifying the common values of the NHS as well as bringing together the rights, commitments and obligations of all stakeholders. However it could benefit from further development to give proper prominence and status to the values that need to be embraced by all who work in healthcare.

21.104 The standards required of healthcare provision derive from the common values and need to be defined in a way which results in their practical, as well as theoretical, acceptance by all who work in the service, and a better understanding of their significance on the part of the public. The standards should be effective in protecting patients and maintaining public confidence in the healthcare service.

21.105 The various changes made in the system of standards since regulatory system standards were first introduced have seen progressive improvement in the concept, but there is more that could be done. The objectives of standards need to be articulated more clearly and aligned with the very clear objectives of the regulation of healthcare professionals.

21.106 Standards should be more clearly divided into:

- Fundamental standards of safety and quality;
- Enhanced quality standards;
- Developmental standards which set out longer-term goals for providers.

21.107 Fundamental safety and quality standards would be defined to make it clear what is the minimum required to protect patients from avoidable harm, and what is treatment and care which falls below a tolerable standard. Failure to comply with such fundamental safety and quality standards should not be tolerated, whether in individual cases or within an organisation. It should be recognised that a service incapable of meeting such standards should not be permitted to continue. Breach of these standards should result in regulatory consequences an for organisation in the case of a system failure and individual accountability where individual professionals are responsible. Where harm to a patient has resulted, failure to disclose breaches of these standards to the affected patient and a regulator should also attract such measures. Breaches not resulting in actual harm but which have exposed patients to the risk of harm should also be regarded as unacceptable.

21.108 More general enhanced quality standards may depend more on available resources, and be capable of being achieved by improvements in management and professionalism. They will focus on improvements in effectiveness and are more likely to be the focus of commissioners and progressive provider leadership than the regulator. Information about attainment of such standards is likely to assist patients in making a choice of provider.

21.109 Developmental standards can be a reflection of the constant striving within healthcare for excellence and progress.

21.110 Although it is acceptable for fundamental standards to be identified by the Government in consultation with the public and stakeholders, the practical underpinning of the route to compliance can be more effectively provided by a body widely accepted as the authority in evidence-based, consensus-driven standards, NICE. Their task in developing clinical standards should be broadened and accelerated to identify the general and particular procedures required to comply with fundamental safety and quality standards in as many spheres of activity as possible. These standards should include both outcome and process-based standards, the sole criterion being whether the available evidence indicates that compliance with them protects patients from harm and ensures the minimum level of acceptable quality. All such standards should include evidence-based means of measuring compliance, as far as possible building on information already available within the system or on readily observable behaviour.

21.111 The regulator should then be left free to focus more on the policing of compliance with fundamental standards using the indicators and measures identified by NICE, by way of audit and physical inspection and investigation, and less on their formulation. It should be the part of the regulator's duty to monitor the accuracy of information disseminated by providers and commissioners in compliance with fundamental standards and their compliance with the requirement of honest disclosure. Because of the need for zero tolerance of non-compliance, the regulator must be willing to consider individual cases as well as systemic causes for concern.

21.112 Other standards should be recognised as being in the domain of providers themselves and commissioners.

Summary of recommendations

Recommendation 3

The NHS Constitution should be the first reference point for all NHS patients and staff and should set out the system's common values, as well as the respective rights, legitimate expectations and obligations of patients.

Recommendation 4

The core values expressed in the NHS Constitution should be given priority of place and the overriding value should be that patients are put first, and everything done by the NHS and everyone associated with it should be informed by this ethos.

Recommendation 5

In reaching out to patients, consideration should be given to including expectations in the NHS Constitution that:

- Staff put patients before themselves;
- They will do everything in their power to protect patients from avoidable harm;
- They will be honest and open with patients regardless of the consequences for themselves;
- Where they are unable to provide the assistance a patient needs, they will direct them where possible to those who can do so;
- They will apply the NHS values in all their work.

Recommendation 6

The handbook to the NHS Constitution should be revised to include a much more prominent reference to the NHS values and their significance.

Recommendation 7

All NHS staff should be required to enter into an express commitment to abide by the NHS values and the Constitution, both of which should be incorporated into the contracts of employment.

Recommendation 8

Contractors providing outsourced services should also be required to abide by these requirements and to ensure that staff employed by them for these purposes do so as well. These requirements could be included in the terms on which providers are commissioned to provide services.

Recommendation 9

The NHS Constitution should include reference to all the relevant professional and managerial codes by which NHS staff are bound, including the Code of Conduct for NHS Managers.

Recommendation 10

The NHS Constitution should incorporate an expectation that staff will follow guidance and comply with standards relevant to their work, such as those produced by the National Institute for Health and Clinical Excellence and, where relevant, the Care Quality Commission, subject to any more specific requirements of their employers.

Recommendation 13

Standards should be divided into:

- Fundamental standards of minimum safety and quality – in respect of which non-compliance should not be tolerated. Failures leading to death or serious harm should remain offences for which prosecutions can be brought against organisations. There should be a defined set of duties to maintain and operate an effective system to ensure compliance;
- Enhanced quality standards – such standards could set requirements higher than the fundamental standards but be discretionary matters for commissioning and subject to availability of resources;
- Developmental standards which set out longer term goals for providers – these would focus on improvements in effectiveness and are more likely to be the focus of commissioners and progressive provider leadership than the regulator.

All such standards would require regular review and modification.

Recommendation 16

The Government, through regulation, but after so far as possible achieving consensus between the public and professional representatives, should provide for the fundamental standards which should define outcomes for patients that must be avoided. These should be limited to those matters that it is universally accepted should be avoided for individual patients who are accepted for treatment by a healthcare provider.

Recommendation 17

The NHS Commissioning Board together with Clinical Commissioning Groups should devise enhanced quality standards designed to drive improvement in the health service. Failure to comply with such standards should be a matter for performance management by commissioners rather than the regulator, although the latter should be charged with enforcing the provision by providers of accurate information about compliance to the public.

Recommendation 18

It is essential that professional bodies in which doctors and nurses have confidence are fully involved in the formulation of standards and in the means of measuring compliance.

Recommendation 20

The Care Quality Commission should be responsible for policing the fundamental standards, through the development of its core outcomes, by specifying the indicators by which it intends to monitor compliance with those standards. It should be responsible not for directly policing compliance with any enhanced standards but for regulating the accuracy of information about compliance with them.

Recommendation 21

The regulator should have a duty to monitor the accuracy of information disseminated by providers and commissioners on compliance with standards and their compliance with the requirement of honest disclosure. The regulator must be willing to consider individual cases of gross failure as well as systemic causes for concern.

Recommendation 22

The National Institute for Health and Clinical Excellence should be commissioned to formulate standard procedures and practice designed to provide the practical means of compliance, and indicators by which compliance with both fundamental and enhanced standards can be measured. These measures should include both outcome and process based measures, and should as far as possible build on information already available within the system or on readily observable behaviour.

Recommendation 24

Compliance with regulatory fundamental standards must be capable so far as possible of being assessed by measures which are understood and accepted by the public and healthcare professionals.

Recommendation 25

It should be considered the duty of all specialty professional bodies, ideally together with the National Institute for Health and Clinical Excellence, to develop measures of outcome in relation to their work and to assist in the development of measures of standards compliance.

Recommendation 28

Zero tolerance: A service incapable of meeting fundamental standards should not be permitted to continue. Breach should result in regulatory consequences attributable to an organisation in the case of a system failure and to individual accountability where individual professionals are responsible. Where serious harm or death has resulted to a patient as a result of a breach of the fundamental standards, criminal liability should follow and failure to disclose breaches of these standards to the affected patient (or concerned relative) and a regulator should also attract regulatory consequences. Breaches not resulting in actual harm but which have exposed patients to a continuing risk of harm to which they would not otherwise have been exposed should also be regarded as unacceptable.

Recommendation 29

It should be an offence for death or serious injury to be caused to a patient by a breach of these regulatory requirements, or, in any other case of breach, where a warning notice in respect of the breach has been served and the notice has not been complied with. It should be a defence for the provider to prove that all reasonably practicable steps have been taken to prevent a breach, including having in place a prescribed system to prevent such a breach.

Chapter 22
Openness, transparency and candour

Key themes

- Openness, transparency and candour are necessary attributes of organisations providing healthcare services to the public. There is strong evidence based on the actions in particular of the Trust and the Care Quality Commission (CQC) that insufficient observance of these requirements has been prevalent.

- The Trust made inaccurate statements about its mortality rates, information about serious concerns was not passed to the regulator, and a report critical of the care provided was not disclosed to the coroner. Frank and accurate information about the cause of death of patients was not universally conveyed to relatives. Exaggerated claims of success were made to the public.

- The CQC made inappropriate use of non-disparagement clauses, and exhibited an inappropriately hostile reaction to communications of relevant concerns to the Inquiry – a reaction incompatible with its aspiration to be an open organisation welcoming and reflective of constructive criticism.

- Insufficient openness, transparency and candour lead to delays in victims learning the truth, obstruct the learning process, deter disclosure of information about concerns, and cause regulation and commissioning to be undertaken on inaccurate information and understanding.

- There is a requirement not only for clinicians to be candid with patients about avoidable harm, but for safety concerns to be reported openly and truthfully, and for organisations to be accurate, candid and not provide misleading information to the public, regulators and commissioners.

- Current requirements for openness, transparency and candour do not cover uniformly and consistently the areas in which these are needed.

- Statutory duties should be created, supported by commensurate sanctions and remedies, creating obligations on healthcare providers believing or suspecting injury has been caused to patients to give them the information they require and on registered healthcare professionals who hold such a belief or suspicion to inform their employer. A further statutory duty should be imposed on directors of healthcare organisations to be truthful in any information required to be given personally or by their organisation to a regulator or commissioner in pursuance of a statutory obligation. There should be criminal liability for deliberately or recklessly made untruthful statements.

- All relevant policies and guidance should be reviewed and amended to give effect to the requirements of openness, transparency and candour.

Introduction

22.1   Much has been said at this Inquiry about a duty of candour. This chapter examines the need for openness, transparency and candour in healthcare and considers what steps should be taken to ensure it is not only enshrined as a principle, but is actually universally observed in practice. These terms may have different meanings and applications, but in this chapter, they have, unless the context otherwise requires, the following meanings:

- *Openness*: the proactive provision of information about performance, negative as well as positive;
- *Transparency*: the provision of facilities for all interested persons and organisations to see the information they need properly to meet their own legitimate needs in assessing the performance of a provider in the provision of services;
- *Candour*: the volunteering of all relevant information to persons who have, or may have, been harmed by the provision of services, whether or not the information has been requested, and whether or not a complaint or a report about that provision has been made.

22.2   At first sight it is surprising that consideration of this subject is needed at all. The statements made over the decades supporting the principle of candour are legion, as are policies adopting it. However, large organisations have a tendency to want to conduct their business behind closed doors, as do governments and professions. This is not always the result of ulterior motives, such as a wish to avoid paying compensation even where there is an entitlement to it. For example, the frank exchange of views thought to be required to enable informed decisions can sometimes be thought to be inhibited by being obliged to hold such discussions in public.

The Trust

22.3 There were a number of episodes exposed by the evidence before the Inquiry, that showed a lack of candour on the part of the Trust and the deleterious effects of this.

Inaccurate statements about mortality

22.4 The Trust repeatedly asserted that it had received a report from CHKS (a provider of healthcare information) which indicated that its mortality rate was below the national average of 2%. Such an assertion appeared in the information given to the board-to-board meeting with Monitor on 5 December 2007.[1] The 2% figure from the purported CHKS report was repeatedly referred to at a presentation given on mortality to the West Midlands Strategic Health Authority (WMSHA) on 16 May 2007, when it was suggested that CHKS had produced quite different figures from Dr Foster. On 15 June, a report from the Trust to the SHA referred to CHKS, as reassurance that the Trust's mortality was at the low end of the national benchmark.[2] On 17 July, the Trust again referred to CHKS in a letter to the WMSHA in support of its conclusion that:

> *Clearly this gives the organisation, and particularly our clinicians some comfort that in overall terms, our mortality rates do not appear to provide any significant concern.*[3]

22.5 When asked to produce it to the Inquiry, no report by CHKS the Trust found and CHKS has denied that it ever produced any such report. Indeed, Mr Paul Robinson, Head of Marketing Intelligence at CHKS, has stated to the Inquiry that it had not been commissioned to analyse mortality data, and that the language quoted in the Monitor document is not language the firm would have used and nor is it indicative of a methodology it would adopt. Mr Robinson assumes that a member of the Trust staff must have taken advantage of the access granted to CHKS online data as part of a tendering process to undertake a separate analysis of which CHKS was unaware.[4]

22.6 A number of Trust witnesses have asserted that there was an analysis from CHKS, on which the information given to the SHA and Monitor must have been based.[5] Mrs Toni Brisby claimed that a CHKS analysis had shown that the Hospital Standardised Mortality Ratio (HSMR) results for the year were "artefactual".[6] Dr Val Suarez, the Trust's Medical Director at the time, told the Inquiry, in her statement that the Trust commissioned CHKS "to undertake a report into our data", and that they could not demonstrate figures similar to Dr Foster's.[7] She drew attention to a report, dated 7 June 2007 and authored by herself and Dr Helen Moss, which

---

1   HM/40 MON00030001251
2   IRC/48 WS0000017766, pp4–5
3   RS/26 WS0000018853
4   Robinson WS0000069267, para 9
5   Coates WS(2) WS0000076945
6   Brisby WS0008000075, paras 283–286
7   Suarez WS0000012508, para 122

was presented to the Trust Board, informing directors of a conclusion said to be drawn from the CHKS review, namely that:

> It appears that the Trust's mortality rates are at the lower end of the national benchmark ... The Trust can therefore be reassured that there are no obvious underlying problems.[8]

22.7 This report was shared with the SHA on 15 June.[9] The SHA had already noted the Trust's identification of the different mortality rates produced by the CHKS methodology as one factor in explaining its excess mortality rates under Dr Foster.[10]

22.8 In the absence of a document, Dr Philip Coates suggests that he, Dr Suarez and Mr John Newsham (the Trust's finance director), who he says commissioned the work from CHKS, must have been given the information by CHKS orally or that they misunderstood the position.[11]

22.9 The only document from which the Trust could conceivably have acquired some of its figures was a letter from the Chief Executive of CHKS sent to the chief executives and medical directors of all acute trusts at the time.[12] It was written in response to a *Daily Telegraph* article on NHS mortality rates, published on 24 April 2007.[13] The letter disputed the efficacy of the HSMR methodology and objected, in general terms, to the reporting of the Dr Foster data. It specifically mentioned a general mortality rate of 2% and suggested that a rate of variation between 1.5% and 3% was not unreasonable. A copy of this letter was sent to trusts with an offer to look at their data if they were worried.[14]

22.10 Having considered the evidence, the Inquiry is satisfied that there was no report from CHKS which analysed mortality or produced the conclusion claimed by the Trust. Mr Robinson's evidence that the only work commissioned was on coding issues, of which there is ample documentary evidence, is accepted. It would have been very strange if CHKS undertook work on mortality at the Trust and then did not reduce it to a report. It is highly unlikely that any representative of CHKS would have given any advice to the Trust intending that it be relied on in relation to such an important topic, without it being reduced to writing. It is possible that a Trust employee, as suggested by Dr Coates, undertook their own analysis using figures derived from CHKS, but such work would obviously not have had the same authority as work undertaken by an independent and reputable expert in the field. It may well be that Martin Yeates, Dr Moss, Dr Suarez, Dr Coates and others believed the assertions that were being made about CHKS advice. This may have originated from confusion surrounding the

---

8   Suarez WS0000012508, para 123; VS/22 WS0000012703–4, SHA0031000310
9   IRC/48 WS0000017766, pp4–5
10   RS/20 WS0000018805
11   Coates WS(2)11 WS0000076947, para 11
12   Robinson WS0000069265, PR 6 WS0000069327
13   *Revealed: Lottery of death rates in hospitals, Daily Telegraph* (24 April 2007);
     www.telegraph.co.uk/news/uknews/1549493/Revealed-Lottery-of-death-rates-in-hospitals.html
14   Robinson WS0000069265, para 14

CHKS letter and the work undertaken internally, but this is speculation. What is apparent is that none of them could have seen a report by CHKS containing such information, and yet the clear impression was given that such a report existed. They could have been expected to have reviewed such an important document personally, rather than accept someone else's apparent summary of its contents, but plainly they could not have done so. To that extent, at least the assertions persistently made in this regard by and on behalf of the Trust in 2007 were misleading, albeit through carelessness rather than dishonesty.

22.11 The Director of Nursing, Dr Moss, assured Monitor at the board-to-board meeting on 5 December 2007 that "We do not have a problem with mortality".[15] She is also recorded as saying that the Trust had "robust" governance arrangements and that "Quality is what drives our business". As *Chapter 5: Mortality statistics* shows, at the time of this meeting, the Trust had been subject to a large number of mortality alerts, in addition to the Dr Foster HSMR report. These were not mentioned to the Healthcare Commission (HCC), nor was an explanation offered as to how there could be no "problem" while they were current.

Lack of openness in foundation trust application

22.12 The Trust's Integrated Business Plan (IBP), the final version of which was produced in September 2007, was an essential part of the material made available by the Trust to Monitor to assess its application for foundation trust (FT) status.[16] It was signed off by all Board members personally.[17] The Board's "Message" at the front of the document made bold statements about the health of the Trust:

> *The Trust has been transformed over the last two years, the organisation is now focused, lean and hungry, well managed and increasingly well respected for its ambition and its delivery ...*
>
> *We do not underestimate the challenges or the risks facing a Trust of our size or in our location. We are aware of our weaknesses as well as our strengths and we have assessed our limitations ...*
>
> *We have developed our governance arrangements and put in place excellent leaders.*[18]

22.13 It purported to contain the "current key risks" to the Trust, including those relating to clinical quality. Reference was made to a risk of failure to manage and deliver effective emergency care.[19] The mitigating actions were: completing the refurbishment of A&E, continuing to attend patients in the area available, and reviewing the risk on a regular basis. The plan failed to mention the concerns raised by the peer review of children's services, the mounting concerns

---

15   HM/41 MON00030012478
16   HM/37 WS0000010103
17   HM/37 WS0000010106
18   HM/37 WS0000010113
19   HM/37 WS0000010234

about the surgical division (areas which were both suffering from a serious deficiency of leadership), or the continuing issues about mortality, even if the latter were in substance known to Monitor.

22.14 In the course of Monitor's assessment of the Trust's application for FT status, the Trust either made misleading statements or failed to pass on information raising concerns about mortality:

- At a meeting on 8 October 2007 between Monitor officials and the Trust leadership, including the Chair, Chief Executive, Medical Director and Director of Nursing, the issue of mortality rates was raised, but apparently dismissed by the Trust, whose position was recorded as follows: "There was an issue with mortality rates due to data capture and initial diagnosis. Data capture/initial diagnosis has been improved and this is no longer an issue."[20]
- The issue came up again at a meeting with Monitor officials on 16 October. The same position was repeated: "Per Dr Fosters the Trust had a high mortality rate. This was due to the quality and depth of coding."[21]
- At the board-to-board meeting on 5 December 2007, Dr Moss was recorded as saying *"We do not have a problem with mortality."*[22]

22.15 Dr Moss thought she might have said more than this on the subject, and pointed out that at the time the overall mortality rate had been 101. However, she accepted:

I think that was probably a brave statement but taking each of the individual facts they were facts at the time. But we know now that coding wasn't purely the issue.[23]

22.16 Mrs Brisby, on the other hand, told the Inquiry she thought that statement was accurate, and was neither actually, nor intended to be, misleading.[24]

22.17 Unfortunately, this statement about mortality was in fact misleading and inaccurate, albeit not intentionally so, and was made at a time when there was insufficient evidence available to justify it.

22.18 Monitor was not informed about the mortality alerts. Neither, before it took the decision to authorise the Trust, was Monitor informed of the letter from the HCC of 28 January 2008 requiring information to enable it to consider what action to take, with specific reference being made to its power to launch a formal investigation (see *Chapter 4: The foundation trust authorisation process*).

---

20   HM/38 MON00030002686
21   HM/39 MON00030002664
22   HM/41 MON00030012478
23   Moss T62.167
24   Brisby T129.92

Chapter 22 Openness, transparency and candour

22.19 For the reasons analysed in *Chapter 5: Mortality statistics*, to state that between September and December 2007 the Trust had no problem with mortality was misleading. The figure of 101 related to a very short period and was not comparable to the HSMR reported by Dr Foster. While there were undoubtedly coding issues, these could not fully explain the figures, and in the absence of thorough review of clinical quality in affected areas, there was a serious risk that the figures represented, at least in part, avoidable mortality. Therefore, to say there was "no problem" was, putting the most charitable construction on it, hyperbole. Those responsible at the Trust for making these statements appear to have convinced themselves of the coding explanation without adequate justification or thought for the implications for patients.

22.20 Dr William Moyes, former Executive Chairman of Monitor, when asked for his view on the failure of the Trust to inform Monitor about the HCC's formal request for information in January 2008, responded as follows:

> THE CHAIRMAN: Well, obviously, as we know, this letter arrived on the chief executive's desk at the trust days before your authorisation, but would you have expected something of this magnitude to be sent to you immediately, or would you have to give it a week or so before it came to your attention?
>
> A. No. I mean ... had this been a financial issue, [and] the auditor [had] said, "There's a major fraud in the trust", I've not the slightest doubt that the chief executive, a responsible chief executive, if I can put it that way ... would have said to Monitor, "We better tell you about this and you better think what you're going to do". And this is at least as serious as that, if not much more serious. So I think, again with the benefit of hindsight and having seen documents now I hadn't seen then, it is a great pity that Martin [Yeates] didn't take his courage in both hands and say to Monitor, "I ought to tell you that there's a – a real problem on the horizon".[25]

Helene Donnelly's experience

22.21 In her evidence, Helene Donnelly described how staff were told to move patients on trolleys out of sight in anticipation of a visit from Monitor:

> Before Monitor arrived I was told to get the patients out of the corridor, although there was nowhere to move them to. There were no trolleys to put patients on and no beds on the wards.[26]

---

25 Moyes T93.25–26
26 Donnelly WS0000022301, para 16

... we knew that they were going to come and look round and so there was a lot of pressure put upon us to have everything moved out and not to display things as they actually genuinely generally were. I don't actually know what happened to these patients. I don't know if they were perhaps moved inappropriately to a different area. I can't actually remember what happened to them in the end.[27]

Q. Did you form the view that this was a deliberate attempt to mislead Monitor by portraying A&E in a better light than you would otherwise have found it?

A. Yes.

22.22 Her experience, which resulted in her making a whistleblowing report, is described in *Chapter 1: Warning signs*. She discovered that her reports of misconduct in A&E were not disclosed by the Trust to the HCC, even after Dr Heather Wood asked for details of any complaints made by staff.[28] She felt that there was a clear message from senior management that the investigation was not to be mentioned to the HCC.[29]

22.23 The Inquiry accepts that Ms Donnelly truly felt this was the case and that the HCC was not told of her complaints, but the fact that she believed this is not of itself evidence of any deliberate intent to mislead on the part of the Trust or the officers she named. However, the fact that the Trust did not volunteer to the HCC the concerns raised by Ms Donnelly is evidence that the Trust was not a transparent organisation doing its best to help an investigation being conducted in the interests of patients.

Lack of openness with the coroner about serious untoward incidents

22.24 The episode following the tragic death of John Moore-Robinson, in which serious concerns about the case were not conveyed to the coroner by the Trust, raises issues about a practice which may well not be confined to the two lawyers from whom the Inquiry heard, or to this Trust. The facts were considered in detail at both the first inquiry and the hearings of this one. The events are considered in *Chapter 2: The Trust*, and it is sufficient for present purposes to refer to the summary provided by Counsel to the Inquiry (Mr Tom Kark QC) in his closing submissions, which is gratefully adopted here:[30]

- Mr Moore-Robinson was examined in A&E at the Trust on 1 April 2006, following an accident on his mountain bike. It is now known that he had ruptured his spleen. He was examined by a relatively junior doctor, who did not suspect the correct diagnosis and discharged Mr Moore-Robinson, with the advice to take analgesia. He died the following day at another hospital.[31]

27 Donnelly T96.167–168
28 Donnelly WS0000022306, para 38
29 Donnelly WS0000022305, para 31; T96.169–170
30 CLO0000003459, para 221, *Counsel to the Inquiry's closing submissions*, Chapter 9: The Trust
31 First report of Ivan Phair, within SK6 at WS0000074824

- On 20 April 2006, Rebecca Southall (Kate Levy's predecessor as Head of Legal Services at the Trust), noting that the junior doctor had left the employment of the Trust, asked Ivan Phair (a consultant in A&E) for a "report addressed to the coroner for use in the inquest".[32]

- Mr Phair produced a report dated 26 April 2006.[33] The report gave a factual analysis of the admission to A&E and the opinion that the attending doctor should have interpreted that Mr Moore-Robinson could have been suffering from some form of bleeding.[34] On the last page, Mr Phair went on to say:

  I would also conclude that as a result of my examination of the Doctor's medical notes I cannot find enough evidence which would lead me to conclude that a thorough abdominal examination was carried out on Mr Moore-Robinson on his attendance to the A&E department of Mid Staffordshire General Hospitals NHS Trust.

  I remain gravely concerned that Mr Moore-Robinson died from the effects of his accident on 1 April 2006. I would therefore raise the possibility that his unfortunate, untimely death may have been avoided, had he been more properly assessed on his initial attendance to the A&E department at the Mid Staffordshire General Hospitals NHS Trust.[35]

- In May, Ms Levy came into post and took over conduct of the matter. On 25 May 2006, she wrote to Mr Phair of the report:

  Rebecca has not forwarded it to the Coroner and on reviewing it I have some concerns as to its content. Whilst it would be entirely appropriate as a report in respect of a clinical negligence claim it goes beyond the issues which concern the Coroner. The Coroner is undertaking a fact finding exercise and does not concern himself with matters of blame or potential negligence. I would therefore like to suggest that the section of your report headed "Conclusion" with the exception of the final para be removed.[36]

- Mr Phair initially refused. He wrote to Ms Levy on 30 May 2006, stating that he had included such opinions in previous reports to the Coroner, that he could deliver a verdict of "death due to unnatural situations" and could "also make a judgement on suspicions of inadequacy of medical care".[37]

- Ms Levy met with Mr Phair on 21 June to discuss the matter. On 22 June, she wrote to him:

  With regards to the content of reports for the Coroner I entirely agree that issues in respect of care can be relevant to the decision as to how a patient came about his/her death. However, as reports are generally read out in full at the Inquest and the press and family will be present, with a view to avoiding further distress to the family and adverse publicity I would wish to avoid stressing possible failures on the part of the Trust.

---

32 TRU00000001054, Rebecca Southall request to Ivan Phair for a report of the treatment of John Moore-Robinson
33 First report of Ivan Phair, within SK/6 at WS0000074824
34 Page 3 of first report of Ivan Phair, within SK/6, WS0000074824
35 Page 4 of first report of Ivan Phair, within SK/6, WS0000074824
36 SK/6, WS0000074843
37 SK/6, WS0000074845

- She suggested removing the two paragraphs on page four of the report (mentioned above). As to the removal of the suggestion that the death could have been avoided:

  In my opinion it is self evident from your report that that is probably the case but I feel such a concluding statement may add to the family's distress and is not one which I would wish to see quoted in the press.[38]

- Mr Phair amended his report in accordance with this request, producing a report dated 29 June 2006.[39]

- Meanwhile, a statement was obtained from the treating doctor. Ms Levy disclosed this to the coroner.

- Ms Levy did not in fact disclose either version of Mr Phair's report to the coroner. In August 2006, Mr Stuart Knowles took over conduct of the file. He did not disclose either version to the coroner either.

- The Inquest took place on 3 April 2007. The family of Mr Moore-Robinson were not aware of the reports from Mr Phair until the time of the first inquiry, despite the inquest process and the fact that civil litigation was pursued and settled by the Trust.

22.25 The first issue requiring consideration is why the coroner was not told of Mr Phair's views. This requires an examination of what, if any, decision was taken by the Trust's legal department, there being no suggestion that the matter was referred to the Chief Executive or other Trust Director, and of the reasons for such a decision.

22.26 Neither Ms Levy nor Mr Knowles accepted that they had made a decision not to disclose Mr Phair's unexpurgated opinion:

- Ms Levy said that after taking the steps described above, she had no opportunity to review the file before handing it over to Mr Knowles and had no recollection of making a decision whether or not to disclose Mr Phair's report to the coroner. The Inquiry accepts that, as there was no immediate need for her to have made a decision before she handed the conduct of the file to Mr Knowles, she probably did not make any final decision about it. At the time of giving evidence to the Inquiry, she felt that if she had reviewed the file, she would have forwarded Mr Phair's amended report to the coroner.[40]
- Mr Knowles gave reasons why non-disclosure would have been justified in retrospect, but emphasised that he had no recollection of making such a decision. For the reasons set out in *Chapter 2: The Trust*, he either made a positive decision not to, or by inaction did not, disclose the report.[41]

---

38   SK/6, WS0000074846
39   SK/6, WS0000074831
40   Levy WS/69 WS0000076132, para 70
41   Knowles WS0000074656, para 67

22.27 The justifications put forward by Ms Levy and Mr Knowles for not disclosing Mr Phair's negative opinion were as follows:

- The report contained inaccuracies of fact.
- Mr Phair's negative opinion was inappropriate to include in a report to the coroner because:

  ... negligence issues were not for the Coroner and making admissions in this form was inconsistent with our duties to the NHSLA [NHS Litigation Authority].[42]

- Mr Phair had apportioned blame to a junior doctor for causing a death when at that stage the cause of death was unknown.[43] To have suggested in these circumstances that the death was avoidable would have caused distress to the patient's family.[44]
- While a clinical negligence claim had not been intimated at that time, if Mr Phair was right:

  It was reasonably clear that a clinical negligence claim was a possibility. It was not in the interests of the Trust to make admissions of liability and in particular admissions that substandard care had led to the death of a patient, when, at this stage, it was not clear whether this was correct or not.[45]

- Ms Levy accepted that what she had said about adverse publicity could have been better phrased but:

  The potential publicity for the Trust was always a legitimate concern in my role as the Trust's solicitor. Maintaining the reputation of the Trust was important in order to maintain public confidence in the services provided.[46]

- It was difficult to see how Mr Phair could have been a witness at the inquest as he had had no involvement in the care of Mr Moore-Robinson, and the junior doctor who had attended Mr Moore-Robinson had been found. Mr Phair could not have been an expert witness as he lacked the necessary independence as an employee of the Trust.[47]
- The patient's family had not "engaged" with the Trust at the time Mr Phair's report was compiled: there had been no complaint and the first notice the Trust had of an issue was a letter from the coroner indicating that there was going to be an inquest.[48]
- The Trust had no duty to disclose the report.[49] This had been confirmed by legal advice from counsel.[50]

---

42   Levy WS0000076128, para 56(b)
43   Levy WS/56 WS0000076128, para 56
44   Levy WS/83 WS0000076136, para 83
45   Levy WS0000076131, para 65
46   Levy WS0000076131, para 67
47   Levy WS0000076132, para 70; Knowles WS0000074655–656, para 65
48   Knowles WS0000074654, para 60
49   Levy WS0000076135, para 80
50   SK/8 WS0000074912–3

- Both solicitors considered that their primary duty was to act in the best interests of their client, the Trust.[51]

22.28 Mr Knowles thought there had been a shift in practice since 2006 towards greater openness; for instance many trusts, he said, now voluntarily disclose serious untoward incident (SUI) reports to coroners when they are not obliged to do so.[52]

22.29 Mr Andrew Haigh, the Coroner, was asked by this Inquiry in 2011 to comment on the non-disclosure of Mr Phair's reports to him; he considered the file and was "disappointed" at the non-disclosure. He thought that it was difficult to conclude whether the outcome of the inquest would have been different if this material had been in his possession at the time, but he would have been able to draft a more focused Rule 43 report. He told the Inquiry that he would have called Mr Phair as a witness.[53] However, he doubted that this would have changed his conclusion or his decision to give a narrative verdict.[54] He told the Inquiry that it would have been "appropriate" for Mr Phair (or at least some senior doctor) to have attended the inquest.[55] In his letter to the Trust, he said that in future he would appreciate receiving copies of relevant complaint letters, SUI reports, and reports and records from clinicians not actually involved in the case, as well as those specifically involved.

22.30 This episode has already been considered in the report of the first inquiry, and Ms Levy and Mr Knowles have taken the Inquiry to task for what was said there, which they assert was based on incomplete evidence. They also complain about the fairness of a report of an investigation into the matter commissioned by the Trust and undertaken by Mr Michael Taylor.[56] Ms Levy was dismissed by the Trust as a result of its view of this matter, and it is right to record that her claim for wrongful and unfair dismissal was settled on terms that the Trust would pay her a substantial sum in compensation and acknowledge that the dismissal was unfair.[57] In view of these arguments, and the fact that the evidence received at this Inquiry is more extensive and detailed than that considered at the first, the issues have been considered completely afresh and without regard to any adverse findings made in the first inquiry.

22.31 This starts with considering what happened from the point of view of Mr Moore-Robinson's bereaved family. The natural shock and distress caused to loving parents by the sudden loss of a much loved son was compounded for them by the fact that the first they heard of the accident was when they were summoned to Leicester Royal Infirmary, where they arrived to be told that their son had died. There was no one there to talk to them or to explain what had

---

51   Levy T131.136–142
52   Knowles WS0000074650, para 53
53   See also Haigh T48.135
54   Haigh WS0000005705, para 71; AH/26 WS0000005847
55   Haigh T48.135–7
56   Knowles WS0000074653, para 59; SPK/7 WS0000074886; Levy WS0000076152, paras 135–6; KL10 WS0000076372; KL/11 WS0000076384
57   Email from the Trust to the Inquiry, 1 February 2012

happened, other than that everything possible had been done there to try to save him.[58] It was a few days later, when a friend who had been cycling with their son visited, that they were told the barest outline of the events leading to his death. In due course, they instructed a solicitor with a view, not so much to pursuing compensation, but to finding out what had happened.[59] A settlement was reached, which involved the payment of a small sum of money to the Robinsons, and a letter containing a form of apology arrived from Mr Yeates, the Trust Chief Executive.[60] Mr Yeates expressed the hope that:

> ... the fact that matters have been resolved speedily will go some way to enable you to put this matter behind you and move on.

22.32   Whether such a sentiment was appropriate in any event, and many would agree with Mrs Robinson[61] that it was not, the handling of the case by the Trust, including the non-disclosure of Mr Phair's report, meant that the Robinsons had no prospect of "moving on". The Robinsons understood the Trust to have admitted liability, but when an acquaintance of the family who worked in the media contacted the Trust some time later regarding John Moore-Robinson's death, the Trust issued a press statement to the effect that liability had not been admitted. The family did not discover, until participating in the first inquiry, that any report had been written by Mr Phair or that he had been immediately critical of the care their son had received.

22.33   The effect of these events was described by Mrs Robinson:

> Having to struggle and cope with the death of our son John is every parent's worst nightmare but discovering the events that followed with people in public office ... withholding evidence from the Inquest and asking for reports to be altered is hard to bear.[62]

22.34   They were "shocked and distraught" that the press statement said liability had not been accepted.[63] Mrs Robinson's reaction to learning that Mr Phair had been asked to alter his report was that this was:

> ... absolutely despicable. I mean these are legal people. That should never, never happen ... it really upsets me ... to think that ... that happened.[64]

---

58   Robinson WS0000000045, para 21; T10.143–145
59   Robinson WS0000000046, paras 25–28; T10.145–149
60   Robinson T10.149–151; JR/2 WS0000000067
61   Robinson T10.151
62   Robinson WS0000000052, para 53
63   Robinson WS0000000048, para 35
64   Robinson T10 transcript for closed session, p5

22.35 Asked to comment on Ms Levy's remark, quoted above, that Mr Phair's adverse opinion might be distressing for the family, she said:

> *It's caused us more distress finding out that she'd actually asked Mr Phair to take out the paragraphs, and distress that the document never even reached the coroner anyway. I think that's – that's more distressing.*[65]

22.36 The discovery of concealment of information, which suggests that a death or serious injury has been caused by the avoidable act or omission of the Trust or a member of its staff, is likely to have just the impact described by Mrs Robinson. This will be even more pronounced where it turns out that the inquest had not had the benefit of all the information available to the Trust.

22.37 While it is not doubted that Ms Levy and Mr Knowles acted in good faith, believing they were doing their duty as solicitors, their actions jointly resulted in the Trust behaving contrary to the standards of openness the Robinsons and the coroner were entitled to expect, and their client, the Trust, was expected to adopt. Each of their justifications is dealt with in turn.

22.38 *Factual inaccuracy*: this is not a good reason for failing to disclose a corrected report. The corrections were based in large part on a misreading of the records. Mr Phair later made the alterations requested of him.

22.39 *Criticism of the standard of care*: while it is quite correct that an inquest is not permitted to make findings of criminal or civil liability of named individuals, that does not mean that it is not appropriate for the coroner to be made aware of the opinions of the senior consultant in the department which was attended by the deceased. It is for the coroner, not for interested parties, to decide what is, and is not, admissible evidence at an inquest under his or her control. Even in a case where gross neglect is not a likely or possible verdict, that should be for the coroner to decide, not an interested party with a self-interest in not disseminating matters adverse to itself. Even if an opinion of this nature is not one a coroner would wish to admit as evidence in the inquest, it could assist him or her in deciding what further inquiries to make, including whether or not to instruct an expert of his or her own. Further, as would probably have been the case here, had the report been disclosed to the coroner, he would have called Mr Phair as a witness.

22.40 The points made in this regard by Ms Levy and Mr Knowles might have had more force if any steps had been taken to draw the opinion of Mr Phair to the attention of those responsible for ensuring that a proper standard of care was provided in the A&E department. If Mr Phair was correct, a junior doctor had been unintentionally responsible either for causing the avoidable death of a patient, or for at least exposing the patient to the risk of death. That required at the

---

65   Robinson T10 transcript for closed session, p6

very least an internal review, an SUI report, and consideration of what action should be taken with regard to junior doctors' training and supervision, and the systems in A&E. None of this was done. At no time was any step taken to check whether Mr Phair's opinion had the substance we now know it had (if only from the expert independent report obtained by the Robinsons' solicitor).

22.41   *Prematurity of the opinion*: the fact that Mr Phair's opinion was offered at a time when the cause of death was unknown is irrelevant. His report made it clear that he was aware of that and that he had expressed his view conditionally. It would still have been helpful to inform the coroner of what the issues were concerning the circumstances surrounding the death. Such an opinion might in some cases assist the coroner in formulating questions to ask of the pathologist.

22.42   *The danger of causing distress to the family of the deceased*: the evidence to this Inquiry given by Mrs Robinson leaves no room for doubt that apparent concealment is likely to cause more distress than openness. A family is highly likely to be distressed by hearing that a loved one has met an avoidable death. They will be distressed even more if they find out that the organisation responsible has hidden an opinion to that effect, and furthermore has done nothing with it. Of course, the risk of causing unnecessary distress, because of an opinion expressed before the facts are fully known, must be addressed. There is nothing wrong in ensuring that a report of this nature is phrased in sufficiently conditional terms. If there is reason to believe that an adverse opinion of this type is wrong or debatable, then the best approach is not one of concealment but of obtaining another opinion in which the organisation has confidence.

22.43   *Lack of independence and reliability*: if the Trust was concerned on either of these grounds, again the proper and wise thing to do would have been to obtain a second independent opinion from a source in which it had confidence, not to conceal a reasoned and genuinely held adverse opinion from a senior member of staff with responsibility for the department in question, and through that, for the patient in question.

22.44   *Concern at adverse publicity:* while such concern is understandable, it should never be considered by a trust as a reason for non-disclosure. The mere knowledge that healthcare organisations might fail to disclose information about substandard care is likely to undermine public confidence to a far greater extent than exhibiting openness about matters of concern and demonstrating that they are being addressed.

22.45   *No complaint had been made*: the implication of this argument is that a report of this nature or information about the opinion in it need not be disclosed unless there is a complaint. This suggests that a patient's family who are unaware that the patient has died from an avoidable cause need not be told that there are concerns about the treatment received. In any event, whether or not there has been a complaint should be irrelevant to the consideration of whether material should be disclosed to the coroner. The very purpose of an inquest in this situation is to establish the cause and circumstances surrounding the death. The coroner needs the fullest information in order to achieve that.

22.46 *No duty of disclosure*: the analysis in the legal opinion produced by Mr Knowles is impeccable. The Inquiry accepts that there is no legal duty to volunteer disclosure to a coroner of all possibly relevant material in the same way as there is in a civil action. The issue of concern here is not one of strict legal rights and responsibility, but of judgement and adherence by the Trust to the spirit if not the letter of what is clearly expressed NHS policy. In this case the coroner had actually asked for a report[66] and, although the Trust did obtain a report in response to this request, it never submitted it. A unilateral decision not to do so on the basis that the junior doctor involved had been found was unjustified. The Trust never asked the coroner whether he still wanted a report, one having been obtained. While it is fair to note that the coroner himself never pursued the request, it is inconceivable that he would have turned down the offer of the report if such an offer had been made. In this case, a lawyer took the relevant decision, or otherwise allowed non-disclosure, without taking the instructions of the Trust, thereby putting himself into the position of his client. What is in issue here is not the duty of a solicitor under his or her professional code, but the duty as a representative of an NHS trust which is required to follow guidance encouraging openness and candour.

22.47 *Duty to act in client's best interests*: the impression given by Ms Levy and Mr Knowles was that there would be an initial presumption that disclosure of material raising criticisms of the Trust would be against its interests. This is not the correct starting point. It should almost invariably be regarded as in a trust's best interests to volunteer, to those affected, any information in its possession that reasonably suggests that avoidable harm has been inflicted on a patient. If that is correct it should follow that the same applies with regard to disclosure to the coroner, who has the duty of investigating many hospital deaths. A solicitor who takes a decision not to disclose information to the coroner and who forms a view as to the client trust's best interests without taking explicit instructions from that client must have regard to all the considerations the trust should take into account, and not assume that a narrow and legalistic interpretation of a client's apparent interests in litigation and reputation should prevail.

22.48 Therefore, it was a serious error of judgement for the Trust not to disclose to the coroner the original report of Mr Phair. The ultimate responsibility was that of Mr Knowles, as he held the file at the time of the inquest, was aware of the report's existence – or should have been if he had read the file thoroughly – and either took a positive decision not to disclose, or allowed non-disclosure by inaction. Most importantly, he conducted the case in this way without

---

66 TRUST00040000196

taking instructions on the matter from the Trust, thereby depriving it of the ability to make an informed decision on the matter.

22.49 In fairness, it is possible that many solicitors would have acted in the same way: there was clearly a culture in which the imperative for openness in matters concerning harm to patients took second place to a misconceived perception that the client's best interests were restricted to protecting its position in respect of possible adversarial litigation, and in protecting its reputation against suggestions of having caused avoidable harm.

Experience of other patients and their carers

22.50 At least one patient relative, in evidence, referred to not having it explained to him/her by hospital staff that his/her mother had contracted *C. difficile*, clearly making it difficult for the family to understand and accept subsequent events.[67]

22.51 A report produced of the themes arising in the Independent Case Note Review (ICNR), overseen by Dr Mike Laker following the HCC's report, found that in nearly 60% of the cases reviewed care had not met the standards it would have been reasonable to expect. The report also indicated that there were in fact a large number of cases where families of patients only found out about a hospital-acquired infection by seeing it mentioned on the death certificate. In other cases, families complained about the failure to communicate the need for urgent cancer care.[68] While this might be attributed to incompetence or late diagnosis, a disturbing possibility is that staff did not want to admit something which could affect the hospital's reputation. The same report suggests a concerning reluctance to communicate with families or record what was said. The ICNR uncovered instances of there being no record of interaction with patient or relatives, no documentation regarding a conversation with the family, poor response times to ongoing inquiries by families and inappropriate and defensive handling of complaints.[69]

Exaggeration by the Trust

22.52 The hyperbolic statements of the Board introducing the Integrated Business Plan in September 2007 are described above. On achieving FT status, the Trust issued a statement saying it was now in the "premier league". Mr Yeates was quoted as saying:

---

67   Cowie T14.34–37
68   MON00030009268, Themes arising from the Mid Staffordshire Independent Case Note Review, Jan 2005 – March 2009 paper
69   MON00030009274–5 Paper on themes arising from the Independent Case Note Review, Jan 2005 – March 2009

This is the healthcare equivalent of promotion to the premier league and heralds an exciting new era for our hospitals, in which local people will have more say than ever in helping us make improvements and to achieve the best services for our local population ... we know that, although we have made many improvements ... there are times when we could do better ... We have been on a remarkable journey as we aimed to achieve our aim of becoming a Foundation Trust. And today, after a rigorous process to check on our financial stability and our arrangements for ensuring the quality and safety of our healthcare, I am delighted to say "we did it!".[70]

"Gagging" clauses and obligation of confidentiality

22.53 The Inquiry has heard of the use by organisations of contractual terms to prevent or inhibit disclosure by employees or former employees of information critical of the organisation.

The Care Quality Commission

22.54 Dr Heather Wood and Roger Davidson were subject to "non-disparagement" clauses in the terms of settlement around the cessation of their employment with the Care Quality Commission (CQC).[71] Dr Wood's agreement read as follows:

> *That Dr Wood will not at any time hereafter make or repeat any statement which disparages or is intended to disparage the goodwill or reputation of the CQC, or any specified person and the CQC will use reasonable endeavours to ensure that no senior manager, tier 3 or above, with whom Dr Wood had direct dealings with her employment with the CQC, nor any specified person involved in the correspondence process surrounding the termination of Dr Wood's employment will make or repeat any statement which disparage or are intended to disparage the goodwill or reputation of Dr Wood.*[72]

22.55 There was a term which excluded evidence to a public inquiry from the scope of this clause:

> *CQC confirm that it is not intended that any term of this Agreement shall prevent and/or restrict Dr Wood in any way from attending and/or taking part fully (including giving evidence) in any public inquiries connected to work which she carried out during her employment with the CQC.*[73]

22.56 In spite of that latter provision, both witnesses felt concerned about giving evidence to the Inquiry and required reassurance. The CQC assured the Inquiry and the witnesses that they were free to give evidence. Nonetheless, it was necessary for the Inquiry to issue orders

70 MON0000000253, *Press Release from Mid Staffordshire NHSFT* (31 January 2008); www.midstaffs.nhs.uk/Get-Involved/Membership/Members-Newsletter/docs/2008/Issue-4-Feb-2008.aspx
71 Davidson T84.3–5, Wood T81.2
72 Bower T87.101
73 Bower T87.102; OI00000000205

directing that they give evidence to provide them with further assurance; Mr Davidson requested a Direction Order in order to clear up any ambiguity there might be.[74]

22.57 Cynthia Bower, then Chief Executive of the CQC, told the Inquiry that such non-disparagement clauses were common practice. Dame Jo Williams, then Chair of the CQC, justified this practice in these terms:

> I think our approach was to follow normal practice, and so a compromise agreement, in my understanding, is there to not only protect the interests of the organisation, but the interests of the individual. And so, in the way in which we dealt with Mr Davidson, we followed what is common practice, public sector, private sector and my own experience too in the voluntary sector. The question you're raising, I must say I haven't given a great deal of reflection on that very point. But it does seem to me that it would be a very great pity to see arguments between employees and their previous employer highlighted in the press. I mean, it's very difficult to know under what circumstances that might happen, but I would look for, if ... there was an issue, actually that people would be able to sit down and have a dialogue and a proper conversation ...
>
> Q. But what if what was sought to be publicised was not an argument but a legitimate criticism that the former employee wished to make in a forum other than a public inquiry, wouldn't then the clause in the compromise agreement stifle legitimate debate?
>
> A. Well, it potentially could do, because, you know, that's how it would have been written. So I take the point that you're making ...
>
> Q. Do you think that the answer might be to very tightly define such a clause so that it covers only commercially sensitive information and/or personal data?
>
> A. Indeed, that might be an appropriate suggestion.[75]

22.58 Ms Bower thought that the clause would not apply to disclosures in the public interest or to comments made by a former employee as a member of the public, but agreed that this was not made clear.[76]

22.59 Non-disparagement clauses are not compatible with the requirement that public service organisations in the healthcare sector, including regulators, should be open and transparent. They are to be distinguished from confidentiality clauses: there is obviously a need to preserve confidentiality in particular areas, either permanently or temporarily. Examples of this include:

---

74 Davidson T84.4
75 Williams T84.155–156
76 Bower T87.103

- Patient confidentiality: it is important that details capable of identifying patients and their families should not be placed in the public domain;
- Prevention of prejudice to investigations: it will sometimes be against the public interest for details of current investigations to be allowed into the public domain until such time as the danger of prejudice has passed. For example, it would be wrong for an intention to make an unannounced visit to be leaked to the trust to be visited;
- Employee confidentiality: employees may be entitled to privacy with regard to their pay and the terms of any settlement on their departure. It is less easy to envisage many cases in which the employer is entitled to confidentiality about such matters should it be waived by the employee.

22.60 Even in areas where confidentiality is potentially justifiable, consideration will have to be given to whether there is a public interest in disclosure which outweighs the need or justification for confidentiality.

22.61 It is unjustifiable in almost all circumstances:

- To prevent any employee or past employee making disclosure to a public authority, including a regulator, a Government department, or an inquiry, of matters internal to the organisation, which he or she honestly believes to be in the public interest to make;
- To prevent any past employee publishing or communicating any criticism of or adverse comment about the organisation, except to the extent that to do so would disclose information justifiably required to be held confidential.

22.62 A clause of the type contained in the agreement with Dr Wood is an impermissible inhibition on free speech, and, just as importantly, is against the public interest in dissemination and consideration of genuinely held concerns about matters of patient safety. It is doubtful that clauses as restrictive as this are common practice in the private sector, but even if they are, the practice should cease in the public sector. Any clause restricting an individual's liberty to make a disclosure or imposing a duty of confidentiality, should be limited to the minimum necessary to protect the public interest, and not the reputation of any organisation or individual. The CQC has suggested that non-disparagement clauses of the type it has used do not, as a matter of law, prevent disclosure being made in the public interest. While, without expressing a legal opinion on the point, that may be correct, employees cannot be expected to understand this unless they are specifically informed of the exception, preferably by it being referred to in the contractual clause. In any event, such an exception is likely to cause sufficient doubt as to its meaning in the mind of an employee that further clarification of the true intended limits of a non-disparagement clause would still be required. Therefore, the recent assurance received from the CQC that it now has no intention of using such clauses again in termination agreements, unless there are exceptional circumstances, is to be welcomed as a step in the right direction.

Chapter 22 Openness, transparency and candour

Care Quality Commission – reaction to bona fide public disclosures

22.63　While the terms of reference of this Inquiry do not include an investigation of the performance of the CQC, it is important that the way in which the CQC operates is adequately understood, as the Inquiry is charged to take into account the system as it works today.

22.64　There was evidence before the Inquiry that the CQC actively discouraged those within the organisation to raise concerns they might have with the Inquiry. In the course of the Inquiry, a document was prepared internally in the CQC detailing statements in the evidence given to the Inquiry by CQC officers which it was thought might not reflect reality on the ground. Members of the CQC field force became concerned. The document, and the evidence to which it led the Inquiry, suggested that the CQC might not be managing its inspections in the most effective way and that its strategy was not entirely effective. These issues are explored in *Chapter 11: Regulation: the Care Quality Commission*, where it will be seen that the evidence obtained was very helpful for the work of the Inquiry.

22.65　The document, which at the time it was produced to the Inquiry was still in draft form, had been prepared by Rona Bryce, a senior operations analyst in the Operations Intelligence Directorate, headed by Sampana Banga. She told the Inquiry that Mr Banga had asked her to produce a report listing all the references to the Directorate's work in the CQC's evidence to the Inquiry. She told the Inquiry that she understood the purpose of this work to be to help:

> *... standardise expectations of what the intelligence directorate should deliver across the country.*

> *... there were concerns that RIEOs* [regional intelligence and evidence officers] *could and in fact already had read the transcripts of evidence and that there may be confusion as to the statements made and what the beliefs of the RIEOs were as to their function.*[77]

22.66　She also hoped it would contribute towards the "service level agreement" which was to define the relationship between various teams. Mr Banga, however, told the Inquiry that the purpose of the work was to fulfil one of the personal objectives set for him:

> *My intention was that this would then be used by me to produce a report which would be appended to my personal objectives which I would discuss with Mr Hamblin.*[78]

22.67　It does not appear, therefore, that it was Mr Banga's initial intention that this document should be given any wider disclosure, whereas Ms Bryce's understanding was consistent with an intention for, at least, some degree of internal disclosure beyond Mr Banga and Mr Richard Hamblin.

77　Bryce WS0000073789, paras 12–14
78　Banga WS0000073891, para 15; T132.29

22.68 Ms Bryce said that in preparing the document she went beyond what she had been asked to do, by carrying out what she termed, a "gap analysis", the "gap" being between the expectations of the senior management team, as she interpreted them from their evidence, and the weaknesses in the system in practice, which could reduce the effectiveness of the role of a CQC regional intelligence officer.[79] To assist her in this, she circulated her draft for comment among a small group of colleagues. She had expected her document to be discussed at a scheduled meeting with Mr Banga on 15 June 2011, but that meeting was taken up with a discussion about the case of Winterbourne View (a private hospital where instances of abuse were discovered). However, Ms Bryce felt that certain issues raised in the Winterbourne View affair illustrated the inconsistency in practice which her review of the CQC's evidence had brought to light, and she wanted to be assured something was going be done about the points raised:

> I wanted an assurance that something was going to happen with regards to the concerns and queries raised in my document, since it seemed to me that the Inquiry might potentially have a distorted view of what was happening in Operations Intelligence. I do not think that every issue I raised was important, but it seemed to me that on some of the issues it was imperative that the Inquiry got the correct view.[80]

22.69 Mr Banga told her that he would discuss the document with his superior Mr Hamblin, who had given evidence to the Inquiry, and she was also assured that any inconsistencies identified would be drawn to the Inquiry's attention in the CQC's final submissions. In her oral evidence, Ms Bryce said that no one at this meeting seemed to disagree that there were discrepancies in the evidence given to the Inquiry.[81]

22.70 Mr Banga did raise the document briefly with Mr Hamblin at a meeting on 23 June 2011. At some point, possibly later, Mr Hamblin made handwritten notes on the document which suggested, as was the case, that he substantially disagreed with its contents in so far as they related to evidence to the Inquiry.[82]

22.71 Information about the existence of this document came to the Inquiry's attention via an anonymous source; this led to a request being made to the CQC to produce it. Initially, the Inquiry sent a letter which was hand delivered directly to Mr Banga on his return home from work on the evening of 13 July 2011, asking him to contact the Inquiry.[83] He emailed Mr Hamblin to tell him about the letter and later spoke to him on the telephone.[84] The email shows that Mr Banga informed Mr Hamblin that he had no idea what this approach was about, but that he was upset by being contacted in this way at home, and assumed others

79   Bryce T130.99
80   Bryce WS0000073796–7, para 30
81   Bryce T130.142–3
82   SB/6 WS0000073942
83   SB/7 WS0000073953
84   Hamblin T132.142–143

had been contacted as well. Mr Banga told the Inquiry that, at the time, he thought the approach might be about his former role as Head of Region at the HCC, and that it did not occur to him that there was a connection with anything he was currently working on.[85] This suggestion was passed on to the CQC's solicitors in a letter of the following day.[86]

22.72　As soon as he got to work the following day, Thursday 14 July 2011, Mr Banga emailed a number of people asking for comments on Ms Bryce's document.[87] The email did not mention the letter he had received from the Inquiry, and he assured the Inquiry there was no connection between his receipt of the Inquiry's letter and this email. His purpose in sending it was, he said, to be prepared for a meeting with Mr Hamblin the following week. He had assumed that the approach from the Inquiry related to his work for the HCC. He said that he did not see any connection between the document, although it was about evidence to the Inquiry, and the letter from the Inquiry, which was on his desk, or in his pocket, as he sent out the email to his colleagues. Later that day, he attended an internal meeting to discuss the approach from the Inquiry. He then discovered that none of his colleagues who had also worked at the HCC had received any approach from the Inquiry. Although still unaware, according to his evidence, that the Inquiry was interested in the document, he then put a stop to any work on it.[88] His evidence was that he only discovered that the Inquiry wanted to see the document when a further letter arrived the following week. His explanation for stopping the work on the document when he did, namely on 14 July, was as follows:

> *Q. Well, I'm sorry, I'm missing something. When you got this letter at home, you didn't know what it related to?*
>
> *A. That's correct.*
>
> *Q. You had a meeting; yes?*
>
> *A. Yes.*
>
> *Q. You still didn't know what it related to?*
>
> *A. Correct.*
>
> *Q. But on the 14th you put a stop on all work on this document?*
>
> *A. That's correct.*
>
> *Q. Why?*

85　Banga T132.69
86　Hamblin T132.145
87　SB/8 WS0000073885/955; Banga T132.72–73
88　Banga T132.81

A. Because I didn't know what it related to. What I felt was that I was being misrepresented to the inquiry. I didn't know by whom, I didn't know why. I had an adverse reaction to being contacted by the inquiry about a work-related matter at home. I, therefore, took the personal decision that anything to do with Mid Staffs that I was aware of should come to a pause until we had clarification from the inquiry exactly what it was they were seeking assistance with.[89]

22.73   The reaction of the senior leadership of the CQC to this development was not favourable. As soon as the matter came to the attention of Richard Hamblin an investigation was launched in an attempt to find out who had informed the Inquiry about the document.

22.74   Ms Bryce heard no more after her meeting with Mr Banga on 15 June 2011, until she was summoned to see Mr Hamblin on 8 August 2011. She was informed that the document had been "leaked" to the Inquiry and that the CQC was investigating how information about the document had been disclosed. She described the meeting as "not a pleasant experience".[90] She:

… felt intimidated and upset by the manner in which the interview was conducted.[91]

22.75   She told the Inquiry that, in contrast to her earlier meeting with Mr Banga, when it had apparently been accepted that the work had disclosed inconsistencies, at this meeting the position was that the document was:

… considered to just be inaccurate, full stop. I felt that there was an assumption that I had written the document with the expression [sic] intention of proving that individuals had given inaccurate evidence to the inquiry and that I had gone through the transcripts cherry-picking statements and distorting the context in which those statements were made to that end.[92]

22.76   After the meeting Mr Hamblin told her:

… That they were not going to take any action at that point but that they would be in touch when they had made a decision about what they intended to do next. I was left with the clear impression that a decision was ongoing as to whether to proceed to a formal investigation and if the decision was made to proceed with a formal investigation then I would be immediately suspended.[93]

89   Banga T132.81–82
90   Bryce WS0000073812, para 79
91   Bryce WS(2) WS0000078643, para 2
92   Bryce T130.144
93   Bryce WS(2) WS0000078643–4, para 2

22.77 Mr Hamblin told the Inquiry that he had not intended to intimidate or cause upset to Ms Bryce. The meeting was one of the last he conducted as part of his investigation into the leak. He said that he had told her that the meeting was not a formal disciplinary investigation. He was concerned that it might become necessary, in the course of what was intended to be an informal meeting, to turn it into a disciplinary meeting and therefore wanted to ensure he followed the correct procedure. He had acted in accordance with advice from the HR department. He had wanted to make clear to her that she was not under investigation but was seeking to understand what had happened. The reference to suspension was only that this was one potential element of a formal disciplinary process, if one became necessary.[94] He pointed out that suspension, if it occurred, should be understood as a neutral act, and in accordance with the CQC's policy. His account of what he told Ms Bryce after the meeting differs in emphasis from hers:

> ... immediately after the meeting, within five minutes of it closing, I went to tell Ms Bryce that we weren't progressing to a formal investigation and there was no question of her suspension.[95]

22.78 It was clear by the manner in which Ms Bryce gave evidence that she had been deeply distressed by what she saw to be unfair treatment: she had only prepared a document at her manager's request, to which, in accordance with what she saw as the culture of the CQC of encouraging the use of initiative, she had added comments. She effectively felt she had been accused of leaking the document, when she had done no such thing.

22.79 On 9 August 2011, Ms Bryce went to her line manager, Mr Banga, to inform him that she was suspected of leaking the document and had been threatened with suspension. She asked him to confirm in writing that she had not exceeded her authority and he verbally assured her that he would take responsibility.

22.80 On 18 August 2011, Ms Bryce was invited to a further meeting with Mr Hamblin and three other employees to whom she had sent the document. The Head of HR, Alison Beal, was also present. She said she would be taking a decision over the weekend as to whether the CQC would proceed with a formal investigation, and offered Ms Bryce and the others an opportunity to come forward with further information. Ms Bryce understood this to be an opportunity to admit having leaked the document. It was made clear that this might not avoid disciplinary action, but would be a factor in the employee's favour.

22.81 Nothing more was heard until 9 September 2011 when Mr Hamblin confirmed that the investigation had closed. It had not revealed who had been responsible for the "leak". Mr Hamblin still seems to have been under the misapprehension that someone had actually

---

94   Hamblin T132.140
95   Hamblin T132.140

supplied the Inquiry with a copy of the document, and he was at pains to ensure that nothing like that happened again. In his email he said:

> ... I want to reiterate my disappointment that a premature and thus misleading document was released to the Mid Staffordshire Inquiry in this way. I know, as you have told me this, that some of you share this disappointment. CQC has reasonable expectations of loyalty to the organisation, and releasing a document such as this without an explanation of context and without any discussion with senior managers, I find unacceptable, and frankly a malicious act. I am therefore pleased that there is no evidence that the leak to the Inquiry came from within Intelligence. However, I would want to make sure that this sort of thing does not happen again.

> Please think carefully about what you write. This is a lesson I too have had to learn. In the wrong hands, loose wording can be twisted into saying much more than was originally meant. The message has to be that you need to be comfortable about anything you write being on the front page of a newspaper.[96]

22.82 On 18 August, the CQC's solicitors, writing to the Inquiry in response to a request for disclosure of the document, asserted that Mr Hamblin, having read the document, considered it to be inaccurate in many ways, both in terms of how it portrayed the evidence which had been given, and in representing the work of Operations Intelligence, and did not believe it raised concerns about the CQC's evidence.[97] The letter went on to set out a detailed case in relation to each of the potential inconsistencies raised by the document. The letter concluded:

> ... we do not believe the draft documents are particularly helpful. CQC considers it unfortunate that this matter has been referred to the Inquiry and raised suspicions as to the accuracy of its evidence when, in fact, there are inaccuracies within the draft review documents themselves.

22.83 The letter went on to say that the principal purpose of the CQC's evidence had been to set out its processes, but that it was inevitable there would be some variability in their implementation.

22.84 Lauren Goodman, a CQC Regional Intelligence Officer (RIEO) had been asked to comment on observations made in draft in the document by Ms Bryce. She told the Inquiry that she thought such a request had been entirely appropriate.[98] Indeed, she thought that documents of this type were "a massive positive feature" of CQC work.[99] She said there had been some concern among RIEOs that if some of the evidence given was taken literally, a very heavy

---

96   Bryce WS(2) RB 2 WS0000078650
97   RB/13 WS0000073871–2
98   Goodman WS0000073973, para 23
99   Goodman WS0000073998, para 138

responsibility would fall on them, and that some of it was inconsistent with the way RIEOs actually worked.[100] She stated that she felt "aggrieved" that it was leaked to the Inquiry, and that it was not in a form she would have chosen to circulate to her superiors, let alone the public. She felt the leak had impeded progress on the work. She was contacted by Mr Hamblin by telephone and asked about her involvement in the preparation of the document. She told the Inquiry that he had alluded to the fact that he felt there were misinterpretations of what had been said, but he did not threaten her with suspension.[101]

22.85 Mr Banga told the Inquiry that the episode had had a "profound impact on the bond of trust" he required within his team. He said he welcomed challenge and encouraged it. It did not surprise him that people had different views, but he was disappointed at the breach of trust.[102] He had no objection to a member of staff raising concerns directly with the Inquiry, but he would have hoped that, in a matter concerning a document he had commissioned, those concerns would have been discussed with him, rather than finding out about them from a hand-delivered letter from the Inquiry.

22.86 The story of the "leak" from the CQC has been set out at some length because it exposes what the Inquiry considers to be an unhealthy culture in which loyalty to the organisation is considered a higher priority than provision of assistance to a public inquiry seeking to contribute to the improvement of the regulation and oversight of the NHS. Someone, whose identity is unknown, was sufficiently concerned about what was going to happen to this project to want to alert the Inquiry to its existence. As the existence of the document in question is likely to have been known only internally, the unknown person was probably a member of staff at the CQC. This person felt sufficiently afraid of the potential consequences of such disclosure that they not only remained completely anonymous, but also refrained from raising the issue explicitly. Instead, they steered the Inquiry on to a line of enquiry.

22.87 Mr Hamblin's reaction in launching an investigation and interviewing Ms Bryce, even though there was no evidence to suggest that she was responsible for the "leak", is clear evidence that such a fear was justified. The placing of such pressure on Ms Bryce caused her considerable distress, even though this was unintentional on Mr Hamblin's part. It is perhaps understandable that a senior manager should feel concerned that someone in his organisation has felt it desirable to act in this way. However, it should immediately prompt the question why it has happened and what in the culture of the organisation has contributed to it, rather than the immediate assumption that the motivation was malicious or mischief-making and worthy of investigation. While the investigation was not said to be disciplinary, whatever was said to her in the immediate aftermath of the first meeting, the reference to and threat of a possible suspension was perceived by Ms Bryce to be very real, and it was not, in reality, lifted until the second meeting with Ms Bryce, held on 18 August 2011. Even though this was

---

100 Goodman T130.16
101 Goodman T130.74–5
102 Banga T132.79–80

probably not the intention of those conducting the investigation, such a reaction is likely to breed a repressive and fearful atmosphere inimical to the open and challenging culture to which it is claimed the CQC aspires.

22.88　Mr Banga's evidence, to the effect that it was pure coincidence that he circulated the draft document to colleagues the morning after he received the written approach from the Inquiry, is implausible. He had taken no such action in relation to the document after his meeting with Mr Hamblin on 23 June (at which the document appears to have been mentioned, but not considered in detail). On any view, he had left requesting input from colleagues on a complicated subject until one working day before he was apparently due to discuss it with his superior. It is difficult to believe that he had made no connection by that time between the approach by the Inquiry and a document so intimately connected with the CQC's evidence to the Inquiry, even if he had harboured an immediate uncertainty about this the previous evening, as expressed in his email to Mr Hamblin. It is more probable that he was motivated to circulate the document in the hope that the responses he was seeking would either provide support for its conclusions or discredit them, so that he either had support should the suggested inaccuracies be substantiated, or else could downplay the incident and show that the matter had been dealt with.

22.89　Even if Mr Banga made no connection between the approach from the Inquiry and Ms Bryce's work before the meeting at which he discovered that no colleague had received a letter like the one he had received, it is improbable that his reason for putting a stop to that work after the meeting was not motivated by a fear that there was a connection. His explanation given to the Inquiry was that he believed he had been "misrepresented" to the Inquiry. Although he insisted he did not know what he had been misrepresented about, on his own account, the relevance of any previous role at the HCC had been ruled out. The most obvious possibility was the "Bryce document". It is therefore probable that he stopped further work on it because he did not want to expose himself to the risk of further trouble.

22.90　There are serious doubts whether the concerns of which the draft document was evidence would have seen the light of day had that process been completed. While the work was not complete, and there was no reason why it should have been offered to the Inquiry in an unconsidered form, the reaction of Mr Banga in stopping work on it suggests a reluctance to continue a piece of work which had the potential to embarrass the CQC. In evidence, in reply to the suggestion that the "Bryce document" would never have been disclosed to the Inquiry, he said:

In terms of the format in which it's currently exhibited, definitely not. What I outlined earlier was that there were – it would have gone through, given that these were issues that have been raised, a process which would have arrived at a conclusion not dissimilar from that which was shared with the inquiry on the 19th. Whether or not we then took a view that that was something that the inquiry needed to be appraised of, I'm not sure.[103]

22.91 This answer is inconsistent with the existence of a healthy corporate instinct of transparency: it might be expected of a manager in Mr Banga's position that he would swiftly agree that if it were confirmed that incorrect evidence had been given, that the Inquiry would be notified about it.

22.92 Mr Hamblin told the Inquiry:

It would depend on what – what one eventually found. Now, clearly if we had found evidence that we'd got something wrong, we would have told you. However, I don't – my point about premature was that it hadn't gone through its full process of being checked and validated at the time ...

... so many of the issues lay in the interpretation of the person speaking that actually I do hold the view that the only person who can accurately say what somebody meant by what they said is the person who said it. So the issues that are in there are not really arguments so much about fact [sic] of what we do, but interpretation about what we said we did. So I don't think that issue would have arisen ...

22.93 This appears to suggest that if he, Mr Hamblin, or his senior colleagues had not agreed that their evidence had been potentially incorrect, no disclosure would have taken place, whatever might have been thought by more junior employees. An approach to assisting a public inquiry which depends on witnesses judging for themselves what is relevant, rather than one of full disclosure where issues have been raised, is not an appropriate one, particularly for a regulator.

22.94 Unfortunately, it seems that Mr Banga was afraid to admit the connection between his actions in relation to this work and the letter from the Inquiry because he was afraid of the light in which it would put him and his superiors, and of their reaction to what he had done.

The Care Quality Commission reaction to the evidence of Kay Sheldon

22.95 At an extremely late stage in the Inquiry proceedings, Ms Sheldon, a commissioner of the CQC, came forward to express her concerns about the way in which the organisation was being run, including a wide-ranging and personally directed criticism of the leadership offered by the Chair and Chief Executive. In so far as the substance of her criticisms are relevant to the

---

103 Banga T132.77

Inquiry's terms of reference, conclusions are to be found in *Chapter 11: Regulation: the Care Quality Commission.*

22.96 Following the Board strategy day on 29 September 2011, at which Ms Sheldon became distressed, Dame Jo Williams, Chair of the CQC, contacted her to say she was concerned about her well-being and mental state. Dame Jo asked Ms Sheldon to see an occupational health nurse so that she could assure herself that Ms Sheldon was fit to attend board meetings. Ms Sheldon saw the nurse on 12 October 2011 and was deemed fine, although a little stressed. The Inquiry accepts that, as CQC Chair, Dame Jo felt a duty of care towards Ms Sheldon and a duty to ensure the effective operation of the Board.

22.97 However, the way in which the request to see a nurse was raised, and the repeated references to her health, clearly gave Ms Sheldon the strong impression that her distress had been seen as an opportunity to remove her from the Board. She, herself, was clear her distress had nothing to do with her mental health, but reflected her frustration at the response to the issues she was raising. Dame Jo's focus seems to have been primarily on Ms Sheldon's health record, rather than on the merits of what she had to say. This seems to be a particularly personal approach to dealing with the issues Ms Sheldon was raising, and it could be questioned whether seeking to end her attendance at Board meetings was, in any case, an appropriate response.[104]

22.98 On the Friday before Ms Sheldon gave her oral evidence to the Inquiry, Dame Jo issued a letter to all CQC staff. Although intended as a rallying note ahead of some likely difficult media attention, its tone left little doubt as to the Board's view of Ms Sheldon's decision to give evidence, and clearly implied that she was undermining the organisation. Looked at from the perspective of a CQC employee, it seems unlikely that any member of staff reading this letter could be left reassured about the CQC's approach to whistleblowing and, by implication, the response they would get should they ever wish publicly to raise concerns of their own:

> *Next week is going to be challenging for CQC. As you may know, a Board member and a member of staff have decided to air their opinions about CQC at the public inquiry into Mid Staffs. This could generate a lot of media coverage about us. This may be difficult, but we must not lose confidence in the great work we are doing and the huge progress we have made ...*

> *... The kind of coverage we may get next week damages our reputation, damages our colleagues and weakens the future of the organisation, which we have all worked tirelessly to build over the last two and a half years. It is not in our interests, nor the public's whom we seek to serve, to have damaging accusations and personal opinions voiced in the media, because a weaker CQC will find it harder to challenge poor care.*[105]

---

104 Sheldon WS0000078501, paras 84–88
105 CQC00000000437 All staff letter from Dame Jo Williams (25 Nov 2012)

22.99 On Monday 28 November 2011, the day Ms Sheldon gave her oral evidence, the three other CQC commissioners issued a joint statement expressing their support for the CQC Chair and Chief Executive and expressing their disappointment in Ms Sheldon's view of the organisation. As with the staff letter, the statement's focus is on rebutting Ms Sheldon's criticisms. It is understandable that the CQC would want to respond to the concerns raised, and indeed the organisation had an opportunity to do this through the Inquiry. However, the implicit message to any member of staff reading this statement is that the Board is concerned more with distancing itself publicly from Ms Sheldon and dissembling her evidence, than with reflecting carefully on the criticisms made and the reasons why a member of the organisation may have felt compelled to approach the Inquiry in this way:

> [Kay Sheldon's] *statement is not an accurate representation of CQC, its leadership or its culture. In addition, it contains a number of factual inaccuracies relating to the functioning of the Board and the operational aspects of CQC. These have been addressed in CQC's most recent statement to the inquiry, which we endorse ...*

> *... We are disappointed that Kay believes that the Board lacks rigour in its governance, decision-making and direction. We are fully confident that we are able to effectively fulfil our governance role ... we do not recognise the criticisms Kay is referring to.*[106]

22.100 It has since become public that, on the same day Ms Sheldon gave her oral evidence to the Inquiry, Dame Jo Williams wrote to the Secretary of State, asking that he use his powers to remove Ms Sheldon from the CQC Board.[107] Dame Jo has since told the Inquiry that she took this step because she considered that Ms Sheldon's actions evidenced a departure from the collegiate and corporate approach, and a breach of trust in approaching the Inquiry without first discussing it with her fellow commissioners.

22.101 Whatever view is held of Ms Sheldon's criticisms, the evidence is that she made them honestly and in a genuine belief that the public interest required her to do so. In her evidence to the Inquiry, she stated that she had raised her concerns on numerous occasions to no avail. She, therefore, felt she had no option but to approach the Inquiry.[108] She has a long history of involvement in healthcare regulation, having been a Mental Health Act Commissioner and on its board for five years. She brought to her work her perspective as a sometime user of mental health services and involvement in various service-user forums. She is a trustee of an established mental health charity. The Inquiry accepts she is not someone who would take action of this nature lightly.

22.102 It took considerable courage for her to approach the Inquiry, as it meant exposing herself not only to the public eye, but to the fierce disapproval of the Chair, the Chief Executive and her

---

106 CQC Commissioners WS0000078638
107 www.publications.parliament.uk/pa/ld201213/ldhansrd/text/120522-gc0001.htm, 5.26pm
108 Sheldon WS0000078478, para 1

fellow CQC commissioners. The organisation, its leaders and others within it are obviously permitted to voice disagreement with criticism and to support their disagreement with evidence and argument. Robust discussion is, or should be, the lifeblood of any effective organisation. However, responses become a matter of concern where they focus on an attack on an individual for placing a *bona fide* disagreement in the public domain where it concerns a matter honestly believed to be a matter of public interest. Unhappily, the reaction of the CQC did cross such a line in:

- The tone of the circular to staff;
- The response from other commissioners;
- The suggestion of the need to seek the assistance of occupational health;
- A request for removal of a commissioner from her post without at least a pause for consideration of the possible reasons she might have had for such an apparently difficult and challenging step.

Such an approach was unlikely to achieve the purpose claimed for it by the CQC, namely to build confidence internally within the organisation.

Overview of a duty of candour

Legal background

22.103 The argument in favour of a duty of candour where medical treatment has gone wrong was advanced as long ago as 1985 by the then Master of the Rolls, Lord Donaldson, when, "with undisguised reluctance", the Court of Appeal refused to order the disclosure of a report from one health authority to another about the circumstances of an adverse incident, on grounds of legal professional privilege:

> *We think there is something seriously wrong with the law if [the patient's] mother cannot find out exactly what caused this brain damage. It should never be forgotten that we are here concerned with a hospital patient relationship ... a doctor is under a duty to answer his patient's questions as to the treatment proposed. We see no reason why there should not be a similar duty in relation to hospital staff. The duty is subject to the exercise of clinical judgement as to the terms in which the information is given and the extent to which, in the patient's interests, information should be withheld. Why, we ask ourselves, is the position any different if the patient asks what treatment he has in fact had? Let us suppose that a blood transfusion is in contemplation. The patient asks what is involved. He is told that a quantity of blood from a donor will be introduced into his system. He may ask about the risk of AIDS and so forth and will be entitled to straight answers. He consents. Suppose that, by accident, he is given a quantity of air as well as blood and suffers serious ill effects. Is he not entitled to ask what treatment he in fact received, and*

is the doctor and the hospital authority not obliged to tell him, "in the event you did not only get a blood transfusion. You also got an air transfusion"? Why is the duty different before the treatment from what it is afterwards?

If the duty is the same, then if the patient is refused information to which he is entitled, it must be for consideration whether he could not bring an action for breach of contract claiming specific performance of the duty to inform. In other words, whether the patient could not bring an action for discovery, albeit upon a novel basis.

We consider that some thought should be given to what is the duty of disclosure owed by a doctor and a hospital to a patient after treatment ...[109]

22.104 Lord Donaldson went further in 1987:

I personally think that in professional negligence cases, and, in particular, medical negligence cases, there is a duty of candour resting upon the professional man. This is recognised by the legal professions in their ethical rules requiring their members to refer the client to other advisers, if it appears that the client has a valid claim for negligence. This also appears to be recognised by the Medical Defence Union whose view is that "the patient is entitled to a prompt, sympathetic and above all truthful account of what has occurred" ...[110]

22.105 After referring to what he said (see above), he expressed concern that it had been suggested that a contractual duty, if it existed, would not assist an NHS patient as there was no legal contract between the patient and the doctor or hospital. He repudiated this suggestion:

In my judgement, still admittedly and regretfully obiter, it is but one aspect of the general duty of care, arising out of the patient-medical practitioner or hospital authority relationship and gives rise to rights both in contract and in tort ...

22.106 Lord Donaldson was later to admit publicly that he was "riding [his] personal hobby horse or, if you like, flying a kite".[111]

22.107 A series of reforms was made to procedural rules making it possible for patients to gain access as of right to their own medical records.[112] The Data Protection Act 1998 allows a patient to make an application to see his/her medical records.[113] The Access to Health Records

---

109 *Lee v SW Thames Regional Health Authority* [1985] 2 All ER 385, 389 (CA)
110 *Naylor v Preston Area Health Authority* [1987] 2 All ER 353, 360
111 (1985) 53 Medico-Legal Journal 148, 157, cited in *Medical Law, Text and Material,* Kennedy & Grubb (Butterworths, 1989) pp533–534
112 See now, for example, Civil Procedure Rules CPR3.16 for availability of pre-action disclosure in personal injury cases, www.justice.gov.uk/courts/procedure-rules/civil/protocol/prot_pic#IDACJKCC
113 See *Guidance for Access to Health Records Requests*, Department of Health (February 2010) for current guidance on application of these provisions.

Act 1990 allows the patient's personal representatives access after death to the records and, where the records are unintelligible, to an explanation of the terms used.[114]

22.108 However, this welcome development did nothing to confirm any duty to disclose information that was not reduced to a record of some sort, or to volunteer any information when things had gone wrong, unless a request was made for information. Lord Donaldson's "kite" was decisively pulled down by the Court of Appeal in 1997, in a case involving an alleged "cover-up" of a failure of diagnosis resulting in the death of a child, and falsification of medical records. Lord Justice Stuart-Smith, referring to what Lord Donaldson had said, stated that the remarks afforded no authority for there being:

> ... some kind of free standing duty of candour irrespective of whether a doctor-patient relationship exists in a healing or treating context, breach of which sounds in damages ... This would involve a startling expansion of the law of tort.[115]

22.109 This case was then taken to the European Court of Human Rights, to which it was submitted that under Articles 2, 8 and 10 of the European Convention on Human Rights, a bereaved parent of a child who had died as a result of negligence by a state agent had a right to a truthful and accurate account of the circumstances surrounding the death and, at the very least, those Articles prohibited the deliberate provision of false information and falsification of official records.[116] The Court rejected the claim for a combination of reasons, and principally because the applicants had settled a civil claim for negligence. It held that, even if Article 8 did require a full and frank disclosure of medical records to the parents, they had denied themselves the chance of confirming their concerns by various procedural steps they took. The Court made no decision about the existence of such a right.

House of Commons Health Select Committee 1999

22.110 In 1999, the Health Select Committee published a report in which it considered a variety of issues relating to adverse outcomes.[117] The Committee reviewed the Powell case and noted that the General Medical Council (GMC) had introduced a professional duty to explain the reasons and circumstances of a child patient's death to those with parental responsibility. It was observed that such a duty was to inform relatives of matters going beyond what had to be included on the death certificate. The Committee concluded that:

---

114 Access to Health Records Act 1990, section 3
115 *Powell v Boldadz* [1998] Lloyds Rep Med 116, 125 (CA)
116 *Powell v United Kingdom* ECHR 3rd Section Admissibility decision, Application No, 45305/99 (4 May 2000), (2000) 30 EHRR CD362
117 *Sixth Report: Procedures Related to Adverse Clinical Incidents and Outcomes in Medical Care* (28 October 1999) House of Commons www.publications.parliament.uk/pa/cm199899/cmselect/cmhealth/549/54902.htm

Doctors should tell relatives these facts unless the patient has requested them not to do so.[118]

22.111 The Committee concluded that they could expect a professional duty to provide such information to deliver this objective, but:

... in case it does not we consider that there should be a statutory duty to provide information.[119]

Bristol Royal Infirmary Inquiry

22.112 Professor Sir Ian Kennedy, Chairman of the Bristol Inquiry, recommended that:

A duty of candour, meaning a duty to tell a patient if adverse events have occurred, must be recognised as owed by all those working in the NHS to patients.[120]

22.113 He set out a powerful argument for this recommendation:

For respect, honesty and openness to flourish between healthcare professionals and individual patients there must be a culture of openness and honesty within the healthcare system as a whole. The hospital as an institution must be open with patients as to what they can expect, where and to whom they can go if they do not understand something, and what they may do if they wish to pass on suggestions or comments. During our oral hearings, we heard the frustration of parents at not being able to discover what was happening as regards the care of their child. A hospital committed to openness would involve and integrate the parent (or patient) into the pattern of care, rather than exclude them.

Historically, of course, while hospitals may have been willing to disclose and discuss accidents, they have been unwilling to do so in the case of an error or a mistake because of the legal repercussions ... What we say here is that even in the case of a mistake which might bring legal liability there is a duty of candour. This duty is part of and grows out of the culture of openness which we have called for. It is also a duty that is implicit in the notions of respect and honesty in dealings with patients.

---

118 *Sixth Report: Procedures Related to Adverse Clinical Incidents and Outcomes in Medical Care* (28 October 1999) House of Commons www.publications.parliament.uk/pa/cm199899/cmselect/cmhealth/549/54902.htm, para 28
119 *Sixth Report: Procedures Related to Adverse Clinical Incidents and Outcomes in Medical Care* (28 October 1999) House of Commons www.publications.parliament.uk/pa/cm199899/cmselect/cmhealth/549/54902.htm, para 28
120 HCC0015000235 The Report of the Public Inquiry into Children's Heart Surgery at the Bristol Royal Infirmary 1984–1995, Learning from Bristol (July 2001) Recommendation 33, p 441

With specific regard to an unplanned event which results in harm to the patient, the duty of candour should still apply even when mistakes are not immediately apparent and come to light later. This is so particularly when the patient may otherwise be unaware. There is already evidence that such an approach is being adopted within the NHS, for example in circumstances of misdiagnosis ...

... It stated that when serious problems occur, patients may want compensation, but they also want an admission; the prevention of future incidents; an explanation; and an apology. When things go wrong, patients should not have to struggle against the system and raise formal complaints. Thus, we believe that hospitals have a responsibility to be active and to investigate adverse events. Whenever it is clear that what went wrong is the result of action or inaction on the part of the hospital or its staff, they should be under a duty to be open and honest and to acknowledge this as early as possible, ensuring that any compensation due is paid swiftly. Difficult and uncomfortable though it will be, we are convinced that this degree of openness by hospitals and healthcare professionals is essential to the maintenance of patients' trust. It is the essence of respect for and honesty towards patients. And, as we argue later, the more that is known and understood about adverse events generally, the more it will become possible to address their causes and to prevent them in the future.[121]

22.114 In his evidence to this Inquiry, Sir Ian advocated a very broad culture of transparency: for instance, he thought that all information that should be considered by a Trust Board should also go to the regulator:[122]

... one of the things that you would oblige a trust and/or a hospital to do is to publish, make open and transparent, those aspects of its activity which touch upon the care of patients, and include the engagement with patients. And those should be the currency of – of local debate and discussion.[123]

The Shipman Inquiry: The Fifth Report, 9 December 2004

22.115 Dame Janet Smith's Inquiry dealt with issues arising from concerns about GPs, but she did observe that patients should be told in advance if a doctor who is to operate on them is subject to GMC conditions. She expressed concern that the GMC had not progressed its consideration of this issue.[124]

---

121 HCC0015000235, *The Report of the Public Inquiry into children's heart surgery at the Bristol Royal Infirmary 1984–1995, Learning from Bristol (July 2001),* chapter 23, pp298–299, paras 51–53
122 Kennedy T77.80–81
123 Kennedy T77.81
124 *Shipman Inquiry: The Fifth Report – Safeguarding Patients: Lessons from the Past – Proposals for the Future* (9 December 2004) p916 para 24.151, and p1146, para 27.199

Guidance and policy on candour

22.116 There has been a consistent theme in Government guidance and policy favouring openness in dealings with patients about their care and treatment where things have gone wrong.

Making amends

22.117 In 2003, the Chief Medical Officer at the time (Professor Sir Liam Donaldson), in his seminal report *Making Amends,*[125] proposed a statutory duty of candour comprising several elements:

> *a duty of candour requiring clinicians and health service managers to inform patients about actions which have resulted in harm;*

> *exemption from disciplinary action for those reporting adverse events or medical errors (except where there is a criminal offence or where it would not be safe for the professional to continue to treat patients);*

> *legal privilege would be provided for reports and information identifying adverse events except where the information was not recorded in the medical record.*[126]

22.118 In making these recommendations, Sir Liam recognised the chilling effect which the threat of disciplinary action and litigation could have on reporting, particularly self-reporting of adverse incidents.[127] He called for a system in which:

> *... risks of care are reduced and patient safety improves because medical errors and near misses are readily reported, successfully analysed and effective corrective action takes place and is sustained.*[128]

22.119 He observed that:

> *Overall too many families are left with the impression that the NHS closes ranks when something goes wrong, to exclude the victim.*[129]

---

125 *Making amends: a consultation paper setting out proposals for reforming the approach to clinical negligence in the NHS: A report by the Chief Medical Officer* (30 June 2003)
126 *Making amends: a consultation paper setting out proposals for reforming the approach to clinical negligence in the NHS: A report by the Chief Medical Officer* (30 June 2003), p18
127 *Making amends: a consultation paper setting out proposals for reforming the approach to clinical negligence in the NHS: A report by the Chief Medical Officer,* (30 June 2003), pp27–28
128 *Making amends: a consultation paper setting out proposals for reforming the approach to clinical negligence in the NHS: A report by the Chief Medical Officer,* (30 June 2003), p13
129 *Making amends: a consultation paper setting out proposals for reforming the approach to clinical negligence in the NHS: A report by the Chief Medical Officer,* (30 June 2003), p42

22.120 In his evidence to the Inquiry, Sir Liam said that he had always been in favour of a statutory duty of candour because:

> ... professionals should be encouraged to take responsibility when they have done something wrong, rather than withhold instances of harm.[130]

22.121 He thought it important that the duty extend to organisations, as well as to individual professionals, because the latter would invariably need support when seeking to disclose something which had gone wrong:

> I think it probably works best is if the organisation does it with the professional involved ... We need to think as well about the second victim, that often they [the professionals] are devastated by what's happened. I've seen it happen. And so I think it's important that when information is disclosed to a family ... it needs to be done by people with skill and sensitivity. You can't just send a distressed nurse straight down the corridor to disclose something. For it to work in a way that's as positive as possible, given the very bad circumstances, I think it needs to be done with skill and in an organised way and as part of a team, in which the individual professional who has made the mistake is involved.[131]

22.122 While he was against the open-ended use of criminal sanctions in relation to cases of harm caused by medical error, he did think that a failure to be candid and covering up the truth should be regarded as serious matters:

> I think it should be viewed very, very seriously. I have a little quote of myself, which I think people tend to find helpful in looking at the balance of these things, I said a few years ago, "To err is human, to cover up is unforgivable, to fail to learn is inexcusable", and I think it's the failure to learn that is the worst offence. The covering up isn't very good but the erring is human, and sometimes it can be forgiven.[132]

22.123 Peter Walsh, Chief Executive of Action against Medical Accidents (AvMA), made a similar point in his evidence:

> THE CHAIRMAN: Would you suggest that a failure to be candid can in many circumstances be considered a more serious breach of duty than the error, professional though it may be, that took place in the first place?

---

130 Donaldson WS0000070165, para 181; also covered at T122.160–161
131 Donaldson T122.161–162
132 Donaldson T122.177

A. Certainly that's the way that I look upon it and that my organisation looks upon it. If I give it from a personal perspective, I'd far rather be treated by a doctor who at some stage in their career has made a mistake, owned up to it, learnt from the mistake and become a better doctor as a result of that. I mean, anyone can make a mistake. I certainly make a lot of mistakes in my professional capacity. I think that can be respected. Patients and family who have been the subject of a medical accident show, in our experience, a remarkable capacity to actually sympathise with someone who's been involved in an unintentional error or system failure, especially if they're dealt with openly and honestly. But, yes, the cover-up or deceit, lack of candour is, in our view, not only totally unacceptable, but it leads to other consequences that are not good for anyone.[133]

22.124 He said that frequently people felt driven to take legal action, not by the original medical accident, but by what they regarded as unreasonable denial or dishonesty.

Health Select Committee, 2011

22.125 In its report on complaints, the Health Select Committee considered the question of a duty of candour.[134] It welcomed the Government's announcement of an intention to introduce a contractual duty of candour and expressed doubt as to whether a statutory duty would produce the required cultural shift. The Committee recommended that a duty of candour between commissioners and providers be introduced into commissioning contracts; that a duty of candour to patients from providers should be part of the terms of authorisation of foundation trusts by Monitor; and that commissioning authorities should be placed under a duty of candour to their local populations and their Local Healthwatch organisations.

Professional obligations

22.126 Registered medical practitioners and nurses are required by their regulators to be open with patients.

22.127 The GMC's *Good Medical Practice* states:

If a patient under your care has suffered harm or distress, you must act immediately to put matters right, if that is possible. You should offer an apology and explain fully and promptly to the patient what has happened, and the likely short-term and long-term effects.[135]

---

133 Walsh T23.91–92
134 *Complaints and Litigation Sixth Report of Session 2010–12* (23 June 2011) House of Commons Health Committee, paras 80–82, Conclusions and recommendations paras 21–22
135 GMC0003000047, para 30

22.128 The Nursing and Midwifery Council (NMC) Code of Conduct says:

> *You must act immediately to put matters right if someone in your care has suffered harm for any reason.*

> *You must explain fully and promptly to the person affected what has happened and the likely effects.*[136]

Reporting of adverse incidents

22.129 An organisation registered by the CQC is obliged to report to the National Patient Safety Agency (NPSA) (whose functions have now moved to the NHS Commissioning Board) or the CQC a wide range of incidents, including most incidents involving injury, abuse or alleged abuse of a patient.[137] As AvMA has pointed out, it seems strange that a statutory requirement to inform a regulator is imposed but not a duty to inform the patient.[138]

Guidance on disclosure of records

22.130 The DH encourages the voluntary disclosure of records and information to coroners:

> *It is the Department of Health's view that the public interest served by Coroners' inquiries will outweigh considerations of confidentiality unless exceptional circumstances apply.*

> *When an NHS organisation feels that there are reasons why full disclosure is not appropriate, e.g. due to confidentiality obligations or Human Rights considerations, the following steps should be taken:*

> > *a) the Coroner should be informed about the existence of information relevant to an inquiry in all cases;*

> > *b) the concern about disclosure should be discussed with the Coroner and attempts made to reach agreement on the confidential handling of records or partial redaction of record content;*

> > *c) where agreement cannot be reached the issue will need to be considered by an administrative court.*

---

136 NMC00010000114, *The Code: Standards of conduct, performance and ethics for nurses and midwives* (1 May 2008), Nursing and Midwifery Council, paras 54–55
137 The Care Quality Commission (Registration) Regulations 2009 [SI 2009/3112], Reg 18
138 *The Need for a Statutory Duty of Candour in Healthcare* (October 2011 edition), AvMA

[note] *Coroners' inquiries are an important part of determining cause of death in a huge number of cases in the UK. Prompt access to confidential information regarding patients and others involved in an investigation is often vital to the reliability of the outcome of an inquiry.*[139]

NHS Constitution

22.131 The NHS Constitution offers a "pledge" of at least a degree of openness and honesty:

> *The NHS also commits:*
>
> *to ensure you are treated with courtesy and you receive appropriate support throughout the handling of a complaint; and the fact that you have complained will not adversely affect your future treatment (pledge);*
>
> *when mistakes happen, to acknowledge them, apologise, explain what went wrong and put things right quickly and effectively (pledge); and*
>
> *to ensure that the organisation learns lessons from complaints and claims and uses these to improve NHS services (pledge).*[140]

22.132 As a "pledge" this ranks as something NHS trusts only have to have regard to, and could possibly be read to cover only the organisation's behaviour if a complaint is made, as opposed to situations where it is aware of an adverse incident causing harm but the patient is not.[141] The guidance on the NHS Constitution seems to refer only to the processing of complaints in this section.[142]

The Code of Conduct for NHS Managers

22.133 The Code of Conduct for NHS Managers states:

> *I will respect and treat with dignity and fairness the public, patients, relatives, carers, NHS staff and partners in other agencies ... I will also seek to ensure that ... patients are involved in and informed about their own care, their experience is valued and they are involved in decisions.*[143]

22.134 This statement suffers similar defects to the NHS Constitution: it is not specific about the need for candour in the sense of volunteering information. The Code does not apparently apply

---

139 Guidance for Access to Health Records Requests, (February 2010) Department of Health, p26
140 *The NHS Constitution* (8 March 2010), p8
141 LEG00000001276, Health Act 2009, section 2. FTs appear in practice to be under the same obligation. See the relevant appendix for a paper produced by the Solicitor to the Inquiry on this issue.
142 *The Handbook to the NHS Constitution* (8 March 2012) DH, pp64–65
143 CURE00330017715, *Code of Conduct for NHS Managers* (October 2002), Department of Health, page 4

directly to FT employees.[144] It is also unclear to some whether, or to what extent, they are covered by this Code: Mr Knowles for one thought it did not apply to him.[145] However, it was incorporated into Ms Levy's contract of employment, although her understanding was that she was obliged to act in the best interests of her client.[146] Both accepted they would have regard to the Code in advising their clients.

The NHS Litigation Authority guidance

22.135 The NHSLA is keen to ensure that trusts and professionals feel free to give open and honest explanations and apologies to patients, where appropriate, without it being thought that this would amount to an admission of liability prejudicing their entitlement to indemnity should a claim arise. Its guidance of August 2007 stated:

> ... it is both natural and desirable for **those involved in treatment** which produces an adverse result, for whatever reason, to sympathise with the patient or the patient's relatives and to express sorrow or regret at the outcome. Such expressions of regret would not normally constitute an admission of liability, either in part or in full and it is not our policy to prohibit them, nor to dispute any payment, under any scheme, **solely** on the grounds of such an expression of regret.

> Explanations: ... In this area, too, NHSLA is keen to encourage both **clinicians and NHS bodies** to supply appropriate information whether informally, formally or through mediation. Care needs to be taken in the dissemination of explanations so as to avoid future litigation risks, but, for the avoidance of any doubt, NHSLA will not take a point against any NHS body or any clinician taking NHS indemnity, on the basis of a factual explanation offered in good faith before litigation is in train. We consider the provision of such information to constitute good clinical practice, and provided that facts, as opposed to opinions, form the basis of the explanation, nothing is likely to be revealed which would not subsequently be discloseable in the event of litigation.[147]

22.136 While this advice is a commendable attempt to promote openness, it might, from today's perspective, be thought to be overcautious. While it did not seek to restrict explanations to cases where a complaint had already been made, it counselled caution by the use of words such as "normally", and "solely" in relation to the effect of an apology on the indemnity. There was a warning to take care to avoid litigation risks and the letter discouraged the offering of opinions, the very matter which has caused such consternation to the Robinsons (as described

---

144 *The Code of Conduct for NHS Managers Directions 2002* (4 October 2002), Department of Health; also *The Regulation and Development of NHS Managers: A discussion paper* (18 October 2011), Dr Judith Smith and Professor Naomi Chambers, p9 – produced for the Inquiry seminars
145 Knowles T131.12–13
146 Levy T131.136
147 TRUST00030003735. Letter of 15 August 2007 from Steve Walker (Chief Executive of the NHSLA) to chief executives and finance directors of all NHS bodies, regarding apologies and explanations (emphasis added)

above). There is an implication that what is disclosed should be what would, in any event, have to be disclosed in litigation.

22.137 The 2009 version of this advice was subtly different:

> It is both natural and desirable for **clinicians** who have provided treatment which produces an adverse result, for whatever reason, to sympathise with the patient or the patient's relatives; to express sorrow or regret at the outcome; and to apologise for shortcomings in treatment. It is most important to patients that they or their relatives receive a meaningful apology. We encourage this, and stress that apologies do not constitute an admission of liability. In addition, it is not our policy to dispute any payment, under any scheme, **solely** on the grounds of such an apology.
>
> Explanations: Patients and their relatives increasingly ask for detailed explanations of what led to adverse outcomes. Moreover, they frequently say that they derive some consolation from knowing that lessons have been learned for the future ...
>
> ... Explanations **should not contain admissions of liability**. For the avoidance of doubt, the NHSLA will not take a point against any NHS body or any clinician seeking NHS indemnity, on the basis of a factual explanation offered in good faith before litigation is in train. We consider that the provision of such information constitutes good clinical and managerial practice.
>
> To assist in the provision of apologies and explanations, clinicians and NHS bodies should familiarise themselves with the guidance on being open, produced by the [NPSA] ... this circular is intended to encourage scheme members and their employees to offer the earlier, more informal, apologies and explanations so desired by patients and their families.[148]

22.138 The advice retained the spectre of the need to avoid admissions of liability, and continued to restrict the protection of the indemnity to factual explanations as opposed to opinions. It can be difficult when addressing medical issues to disentangle facts from opinions. For instance, in explaining what a diagnosis was, it is likely that a clinician will import a personal opinion into an interpretation of the records. An apology may not make much sense, or carry much meaning, unless accompanied by an acknowledgement that something has happened which should not have. While such an acknowledgement made by an individual clinician is unlikely in law to amount to a formal admission by the trust who employs the clinician, if it is made by a trust officer it might be an admission. If there is any confusion in this area, and there is, the reaction of clinicians and officers is likely to be one of caution and erring on the side of not being as open and frank as they would like to be.

---

148 NHSLA0001000001. Letter of 1 May 2009 from Steve Walker (Chief Executive of the NHS Litigation Authority) to chief executives and finance directors of all NHS bodies, regarding apologies and explanations. (emphasis added)

22.139 This advice was endorsed by all the medical defence organisations, the NPSA and the GMC. The chief executives of these organisations signed a joint statement in support of it, which was included at the bottom of the NHSLA guidance:

> *For many years we have advised our members that, if something goes wrong, patients should receive a prompt, open, sympathetic and above all truthful account of what has happened. Any patient who has had the misfortune to suffer through an error of whatever nature should receive a full explanation and a genuine apology. We encourage members to adopt this approach. There are no legal concerns about taking this course of action: it is quite different from admitting liability.*[149]

22.140 This statement appears to go further than the NHSLA guidance and appears to encourage a full explanation, which presumably could include an opinion, and gives a wider, less qualified degree of assurance with regard to indemnity.

22.141 The NPSA's guidance, *Being Open*, state categorically:

> *Being open involves:*
> * *Acknowledging, apologising and explaining when things go wrong;*
> * *Conducting a thorough investigation into the incident and reassuring patients, their families and carers that lessons learned will help prevent the incident recurring;*
> * *Providing support for those involved to cope with the physical and psychological consequences of what happened.*[150]

22.142 This guidance offers an articulate and comprehensive guide to the disclosure to patients of incidents which have caused harm to them. It expressly does not advocate telling patients about incidents where harm has been prevented, or "near misses". While it does not appear to say so expressly, the guidance only makes sense if it applies to cases where the patient would otherwise be unaware, and where no complaint has been lodged. For example, there is a requirement that an incident be discussed with the patient "as soon as possible after recognition of the patient safety incident".[151]

---

149 NHSLA0001000001. Letter of 1 May 2009 from Steve Walker (Chief Executive of the NHS Litigation Authority) to chief executives and finance directors of all NHS bodies, regarding apologies and explanations.
150 *Being Open: communicating patient safety incidents with patients, carers and their families* (November 2009) National Patient Safety Agency, p2 and p6
151 *Being Open: communicating patient safety incidents with patients, carers and their families* (November 2009) National Patient Safety Agency, p22

Consideration of a statutory duty of cooperation to share information about healthcare workers

22.143 In March 2010, the DH issued a consultation on proposed regulations to impose a duty of cooperation on specified bodies with regard to sharing information about the performance or conduct of healthcare workers, providing information in response to requests from other designated bodies for information on this subject, and in considering any issues arising as a result of sharing such information.[152] In February 2012, the Government published a summary of responses to the consultation and an announcement that it did not now intend to continue with this proposal.[153] It was accepted that the new regulations were not needed because of a number of developments since the regulations were proposed:

- The GMC had undertaken research showing that systems to identify problems among healthcare workers were improving and employers were giving priority to detecting and dealing with concerns.
- Existing and prospective provisions for duties to provide information or report matters were sufficient. These included:
  - The introduction of Responsible Officers: these are obliged to ensure that appraisals of staff take into account all available information about fitness to practise in work for the officer's organisations and for any other body; to cooperate with the GMC; and to have regard to guidance issued by the GMC and the Secretary of State;[154]
  - The amendment of NHS Terms and Conditions to include a contractual right and a duty for employees to raise genuine concerns with their employer about malpractice, patient safety, financial impropriety or any other serious risks they consider to be in the public interest.[155] The handbook contains a recommendation that local policies include an option to raise concerns outside the line of management, ultimately with the Secretary of State or any designated body.[156] This document does not address the issue of cooperation with other bodies or the provision of information to patients. The Secretary of State had announced that the NHS Constitution would be updated to include an expectation that staff would raise concerns at the earliest opportunity and a pledge that staff would be supported in doing so, and to "highlight" the existing legal right for them to do so;[157]
  - A memorandum of understanding was to be developed between the NHS and the independent healthcare sector.

---

152 AS/20 WS0000048532 *Consultation on proposed regulations on "duty of cooperation"* (5 March 2010) Department of Health

153 *Consultation on proposed regulations on "duty of cooperation" – Summary of consultation responses* (Feb 2012) Department of Health, p32

154 Medical Profession (Responsible Officers) Regulations 2010 *[2010 SI 2841] reg 11(3), (5)*

155 *NHS Staff Terms and Conditions of Service Handbook,* Amendment number 26, Pay Circular (AforC) 2/2010, The NHS Staff Council, section 21.1

156 *NHS Staff Terms and Conditions of Service Handbook,* Amendment number 26, Pay Circular (AforC) 2/2010, The NHS Staff Council, section 21.3

157 *The NHS Constitution and Whistleblowing – Consultation Report: September 2011,* Department of Health (17 October 2011); for press release see http://nds.coi.gov.uk/content/Detail.aspx?ReleaseID=421644&NewsAreaID=2

Views of witnesses

Action against Medical Accidents

22.144 Since the Powell case (described above) AvMA, acting in conjunction with the patient's family, has been seeking to promote a statutory duty of candour, under the banner of "Robbie's law". Mr Walsh, Chief Executive of AvMA, told the Inquiry that there was some tension in the system between the recognition of the need for openness and the fear of litigation. However, he did not think this ought to be the case:

> There should be nothing in the way that the NHS or indeed other healthcare providers operate which is designed to reduce the risk of people attaining their quite proper right to litigate in order to get compensation. That's what people in the Department of Health, as well as the NHS, say. So it's more a question of educating people. The problem we find is that whilst that's said from the centre, if you speak to the rank and file complaints officers, perhaps PALS officers, risk management staff, they say that in reality they do feel under pressure to reduce the risk for the organisation.[158]

22.145 He thought that this phenomenon had been seen at work in this Inquiry in the Trust's handling of information in its possession about the Moore-Robinson case (described above) and the Astbury case (see *Chapter 1: Warning signs*), where it appeared that the guidance referred to above had been ignored. Mr Walsh spoke from AvMA's experience that this was not uncommon:

> ... we come across, not infrequently, examples of the NHS being at best economical with the truth, or at worst even covering up, which flies in the face of all ... guidance. We've dealt with two cases here from Stafford already, the Robinson case, the Moore-Robinson case and also Ron Street's evidence about a serious untoward incident being kept secret from the family for the best part of a year. They're not isolated cases entirely because at AvMA we have examples of that happening in other parts of the country. And the fact is that some managers have got it into their heads that that can be acceptable. And the Government to date, whilst giving guidance, have been prepared to tolerate it and not stamp down on it.[159]

22.146 AvMA considers that the measures taken to date have failed to instil a culture of openness and that a statutory duty is a necessary step in this direction.[160] A statutory obligation could workably be imposed on organisations registered with the CQC via the registration requirements.[161] Mr Walsh pointed to the current paradox that CQC rules required reporting to the National Reporting and Learning System (NRLS) at the NPSA (whose functions have now

158 Walsh T23.88–89
159 Walsh T23.90–91
160 CLO000000355, AvMA closing submission, paras 193–194
161 Walsh T23.132–133

transferred to the NHS Commissioning Board), but not to the patient or family concerned.[162] AvMA suggests that the duty of candour to patients should be made statutory by inclusion in the terms of CQC registration with the contractual duty as an adjunct. It also suggests that the duty should extend in most cases to informing patients and families of "near misses", that is incidents which could have caused harm but where this was prevented.

National Clinical Assessment Service

22.147 Professor Alastair Scotland, Chief Executive of the National Clinical Assessment Service (NCAS), contended that there should be a statutory duty of cooperation between healthcare organisations and NCAS, which should be accompanied by a duty of candour to ensure that the service is informed of all the salient facts.[163] If an advisory service of this nature is to be effective, in, for instance, assisting with issues around the contemplated suspension of a consultant, clearly it needs to have the full facts disclosed to it promptly and candidly.

The Department of Health

22.148 Una O'Brien, Permanent Secretary of the DH, gave evidence while the Government was still considering its views on a statutory duty of candour. Understandably, therefore, she was somewhat non-committal. However, she drew attention to the need to ensure that any imposed duty of candour did not have unintended consequences for individuals because of the possible difficulty in identifying when the duty arose; where there was a lack of clarity, for instance, as to whether something had gone wrong and how.[164] She foreshadowed the Government's favoured solution of imposing an obligation by contract, and expressed the desire that the professions rather than external agencies rather than external agencies should promote candour.

22.149 Professor Sir Bruce Keogh, the NHS Medical Director, queried what a statutory duty would add to the current and proposed requirements and guidance, but professed to being "agnostic" on the subject.[165] He accepted, however, that the NHS, and its organisations, needed to be more open.[166]

---

162 See also CLO000000355, AvMA closing submission, para 199
163 Scotland WS0000048165, paras 86–87
164 O'Brien T125.141–143
165 Keogh T123.20–23
166 Keogh T123.23

22.150 For Sir David Nicholson, NHS Chief Executive, the question was not around the principle, but about how best to implement it:

> *It seems to me the principle that if the NHS harms you that it actively tells you that it's harmed you, I think seems to me to be a good one. Certainly if I was a patient I would want to know that, and I think that's right. And I think – but how you do it and how do you create a system which does that I think needs quite a lot of thought and indeed that's why we are consulting round it ...*[167]

Public Concern at Work

22.151 Public Concern at Work is a highly respected charity at the forefront of work to support whistleblowers and to share expertise on the complex law in this area. On its behalf, Cathryn James, its Chief Executive, expressed support for a statutory duty:

> *We ... see this as part of creating an open and transparent workplace culture, as its emphasis appears to be on encouraging health organisations to speak to patients. We see this as complimentary to good whistleblowing arrangements and as quite separate from placing an additional duty on individual doctors and nurses to raise a concern about wrongdoing or malpractice in the workplace.*[168]

Conclusions

22.152 "Openness, transparency and candour", as considered in this chapter, has several elements. The term embraces the concept of being open and truthful about individual incidents in which things have gone wrong. It also involves offering a balanced picture of performance generally that is devoid of the "spin" of downgrading important matters of concern and exaggerating positive achievements. It requires insight into personal and organisational deficiencies and the welcoming of constructive criticism. Above all, it requires a determination to put right what has gone wrong, not only for any who have suffered as a result, but to protect future patients from a repetition of wrong-doing. It requires a willingness to learn and be challenged. Therefore Counsel to the Inquiry is right to warn in his closing submissions about turning the term into a slogan.[169] There is a danger in over-simplification.

22.153 There seems to be near universal agreement that candour is an essential component in today's healthcare. The reasons for this are many, but they include:

- The need to maintain public and patient trust in the service;
- Proper involvement of patients in their own care and treatment;

---

167 Nicholson T128.120–121
168 James WS0000076467, para 66
169 CLO0000003086, Counsel to the Inquiry's closing submissions, Chapter 26: Department of Health, para 427

- Early identification of concerns for individual patients;
- The need of affected patients and those close to them for explanations about what has happened;
- Ensuring those requiring remedial treatment receive it;
- Facilitating receipt of other remedies for poor treatment where appropriate;
- Early identification and remedy of patient safety-related systemic issues and concerns about individual professionals;
- Facilitation of genuine patient choice;
- Reliable identification of good practice.

22.154 This Inquiry has shown that, desirable though the principle of openness, transparency and candour may be, it is frequently not observed. This has had serious consequences which have included:

- Delays in bereaved families learning the truth about the treatment of their loved ones, thereby compounding their suffering, and raising unjustifiable obstacles to receipt of proper remedies;
- Obstruction to the process of learning from and correcting deficient service provision;
- Discouraging disclosure of information about concerns;
- Allowing a foundation trust to be authorised on a false understanding of the facts;
- Potentially allowing commissioning of services to be undertaken on the basis of inaccurate information.

22.155 Great strides have been made in recent years towards recognition of the importance of candour and towards actually behaving in a more open manner. Thus, the Trust has been demonstrably more open about concerns. The DH and others have been swifter in publicly recognising issues and in addressing them. However, the picture is not uniformly encouraging. The lack of the necessary degree of candour has not been confined to one board in one trust at one time. A general culture lingers on within the NHS, including the DH and regulators, in which the truth is often not welcomed; those who seek to convey it are not supported; and issues of concern are ignored by, or not known to, those who could do something about them. In the overwhelming majority of cases this is not a matter of deliberate dishonesty, but of the natural human reaction to potential criticism, and an institutional will to put the best gloss on performance.

22.156 The debate about a duty of candour is often confused because there is insufficient recognition that the need for candour embraces many different aspects of healthcare provision. The most commonly considered context is the need to inform a patient as soon as possible that he or she has or may have been subjected to avoidable harm, but this is far from being the only circumstance in which candour is required:

- Individual clinicians and managers need to report patient safety concerns openly and truthfully to their employers.
- Organisations need to be open and truthful with the public about their performance, poor as well as good.
- Information provided to regulators, commissioners and Government agencies must be accurate, candid and, above all, not misleading.

22.157 While the arguments in favour of extending a duty of candour to patients to require disclosure of "near misses" are powerful, the Inquiry does not agree this is necessary. While such disclosure may in some cases be desirable, in others it is likely to confuse and distress and produce no discernible benefit to either the patient or the public interest. Disclosure of this category of incident to the patient has to remain a matter of judgement, not entitlement. Disclosure of "near misses" should, of course, continue to be made within the system in accordance with current best practice reporting.

22.158 The requirement for candour is therefore multi-faceted, embracing individual clinical and managerial professionals, provider organisations and their collective leadership, in the NHS and the private sector, commissioners, regulators and political leaders.

22.159 The ways in which that requirement is currently recognised are piecemeal and disjointed, and inevitably do not cover the whole of the ground which should be addressed. Thus, while doctors and nurses have similar (but not identically phrased) obligations placed on them, with similar sanctions available, NHS managers are subject to a much vaguer obligation, and no definable sanctions to back up even that. There is no clearly defined uniform obligation imposed on FT (non-clinical) managers and none at all on their counterparts in the independent sector. Organisations have even less well-defined duties in this regard. Unless steps are taken to evidence the importance of candour by creation of some uniform duty with serious sanctions available for non-observance, a culture of denial, secrecy and concealment of issues of concern will be able to survive anywhere in the healthcare system.

22.160 While it is a step in the right direction to propose, as the Government has recently, that a duty of candour should be written into commissioning contracts and terms of authorisation, this is not sufficient. An overarching duty of candour should be defined and enshrined in statute, accompanied in serious, defined situations by criminal sanctions. The duty requires a status higher than a performance standard as it needs to permeate and inform everything that is done when providing healthcare to the public. Observance of the duty can be policed by a regulator with powers in the last resort to prosecute in cases of serial non-compliance or serious and wilful deception. There is no reason why the CQC cannot do this if given that task: it can be supported by monitoring undertaken by commissioners and others. This does not require every statement made to be vetted for accuracy, but does require the investigation of matters when a complaint is made. The creation of such a framework, in which the administrative measures such as those currently proposed can be formulated, will elevate the duty of candour to its rightful position of significance, and will considerably strengthen the hand of those who wish to be open and to volunteer concerns. Peter Walsh is entirely right to say that in many cases a failure to disclose an error leading to harm is more serious than the original error. Similarly, Counsel to the Inquiry is right to observe in his closing submissions that what is required is a change of culture and an increase in organisational "maturity".[170] An overarching statutory duty is likely to assist in achieving this.

Principles

22.161 Some specific recommendations are made in other chapters. Some more generic ones are set out below. Underlying them should be a set of clear principles:

- Every healthcare organisation and everyone working for them, or on their behalf, must be honest, open and truthful in all their dealings with patients and the public.
- Organisational and personal interests must never be allowed to outweigh the duty to be honest, open and truthful.
- Where harm has been, or may have been, caused to a patient by an act or omission of the organisation or its staff, the patient (or, if the patient is deceased, any lawfully entitled personal representative) should be informed of the incident, given full disclosure of the surrounding circumstances and be offered an appropriate level of support.
- Full and truthful answers must given to any question reasonably asked by a patient (or, if deceased, by any lawfully entitled personal representative) about his or her past or intended treatment.
- Any statement made to a regulator or a commissioner in the course of its statutory duties must be completely truthful and not misleading by omission.
- Any public statement made by a healthcare organisation about its performance must be truthful and not misleading by omission.

Statutory duty

22.162 A statutory obligation should be imposed to observe a duty of candour:

- On healthcare providers who believe or suspect that treatment or care provided by them to a patient has caused injury to the patient, to inform that patient as soon as is practicable of that fact and, thereafter, to provide such information and explanation as the patient may reasonably request;
- On registered medical practitioners and registered nurses who believe or suspect that treatment or care provided to a patient by, or on behalf of, any healthcare provider by which they are employed has caused injury to the patient and to report their belief or suspicion to their employer as soon as is reasonably practicable.

---

170 CLO000003086, Counsel to the Inquiry's closing submissions, Chapter 26: Department of Health, para 427

22.163 The statutory provision should make it clear that the provision of information in compliance with this requirement is not of itself evidence or an admission of any civil or criminal liability, but non-compliance with the statutory duty should entitle the patient to a remedy.

22.164 There should be a statutory duty on all directors of healthcare organisations to be truthful in any information given to a healthcare regulator or commissioner, either personally or on behalf of the organisation, in compliance with a statutory obligation on the organisation to provide it. It should be made a criminal offence for any registered medical practitioner, or nurse, or director of an authorised or registered healthcare organisation:

- Knowingly to obstruct another in the performance of these statutory duties;
- To provide information to a patient or nearest relative intending to mislead them about such an incident;
- Dishonestly to make an untruthful statement to a commissioner or regulator knowing or believing that it is likely to rely on the statement in the performance of its duties.

Review of terms of registration and authorisation, guidance and policies

22.165 All organisations with published guidance or policies on disclosure of information about incidents to patients, including the NHSLA, the DH, trusts, FTs, and commissioners, should review their guidance and policies to ensure they include and are consistent with the following requirements:

- Honesty and candour: The *Code of Conduct for NHS Managers* should be amended to include:
  - An express requirement of honesty, candour and open dealing with the public, commissioners and regulators and, in particular, an obligation to be truthful in the provision of any information to commissioners or regulators that to the manager's knowledge they will rely on in the performance of their duties;
  - A duty, parallel to that imposed on registered medical and nursing practitioners, to ensure, where it is within the manager's knowledge, that appropriate steps are taken to inform patients, or, where deceased, their nearest relatives, of any incident in which they have been avoidably harmed (or have been harmed in circumstances which may have been avoidable) by services provided to them, and the circumstances of such incidents;
- Obligation to make truthful public statements: Conditions of registration or authorisation of healthcare organisations should be amended to include a standard requirement that any information provided to the public about services, compliance with statutory standards and statistical results is truthful and not misleading. Compliance with the standard should be regulated by the CQC, which should have power to direct an organisation to correct any information found by the CQC to be untruthful or misleading.

- "Gagging" and non-disparagement clauses: Such clauses should be prohibited in the policies of all healthcare organisations, regulators and commissioners, which should be amended to prohibit the taking of any steps, including the imposition or enforcement of contractual terms, to prevent their employees or former employees communicating to third parties statements they honestly believe to be necessary in the interests of protecting patient safety or to disclose fraud, mismanagement or neglect of duty – except to the extent that is justified by the preservation of patient or employee confidentiality, or the need to avoid prejudicing the organisation's performance of its public duties;
- Information to coroners: The terms of authorisation and registration and any relevant guidance for healthcare providers should be amended to ensure that all relevant information is provided to enable coroners to perform their function. Where a patient dies in hospital, or in circumstances in which it is suspected that the death was caused or contributed to by medical care or treatment, healthcare providers should generally disclose to the coroner investigating the death any documentary material in their possession containing information about or relevant to the patient's condition, treatment provided, the cause of death and the surrounding circumstances, including but not limited to any recorded opinion concerning those matters. Where, exceptionally, a provider considers withholding such material from the coroner, including where reliance is placed on legal professional privilege, such a step should only be taken with the personal authority of a director who is satisfied that it is justified in the public interest;
- Candour about adverse incidents: Guidance and policies should be reviewed to ensure that they will lead to compliance with *Being Open*, the guidance that was published by the NPSA;
- The NHS Constitution: This should be amended to reflect the changes recommended.

22.166 Various other steps are recommended in other chapters which are designed to assist in the observance of this essential duty.

Summary of recommendations

Recommendation 173

Every healthcare organisation and everyone working for them must be honest, open and truthful in all their dealings with patients and the public, and organisational and personal interests must never be allowed to outweigh the duty to be honest, open and truthful.

Recommendation 174

Where death or serious harm has been or may have been caused to a patient by an act or omission of the organisation or its staff, the patient (or any lawfully entitled personal representative or other authorised person) should be informed of the incident, given full disclosure of the surrounding circumstances and be offered an appropriate level of support, whether or not the patient or representative has asked for this information.

Recommendation 175

Full and truthful answers must be given to any question reasonably asked about his or her past or intended treatment by a patient (or, if deceased, to any lawfully entitled personal representative).

Recommendation 176

Any statement made to a regulator or a commissioner in the course of its statutory duties must be completely truthful and not misleading by omission.

Recommendation 177

Any public statement made by a healthcare organisation about its performance must be truthful and not misleading by omission.

Recommendation 178

The NHS Constitution should be revised to reflect the changes recommended with regard to a duty of openness, transparency and candour, and all organisations should review their contracts of employment, policies and guidance to ensure that, where relevant, they expressly include and are consistent with above principles and these recommendations.

Recommendation 179

"Gagging clauses" or non disparagement clauses should be prohibited in the policies and contracts of all healthcare organisations, regulators and commissioners; insofar as they seek, or appear, to limit bona fide disclosure in relation to public interest issues of patient safety and care.

Recommendation 180

Guidance and policies should be reviewed to ensure that they will lead to compliance with *Being Open*, the guidance published by the National Patient Safety Agency.

Chapter 22 Openness, transparency and candour

Recommendation 181

A statutory obligation should be imposed to observe a duty of candour:

- On healthcare providers who believe or suspect that treatment or care provided by it to a patient has caused death or serious injury to a patient to inform that patient or other duly authorised person as soon as is practicable of that fact and thereafter to provide such information and explanation as the patient reasonably may request;
- On registered medical practitioners and registered nurses and other registered professionals who believe or suspect that treatment or care provided to a patient by or on behalf of any healthcare provider by which they are employed has caused death or serious injury to the patient to report their belief or suspicion to their employer as soon as is reasonably practicable.

The provision of information in compliance with this requirement should not of itself be evidence or an admission of any civil or criminal liability, but non-compliance with the statutory duty should entitle the patient to a remedy.

Recommendation 182

There should be a statutory duty on all directors of healthcare organisations to be truthful in any information given to a healthcare regulator or commissioner, either personally or on behalf of the organisation, where given in compliance with a statutory obligation on the organisation to provide it.

Recommendation 183

It should be made a criminal offence for any registered medical practitioner, or nurse, or allied health professional or director of an authorised or registered healthcare organisation:

- Knowingly to obstruct another in the performance of these statutory duties;
- To provide information to a patient or nearest relative intending to mislead them about such an incident;
- Dishonestly to make an untruthful statement to a commissioner or regulator knowing or believing that they are likely to rely on the statement in the performance of their duties.

Recommendation 184

Observance of the duty should be policed by the Care Quality Commission, which should have powers in the last resort to prosecute in cases of serial non-compliance or serious and wilful deception. The Care Quality Commission should be supported by monitoring undertaken by commissioners and others.

Recommendation 273

The terms of authorisation, licensing and registration and any relevant guidance should oblige healthcare providers to provide all relevant information to enable the coroner to perform his function, unless a director is personally satisfied that withholding the information is justified in the public interest.

Chapter 23
Nursing

Key themes

- The evidence shows that a completely unacceptable standard of nursing care was prevalent at the Trust and that this caused serious suffering for patients and those close to them.

- The decline in standards was associated with inadequate staffing levels and skills, and a lack of effective leadership and support.

- Nursing staff at the Trust did not receive effective support or representation from the Royal College of Nursing (RCN).

- The aptitude and commitment of candidates for entry into nursing to provide compassionate basic hands-on care to patients should be tested by a minimum period of work experience, by aptitude testing and by nationally consistent practical training. Effective support and professional development for nurses should be made the responsibility of professionally accountable responsible officers for nursing, and, in due course, reinforced by a system of revalidation.

- The capacity for front-line nursing leadership needs to be increased by enhancing the role, by better support and professional development resources, by placing leaders at the centre of teams caring for patients, and by identifying nurses with personal responsibility for each patient.

- The leadership required for the delivery of excellent nursing care should be recognised and incentivised in the remuneration structure by more explicit reference to the delivery of excellent care, and by use of professionally formulated and accepted performance measures.

- The specialist skills, commitment and compassion needed for the nursing care of the elderly should be accorded the recognition they deserve by creation of a specialist registered status.

- There is an inherent conflict between the professional representative and trade union functions of the RCN which may diminish the authority of its voice on professional issues.

- It is important that the strength of the nursing voice is not diminished by the transfer of the post of Chief Nursing Officer to the NHS Commissioning Board. That voice could be further strengthened by a requirement that all organisations in the healthcare system for which nursing issues are relevant had the advantage of a nurse at board level.

> - Ward nurse managers and named nurses should be an intrinsic part of medical ward rounds and other contacts between doctors and patients.
>
> - Healthcare support workers provide intimate and vital care to patients at their most vulnerable but neither patients nor the public are provided with any effective protection from those who are unfit for this role. There have been authoritative calls for such workers to be regulated, but there have been divergent views expressed about the desirability of this. This Inquiry's conclusion is that the balance of the evidence is strongly in favour of at least a compulsory registration scheme, and the imposition of common standards of training and a code of conduct. Such a register should include a record of the reasons for any termination of employment as a healthcare support worker. The possibility of a wider system for excluding those unfit to hold such posts should be kept under review.

Introduction

23.1   The title of this chapter is deliberately chosen: nursing is an activity partly performed by staff who are not registered nurses and no longer carry "nurse" in their title. This leads to a great deal of confusion among patients and the public who often attribute the incidents of poor care of which they complain to "nurses" when in fact what they have experienced are the actions, or inactions, of a category of staff variously named "healthcare support workers" or "nursing assistants" or some other similar title.

23.2   The role of the registered, professionally qualified nurse is crucial in the provision of healthcare:

> *The fundamental role of the nurse and midwife is to be accountable for providing and overseeing total patient care.*[1]

23.3   A very significant proportion of the complaints of poor care with which the first inquiry and this Inquiry have been concerned have been due to poor nursing and it will be necessary to examine the causes of this. They include:

- Inadequate staffing;
- Poor leadership;
- Poor recruitment;
- Deficiencies in initial and continuing training;
- Undervaluing of the nursing task and those who perform it;
- Declining professionalism.

---

1   *Presentation to the Forward Look Nursing Seminar* (31 October 2011), Professor Katherine Fenton, available at: www.midstaffspublicinquiry.com/inquiry-seminars/nursing, page 6

23.4 It is clear that the nursing issues found in Stafford are not confined to that hospital but are found throughout the country. This is not to deny that much high-quality, committed and compassionate nursing is carried out day in and day out, often with inadequate recognition. However, all in the profession must surely recognise that the challenges to the maintenance of proper standards and protection of patients have never been greater.

23.5 Until this scandalous decline in standards is reversed, it is likely that unacceptable levels of care will persist and therefore it is an area requiring the highest priority. There is no excuse for not tackling it successfully. Much of what needs to be done does not require additional financial resources, but changes in attitudes, culture, values and behaviour.

Nursing in Stafford

The Healthcare Commission findings

23.6 The Healthcare Commission (HCC) found cause for serious concern at the Trust in the following areas:

- Staffing levels;
- High levels of staff sickness;
- Skill mix;
- The standard of care being provided, in particular cleanliness, feeding, continence care, pressure ulcers, and accuracy of medication administration.

Patients and relatives that came to see us also expressed more concerns about nursing care on ward 11 than any other ward. One relative said that "some nights it was a war zone" and that "the family were doing lots for other patients who didn't have their relatives with them. They were helping them to go to the toilet or they were helping them to eat."

Another told us that her mother was in the far corner of a four-bedded bay on ward 11. She said: "The nurses told her to ring the buzzer, but because of her paralysis she could not use the buzzer. When someone else used it on her behalf, it often would not be answered."

A number of staff in different professions raised concerns about the lack of basic nursing care, such as poor hydration and nutrition of patients, and failure to help patients eat or drink. Some said there was a negative attitude among some of the nurses, with relatives who complained about being seen as difficult.

Care was also criticised on the other medical wards on floor two. It was described as being very poor, with buzzers not being answered, privacy and dignity ignored, and patients receiving little or no help with food or drink.[2]

---

2   HCC0015002863, *Investigation into Mid Staffordshire NHS Foundation Trust* (March 2009), Healthcare Commission, page 63

An audit by the trust in January 2008 of the prevalence of pressure damage found that most pressure sores occurred after patients were admitted and wards 10, 11 and 12 had among the highest rates. For example, 55% of 38 patients on ward 10 had some degree of pressure damage.[3]

Patient experience

23.7 The first inquiry report contained many examples of totally unacceptable nursing care, behaviour and attitude.

23.8 For example, the daughter of a patient in Ward 11 said:

In the next room you could hear the buzzers sounding. After about 20 minutes you could hear the men shouting for the nurse, "Nurse, nurse", and it just went on and on. And then very often it would be two people calling at the same time and then you would hear them crying, like shouting "Nurse" louder, and then you would hear them just crying, just sobbing, they would just sob and you just presumed that they had had to wet the bed. And then after they would sob, they seemed to then shout again for the nurse and then it would go quiet ...[4]

23.9 The daughter-in-law of a 96-year-old patient said:

We got there about 10 o'clock and I could not believe my eyes. The door was wide open. There were people walking past. Mum was in bed with the cot sides up and she hadn't got a stitch of clothing on. I mean, she would have been horrified. She was completely naked and if I said covered in faeces, she was. It was everywhere. It was in her hair, her eyes, her nails, her hands and on all the cot side, so she had obviously been trying to lift her herself up or move about, because the bed was covered and it was literally everywhere and it was dried. It would have been there a long time, it wasn't new.[5]

23.10 Further and repeated examples have been given as evidence at this Inquiry. One patient spoke about her husband's experiences with the Trust:

---

3 HCC0015002864, *Investigation into Mid Staffordshire NHS Foundation Trust* (March 2009), Healthcare Commission, page 64
4 *Independent Inquiry into care provided by Mid Staffordshire NHS Foundation Trust January 2005–March 2009,* chaired by Robert Francis QC (February 2010), vol 1, p53
5 *Independent Inquiry into care provided by Mid Staffordshire NHS Foundation Trust January 2005–March 2009,* chaired by Robert Francis QC (February 2010), vol 1, p55

... [W]hen he'd had his operation on the Wednesday, they did change him when he came back from the hospital – from the theatre, but then he was still in the same clothes by the Saturday, and they were all blood-stained. He never had a wash down, as he should have done, and in the end he struggled himself into the bathroom to have a shower, which took him an hour, because his breathing was affected and because he was so weak ...

He felt demeaned. He lost a lot of his dignity, his pride. There was so much taken away from him that – it was just unbelievable to see a man that was so full of life brought down to the – to the state that he was in, that he was frightened to say anything or to be able to stand up to people.

... On one particular day ... and a nurse came in and I said to her "Could you, please, help my husband to the toilet?" And she says "Oh, no", she says "I can't do that", she said "I'm looking after the four beds the other side." And I said "Well, they're all asleep, please can you help him?" "Oh, I suppose I better this time". But she took him into the toilet and then she left ... he came out and he was holding his pyjama trousers up ... he'd lost so much weight he couldn't keep his pyjamas up, and he asked me to hold them up while he washed his hands in the sink in the ward.[6]

23.11   Another patient spoke of the sub-standard care she had witnessed a fellow patient receiving:

... I mean, ten minutes was nothing, sometimes longer. And it was worse, I thought, for the old lady next to me, who couldn't get out of bed, and she was on a commode at least 15 minutes ringing and ringing, and it went on and on, and she was a very ill lady. I mean, everybody seems old to me because I only feel 50, but she did seem very old. And she was ill, truly ill. And ... then at last the nurse came. And she said "Do you want to go back to bed or will you sit in the chair?" And before the lady could answer, the cleaning lady said "If she can sit in the commode – on a commode she can sit in a chair. Don't put her back to bed." So the young nurse didn't, she sat her in a chair.[7]

23.12   One witness recounted his partner's experiences:

... [S]he had been showing symptoms of diarrhoea for two or three days ... [S]he was not tested for C. difficile until the morning of the 10th ... I discovered a faecal smear sample for analysis left on her bed table in amongst her drinking cups, and I had to call one of the nurses to take it ...

Q. It was just sitting there among the other glasses and bottles?

A. Yes ...[8]

---

6   Dalziel T11.50–51
7   Matthews T11.121
8   Street T12.9

23.13 Another witness informed the Inquiry of an incident that occurred whilst his wife was in the care of the Trust:

> *I went up to* [the two nurses] *to say that when they had finished* [changing a bed], [she] *needed some attention. Within five minutes of finishing, they returned to attend to Irene. I was very surprised that they had managed to come back so quickly. However I noticed that they were still wearing the same gloves they had been wearing when they had been changing the dirty bed. They seemed taken aback when* [I] *told them to go and remove the gloves and wash their hands. I had to tell a nurse to wash her bloody hands.*[9]

Staff numbers

23.14 Helene Donnelly, a whistleblower who worked as a nurse in the Trust's accident and emergency (A&E) department and gave evidence to the Inquiry, saw the effects of short staffing there:

> *New staff were recruited, but would arrive just as others were leaving, so that the actual number of nurses on the ward never increased. In addition many of the new recruits were very junior. It used to be the case when I qualified that it was necessary to have at least one year's experience as a nurse before working in A&E. However this did not seem to be the rule in the Hospital. Many of the new recruits had no experience and were terrified at the level of work they were asked to do. My workload increased as a result, as these staff could not be left alone to carry out certain duties. In many ways they were a hindrance and made the situation worse. However, this was through no fault of their own but rather due to poor staff allocation and hospital management.*[10]

23.15 Evidence to this Inquiry suggested that the Trust did not have available to it reliable figures for its nursing establishment, either in theory or in practice. It is one of the reasons given by the former Director of Nursing, Dr Helen Moss, for taking so long with her skill mix review.[11] What is clear is that the numbers had always been tight and declined during the period with which the Inquiry is concerned. Staffing levels were further compromised with the additional levels of sickness and absence.

Table 23.1: Staff Group Establishment (WTE)[12]

	2003/04	2004/05	2005/06	2006/07
Nursing, Midwifery & Health Visitors	695.96	719.22	662.28	616.7

---

9   Guest WS000000127, para 26
10   Donnelly WS0000022297, para 3
11   Helen Moss WS0000009464–5, paras 34–5
12   HM/37 WS0000010133, extract from table 14 in the exhibit

Leadership

23.16 Helene Donnelly witnessed the shocking effects of unprofessional leadership in A&E, particularly around the pressure to fabricate waiting times to meet the 4-hour A&E target:

> *Nurses were expected to break the rules as a matter of course in order to meet targets, a prime example of this being the maximum four hour wait time target for patients in A&E. Rather than "breach" the target, the length of waiting time would regularly be falsified on notes and computer records. I was guilty of going along with this if the wait time was only being breached by 5 or 10 minutes and the patient had been treated, as it seemed unfair and unreasonable to declare a breach just because we were waiting for a porter to come and collect a patient. However, when wait times were being breached by 20–30 minutes or more and the patient had still not been seen, I was not prepared to go along with what was expected.[13]*

> *I then discovered that there were several patients who had breached having recently returned from X-ray and waiting to be reviewed. Upon realising this I immediately informed [Sister] and the CSM [Clinical Service Manager] of the situation. When I telephoned the major side of the department to inform [Sister] I spoke to [Staff Nurse –]. I explained to her the situation and asked her to relay this information to [Sister]. Whilst she did this she kept me on the phone. I heard her tell [Sister] that I had discovered that several patients had breached. I then heard [Sister] tell [Staff Nurse –] to tell me to lie.[14]* [Names redacted]

Professionalism

23.17 Helene Donnelly witnessed repeated poor and even fraudulent practice in relation to waiting times in A&E.[15] This episode has been described in more detail in *Chapter 1: Warning signs* and *Chapter 2: The Trust*. She ascribed her initial reluctance to report it or complain about it to fear of the repercussions and a lack of visible support or feedback when concerns were raised:

> *I have been asked how I reconciled poor practice in the A&E department with my nursing code. I was of course aware of the nursing code but it was not even this that convinced me to raise concerns. My own moral code told me that the standards of care were not right. I would go home in tears because people were being treated so badly in that Hospital and were suffering so unnecessarily.*

---

13   Donnelly WS0000022298, para 8
14   HD/2 WS0000022336
15   Donnelly WS0000022298, para 8

The fear factor kept me from speaking out, plus the thought that nobody wanted to know anyway, due to lack of response to the Incident Report forms I had logged. I felt that any external bodies would have told me that it was necessary to exhaust internal mechanisms first before they would fully consider my complaint(s). Also it would have been a big step for me to go outside the Trust as I was a relatively junior nurse and was being told by people around me that this practice was normal and the same everywhere; that it was just how the NHS was now. I didn't believe that this was the case, as I had trained in a different hospital where standards were much better. Nowhere is perfect and there are of course elements of this practice, I am sure, in every hospital. However, what was going on in Stafford was plainly wrong. The problem is that this practice becomes routine and, because I didn't have any recent point of reference, it was difficult for me to stand out from the crowd and be counted.[16]

23.18   When she did summon up the courage to raise the serious concerns she had, initially the response was positive. However, in the end, the two nursing sisters in the A&E department, against whom she complained, were returned to the department and were publicly described by the Director of Operations, who apparently remained in ignorance of the incomplete investigation and disciplinary process undertaken, as the "A team". She was not offered adequate support at that time. She had to endure harassment from colleagues and eventually left for other employment. Clearly, such treatment was likely to deter others from following her example, and she was aware of colleagues on whom her experience had this effect:

> *... [T]he first sister ... made it very clear that she was very displeased with me and the fact that I'd spoken out ... [T]hreats were made, both directly and indirectly, friends of hers and the other sisters would make threats to me. People were very often coming up to me in – trying I think in a helpful way to tell me to, I quote "watch my back", ... and people were saying, "Oh, you shouldn't have done this, you shouldn't have spoken out."*

> *And then physical threats were made in terms of people saying that I needed to – again, watch myself while I was walking to my car at the end of a shift. People saying that they know where I live, and basically threats to sort of my physical safety were made, to the point where I had to at the end of a shift ... at night would have to have either my mum or my dad or my husband come and collect me from work because I was too afraid to walk to my car in the dark on my own.*[17]

---

16   Donnelly WS0000022299–300, paras 11–12
17   Donnelly T133.134

23.19 This behaviour continued even after she reported it:

It was slightly more subversive and I think people were slightly more guarded in how they were doing it. You know, on one particular occasion another staff nurse followed me into the toilet which was also our locker room and locked the door behind her, locking me in, and demanded to know if I had a problem with her and if I was going to say anything about her, and basically threatening me not to do so if I did. And I immediately then reported that to Paula Gardner at the time, saying that this had happened.

So people were still doing things, but not so publicly, in terms of sort of in the middle of the department where other people could perhaps hear. They were doing it slightly more discreetly, I suppose.[18]

23.20 The conditions in which the staff had to work undoubtedly contributed to low morale as evidenced by the results of staff surveys.

23.21 Just under 50% of staff stated that they would not want to be cared for or treated in the hospital.[19] Although the Trust received an average score for work hours and for the number of staff taking advantage of flexi-hours, it was placed in the worst 20% of acute trusts in a number of areas, including:

- Quality of work-life balance;
- Appraisal, training, learning and development;
- Team working, supervision, communication and staff involvement – including the extent of positive feeling within the organisation and support from immediate managers;
- The percentage of staff reporting errors, near misses or incidents;
- Percentage of staff experiencing harassment, bullying or abuse from staff in the last 12 months;
- Staff attitudes – including staff job satisfaction, work pressure felt by staff, and staff intention to leave jobs.[20]

Union representation: Royal College of Nursing

23.22 The College of Nursing was founded in 1916 and then incorporated by Royal Charter in 1928.[21] Under the Charter, the Royal College of Nursing's (RCN's) objectives are to:

- Promote the science and art of nursing and education and training in the profession of nursing;

---

18 Donnelly T133.137–8
19 HM/37 WS0000010205
20 ESI00047981, *National NHS Staff Survey 2007: Brief summary of results from Mid Staffordshire General Hospitals NHS Trust (2007)*, Healthcare Commission, pp3–7
21 RCN website "Our History", www.rcn.org.uk/aboutus/our_history

- Promote the advancement of nursing as a profession in all or any of its branches;
- Promote the professional standing and interests of members;
- Assist members who by reason of adversity, ill health or otherwise are in need of assistance of any nature; and
- Promote through the medium of international agencies and otherwise the foregoing purposes in other countries as well as in the UK.[22]

23.23   The College began as a professional organisation for trained nurses and has since also become the nurses' union.[23] The College provides legal representation and advice to its members; lobbies the Government and other policy-making bodies on behalf of the profession; develops nursing education; and provides indemnity insurance for its members.[24] It is not the regulator for the nursing profession; that role falls within the jurisdiction of the Nursing and Midwifery Council (NMC).

23.24   Ms Donnelly, following her raising serious concerns about colleagues' conduct in A&E, as described in *Chapter 1: Warning signs* and *Chapter 2: The Trust*, did not receive strong support from the RCN of which she was a member. Effectively Mr Legan, the regional representative, told her there was little that could be done. She later discovered that he was also representing the two sisters against whom she had complained:

> *A week or so later I found out that Mr Legan was representing at least one of the sisters and accompanying her to meetings at the Trust. This really upset me as I felt that he shouldn't have represented us both, or, at the very least, he should have told me that he was doing so. I didn't feel that he could advise me properly if he was advising them too. I therefore didn't see any point in pursuing matters with the RCN ... at the time it felt almost like a conspiracy. I felt completely on my own.[25]*

23.25   Within the Trust the RCN was represented by members of staff elected to the position by the membership. The Inquiry's impression is that this was a little-sought-after honour, and that those who took up the challenge received little training or other support from their union, except for the attendance of a Regional Officer at Joint Negotiating Consultative Committee (JNCC) meetings. Ms Breeze was a nurse of 45 years' experience, most of that time at Stafford, where she started in 1972. She was a union representative for 30 years[26] and, during the relevant period, the staff convenor.[27] She had direct access to Mr Yeates, the Trust's then

22   The RCN Charter (amended 8 March 2012), section 3,
      www.rcn.org.uk/__data/assets/pdf_file/0003/438294/RCN_Royal_Charter_08.03.12.pdf
23   The RCN Charter (amended 8 March 2012) para 4.1,
      www.rcn.org.uk/__data/assets/pdf_file/0003/438294/RCN_Royal_Charter_08.03.12.pdf
24   The RCN Charter (amended 8 March 2012), section 4,
      www.rcn.org.uk/__data/assets/pdf_file/0003/438294/RCN_Royal_Charter_08.03.12.pdf
25   Donnelly WS0000022303–4, paras 26–28
26   Breeze T42.4
27   Breeze T42.52

Chief Executive, and there were meetings with him on roughly a monthly basis.[28] By the time of her retirement in 2010, she was a departmental manager of the outpatients department, only two rungs down from the Director of Nursing.[29] She therefore found herself in the potentially difficult position of having to represent and advise members significantly junior to herself and to juggle her union with her managerial responsibilities. There were other RCN representatives: Sue Adams, Carol Hedley, Sharon Matthews (for a short period) and Mark Elton, a health and safety representative who was based at Cannock.

23.26 Ms Breeze freely conceded that there were insufficient representatives for the number of members,[30] commenting that she believed there ought to have been between eight and 10 such representatives.[31] However, her own involvement in the work did not extend to knowledge of how many nursing staff there were in the Trust or how many of them were members of the RCN.[32] There seemed to be a reluctance to volunteer:

> *Well, you can't pressurise people into being reps, or else they don't do the job they should do, you know, correctly. And a lot of people won't come forward as a rep because they don't like speaking up.*[33]

23.27 This reluctance extended to attendance at union meetings. Out of a nursing staff of over 600, rarely did more than 10 RCN members attend.[34]

23.28 The Trust provided an office for union representatives – a hut adjoining the car park. Ms Breeze did not think it was big enough and, from personal inspection, the Inquiry can certainly agree that it is not large, although large enough for all the representatives to meet together.

23.29 Communication with RCN members may have been limited. Firstly, as indicated above, they did not attend union meetings in numbers, and, secondly, they do not appear to have communicated very freely with their local representatives. For example, Ms Breeze told the Inquiry that she was unaware of the volume of incident reports being filed from Wards 10, 11, and 12 concerning staffing levels.[35] According to the HCC, nearly 200 such reports were filed between 2005 and 2009. She was also unaware that staff felt incident reports were going into a "black hole". She was involved in the JNCC discussion about the proposals for staff cuts in 2007, but had a surprisingly limited memory of whether concerns about patient safety were

28 Breeze T42.76
29 Breeze T42.13
30 Breeze T42.7
31 Breeze T42.7
32 Breeze T42.7–8
33 Breeze T42.10
34 Breeze T42.12
35 Breeze T42.28

raised at the time, in part it seems because she relied on the RCN Regional Officer to lead on this issue:[36]

> *... I was a bit concerned, but, as I keep reiterating, the full-time officer had got this on board. Most of the unions were involved in – full-time officers.*
>
> *THE CHAIRMAN: But if you were a bit concerned, I'm surprised that you can't recall whether the issue was raised.*
>
> *A. Patient care, no, I cannot recall it. No.*
>
> *THE CHAIRMAN: Do you think at the time perhaps it should have been raised or not, or didn't it occur to you?*
>
> *A. I can't really comment on it.*

23.30   The same applied to the proposals for the ward configuration:

> *... But I'm just asking you whether you had any view about the restructuring at all?*
>
> *A. No. No, I didn't – I didn't get involved in that one.*
>
> *Q. So leaving aside the question of whether you were responsible for dealing with it, you personally didn't have any view about the clinical floors?*
>
> *A. No, I didn't – no, because Adrian* [Legan, the Regional Officer] *was dealing with it direct.*
>
> *Q. So you just didn't turn your mind to it at all, is that what you're saying?*
>
> *A. No.*[37]

23.31   It is fair to note that, as Ms Breeze stated, Mr Legan raised concerns about staff reductions, which resulted in the selection criteria being changed, and about the clinical floor reconfiguration, which he regarded as:

> *... merely a mechanism to dispense with senior staff on the ward and reduce the costs ...*[38]

23.32   However, his efforts had little impact; he stated that his:

> *... influence was unfortunately limited.*[39]

---

36   Breeze T42.47–48
37   Breeze T42.50
38   Legan T42.154, 159–60
39   Legan WS0000004004, para 20

23.33 Ms Breeze's interest in the HCC report was also limited. She said that she had not read it and could not recall reading a summary.[40] She later told the Inquiry that she had in fact read sections of the report relevant to her managerial work at the time. Indeed, as at the time of her giving evidence, she appeared unaware of its contents. Her broader knowledge of it came from newspaper reports and she had been "horrified" by them as they did not reflect her own experience in the hospital. Although she had given up being convenor at about the time the report was published, she accepted that as a registered general nurse she should have read the report.[41] She was unable to explain why colleagues had not brought concerns to her about any of the matters which were found by the HCC. She accepted on reflection that, even if Mr Legan took the lead on most issues, as a staff representative, convenor and a registered general nurse, she should have taken more interest in these issues than she did.[42]

23.34 The discussions that took place between the RCN and Trust management caused concern among other union colleagues. Kath Fox, Unison representative, told the Inquiry that:

> ... we made sure we had a full-time officer in attendance at the staff-side meetings. We needed them there. The RCN full-time officer would not come to the staff-side meetings and would just appear at the JNCC meetings without hearing about any of the discussions on the staff side. It was apparent that meetings were taking place between the RCN full-time officer and management at the trust. They would be seen at the trust. Sometimes, when issues were raised the RCN or Adrian Legan would already have been satisfied by a conversation between RCN and the management. It seemed like discussions were taking place with management outside the context of the JNCC, which undermines the JNCC role.[43]

23.35 Other unions felt that the RCN did not share the concerns it had about the service being provided at the Trust:

> The non-nursing representatives like me seemed to know something was wrong, but the RCN did not seem to be concerned. The feeling was that if the RCN was happy at any one time, management were happy.[44]

---

40   Breeze T42.71
41   Breeze T42.73
42   Breeze T42.77
43   Kath Fox WS0000004505, para 46
44   Kath Fox WS0000004504, para 45; Breeze T42.79

23.36 Ms Breeze was asked to comment on a report in a local paper – *The Staffordshire Newsletter* – on a staff survey indicating that 47% would not want a relative to be treated in Stafford.[45] Ms Breeze was quoted in the paper as rejecting this figure:

> *I don't think the survey paints a correct picture. I'm amazed at the result because all the staff and especially the nurses give 100 per cent to provide a good standard of care. Morale here is okay. We have been struggling financially as a hospital but we are getting there.*[46]

23.37 While she could not recollect making that comment, or indeed knowing about the survey figure, she made it clear that she would not have accepted it and would have challenged it on the ground that it might not be correct.[47] She later told the Inquiry that she did "value the significance of this figure", but her focus had been on her own practice area. There is, however, no evidence that she took any action on the matter other than to challenge it to the newspaper.

23.38 A further area in which no action was taken by the RCN was when it received evidence of bullying by managers. In a JNCC meeting on 12 February 2009, reference was made to 30% of staff having experienced or witnessed bullying by a member of management.[48] Although Ms Breeze had been present at this meeting, she did not consider that there was anything the RCN could have done about it.[49] Other figures in the same culture audit revealed, as Ms Breeze conceded in evidence, a serious state of affairs with regard to staff morale, but no action was taken by the RCN.[50]

23.39 One other matter raised in the course of Ms Breeze's evidence was the suicide of a newly qualified staff nurse named Eva Clark. An excerpt from a letter written by the coroner who presided over the inquest into her death was read into evidence by Counsel to the Inquiry in the course of their examination of Ms Breeze. It read:

> *Eva Clark does appear to have made a complaint about being bullied at work. Her ward manager was unaware of the complaint and it seems to have been communicated to the buddy system.*[51]

23.40 Ms Breeze's evidence was that she knew nothing about either the buddy system or Ms Clark's case.[52] Later in her evidence, she said that she did recall something about it.[53] Ultimately,

---

45   WC/2 WS0000003454, "*Hospital staff fear treatment*", The Staffordshire Newsletter (April 2007)
46   Breeze T42.84
47   Breeze T42.86–7
48   TRU00010004369, para 5
49   Breeze T42.90
50   Breeze T42.93–4
51   Breeze T42.87–9
52   Breeze T42.88–9
53   Breeze T42.96

however, her conclusion was that she had not, as the RCN representative, been aware of the extent of the bullying at the Trust, nor sought to make inquiries of her deputies, including the RCN representative who dealt with Ms Clark's case, Carol Hedley, to establish the extent of the problem.[54] Again, it seems that she was prepared to leave the matter to others as Ms Clark had not worked in her department.

Conclusions

23.41   At Stafford, the RCN was sadly ineffective both as a professional representative organisation and as a trade union. The concerns of, and problems faced by, members either were not addressed effectively (although it must be noted that some attempts were made to represent members' interests, for example by Mr Legan) or were simply not addressed, due largely to weakness of representation within the organisation and problems in communication with members. Furthermore, no action seems to have been taken to promote excellence in nursing. Issues on which there was apparent inaction included:

- The suicide of a junior member of staff following an episode of bullying;[55]
- The rash of incident reports about lack of staffing;
- Failure to give effective protection to a member who had justifiably raised serious concerns about nursing conduct in A&E.

23.42   A prime reason for this was the lack of effective representation from elected officers on site. It would be easy to point personal criticism at Ms Breeze, whose evidence has been considered in some detail: given her role as staff convenor she appears to have taken a remarkably small amount of interest in the welfare of her members or issues likely to impinge on the standard of care provided to patients who were her members' responsibility. However, it would be unfair to place all the responsibility for these failures on her. It should have been clear to competent union officials that she was not equipped to undertake the important role of convenor, let alone being a senior representative for so many members. She was an unwilling recruit, yet had been in the job for 30 years. She was in a senior management position within the Trust and therefore close to Mr Yeates and other Trust officers with whom she was meant to be representing her members' interests. The latter were probably inhibited in approaching her with concerns because of her position. Her own view of Trust issues would have been coloured by her management position, as exemplified by her difficulty in believing the results of the culture audit. There may also have been difficulties for her obtaining sufficient time to undertake these duties, of which Mr Legan was aware:

---

54   Breeze T42.96–7
55   Breeze T42.87–9, T42.95–7

My recollection is that ... Denise didn't regularly attend the patch meetings, nor did she attend the stewards' regional committee meetings. But, again, I think in defence of Denise, that was because of the time pressures of the role that she was occupying within the Trust.[56]

23.43 He stated he was concerned about this, but that this was a general problem faced by the RCN:

... I would constantly raise that with senior managers, but as I stated earlier, I would constantly raise that at every other trust with every senior manager. It's a firm belief that trade union representatives don't get anywhere near the time that they should to consider the documents that they're given and actually function appropriately within the role..[57]

23.44 However, he did not recall specifically raising this issue with the Trust with reference to Ms Breeze.

23.45 The support available from RCN officials at a regional and national level was also limited. Mr Legan would have been reliant on information given by local officials and therefore would not have been forewarned of the dreadful things that were happening. His primary concern would understandably have been the negotiation of favourable terms and conditions and, particularly around the time of the proposed staff cuts, to seek to have those minimised. In this regard, he did raise concerns about the proposed staff cuts and the clinical floors' configuration.

23.46 The only visible national involvement was the visit by Dr Peter Carter, Chief Executive and General Secretary of the RCN, to the Trust, which was followed by his offering a paean of praise to the local press:

I found the hospital to be well managed, it was clearly a very clean and efficient hospital, and the quality of nursing and other health-related care was of an exceptionally high standard.

I had the opportunity to talk in private with patients and their relatives, all of whom expressed a high degree of satisfaction with the standard of care.[58]

23.47 Although the RCN is not a regulator but a combination of a professional representative body and a trade union, it does represent a group of qualified professionals and claims, as it should, to promote high standards of service and conduct. It appears that there is a concerning

---

56   Legan T42.121
57   Legan T42.121–3
58   PC/3 WS0000003377

potential for conflict between the professional role of promoting standards, and the union role of negotiating terms and conditions and defending members' material and other narrow interests. It is the combination of these roles that has led this Inquiry to focus on the RCN rather than other trade unions representing nurses.

What is needed?

23.48 The experience from Stafford, echoed by what emerged at the Inquiry seminars suggests that the current university-based model of training does not focus enough on the impact of culture and caring. It is likely that most of those entering the nursing profession do so because of a wish to undertake work helping and caring for others. Even in a well run organisation, the stark differences between nursing as they imagined it to be and the reality will challenge their ability to maintain their motivation. This can be seen even more so in the stresses of working in an understaffed, badly led environment in which the quality of care appears to take a lower priority than throughput and where meeting managerially dictated targets can turn the unacceptable into the mundane. In other words, the internal drive to insist on proper standards of care can all too soon degenerate and be replaced by a meek acceptance of the mediocre or worse.

23.49 There should be an increased focus in nurse training, education and professional development on the practical requirements of delivering compassionate care in addition to the theory. A system which ensures the delivery of proper standards of nursing requires:

- Selection of recruits to the profession who demonstrate:
    - Possession of the appropriate values, attitudes and behaviours, the ability and motivation to enable them to put the welfare of others above their own interests;
    - The drive to maintain, develop and improve their own standards and abilities;
    - The intellectual achievements to enable them to acquire through training the necessary technical skills;
- Training and experience in the delivery of compassionate care;
- Leadership which constantly reinforces values and standards of compassionate care;
- Involvement in, and responsibility for, the planning and delivery of compassionate care;
- Constant support and incentivisation that values nurses and the work they do through:
    - Recognition of achievement;
    - Regular comprehensive feedback on performance and concerns;
    - Encouragement to report concerns and to give priority to patient well-being.

Recruitment, training and development

Demonstrating compassion

23.50 The Prime Minister's Commission on the Future of Nursing and Midwifery, established in March 2009, accepted the importance of promoting care and compassion in nursing:

> *To care with compassion, nurses and midwives must work with their heads, hands and hearts.*[59]

23.51 They quoted the Chief Nursing Officer for England:

> *Nursing is more than the sum of its parts. Any health system needs nurses who are intellectually able and emotionally aware and who can combine technical clinical skills with a deep understanding and ability to care, as one human to another ... This is a constant of nursing. It is the value base on which public trust rests and the profession is grounded. As a profession it is our promise to society.*[60]

23.52 They recommended:

> *To ensure high quality compassionate care, the move to degree level registration for all newly qualified nurses from 2013 must be implemented in full ... There must be effective revalidation, and greater investment in continuing professional development.*[61]

23.53 The recent report *Delivering Dignity*,[62] published by the Local Government Association, the NHS Confederation and Age UK, echoes this approach in its key recommendations for the care of the elderly:

> *Hospitals should recruit staff to work with older people who have the compassionate values needed to provide dignified care as well as the clinical and technical skills. Hospitals should evaluate compassion as well as technical skills in their appraisals of staff performance ...*

---

59 *Front Line Care: Report by the Prime Minister's Commission on the Future of Nursing and Midwifery in England* (2010) p62, www.parliament.uk/deposits/depositedpapers/2010/DEP2010-0551.pdf

60 *Front Line Care: Report by the Prime Minister's Commission on the Future of Nursing and Midwifery in England* (2010), p63, www.parliament.uk/deposits/depositedpapers/2010/DEP2010-0551.pdf

61 *Front line care, Report by the Prime Minister's Commission on the Future of Nursing and Midwifery in England* (2010), p94, www.parliament.uk/deposits/depositedpapers/2010/DEP2010-0551.pdf

62 *Delivering Dignity: Securing dignity in care for older people in hospitals and care homes. A report for consultation* (29 February 2012), Local government Association, NHS Confederation and Age UK, www.nhsconfed.org/Documents/dignity.pdf

Hospitals should introduce facilitated, practice-based development programmes – 'learning through doing' – to ensure staff caring for older people are given the confidence, support and skills to do the right thing for their patients.[63]

23.54 This approach is required across all providers of care to all patients and should not be limited to the elderly, vitally important as that particular group is.

23.55 There needs to be a requirement for a minimum period of experience in the hands-on, fundamental aspects of care to provide an opportunity for aspiring nurses to demonstrate that they have the capacity to be compassionate in practice. What is required is a better opportunity for potential recruits to the nursing service to develop experience in the fundamental but essential tasks involved in hands-on care of physically and emotionally vulnerable patients and to demonstrate their vocation and the values that all good nurses should have.

Practical experience of basic care

23.56 At both the Inquiry seminars and during the hospital visits undertaken, the Inquiry was told of concerns that today's nursing training contains an inadequate quantity of practical experience at an early stage. Most of those with whom the Inquiry had contact agreed that the increasingly technical demands of the role required degree-level training and education. However, they recognised that the progress made in this direction had sometimes been at the expense of exposure to personal experience of the basic tasks that all nurses should be able and willing to do. This has been largely replaced by experience as observers and supernumeraries which, the Inquiry was emphatically told, is not an equivalent.

23.57 During its visit to St Christopher's Hospice the Inquiry was told of their training scheme. Their scheme was carried out by people who themselves did the work in which they provide instruction to others. This not only benefited the trainees, but also conferred a further beneficial dimension to the tutors' work mix, which they appreciated. Healthcare assistants were given structured training that involved induction and mentoring, as were volunteers and new registrants. Staff were encouraged to think about what they would want for themselves and their families as the standard for providing care. Staff were also encouraged to ask for help if they did not know something, and to both train and reflect upon their training on a daily basis. This approach was tied to an effort to minimise the gap between the "top" and "bottom" of the organisation through the creation of a "flatter" managerial structure in which responsibility was "pushed down" to those providing front-line services. This allowed managers on the ground to model other staff behaviours through upfront leadership. Proximity and communication between leadership and staff appeared to create a healthy and constructive environment for informal peer review, it being noted that if leaders strive to

---

63 *Delivering Dignity: Securing dignity in care for older people in hospitals and care homes. A report for consultation* (29 February 2012), Local government Association, NHS Confederation and Age UK, p5, www.nhsconfed.org/Documents/dignity.pdf

notice and provide positive feedback in respect of positive work where appropriate, the recipient will "give you permission to notice bad things" – that is to say, be more amenable to negative feedback that requests improvement – if/when the time comes.

23.58   The Inquiry spoke to the hospice senior staff of their experience of newly qualified nurses. They told the Inquiry that many qualified nurses did not train in the UK and were post-Project 2000, which meant that they had not had "apprenticeships" before practising in the UK. This meant that they had not seen a model of communication with healthcare assistants. They said they felt that nursing had lost personal care to social care and had thus become more task-oriented. They highlighted their views that compassion could be taught and the fact that some nurses may previously not have had experience caring for others. The Inquiry was told that the hospice looked for resilience in prospective nurses at the time of recruitment.

23.59   Other hospitals the Inquiry visited encouraged the acquisition of hands-on experience of care, and assessed candidates' attitudes and values as part of the recruitment process. However, there is no standard requirement to this effect throughout the system. Therefore, a nurse or support worker recruited in one hospital may not have had such assessments or experience, and may not be exposed to them until such practices have become established.

Recruitment for values

23.60   Providing caring, compassionate, sensitive and thorough attention to the basic needs of patients is, and should remain, the highest priority of any nurse at any level of seniority. In the past, it may have been taken for granted that anyone wishing to enter nursing wanted to do so because they were motivated to provide hands-on care for patients. Therefore, it may not have been necessary in the past to assess candidates for their willingness and aptitude for such tasks. It is now clearly very important for patients, the providers of nursing services and those considering a career in nursing that those entering the profession are willing and able to undertake fundamental nursing tasks and are not merely interested in the more technical competencies of the profession. There should be no nurses who are "too posh to wash". At the same time, as pointed out at the Inquiry seminar on nursing, an academic programme and the ability to provide great care for patients are not mutually exclusive.[64]

Basic training

23.61   It can no longer be assumed, if it ever was proper to do so, that so-called basic nursing tasks are "simple". Lifting an immobile patient takes skill, which requires training and sensitivity, talents clearly lacking in the terrible care offered to Julie Bailey's mother Bella, among many others.[65] Washing a patient requires compassion and patience. Providing any form of personal care requires a very high degree of attention paid to the patient, as meticulous observation

64   *Mid Staffordshire NHS Foundation Trust Public Inquiry: Report from the Forward Look Seminars,* Dr Sarah Harvey (18 November 2011)
65   Bailey T9.84–5

helps protect against pressure ulcers and detects early signs of deterioration in a patient's condition. It is important that a nurse undertaking this vital work promotes the patient's self-respect, dignity and well-being. None of this is likely to be achieved by a reluctant or ill-trained nurse. Even when not performing such tasks personally on a regular basis, nurses will be responsible for supervising support workers who do. Any nurse ought to be ready to step in and take over these basic care tasks when this is in the best interests of the patient.

23.62   Therefore, nursing training should be reviewed to ensure that sufficient practical elements are incorporated to ensure that a consistent standard is achieved by all trainees throughout the country. This requires national standards.

Support and development

23.63   Ensuring that recruits to the profession demonstrate commitment to and delivery of the core values required for proper basic care of patients is a necessary but not a sufficient step to embed those values. For the reasons mentioned earlier, these values require constant reinforcement throughout their careers. The experience of the few nurses at Stafford who sought to stand up for proper standards suggests that doing this can result in discouragement and isolation. Professional development is always vulnerable to being treated as a burdensome formality, and subject to reduction in availability through the pressure of increasingly scarce resources. The medical professional regulatory system is addressing these concerns through the introduction of revalidation. The sheer numbers of registered nurses would make this a more formidable task for their profession. However, at present, the principal means of seeking to maintain nursing standards is the presence of a Director of Nursing within an organisation. The Director of Nursing is accountable mainly to her or his own Board, and therefore open to the pressures that accompany the Director's duty to comply with the necessary financial obligations. Accountability to the NMC is less clear.

23.64   It would be possible to introduce the concept of a Responsible Officer for nursing, appointed by and accountable to the NMC. The NMC is now committed to establishing a system of revalidation but not before the end of 2015.[66] However, independently of that development, the NMC could introduce common minimum standards for appraisal and support, setting benchmarks with which responsible officers would be obliged to comply. Such standards could, for example, include a requirement for 360-degree anonymous appraisal by colleagues, feedback from patients, and demonstration from records of continuous training, experience and skills. Responsible officers could be required to report to the NMC on their performance on a regular basis. The existence of this professional obligation would immeasurably strengthen the power of the nursing voice in the leadership of provider organisations.

---

66   www.nmc-uk.org/Registration/Revalidation/

Leadership in nursing

23.65   The ward manager's role as leader of a unit caring for patients is universally recognised as absolutely critical. This is to be distinguished from the additional capabilities required of organisational leaders (currently the province of the NHS Leadership Academy initiative). In Stafford, wards that were well led generally provided an acceptable standard of care. The terrible experiences of which the various inquiries received so much evidence came largely from wards lacking in strong, principled and caring leadership. At the Inquiry seminar on nursing and during its visits to hospitals as part of the Inquiry process, the same message was emphasised repeatedly to the Inquiry. The leadership of wards that the Inquiry visited and that appeared to be successful shared a number of characteristics:

- Visible priority is given to the delivery of safe and excellent care to their patients;
- Ward sisters care for the staff they lead;
- They are empowered by being given responsibility for their budgets and for recruitment of their staff;
- They seek out ways of applying best practice from their team and externally;
- They are listened to by senior management;
- They welcome and accept measurement of their performance;
- They develop a team ethic embracing all staff in their unit;
- They are given training and often seek out personal mentorship and coaching.

23.66   Not all nurses want to undertake, or are capable of undertaking, this challenging but rewarding role, and it is not always easy to identify suitable candidates. More needs to be done to promote professional development in leadership and management within the profession. However, leadership is an essential ingredient of the work of every nurse:

- Nurses frequently have to supervise other staff in their interaction with patients;
- They have to be capable of taking the initiative within the limits of their authority and competence;
- They are the public face of their employer and their profession in their dealings with patients and the public;
- Nurses must be able to engender trust with their patients, making the care of people their first concern;[67]
- They work with others to protect and promote the health and well-being of those in their care, their families and carers, and the wider community;[68]
- They are advocates for patients in assisting them to articulate their needs, helping their patients communicate and cope with an often confusing and fearful process;
- They must take personal responsibility for and be committed to the care of their patients.

---

[67]   NMC00010000108, *The Code: Standards of conduct, performance and ethics for nurses and midwives* (1 May 2008), Nursing and Midwifery Council, p2

[68]   NMC00010000108, *The Code: Standards of conduct, performance and ethics for nurses and midwives* (1 May 2008), Nursing and Midwifery Council, p2

23.67 One way in which such leadership qualities can be encouraged would be to ensure that ward sisters operate in a supervisory capacity. This would mean not being office-bound. As a supervisory leader, the ward sister should, and would, know about the care plans relating to every patient on her or his ward. Ward sisters should make themselves visible to patients and staff alike, and be available to discuss concerns with all, including relatives. Critically, they would work alongside staff as a role model and mentor, developing clinical competencies and leadership skills within the team. As a corollary, they would monitor performance and deliver training and/or feedback as appropriate, including a robust annual appraisal.

23.68 A second way in which this might be done is to reconsider the structure of nurses' remuneration and promotion. Remuneration is governed by a national "banding" structure of terms and conditions that apply throughout the country to all posts, whether or not nursing-related. Local management, and staff bodies, in accordance with the Job Evaluation Scheme, identify the "band" for each post. Lengthy guidance is offered in the *NHS Job Evaluation Handbook*.[69] It is possible for foundation trusts (FTs) to set their own terms and conditions, although only a few appear currently to be doing so.[70]

23.69 National terms and conditions provide for two assessment points (gateways) in each band, one near the beginning and one towards the end.[71] After progression through the first, "foundation" gateway, pay is incremental and generally dependent only on length of service until the "second" gateway is reached.[72] There are a number of "safeguards" that give weight to a presumption of progression up the pay scale. These include:

- A normal "expectation of progression";
- The existence of a clear statement of skills and knowledge required at each gateway;
- Adherence to the Knowledge and Skills Framework;
- The existence of a robust and jointly agreed system of review of decisions;
- A prohibition on deferment of pay progression unless certain procedural steps have been taken.

23.70 Following the introduction of "Agenda for Change" in 2004, a Knowledge and Skills Framework was introduced to assist employers to set out career paths and support for staff in their career and professional development. This framework is intended to drive staff improvement through making entry into entitlement of pay attached to a particular banding dependent on demonstrating progression in the acquisition of skills. This has enjoyed a variable take-up

---

69 *NHS Job Evaluation Handbook,* third edition (February 2010), in which a brief history of NHS conditions and bargaining can be found, www.nhsemployers.org/Aboutus/Publications/Documents/NHS_Job_Evaluation_Handbook_third_edition.pdf

70 *NHS Terms and Conditions of Service Handbook: Amendment No. 26, Pay Circular (AforC) 2/2012* (February 2012), NHS Staff Council, Annex K, available at: www.nhsemployers.org/SiteCollectionDocuments/AfC_tc_of_service_handbook_fb.pdf

71 *NHS Terms and Conditions of Service Handbook: Amendment No. 26, Pay Circular (AforC) 2/2012* (February 2012), NHS Staff Council, pp39–40, section 6, paras 6.16–6.20

72 *NHS Terms and Conditions of Service Handbook: Amendment No. 26, Pay Circular (AforC) 2/2012* (February 2012), NHS Staff Council, p40, section 6, paras 6.21–6.22

owing to its complexity, and a simplified version was produced by the NHS Staff Council in 2010.[73] There are six "dimensions":

- Communication;
- Personal and people development;
- Health, safety and security;
- Service improvement;
- Quality;
- Equality and diversity.[74]

23.71 Every statement made in the framework is unexceptional in terms of defining what are desirable attributes for a nurse. The concept of the framework reflects the need for flexibility in approach because of the wide variation of tasks that different nursing posts and levels of seniority may require to be done. The prioritisation of good and effective patient care and the desirability of development of leadership skills are implicit in the framework. However, neither of those necessary characteristics are explicitly headlined or highlighted specifically for every nursing post.

23.72 Thought needs to be given to the structural means of encouraging professional development and recognition of leadership skills, and to incentivising high standards of performance and professional development. One way of achieving this while fostering a positive teamwork culture is to find a way to measure and disseminate information about personal and collective achievement, perhaps through 360-degree appraisal as suggested earlier.

23.73 In the Inquiry's hospital visits, apparently high-performing wards publicly displayed their results for healthcare acquired infections, pressure ulcers, falls, etc., on corridor walls with pride. As a result of its nursing seminar the Inquiry has been shown work on developing a "Cultural Barometer" which seeks to give the employed nurse the chance to assess the resources and support available for the job; how worthwhile it is; and what opportunities there are for improving teamwork. This is combined with a request that he or she records actions the employee could take in respect of these matters, thus reinforcing personal professional responsibility for the standards applied, and the value placed on personal contribution.

23.74 Leaders need to be present and visible. That means they also need to be informed of and in a position to coordinate patients' care. Unless they personally are in direct communication with other senior members of the team caring for each patient there is a danger that this will not occur. Therefore, wherever possible they should be present on ward rounds and at handovers.

---

73 *Appraisals and KSF Made Simple – a practical guide* (16 November 2010), NHS Staff Council, www.nhsemployers.org/aboutus/publications/documents/appraisals%20and%20ksf%20made%20simple.pdf
74 *Summary description of KSF Core Dimensions* (November 2010), NHS Employers, www.nhsemployers.org/PayAndContracts/AgendaForChange/KSF/Simplified-KSF/Pages/SimplifiedKSF.aspx

23.75 They also need to ensure that each patient has at all times a named key nurse who is responsible for coordinating the nursing and ancillary care provided to each patient. The named key nurse on duty should also, wherever possible, be present for those parts of ward rounds concerning his or her patients. Named nurses need to take personal responsibility for and be committed to the care of their allocated patients. They should be the front-line "faces" to whom patients and those close to them feel comfortable to turn for help and information and on whom ward managers are able to rely to coordinate the provision for each patient's needs.

Nursing care of the elderly

23.76 A significant proportion of the issues that occurred on the wards at Stafford concerned the care of the elderly. While specialised medical and nursing resources were made available to the wards on a visiting basis, mainly through an outreach team, this cannot be the whole answer. Vulnerable patients require, and are entitled to, consistent and attentive care from staff who understand their special needs, whereas what they often receive is nursing to address a defined problem without adequate account being given to the multiple pathologies that are often present in the more elderly patient. Therefore, the level of expertise available on wards where a significant proportion of the patients fall into this category needs to be increased.

23.77 It is to be noted that there is already a specialist register for nurses with expertise and training in paediatric care and mental health, as well as in midwifery. These categories of patients share with the elderly the characteristics of requiring specialist care and of being particularly vulnerable. The elderly may differ from these other vulnerable groups in being more numerous to the extent of constituting the majority of occupants of NHS hospital beds in many general hospitals. This is not a reason for treating them with less specialist attention than they need but one for ensuring that the particular needs of this ever-increasing patient group receive urgently the recognition it demands. The time has gone when the care of the elderly can be comfortably regarded as a backwater of medicine; it is an area which requires a status in accordance with its proper social importance. Nursing of the elderly in particular needs to be recognised for its high value to the patients, and the distinct skill set required to lead its provision. One way such recognition could be provided, and good and effective nursing practice incentivised, would be the creation of a registered older persons nurse status. It would not need to be a requirement that all nurses treating such patients have this status, but, once established, it would be a useful marker for nurses to be able to lead an older persons' ward or other unit where such patients were treated. It could be supported by a programme of specialist training and experience, largely obtainable in post as a registered general nurse. There are naturally numerous training courses available in the care of the elderly leading to various qualifications, including postgraduate diplomas and these can only help spread the requisite knowledge of the specialty. However, this Inquiry suggests that a registered status could be developed into a source of pride for those holding it and a means of spreading and maintaining good practice in this area.

Standing of the profession

The Royal College of Nursing

23.78 The Inquiry heard from a number of witnesses who expressed concern that the effectiveness of the RCN as an authoritative professional voice promoting high-quality standards in nursing was hindered by a perception of a conflict of interest with its other role as a trade union for nurses with a priority of enhancing the employment conditions of its members.

23.79 This topic was discussed at the Inquiry seminar on nursing, where participants agreed that the current situation was not ideal, although a number of different considerations were raised. Some highlighted the benefits of an independent Royal College dedicated to setting and monitoring standards, while others felt that the size and diversity of the nursing profession militated against a single standard-setting body. Professor Katherine Fenton who presented at the seminar described the dilemma inherent in the RCN's current dual functions. On the one hand, as a regional nurse she had found the RCN helpful in its trade union role in highlighting issues where trust management decisions were affecting the quality of nursing practice. On the other, she highlighted a danger that employers too easily dismissed RCN reports on standards because of their trade union associations.[75]

23.80 The evidence reviewed in this report suggests that the RCN has not been heard as might have been expected in pursuing professional concerns about the standard of care. At Stafford, its voice seems to have been muted.

23.81 Sir Stephen Moss, Chair of Mid Staffordshire NHS Foundation Trust between August 2009 and January 2012, himself a highly distinguished registered nurse for over 30 years by background, observed:

> ... the difference between the Royal College of Nursing and the medical Royal Colleges is that it is – the Royal College of Nursing has a dual role, one of professional development and one as a staff association or trade union, and I think there is a – there is a widely held view that those don't sit together as comfortable bedfellows. In fairness to the Royal College of Nursing, I know that they've done a lot of good work in terms of education and development, but the discomfort that I have is that in a sense my comment can best be summed up by saying "We have a Royal College of Surgeons and the Royal College of

---

75   *Mid Staffordshire NHS Foundation Trust Public Inquiry: Report from the Forward Look Seminars,* Dr Sarah Harvey (18 November 2011), p44

Nursing is – is would be better called the Royal College of Nurses at the moment, because it actually inevitably ... it's focus will get sucked into representing their members, who are paying the fees that keep the organisation going, like any other trade union.

So I think there is an issue there for me. It's not a lack of will from the Royal College of Nursing to undertake that role successfully, but I think the odds are stacked against it at times.[76]

23.82 The inherent conflict between the representation of the interests of nurses as employees and the representation of their interests as a profession is capable of diminishing the authority with which the RCN's views are received in relation to the standards of care capable of being provided by its members. An example at Stafford was the inherent conflict between representing, as a trade union, the interests of the nursing sisters who were the subject of Helene Donnelly's whistleblowing complaint, and the promotion of standards of nursing that might be expected of a professional Royal College. It would be very difficult for the same organisation to do both at the same time. Further, the importance of nursing representation in providers needs to be recognised by ensuring that adequate time is given to staff undertaking this role.

The voice of nursing

Chief Nursing Officer

23.83 Until March 2011, the Department of Health (DH) had a post within it of Chief Nursing Officer (CNO) for England, whose functions it summarised as follows:

- *Provides expert advice on nursing, midwifery and health visiting to Government and helps to develop, implement and evaluate Government health policy, leading on nursing, midwifery and health visiting policy and strategy in support of the Government's objectives;*
- *Provides professional leadership to the nursing, midwifery and health visiting professions in England, working closely with the professional statutory bodies, professional and staff associations, NHS managers and the voluntary and independent sectors;*
- *Ensures an effective UK contribution to nursing and health policy in international forums, including the World Health Organization, the Commonwealth and Europe;*
- *Contributes to the Department's central task of managing the NHS.[77]*

23.84 It was announced in November 2010 that the then current postholder, Dame Christine Beasley, was to step down and that an interim appointment would be made. Following this, a new post of CNO for England was created as a member of the NHS Commissioning Board. The

---

76   S. Moss T58.194–5
77   Description set out on the Department of Health website: www.dh.gov.uk/health/category/chief-professional-officers/cpo-cno/

post of CNO at the DH was discontinued, but there is now a Director of Nursing, Department of Health. The holder of this post is also the Government's principal adviser on public health nursing. This post reports to one of the Department's directors-general. In her evidence to the Inquiry,[78] Dame Christine pointed out that the post of CNO had not been comparable to that of Chief Medical Officer owing to the history of the latter post and its particular role in being the Chief Medical Adviser across Government. Nonetheless, the effect of the new changes is to move the post regarded as being the most senior nursing post in England to a body charged with commissioning NHS services.

23.85 The intended role of the CNO for England has been clarified since the close of the oral hearings. Sir David Nicholson, in new evidence, has told the Inquiry that the CNO is the head of the nursing profession in England and is the equivalent in rank to the National Medical Director, both of whom are accountable to him as Chief Executive of the Board. It is believed that by being positioned on the Board, the CNO will have the greatest opportunity to lead and directly influence nursing in the NHS. The CNO will also be the principal adviser to the Government on NHS nursing matters. The Board also intends to have four regional chief nurses, and each clinical commissioning group (CCG) will be required to have a senior nurse in its governing body.

23.86 An example of the work of these two new appointees at the DH and the NHS Commissioning Board is their joint report *Compassion in Practice.*[79] The report identified six values:

> *... care, compassion, competence, communication, courage and commitment.*

which the authors wish to see made a reality. A full implementation plan of their vision is promised for March 2013. They observe that these values are not just the business of nurses and care workers but of all staff, including porters, ancillary professionals and managers. They identify a number of things required to bring their vision about:

- A supportive organisational culture;
- Leadership at every level to create that culture;
- Recognition of the demands of caring for vulnerable sick and dying patients;
- Time and space for reflection, sharing experiences, support and building emotional resilience.

---

78   Beasley T117.148–50
79   *Compassion in Practice, Nursing: midwifery and care staff; our vision and strategy* (December 2012), DH/NHS Commissioning Board Gateway ref. 18479, www.commissioningboard.nhs.uk/files/2012/12/compassion-in-practice.pdf

23.87 Six areas for action are proposed:

- Helping people to stay independent, maximising well-being and improving health outcomes;
- Working with people to provide a positive experience of care;
- Delivering high-quality care and measuring the impact of care;
- Building and strengthening leadership;
- Ensuring we have the right staff, with the right skills, in the right place;
- Supporting positive staff experience.

23.88 Among steps they recommend should be taken are:

- Regular board-level discussions of the staffing levels agreed by the Director of Nursing twice a year;
- Commissioners to review staffing levels using evidence-based tools;
- Development of access to pre-registration nurse training, possibly through foundation courses or apprenticeships;
- Health Education England to work with stakeholders to ensure that the values are embedded in all education and training;
- Employers to develop the use of the values in recruitment and appraisal systems;
- The use of the "cultural barometer" on a trial basis;
- Ward leaders to be supervisory to give them time to lead.

23.89 While these proposals have obviously not been the subject of examination in the evidence sessions or the seminars held by the Inquiry, their essential direction seems to be entirely consistent with the proposals made in this report.

23.90 While the joint report just considered may show that in itself the location of the desk of the CNO may matter little, it is important that the postholder retains the full freedom to offer independent professional advice to the Government, and to provide leadership for the profession as a whole, including that part working in the independent sector. It is clear that there is a continuing need at the heart of Government for a strong and independent professional nursing voice, similar to that provided in medical matters by the Chief Medical Officer. As much is demonstrated by two successive prime ministers seeing the need to appoint an *ad hoc* nursing advisory body to report directly to them on nursing issues.

23.91 It would be unfortunate at a time of such challenge to the nursing profession if its voice were to be diminished just when its standing and self-regard need to be enhanced for the good of the patients it serves. Clearly, it is not the intention of the changes described to do that, but the effectiveness of the new arrangements should be kept under review.

23.92 Senior nurses can provide invaluable advice and support to boards on a whole range of matters. They can bring their professional perspective to the table. By reason of their professional standards, training and regulatory obligations, they are well placed to resist corporate pressures to "toe the line" when patient safety is at stake.

23.93 All NHS provider organisations, including FTs, will have a registered nurse on the board as an executive director. FTs are under an obligation to do this by the standard terms required by Monitor to be included in their constitution.[80] The role they play varies from organisation to organisation but the posts will have in common the responsibility to advise the board on nursing matters. Strategic health authorities (SHAs) also had directors of nursing. It is intended that the governing bodies of CCGs include at least one nurse along with at least one secondary care specialist and two lay members.[81] There is no such requirement imposed on regulators and other bodies required to oversee healthcare. Even where there is such a requirement, there is potential for conflict between the professional duty of nursing directors and their corporate duty. For example, it is emphasised in guidance for CCGs that non-GP members of governing bodies are not there to represent constituencies. It would be helpful in ensuring a proper voice, for nursing in particular, if the requirement for a nursing director were consistently imposed over all parts of healthcare, including the independent sector.

The importance of ward rounds

23.94 At the Inquiry nursing seminar on 31 October 2011,[82] the point was raised that nurses should be present on ward rounds in order to act as a central point of communication between the patient and medical staff. The nurse both acts as advocate for the patient and communicates information that only the nursing staff will know from the last 24 hours of the patient's care.

23.95 This point was picked up by the Royal College of Physicians and the Royal College of Nursing who, in October 2012, jointly published *Ward Rounds in Medicine: Principles for best practice*. The publication highlights the importance of ward rounds as an opportunity for the multidisciplinary team to come together to review a patient's condition and develop a coordinated plan of care, while facilitating full engagement of the patient and/or their carer in making shared decisions about care:

---

80 MON00030012148, *Authorisation of Mid Staffordshire NHS Foundation Trust: Schedule 1, The Constitution (and Annexures)*, Schedule 1, para 20.8; National Health Service Act 2006, Schedule7, section 16(2); CURE0029000183, *NHS Foundation Trust Model Core Constitution*, (September 2008), Monitor, clause 20.7, p15

81 *Towards Establishment: Creating responsive and accountable clinical commissioning groups* (2 February 2012), NHS Commissioning Board, p33, www.commissioningboard.nhs.uk/files/2012/01/NHSCBA-02-2012-6-Guidance-Towards-establishment-Final.pdf; *Model Constitution Framework* (5 April 2012), NHS Commissioning Board, para 6.6.2(e), p32, www.commissioningboard.nhs.uk/files/2012/04/ccg-model-cons-framework.doc; for guidance generally on CCG constitutions see: www.commissioningboard.nhs.uk/resources/resources-for-ccgs/

82 Nursing seminar held by the Mid Staffordshire NHS Foundation Trust Public Inquiry; podcast available at: www.midstaffspublicinquiry.com/node/525, Plenary Question 4

Nurses have a crucial role on ward rounds, not only sharing key information between the patient and the healthcare team, but also supporting patients in articulating their views and preferences. Absence of a nurse at the bedside has clear consequences for communications, ward-round efficiency and patient safety. Although time pressures have grown for all professions, the responsibility to set aside time for ward rounds should be a collective one for doctors, nurses, pharmacists and therapists. This can and should be negotiated by local teams.[83]

23.96 The publication recommended that ward rounds should be seen as a priority by all members of the multi-professional team. It further recommended that a senior nurse should be present at every bedside patient review as part of a ward round, adding that the senior nursing team should be informed of all key decisions made on the ward round.

23.97 This is clearly a key aspect of patient care and the recommendation that nurses should be actively involved in ward rounds is an essential ingredient to be incorporated into patient care best practice. No consultant ward round or visit should take place without the presence of the nurse or an appointed deputy or other replacement in charge of the patients that are to be visited. Nurses are the one constant on the ward, and with proper handovers between nurses at the end of shifts, they can ensure that the information they pass on to doctors and their teams is up to date and relevant.

23.98 As well as improving communication and, consequently, the flow of information between medical staff, nurses' involvement in ward rounds is an important learning tool. As part of a nurse's development, senior nurses should ask student nurses to present bedside updates. The effect is twofold: firstly, it ensures that the student nurse is fully informed about the condition and care plan of their patient; secondly, it gives experience to the student nurse while providing the senior nurse with an understanding of the student nurse's abilities.

Healthcare support workers

The current position

23.99 The health sector is large and complex, comprising large public sector employers, collectively called the National Health Service large independent healthcare employers, and a very large number of small- and medium-sized enterprises, which may be independent or voluntary organisations.

23.100 Healthcare support workers (HCSWs) constitute a very large proportion of the healthcare workforce. It is of some significance that there is uncertainty about how many HCSWs there are, but the 2011 census indicated that in the NHS there were just over 270,000 providing

---

83   *Ward Rounds in Medicine: Principles for best practice* (October 2012), the Royal College of Physicians and the Royal College of Nursing, p3

support for doctors and nurses and a further 62,000 among the scientific and technical staff.[84] The number working in the independent sector was unknown but likely to be greater.[85] Healthcare assistants, unqualified nurses, unqualified staff, etc., earn around £16,000 to £17,000 per annum[86] meaning their earnings represent roughly 5–6% of the NHS budget.[87]

23.101 HCSWs are involved in delivering intimate, sensitive care for almost all patients who are unable to care for themselves. They will wash, dress and assist with feeding patients. They may well be the first to be told by the patient of a new symptom or to observe a new sign or development. Patients or relatives may seek clinical or other important information from them. They have access to patients' confidential information and may be expected to make accurate entries in patient records. While they will, or should, undertake these important tasks under an appropriate degree of supervision by a qualified and registered nurse, in practice they will often be left to their own devices. Even if it is accepted that only a small proportion of this workforce is unfit to provide this form of care, that will amount to a very large number of individuals and an exponentially greater number of patients who are exposed to the risk of unacceptable care as a result.

23.102 The patients they care for should all be regarded as part of a vulnerable group: all sick and vulnerable people, not just the elderly, have to be able to have confidence that those providing this care have had the appropriate training, and possess the necessary competence to care for them. None of us would willingly consent to allowing intimate care to be performed by insufficiently trained, or incompetent, employees.

23.103 The Inquiry has not been charged with investigating the wider healthcare economy outside the hospital setting, but HCSWs provide similar services to patients in their own homes and in care homes. Some are directly employed; others are employed by agencies.

23.104 Currently, workers in this category are not subject to any regulatory or other standard requirement, except for the basic requirement of a Criminal Records Bureau (CRB) check. Each employer will have its own recruitment policy, job specifications, code of conduct and training requirements. The degree to which such workers are supervised within a hospital or care home setting will be a matter of judgement for ward and departmental managers and the quality of supervision will often be vulnerable to constraints on resources. The range of competence and experience will range from recent school leavers with limited educational attainment or life experience, and workers from overseas with limited linguistic and cultural

---

84 *NHS Workforce: Summary of staff in the NHS: Results from September 2011 Census* (30 September 2011), NHS Health and Social Care Information Centre, p29, www.ic.nhs.uk/webfiles/publications/010_Workforce/nhsstaff0010/Census_Bulletin_March_2011_Final.pdf

85 *Moving Forward with Healthcare Support Workforce Regulation*, (Jul 2010), Paul Griffiths and Sarah Robinson, Kings College London, pp10–11, www.nmc-uk.org/Documents/ResearchPapers/NNRUreportMovingForwardWithHealthcareSupportWorkforceRegulation2010 July2010.pdf

86 *NHS Staff Earnings Estimates* (September 2011), NHS Health and Social Care Centre, p4, www.ic.nhs.uk/webfiles/publications/010_Workforce/staffearnjulsep2011/staff_earn_est_julsep2011_rep.pdf

87 NHS budget for 2011/12 is around £106 billion: www.nhs.uk/NHSEngland/thenhs/about/Pages/overview.aspx

familiarisation, to highly experienced, long-serving employees with special skills and increased technical competency. They are on the whole modestly paid and often have little if any voice that is heard.

23.105 The supervision of support workers is a matter referred to in the NMC code of conduct:

You must establish that anyone you delegate to is able to carry out your instructions.

You must confirm that the outcome of any delegated task meets required standards.

You must make sure that everyone you are responsible for is supervised and supported.

You must act without delay if you believe that you, a colleague or anyone else may be putting someone at risk.[88]

23.106 The level of supervision expected will depend on the qualifications, competence and experience of the worker.[89]

23.107 There is almost no protection available to patients or the public. There are no minimum standards of training or competence. Should a healthcare support worker be dismissed by an employer for being unfit to undertake this form of work, there is no system which prevents the worker being re-engaged by another employer, or even to ensure that a prospective employer is aware of any adverse past history. There is no system whereby changes of name (a not uncommon event among a largely female work force) can be tracked.

23.108 There is currently no common title for support workers. As stated by the UNISON representative at the Inquiry's nursing seminar, there is:

no consistency in what unregistered care staff do, what they are expected to do or training to underpin their roles.[90]

23.109 The result is that patients and the public have little idea of the professional status of those who are caring for patients. Patient participants at the nursing seminar noted that:

[i]t is confusing for patients – we don't know which people are nurses and what we can expect of different staff.[91]

88   NMC00010000108, *The Code: Standards of conduct, performance and ethics for nurses and midwives* (1 May 2008), Nursing and Midwifery Council, p5, paras 29–32
89   *The Regulation and Training of Healthcare Assistants: Presentation to the Mid Staffordshire NHS Foundation Trust Inquiry Nursing Seminar* (31 October 2011), Gill Heaton, slide 7
90   *Mid Staffordshire NHS Foundation Trust Public Inquiry: Report from the Forward Look Seminars*, Dr Sarah Harvey (18 November 2011), p45
91   *Mid Staffordshire NHS Foundation Trust Public Inquiry: Report from the Forward Look Seminars*, Dr Sarah Harvey (18 November 2011), p45

Proposals for change

23.110 The Prime Minister's Commission on the Future of Nursing and Midwifery in England recommended that this category of healthcare worker should be better trained and regulated. In its report, the Commission stated that:

- The move to degree-level registration for nurses was likely to stimulate employers to make more use of support workers;
- Training for support workers was very variable and they noted UNISON's advocacy of a national competency framework for this category;
- The public would be better protected through "some form of regulation of staff to whom nurses and midwives delegate tasks".[92]

23.111 They welcomed the NMC's decision to commission research on the potential risks and benefits of regulating this sector.

23.112 The Government has resisted calls for the regulation of support workers, principally on the grounds of cost, but has taken steps designed to improve training and standards. In particular it has commissioned Skills for Health and Skills for Care to work together to develop a code of conduct and minimum induction and training standards, including a core framework on both technical and core competencies, for support workers working in support of nurses and for adult social care workers. It also proposed to introduce a voluntary register, eligibility for which would be based on these requirements. It intends to commission a strategic review of the effectiveness of these arrangements within three years.[93]

23.113 The Prime Minister has created and commissioned the Nursing Care Quality Forum to identify best practice in the areas of: promoting nurse leadership; ensuring the right culture; obtaining and using feedback from patients; and enabling carers to have the time to perform their tasks.[94] A code of conduct for support workers is being considered, as is the formulation of standards of good practice.

23.114 Sir David Nicholson supported the Government's stance in his evidence to the Inquiry. He accepted the importance of maintaining and improving standards among this group of workers but questioned whether regulation was necessary. He pointed out the large numbers involved, and suggested that creating a regulatory system from scratch was not likely to be a top priority at the present time. He felt that focusing on training was likely to be a more

---

92 *Front Line Care: Report by the Prime Minister's Commission on the Future of Nursing and Midwifery in England* (2010), pp61–2, www.parliament.uk/deposits/depositedpapers/2010/DEP2010-0551.pdf

93 *Third Reading of the Health and Social Care Bill* (19 March 2012), Earl Howe, Hansard House of Lords Debates, col 698–700; Skills for Health Newsletter (Winter 2011/12), www.skillsforhealth.org.uk/newsletter/Newsletter-Winter-11-12.html#5

94 "Nursing and Care Quality Forum outlines work to improve nursing care" (17 April 2012), Department of Health press release, www.dh.gov.uk/health/2012/04/nursing-quality/. Tricia Hart, an assessor for this Inquiry, is a member of the Forum.

beneficial use of available resources.[95] He undertook to consider whether more needed to be done by way of a national initiative in relation to such training and development of healthcare workers.[96]

23.115 Dame Christine Beasley, in her evidence to the Inquiry, expressed strong disagreement with the arguments in favour of compulsory regulation for all HCSWs. She thought it was disproportionate in terms of patient safety and cost. She thought definitions would be difficult, and that regulation would not be capable of coping with the mobility of this part of the workforce. She considered that a "clear licensing policy" and "accreditation" of organisations and individuals would be sufficient. She told the Inquiry that, in spite of her having been a member of the Prime Minister's Commission which had supported regulation of workers to whom nurses delegated tasks (see earlier), she had not changed her views since then:

> My views are the same views as I had then, which is I can see – personally I think there may be a case for regulating that level that – in a way as what's described there, that reports directly at that top level, for want of a better word.
>
> I definitely – I absolutely hold to the view I don't think that – regulation for the whole healthcare support workers across the piece, I don't think is needed.[97]

23.116 Her experience had been that in the past the Government had not been given a "clear steer" from soundings of opinion that had produced mixed messages; there was uncertainty as to how effective regulation would be and the potential size of the task was a difficulty.

23.117 At the Inquiry, Action against Medical Accidents (AvMA) supported the introduction of statutory regulation for HCSWs. It contended in its submissions that:

> [At Mid Stafford] ... the same duties would be shared between qualified nurses and HCAs [health care assistants] and both were responsible for delivering poor standards of day to day care in terms of feeding, drinking, cleaning, toileting, cleanliness and dignity. There can be no justification for nurses being answerable to an external body responsible for protecting the public and HCAs who fail in providing basic standards of care not being so answerable ... One clear advantage of regulation would be the introduction of unequivocal standards, which would provide both a template for providing care and a yardstick against which that care could be assessed. It is acknowledged that the standards to which an HCA would need to adhere should take into account the differing level of their training and the more circumscribed nature of their role.[98]

---

95   Nicholson T128.48–50
96   Nicholson T128.50
97   Beasley T117.122
98   CLO000000428 Closing submissions of Action against Medical Accidents (AvMA), paras 244–5; T134.18–19

23.118 The NMC supports compulsory regulation of these workers. In his evidence to the Inquiry, the then Chief Executive Officer of the NMC (Professor Dickon Weir-Hughes) stated that he thought there was a gap in the regulation of the healthcare workforce:

> *HCSWs have become an increasingly important part of the healthcare workforce, and are taking on more and more roles traditionally undertaken by registered nurses. Very often patients make complaints to the NMC and think they are complaining about a nurse but they are actually talking about a HCSW ...*
>
> *The NMC believes that the public deserve better protection in relation to HCSWs through a national system of regulation.*[99]

23.119 In his oral evidence he said:

> *... we know that even if people are well managed in the NHS, that if they're dismissed from their post in the NHS they will walk down the road and get a job in a nursing home tomorrow.*
>
> *So unless they have done something that's criminal, and, of course, ... that gives a lot of room for ... being unpleasant or rude or, you know, a whole range of other things, there's a problem. So we feel quite strongly that healthcare support workers should be consistently trained, across the four countries. We believe that they should be consistently regulated across the four countries. We don't believe that needs to be an expensive procedure ... We think it's a really key issue in public protection.*[100]

23.120 NMC research showed that there had been instances of HCSWs obtaining employment with a healthcare provider after having been dismissed for misconduct by a previous employer. It also found evidence that such workers often undertook tasks for which they were not trained, that they were left unsupervised, and that deployment often depended on workforce and cost constraints rather than qualifications and competence. The conclusion of this scoping research was that there was a strong, although not unequivocal, case for regulation.[101]

23.121 Mr Dickson, Chief Executive of the General Medical Council, although not asked directly about this issue, in another context cautioned against making regulators too large.[102]

23.122 The Royal College of Nursing favours regulation of support workers. Their Chief Executive, Dr Carter, pointed out to the Inquiry that only some 8,000 are members of his organisation,

99   Weir-Hughes WS0000047524–5, paras 194–5
100 Weir-Hughes T106.125–6
101 Weir-Hughes WS0000047525, para 196; *Moving Forward with Healthcare Support Workforce Regulation* (July 2010), Paul Griffiths and Sarah Robinson, King's College London, p5, www.nmc-uk.org/Documents/ResearchPapers/ NNRUreportMovingForwardWithHealthcareSupportWorkforceRegulation2010July2010.pdf
102 Dickson T105.174–5

and a very small proportion are members of any organisation at all. He gave a number of reasons for being in favour of regulation and mandatory training:

- There are nearly half a million HCSWs working in hospitals, care homes and residential homes.
- There is no mandatory training.
- Such training as is offered is inconsistent:

    there are some trusts that do it really well. They employ people, they induct them, they train them and teach them all of the skills that are needed. Sadly, at the other end of the spectrum, we've come across instances where people have no training at all. They're literally given a tunic, it looks like a nurse's uniform. They're put on wards and they pick it up as they go along. Now, we say that's wholly unacceptable. Now, you wouldn't do that in a supermarket, where you're dealing with merchandise.

- The work done by this type of worker is becoming increasingly difficult, involving, for example, matters such as pressure sore care, feeding and hygiene of the elderly.[103]

23.123   The RCN-commissioned Willis Report was published in 2012.[104] The purpose was to "establish an independent commission to examine the 'health' of pre-registration nursing education".[105] It recommended the following:

1. *Evidence of the positive impact of registered nurses on patient outcomes must be utilised by healthcare providers in planning the nursing skill mix.*

2. *Employers must make use of the enhanced skills of the emerging graduate nursing workforce, as an opportunity to drive up standards and provide effective leadership and supervision of the clinical nursing workforce.*

3. *Graduate nurses, as leaders of clinical teams, should supervise and delegate work to registered healthcare assistants with clearly defined roles.*

4. *The numbers and roles of healthcare support workers who deliver patient care must be properly planned and regulated, in the interests of patient safety and care quality.*

5. *All staff at Agenda for Change bands 3–4 (and their equivalents outside the NHS) who deliver patient care should be trained to NVQ level 3 as the minimum UK standard, delivered by healthcare providers and further education.*

---

103 P. Carter T52.88–9
104 *Quality with Compassion: The future of nursing education*, report of the Willis Commission on Nursing Education (2012, www.willliscommission.org.uk/__data/assets/pdf_file/0004/489028/The_Willis_Report_2012.pdf
105 *Quality with Compassion: The future of nursing education*, report of the Willis Commission on Nursing Education, 2012, p4 www.willliscommission.org.uk/__data/assets/pdf_file/0004/489028/The_Willis_Report_2012.pdf

6. *A planned programme of regulation should begin with the mandatory registration of all staff who deliver patient care at Agenda for Change bands 3–4 (and their equivalents outside the NHS) by an independent regulator.*

7. *Governments, education institutions and employers must fulfil longstanding policy commitments to develop educational and employment models that widen access to nursing education, and provide career pathways for healthcare support workers including those who wish to train as nurses or midwives.*[106]

23.124 Sir Stephen Moss strongly supported regulation:

> *... anybody that could cause a patient some harm, looking at it negatively, ought to be tightly controlled by regulation or by a set of standards that they live and work by...*[107]

23.125 He advocated a return to the sort of regulation that surrounded state enrolled nurses.[108]

23.126 The House of Commons Health Select Committee was concerned that the Government's approach did not go far enough to protect patients and the public:

> *... [T]he Committee has ongoing concerns about the care and treatment of older people both in hospitals and care homes. Of particular concern to the Committee is the lack of regulation of a range of groups who undertake many basic nursing care tasks.*
>
> *The Committee endorses mandatory statutory regulation of healthcare assistants and support workers and we believe that this is the only approach which maximises public protection. The Committee notes that the Government intends to give powers to the relevant regulators to establish voluntary registers for non-regulated professionals and workers, but would urge it to see healthcare assistants, support workers and assistant practitioners as exceptions to this approach who should be subject to mandatory statutory regulation.*[109]

23.127 The Committee, however, recommended that changes needed to be made to the NMC before such regulation was introduced.

23.128 There was, with some dissenting voices, broad agreement at the Inquiry's nursing seminar that there should be some form of regulation for this category of worker. However, participants were anxious to emphasise that regulation on its own would be insufficient to

---

106 *Quality with Compassion: The future of nursing education*, report of the Willis Commission on Nursing Education (2012), p29
www.williscommission.org.uk/__data/assets/pdf_file/0004/489028/The_Willis_Report_2012.pdf
107 S. Moss T58.197
108 S. Moss T58.198
109 *Annual Accountability Hearing with the Nursing and Midwifery Council: Seventh report of session* 2010–12 (26 July 2011), House of Commons Health Committee, p17, paras 63 and 64,
www.publications.parliament.uk/pa/cm201012/cmselect/cmhealth/1428/1428.pdf

safeguard patients and that improvements and standardisation were required with regard to training and support.

23.129 It is relevant to note, as referred to earlier, that the recent report of the CNO for England and the Director of Nursing at the DH suggests that pre-registration experience on wards as support workers or apprentices should be developed. Therefore either by that route or by way of other implementation of the training recommendations of this report, working as a support worker is likely to become a recognised route to qualification as a registered nurse, with patients being exposed to hands-on care by such students.

23.130 Regulation is not something that should be introduced for its own sake. While there is a wide range of matters that could be regulated in relation to HCSWs, it is necessary to consider what concerns can best be addressed in the public interest by a regulator as opposed to other means.

23.131 The experience at Stafford and the multiple reports of appalling care elsewhere, often delivered by HCSWs, clearly demonstrate a need for visible and accessible protection of patients and the public from being exposed to care and treatment by people who are unfit, unqualified or incapable of performing their duties to an acceptable standard. A responsible employer with effective systems of governance may be able to detect and root out such people from their organisations, but they can do nothing at the moment to prevent such people from obtaining work elsewhere from employers ignorant of their past. There is no consistency in the training of HCSWs and therefore no common standard against which to assess the competence of this grade of worker. They are governed by no standard code of conduct. They undertake work that, if not carried out or if undertaken carried out badly, may endanger patients' health. The work carried out by HCSWs requires skill and training to be done properly and yet no common information is available to the public about them.

23.132 It seems strange that a number of other activities involving a low level of skill but giving rise to a risk to members of the public are thought to be more suitable for regulation by registration or licensing. Certain categories of security guards, nightclub security staff and key holders require licences administered by the Security Industry Authority.[110] A private hire vehicle driver requires a licence from a licensing authority.[111] Thus the minicab driver who takes a patient to hospital and the security guard who may be at the door when the patient arrives are likely to be subject to regulation under which they can be disqualified from the role if not a fit and proper person, but the HCSW who washes the patient and accompanies him or her to the toilet is not.

---

110 Private Security Industry Act 2001, Schedule 2
111 Private Hire Vehicles (London) Act 1998; Local government (Miscellaneous Provisions) Act 1976, section 51

23.133 At its simplest, regulation can help protect patients and the public by providing a register of individuals who are undertaking a defined type of work, to enable a sharing of information about them in the public interest. Regulation could also provide a means of ensuring that individuals identified as being unfit to work with patients can be prevented from doing so, or, at the very least, prospective employers can be made aware of matters of concern before exposing patients to them. The very existence of a register, even if a simple one, would help to drive up standards.

23.134 The Government intends to create a voluntary rather than a compulsory register.[112] A voluntary register has little or no advantage for the public. Employers will not be compelled to employ only those on the register, although no doubt they could be incentivised to do so. It is not generally those who would seek voluntary registration who are the concern, but those who will or could not do so, but are still able to obtain employment in contact with vulnerable patients.

23.135 A register need not be unduly costly and can be self-financing through registration fees. Currently, registered nurses pay a fee of £76 a year. The Inquiry advised that the vast majority of nurses are expected to pay this for themselves. After a 12-week consultation on the proposal that this fee be increased by 58%, to £120 a year, the NMC has decided to increase its fees to £100.

23.136 The major costs of most professional regulators arise from their casework in investigating and pursuing fitness to practise cases. While it would be desirable for a regulator of support workers to have such a jurisdiction, it would be possible, at least initially, to consider requiring a regulator to perform the functions of keeping the register. Employers should have a duty imposed on them to report adverse disciplinary decisions involving support workers to the regulator.

23.137 It would also be possible to restrict the scope of workers to be regulated, again initially to those employed to provide care to patients in hospitals and other organisations registered by the Care Quality Commission (CQC) under the supervision of nurses. This Inquiry has not been charged with considering care provided privately in patients' homes, and therefore it is not possible to comment on the need for regulation in those settings. However, the recently reported incidents at Winterbourne View and Ash Court suggest that there is a need for the ambit of regulation to extend beyond hospital care.

23.138 The essential ingredients of a minimal system designed to offer protection to the public would be a register kept and managed by a healthcare professional regulator, which in respect of each person working in a regulated activity would record:

---

112 www.legislation.gov.uk/ukpga/2012/7/section/228?view=plain Health and Social Care Act 2012, section 228

- A unique identifier;
- A registered address;
- Current and past employers;
- The reasons for termination of previous employments as reported by the employer;
- Any observations on those reasons recorded by the registrant.

23.139 In order to restrict disclosure of what would normally be confidential items of information to that reasonably required in the interests of patient safety, access to information under the last two categories would need to be restricted to any employer to whom the registrant applied for employment, and to any other person who satisfied the regulator that they had a good reason for requiring the information.

23.140 Following development of this limited system of registration, its effect should be reviewed for consideration of whether the public interest required the development of a fitness to practise regulatory system comparable to that in force for registered nurses.

23.141 A further step that would assist in protecting patient safety would be the development of a system facilitating the exchange of information about previous employments of workers in this category. This should be designed to enable prospective employers to obtain information from previous employers that might otherwise be confidential but would be relevant to an applicant's fitness for an HCSW post. This would be less necessary if a fitness to practise regulatory system were created, but even then would be an additional safeguard.

23.142 Many HCSWs are mistaken for nurses. A national uniform description of such workers should be established. The Inquiry suggests that the relationship with (currently) registered nurses should be made clear by the title. The Inquiry suggests "nursing assistant", "community nursing assistant" and "midwifery assistant".

23.143 A registration system, as described earlier, should be created under which no unregistered person should be permitted to provide, for reward, direct physical care to patients currently under the care and treatment of a registered nurse or a registered doctor, (or who are dependent on such care by reason of disability and/or infirmity). The system should apply to HCSWs whether they are working for the NHS or for independent healthcare providers, in the community, for agencies or as independent agents. (Exemptions should be made for persons caring for no reward for members of their own family or those with whom they have a genuine social relationship.)

23.144 There should be a uniform code of conduct for HCSWs.

23.145 There should be a common set of national standards for the education and training of this grade of worker.

23.146 The code of conduct, education and training standards and requirements for registration should be prepared and maintained by a regulator after due consultation with all relevant stakeholders, including the DH, other regulators, professional representative organisations and the public, and incorporated into the contracts of employment of all HCSWs employed by NHS acute care providers.

23.147 Because of the close connection with registered nursing, the regulator performing the functions described earlier should be the NMC.

23.148 The DH and the CQC should institute a system for the confidential exchange of information between employers, under which an applicant for employment as an HCSW:

- Would be required as a condition for the consideration of the application to identify all previous employers in such posts;
- To consent to the employers to whom the application is made to have access to information from any previous employer relevant to the fitness of the applicant to practise as an HCSW arising during previous employment.

23.149 This system should be supported by fair due process in relation to employees in this grade to allow them a fair opportunity to respond to adverse information obtained through this system who have been dismissed by employers on the grounds of a serious breach of the code of conduct, or otherwise being unfit for such a post.

23.150 Commissioning arrangements should require provider organisations to ensure, by means of identity labels and uniforms, that this grade of worker is easily distinguishable from a registered nurse.

Summary of recommendations

Recommendation 185

There should be an increased focus in nurse training, education and professional development on the practical requirements of delivering compassionate care in addition to the theory. A system which ensures the delivery of proper standards of nursing requires:

- Selection of recruits to the profession who evidence the:
  - Possession of the appropriate values, attitudes and behaviours;
  - Ability and motivation to enable them to put the welfare of others above their own interests;
  - Drive to maintain, develop and improve their own standards and abilities;
  - Intellectual achievements to enable them to acquire through training the necessary technical skills;
- Training and experience in delivery of compassionate care;
- Leadership which constantly reinforces values and standards of compassionate care;
- Involvement in, and responsibility for, the planning and delivery of compassionate care;
- Constant support and incentivisation which values nurses and the work they do through:
  - Recognition of achievement;
  - Regular, comprehensive feedback on performance and concerns;
  - Encouraging them to report concerns and to give priority to patient well-being.

Recommendation 186

Nursing training should be reviewed so that sufficient practical elements are incorporated to ensure that a consistent standard is achieved by all trainees throughout the country. This requires national standards.

Recommendation 187

There should be a national entry-level requirement that student nurses spend a minimum period of time, at least three months, working on the direct care of patients under the supervision of a registered nurse. Such experience should include direct care of patients, ideally including the elderly, and involve hands-on physical care. Satisfactory completion of this direct care experience should be a pre-condition to continuation in nurse training. Supervised work of this type as a healthcare support worker should be allowed to count as an equivalent. An alternative would be to require candidates for qualification for registration to undertake a minimum period of work in an approved healthcare support worker post involving the delivery of such care.

Recommendation 188

The Nursing and Midwifery Council, working with universities, should consider the introduction of an aptitude test to be undertaken by aspirant registered nurses at entry into the profession, exploring, in particular, candidates' attitudes towards caring, compassion and other necessary professional values.

Recommendation 189

The Nursing and Midwifery Council and other professional and academic bodies should work towards a common qualification assessment/examination.

Recommendation 190

There should be national training standards for qualification as a registered nurse to ensure that newly qualified nurses are competent to deliver a consistent standard of the fundamental aspects of compassionate care.

Recommendation 191

Healthcare employers recruiting nursing staff, whether qualified or unqualified, should assess candidates' values, attitudes and behaviours towards the well-being of patients and their basic care needs, and care providers should be required to do so by commissioning and regulatory requirements.

Recommendation 192

The Department of Health and Nursing and Midwifery Council should introduce the concept of a Responsible Officer for nursing, appointed by and accountable to, the Nursing and Midwifery Council.

Recommendation 193

Without introducing a revalidation scheme immediately, the Nursing and Midwifery Council should introduce common minimum standards for appraisal and support with which responsible officers would be obliged to comply. They could be required to report to the Nursing and Midwifery Council on their performance on a regular basis.

Recommendation 194

As part of a mandatory annual performance appraisal, each Nurse, regardless of workplace setting, should be required to demonstrate in their annual learning portfolio an up-to-date knowledge of nursing practice and its implementation. Alongside developmental requirements, this should contain documented evidence of recognised training undertaken, including wider relevant learning. It should also demonstrate commitment, compassion and caring for patients, evidenced by feedback from patients and families on the care provided by the nurse. This portfolio and each annual appraisal should be made available to the Nursing and Midwifery Council, if requested, as part of a nurse's revalidation process.

At the end of each annual assessment, the appraisal and portfolio should be signed by the nurse as being an accurate and true reflection and be countersigned by their appraising manager as being such.

Recommendation 195

Ward nurse managers should operate in a supervisory capacity, and not be office-bound or expected to double up, except in emergencies as part of the nursing provision on the ward. They should know about the care plans relating to every patient on his or her ward. They should make themselves visible to patients and staff alike, and be available to discuss concerns with all, including relatives. Critically, they should work alongside staff as a role model and mentor, developing clinical competencies and leadership skills within the team. As a corollary, they would monitor performance and deliver training and/or feedback as appropriate, including a robust annual appraisal.

Recommendation 196

The Knowledge and Skills Framework should be reviewed with a view to giving explicit recognition to nurses' demonstrations of commitment to patient care and, in particular, to the priority to be accorded to dignity and respect, and their acquisition of leadership skills.

Recommendation 197

Training and continuing professional development for nurses should include leadership training at every level from student to director. A resource for nurse leadership training should be made available for all NHS healthcare provider organisations that should be required under commissioning arrangements by those buying healthcare services to arrange such training for appropriate staff.

Recommendation 198

Healthcare providers should be encouraged by incentives to develop and deploy reliable and transparent measures of the cultural health of front-line nursing workplaces and teams, which build on the experience and feedback of nursing staff using a robust methodology, such as the "cultural barometer".

Recommendation 199

Each patient should be allocated for each shift a named key nurse responsible for coordinating the provision of the care needs for each allocated patient. The named key nurse on duty should, whenever possible, be present at every interaction between a doctor and an allocated patient.

Recommendation 200

Consideration should be given to the creation of a status of Registered Older Person's Nurse.

Recommendation 201

The Royal College of Nursing should consider whether it should formally divide its "Royal College" functions and its employee representative/trade union functions between two bodies rather than behind internal "Chinese walls".

Recommendation 202

Recognition of the importance of nursing representation at provider level should be given by ensuring that adequate time is allowed for staff to undertake this role, and employers and unions must regularly review the adequacy of the arrangements in this regard.

Recommendation 203

A forum for all directors of nursing from both NHS and independent sector organisations should be formed to provide a means of coordinating the leadership of the nursing profession.

Recommendation 204

All healthcare providers and commissioning organisations should be required to have at least one executive director who is a registered nurse, and should be encouraged to consider recruiting nurses as non-executive directors.

Recommendation 205

Commissioning arrangements should require the boards of provider organisations to seek and record the advice of its nursing director on the impact on the quality of care and patient safety of any proposed major change to nurse staffing arrangements or provision facilities, and to record whether they accepted or rejected the advice, in the latter case recording its reasons for doing so.

Recommendation 206

The effectiveness of the newly positioned office of Chief Nursing Officer should be kept under review to ensure the maintenance of a recognised leading representative of the nursing profession as a whole, able and empowered to give independent professional advice to the Government on nursing issues of equivalent authority to that provided by the Chief Medical Officer.

Recommendation 207

There should be a uniform description of healthcare support workers, with the relationship with currently registered nurses made clear by the title.

Recommendation 208

Commissioning arrangements should require provider organisations to ensure by means of identity labels and uniforms that a healthcare support worker is easily distinguishable from that of a registered nurse.

Recommendation 209

A registration system should be created under which no unregistered person should be permitted to provide for reward direct physical care to patients currently under the care and treatment of a registered nurse or a registered doctor (or who are dependent on such care by reason of disability and/or infirmity) in a hospital or care home setting. The system should apply to healthcare support workers, whether they are working for the NHS or independent healthcare providers, in the community, for agencies or as independent agents. (Exemptions should be made for persons caring for members of their own family or those with whom they have a genuine social relationship.)

Recommendation 210

There should be a national code of conduct for healthcare support workers.

Recommendation 211

There should be a common set of national standards for the education and training of healthcare support workers.

Recommendation 212

The code of conduct, education and training standards and requirements for registration for healthcare support workers should be prepared and maintained by the Nursing and Midwifery Council after due consultation with all relevant stakeholders, including the Department of Health, other regulators, professional representative organisations and the public.

Recommendation 213

Until such time as the Nursing and Midwifery Council is charged with the recommended regulatory responsibilities, the Department of Health should institute a nationwide system to protect patients and care receivers from harm. This system should be supported by fair due process in relation to employees in this grade who have been dismissed by employers on the grounds of a serious breach of the code of conduct or otherwise being unfit for such a post.

Chapter 24
Leadership in healthcare

Key themes

- The role of leadership in a provider trust is challenging and carries huge responsibility. The NHS suffers from difficulties in recruiting and retaining leaders of suitable calibre.

- Good leadership must be visible, receptive, insightful and outward looking. Leadership and managerial skills are not the same but both are required. Leadership skills are required to be shared at all levels in an organisation, from board to ward, and all staff must be empowered to use their own judgement in providing the best possible care for patients.

- Clinicians must be engaged to a far greater degree of engagement in leadership and management roles. The gulf between clinicians and management needs to be closed.

- Effective management and leadership development is essential to remedy these issues; initiatives have come and gone leading to a patchwork of provision. The Leadership Academy is currently seeking to bring together and promote the various necessary streams of management and leadership training in particular through the introduction of a leadership framework. The number and quality of candidates for leadership posts could be enhanced by provision of some common training in a leadership college. This could in due course lead to the development of an accreditation scheme.

- The Care Quality Commission (CQC) standards include requirements for the fitness of the nominated person responsible for supervising the carrying on of the regulated activity, but there is generally no such provision for other directors or senior managers. Monitor publishes an advisory code of governance applicable to foundation trust (FT) directors and requires evidence of adequate support and training for them. It has power to direct their removal from office. There is no power of general disqualification, but Monitor is consulting on whether to include in proposed licensing conditions a "fit and proper person test" and on the inclusion in that of a requirement of compliance with a code of conduct.

- There is no system of accountability for managers and leaders of NHS healthcare organisations other than by reference to their contracts of employment. Consequently there is nothing to prevent officials who are unfit for such posts through incompetence or misconduct from being appointed to them. There is no regulatory system providing accountability comparable to that imposed on registered healthcare professionals.

- A Council for Healthcare Regulatory Excellence (CHRE) review has set out standards for directors. While there is no consensus in favour of regulation of NHS managers there are strong arguments in support of producing a level playing field in management roles between registered healthcare professionals and those from backgrounds not otherwise subject to professional regulation. As a first step a "fit and proper person" test and an associated power of disqualification for serious incompetence or misconduct should be adopted as part of Monitor's licensing scheme. Consideration needs to be given as to how to extend these requirements to NHS healthcare organisations not regulated by Monitor. The need to extend a regulatory scheme to lower levels of managers and leaders and to set up a separate professional regulatory body should be kept under review.

Introduction

24.1   Effective leadership is essential to a flourishing NHS. Dr Judith Smith and Professor Naomi Chambers[1] drew the Inquiry's attention to the report of the King's Fund Commission on Leadership in the NHS,[2] which identified the importance of leadership throughout the system to making improvements in service and outcomes and promoting professional cultures supporting teamwork, continuous improvement and patient engagement.

24.2   NHS leaders have complex jobs and are responsible for organisations where failures in systems and performance can lead to serious harm or death of their patients, as well as adversely affecting those that work within them.

24.3   Effective leadership was a feature significantly lacking at the Trust during the period under review. In order for a common culture to take root and grow, the healthcare system needs leaders who can adopt and promote the common values of the NHS and have the competence and skills to take forward the complex task of delivering health services to the public in accordance with the required standards and within the allocated resources.

24.4   Professor Sir Ian Kennedy, in the report of the Bristol Inquiry, identified the need to change hospital culture from a "club culture" to one of:

> ... safety and of quality; a culture of openness and one of accountability; a culture of public services; a culture in which collaborative teamwork is prized; and a culture of flexibility in which innovation can flourish in response to patients' needs.[3]

1   Dr Judith Smith and Professor Naomi Chambers *The Regulation and Development of NHS Managers: a Discussion Paper*, (19 October 2011), paper delivered to the Inquiry Leadership Seminar, p5, www.midstaffspublicinquiry.com/sites/default/files/uploads/Judith_Smith_and_Naomi_Chambers_-_paper_2_0.pdf

2   *The Future of leadership and management in the NHS: no more heroes* (2011) King's Fund Commission on Leadership in the NHS, King's Fund, www.kingsfund.org.uk/sites/files/kf/future-of-leadership-and-management-nhs-may-2011-kings-fund.pdf

3   *The Report of the Public Inquiry into Children's Heart Surgery at the Bristol Royal Infirmary 1984–1995* (July 2001), Cm 5207(1), p271 para 23, www.bristol-inquiry.org.uk/final_report/index.htm

24.5   He recommended that healthcare managers, in particular chief executives, required more support, and that managers should be subject to a new body overseeing all aspects relating to the regulation of professional life: education, registration, training, revalidation, continuing professsional development (CPD), and discipline.[4] This recommendation has not been implemented. In his evidence to this Inquiry, Sir Ian said:

> ... we did recommend in Bristol ... that managers and that, in my view, by extension could include non-executive directors, should be in some way validated or accredited or trained, and in the end, of course, if that would be the case, they would have to show not only that they met certain standards but that they continued to meet standards. And ... I think there is ... a plausible argument for a device for holding non-executive directors to account in the performance against certain standards of what a non-executive directors should meet.

> And, I mean, that's what's happened in the world of commerce and the world of finance. The NHS is not an island. It doesn't exist as if the rest of the world didn't take place, although many would argue that it should. In the other parts of the world, non-executive directors are now visited with a great deal more responsibility, rightly so, and appointed with due care as to whether they can meet that responsibility.[5]

24.6   Healthcare, both inside and outside the NHS, has many excellent leaders, but it is a tough environment in which to succeed. Each provider trust, even the "smaller" ones such as the Trust, are complex organisations with turnovers of well over £100 million pounds, employing thousands of staff and responsible for thousands of interactions with patients daily. The tenure of chief executives is, on average, shockingly short. At the time of the Inquiry's oral hearings, the average tenure was said to be no more than two years.[6] Mr Antony Sumara considered there to be an acknowledged problem with the numbers and quality of leaders in the NHS.[7]

24.7   The qualities required by leaders generally have been pithily summarised by General Duane Cassidy, formerly of the US Air Force:[8]

> My 34 years of service have convinced me that there are no experts on the subject of leadership, but I have observed several characteristics that seem to be common to successful leaders. Those characteristics are integrity, selflessness and energy ...

---

4   *The Report of the Public Inquiry into Children's Heart Surgery at the Bristol Royal Infirmary 1984–1995* (July 2001) Cm 5207(1), Recommendation 70, p446 and recommendation 91, p448, www.bristol-inquiry.org.uk/final_report/index.htm
5   Kennedy T77.79
6   Sumara T58.123
7   Sumara T58.124
8   General Duane H Cassidy *A Leadership Perspective*, (2001) www.au.af.mil/au/awc/awcgate/au-24/au24-378.htm

24.8 Of integrity, he said:

> *We must be right, we must be competent. we [sic] must admit our mistakes and correct them when they do occur, and above all we must never permit either the fact or image of duplicity to taint our honor. The watchword must be, as always, the truth, the whole truth, and nothing but the truth ... a leader must not only set high standards, but must, by commitment and example, live up to the same standards.*

24.9 He referred to a well-known saying of Viscount Slim, also quoted by Sir Cyril Chantler at the Inquiry's leadership seminar:

> *Leadership is of the spirit, compounded of personality and vision. Its practice is an art. Management is of the mind, more a matter of accurate calculations, statistics, methods, timetables, and routine. Its practice is a science. Managers are necessary, Leaders are essential.*

24.10 The question considered in this chapter is whether more should now be done to enhance the availability and effectiveness of leaders in healthcare organisations.

Qualities of leadership in healthcare

Visibility and example

24.11 For Professor Sir Bruce Keogh, the NHS Medical Director, the key to effective healthcare lay in clinical teams and their professional leadership, but he also emphasised the importance of effective leadership in supporting such teams:

> *... how the organisation in managerial terms, in leadership terms, supports the clinicians delivering that service is important. The board must be seen to walk the talk. The board must be seen to be talking about effective care, safe care and patient experience. It needs to promote the culture which prevents people drifting away from their own values that drove them into the service in the first place.*[9]

Listening to patients and staff

24.12 Sir Bruce also pointed to the need for leaders at all levels to have direct contact with patients and others with an interest in healthcare quality. He saw the need for patients to act as the "common conscience" of leaders throughout the system, seeking to drive healthcare quality forward.[10]

---

9   Keogh T123.200–201
10   Keogh T123.199

In-depth understanding

24.13 For Sir David Nicholson, Chief Excutive of the NHS, chief executives required a combination of strategic insight and what he termed "operational grip", an understanding of how the organisation they were to lead worked.[11]

Lateral cross-boundary thinking

24.14 The National Leadership Council (NLC), in its 2010 annual report, identified "new behaviours" that were required:

- *Listening to patient and staff experience and acting on it to improve the quality of care and the efficiency of its delivery;*
- *Rethinking and revising the care pathways across organisational boundaries so that patients are treated in the most appropriate setting for their condition;*
- *Making connections across boundaries in partner organisations so that innovation and best practices can be rapidly adopted wherever they are found rather than being reinvented locally;*
- *Eliminating sources of waste and duplication to free up resources for reinvestment back into improving lives for patients and staff.[12]*

Sharing leadership with all staff through empowerment

24.15 As has been indicated in some of the quotations cited above, management and leadership are two different skills, although obviously both are needed in any well-functioning organisation. However, the qualities of leadership are not only requirements of the senior officers of an organisation, but of staff throughout it. As argued by Dr Karen Lynas:

> *Whilst managerial skills are essential to ensure that organisations are run efficiently, effectively and legally – and in effect, provide a solid foundation from which services can run – leadership skills maximise the potential of people working in the NHS, drive innovation and continually seek to change and improve services.[13]*

---

11   Nicholson T127.139–140
12   *The Foundation NLC Annual Report – First Year: Executive summary,* National Leadership Council, p10, www.dh.gov.uk/prod_consum_dh/groups/dh_digitalassets/@dh/@en/@abous/documents/digitalasset/dh_117363.pdf
13   Dr Karen Lynas *The Development and Training of Trust Leaders, (*Paper for the Inquiry seminar on the development of Trust leaders on (18 October 2011), paper delivered to the Inquiry leadership seminar, www.midstaffspublicinquiry.com/sites/default/files/uploads/Karen_Lynas_paper.pdf

24.16 To achieve that, many staff are required to exercise leadership. She went on to quote Sir Terry Leahy, formerly Chief Executive of Tesco:

The key to organisational success is for people from every rung of the corporate ladder to take responsibility. Leadership matters everywhere. The great thing that we always tried to achieve at Tesco was to have thousands of leaders, not just one. You've got to empower people to take responsibility – that is really the type of leadership that works.

24.17 In a complex organisation, staff need to be empowered to use their own judgement in order to improve the quality of the service they provide. Or, as Dr Lynas put it:

This is all the more important for the NHS which is a people driven service, created to provide the best possible care to patients.[14]

24.18 This requires bold senior leaders who instil in their staff the confidence and the ability to act in the organisation's interests – in the case of a healthcare service, by doing what is best for patients:

Structure drives culture. It is not possible to create a world-class service culture as long as we keep structures that are defined by layers of bureaucracy and departmental barriers to speed and responsiveness. The most important single change that can accompany a strong service message is spontaneity, the power of inspired front line staff to say Yes and do the fair or generous thing on the spot.[15]

24.19 The King's Fund has identified this as a need within the NHS:

The old model of 'heroic' leadership by individuals needs to adapt to become one that understands other models such as shared leadership both within organisations and across the many organisations with which the NHS has to engage in order to deliver its goals. This requires a focus on developing the organisation and its teams, not just individuals, on leadership across systems of care rather than just institutions, and on followership as well as leadership.[16]

Clinical engagement

24.20 Clinical engagement in leadership at all levels is vital. As stated in the King's Fund report:

---

14   Dr Karen Lynas *The Development and Training of Trust Leaders,* (Paper for the Inquiry seminar on the development of Trust leaders on (18 October 2011), paper delivered to the Inquiry leadership seminar, www.midstaffspublicinquiry.com/sites/default/files/uploads/Karen_Lynas_paper.pdf
15   Lee F (2004) *If Disney Ran Your Hospital, 9½ Things You Would Do Different Differently,* Second River Healthcare Press, Chapter 5
16   *The Future of Leadership and Management in the NHS: no more heroes* (2011), King's Fund Commission on Leadership in the NHS, pix, www.kingsfund.org.uk/sites/files/kf/future-of-leadership-and-management-nhs-may-2011-kings-fund.pdf

Leadership development needs to extend 'from the board to the ward'. One of the biggest weaknesses of the NHS has been its failure to engage clinicians – particularly, but not only doctors – in a sustained way in management and leadership. Individuals within the service, and its providers, need to be given both the ability and the confidence to challenge poor practice. Management and leadership needs to be shared between managers and clinicians and equally valued by both.[17]

Collective leadership skills

24.21 David Stone, former interim Chair of the Trust, expressed the view that boards required a balance of skills:

> *I think the key is that ... on a group of non-executives on the board you need balance. You need to bring to the board a variety of knowledge and experience in order for it to function effectively and, clearly, one of those, if one's talking about a trust, you need to have clinical, hospital, medical, whatever, background, as well as financial whatever.*[18]

Ability and willingness to challenge others

24.22 Part of that balance is the confidence, competence and judgement necessary to mount the appropriate degree of challenge with regard to executive performance. Elizabeth Buggins, former Chair of the West Midlands Strategic Health Authority (WMSHA), told the Inquiry about her practice as Chair of a Board:

> *The evidence suggests that where a board either errs on the side of too much support or on the side of too much challenge, both result in poor performance. So if there's too much support, group think develops, and the challenge that should be around a board table is absent to some degree.*
>
> *Where there is too much challenge, it's very difficult for openness to reign around that board table. And for people who have concerns to raise them for fear of being chopped down. So that's what I mean by that. The evidence supports that.*
>
> *... my job, as chairman of those meetings, is to make – create the space really for that challenge to happen, either in the meeting or outside as most appropriate, but the open culture, I think, is very important ... I try to model that by – at the end of board meetings, even when the final board meeting' [sic] is in public, asking the board to reflect on how we could have done that meeting better. Whether it's the information that was provided, whether it was the way I handled the debate, whether it was the way the presentations were delivered or in the judgements that we made.*[19]

---

17   *The Future of Leadership and Management in the NHS: No more heroes* (2011), King's Fund Commission on Leadership in the NHS, pix, www.kingsfund.org.uk/sites/files/kf/future-of-leadership-and-management-nhs-may-2011-kings-fund.pdf
18   Stone T54.66
19   Buggins T74.115–116

Summary

24.23 Acknowledging that there are many definitions of leadership, the King's Fund offered a definition for the purposes of their report which summarised many of the qualities required:

> *The commission defines leadership as the art of motivating a group of people to achieve a common goal. This demands a mix of analytic and personal skills in order to set out a clear vision of the future and defining a strategy to get there. It requires communicating that to others and ensuring that the skills are assembled to achieve it. It also involves handling and balancing the conflicts of interests that will inevitably arise, both within the organisation and outside it where, even in the private sector, a wide variety of stakeholders will have a legitimate interest ...*
>
> *Leadership clearly requires considerable management skills. But it is more than just management, which might be concisely summarised as 'getting the job done'. It essentially involves marshalling the human and technical resources needed to achieve the organisation's goals – ensuring that the administration needed to do that is in place, while ideally excising all administration that is not needed. These definitions make clear the Commission's view that leadership in the NHS is needed from the board to the ward and involves clinicians as well as managers.*[20]

24.24 Therefore, a list of the qualities required of leaders in healthcare would include:

- Ability to create and communicate vision and strategy;
- Understanding of how to prioritise and protect patient safety and provision of fundamental standards within available resources;
- Ability to be viewed as a role model;
- Listening and learning from patients and colleagues;
- Inspiration and motivation of colleagues;
- Willingness to challenge;
- Ability to judge and analyse complex issues;
- Probity;
- Openness;
- Courage.

24.25 It is suggested that such qualities are needed at all levels of the healthcare service; it is how they are applied that will differ according to the leadership function undertaken.

---

20 *The Future of Leadership and Management in the NHS: No more heroes* (2011), King's Fund Commission on Leadership in the NHS, p12, www.kingsfund.org.uk/sites/files/kf/future-of-leadership-and-management-nhs-may-2011-kings-fund.pdf

Increasing the leadership pool and the professional status of managers

24.26 It has been observed that it is not healthy for the NHS if the pool of potential recruits for senior management and leadership posts is limited and largely involves the same group of people applying for jobs.[21] Sir David Nicholson told the Inquiry that, at around the time Martin Yeates was recruited to the Chief Executive post at the Trust, there were on average about 1.2 people applying for each such post, meaning that there was very little choice. The NLC's first annual report in 2010 noted a survey result for 2009 suggesting that, on average, one person applied for every chief executive role, but fewer than one for "key director roles".[22] Sir David suggested, however, that the position had improved as a result of the efforts made since.[23] The position had been reached where there was a generally agreed leadership framework describing good leadership, and programmes had been set up throughout the regions to offer training and development to persons identified as potential leaders at director, chief executive and emerging leader level.[24]

24.27 A further challenge is the relatively small proportion of senior NHS leaders who are clinicians. In the NLC's report referred to above, it was stated that only 5% of chief executives were doctors and 15% were clinicians of any sort. There were regional plans for a third of leaders on talent development programmes to be clinicians.[25]

24.28 The Royal Colleges have formed a Faculty of Medical Leadership, the purpose of which is:

> ... to promote the advancement of medical leadership, management and quality improvement at all stages of the medical career from medical student to medical director, for the benefit of patients.[26]

One of the Faculty's declared objectives is to: "advance medical management and leadership as a profession."[27]

24.29 There is little doubt that enhancement of the status of healthcare management and leadership as a profession is sorely needed. The gulf that still exists between some managers and some clinicians would be more bridgeable if there were a mutual perception of grounding as members of a profession, with all the ethical background that entails. It would be easier to develop a shared culture and harder for barriers between "them" and "us" to develop.

21 Nicholson T127.134
22 *The Foundation NLC Annual Report – First Year: Executive summary,* National Leadership Council, p9, www.dh.gov.uk/prod_consum_dh/groups/dh_digitalassets/@dh/@en/@abous/documents/digitalasset/dh_117363.pdf
23 Nicholson T127.135
24 Nicholson T127.136–137
25 *The Foundation NLC Annual Report – First Year: Executive summary,* National Leadership Council, p9, www.dh.gov.uk/prod_consum_dh/groups/dh_digitalassets/@dh/@en/@abous/documents/digitalasset/dh_117363.pdf
26 Please see the Faculty's website at: www.fmlm.ac.uk/about-us/purpose-and-objectives
27 www.fmlm.ac.uk/about-us/purpose-and-objectives

It would also encourage a wider range of potential candidates to aim their careers and personal development at achieving these essential positions in healthcare. That is something to which the Faculty can make a significant contribution, but it cannot do so on its own.

Development of the concept of leadership in the NHS

24.30   In an illuminating review offered to the Inquiry's leadership seminar, Dr Karen Lynas, the then Project Lead for the development of the NHS Leadership Academy and the NHS Top Leaders Programme, stated:

> *The national and local landscape for management and leadership development is prone to change and restructure as the architecture of the NHS changes, and has done so frequently over the last 10 years as successive national restructuring has occurred. Approaches such as the National Management Development Initiative have come and gone as the structures in place to support them go. These national initiatives are often underpinned by the Leadership Qualities Framework ... None of these programmes are mandated and none are pre-requisite for applying to or being appointed to management roles.*[28]

24.31   At the Seminar on leadership, Dr Lynas told the Inquiry of the need for leadership development:

> *Clinicians moving into first line management positions benefit hugely from management and leadership development. The need to successfully help clinicians, and indeed other professionals, transition into managerial and leadership roles, through the acquisition of more deeply held insights and approaches, adds to the case for leadership development beyond simply the acquisition of managerial "skills".*[29]

24.32   The evolution of the need for leadership development in the NHS has run in parallel with the change over time in the approach to the management of the system.[30]

24.33   Before 1979, hospitals were largely led by a team consisting of a senior doctor, a senior nurse and other professional staff, such as a treasurer. The administrator was then someone whose

28   Dr Karen Lynas *The Development and Training of Trust Leaders* (18 October 2011), paper delivered to the Inquiry Leadership Seminar, p2; www.midstaffspublicinquiry.com/sites/default/files/uploads/Karen_Lynas_paper.pdf

29   Dr Karen Lynas *The Development and Training of Trust Leaders, (*Paper for the Inquiry seminar on the development of Trust leaders on (18 October 2011), paper delivered to the Inquiry leadership seminar, pp5–6 www.midstaffspublicinquiry.com/sites/default/files/uploads/Karen_Lynas_paper.pdf

30   Dr Judith Smith and Professor Naomi Chambers *The Regulation and Development of NHS Managers: A discussion paper,* (19 October 2011), paper delivered to the Inquiry Leadership Seminar, pp2–3, www.midstaffspublicinquiry.com/sites/default/files/uploads/Judith_Smith_and_Naomi_Chambers_-_paper_2_0.pdf

duty it was to facilitate the work of the others in a form of consensus management, ensuring that clinical staff were resourced and supported.[31]

24.34 In 1983, following concerns about the effectiveness of this approach, Sir Roy Griffiths recommended a new management model, following his famous dictum:

> If Florence Nightingale was carrying her lamp through the corridors of the NHS today, she would almost certainly be searching for the people in charge.[32]

24.35 Sir Roy recommended that there should be a general manager with greater freedom to organise a structure to suit their needs, with a clear accountability structure, starting centrally and going down to unit level. Crucially, he also recommended that clinicians should be more closely involved in management decisions, and be given a management budget and administrative support.[33] However, as Dr Smith and Professor Chambers pointed out, this focusing of managerial accountability on the general manager had the potential of putting enormous strain on managers if they were going to be autocratic and challenge clinical decisions.

24.36 The introduction of FTs has accelerated the trend towards the autonomous board with a mixture of executive and non-executive directors led by a chair and a chief executive.

Leadership training support in the NHS

Institute in Healthcare Management

24.37 Following the Griffiths reforms, the Institute of Health Services Administrators renamed itself the Institute of Health Services Management. It is now the Institute of Healthcare Management. It is a professional body for NHS managers. Following Griffiths, it awarded a recognised qualification, the Diplomas in Health Services Management, which involved a three-year study programme and 12 public examinations. This was a required qualification for all aspiring senior NHS managers. The Institute also acted as a professional representative for managers and was a source for networking and professional conferences.

24.38 With the changes that occurred as a result of the move to an internal market in the 1990s, Dr Smith and Professor Chambers explained that the status and influence of the Institute appeared to decline. While it has continued to develop professional standards for

---

31 Dr Judith Smith and Professor Naomi Chambers *The Regulation and Development of NHS Managers: A discussion paper*, (19 October 2011), paper delivered to the Inquiry Leadership Seminar, p2, www.midstaffspublicinquiry.com/sites/default/files/uploads/Judith_Smith_and_Naomi_Chambers_-_paper_2_0.pdf
32 www.nhshistory.net/griffiths.html
33 Dr Judith Smith and Professor Naomi Chambers *The Regulation and development of NHS Managers: A discussion paper* (18 October 2011), paper delivered to the Inquiry Leadership Seminar, p4–5, www.midstaffspublicinquiry.com/sites/default/files/uploads/Judith_Smith_and_Naomi_Chambers_-_paper_2_0.pdf

development, management conduct and practice, it does not command the membership among senior NHS staff it used to.[34]

24.39 The Diploma was superseded by a variety of alternatives, such as the Management Education Syllabus and Open Learning initiative of the Institute, the funding of MBAs and bespoke leadership programmes.[35] A range of NHS organisations came and went, including the NHS Training Authority, a National Accelerated Development Programme, Regional Educational Development Groups, NHS Women's Unit, the NHS University, and the NHS Leadership Centre.

24.40 Dr Lynas explained that training and development resources existed at four levels in the NHS: individual, organisational, regional and national.[36]

24.41 At an individual level, staff may, at their discretion, undertake self-funded courses, such as the MBA or other postgraduate degree. In some cases, such efforts may be supported by their employers. Many professional bodies, such as the Royal College of Nursing (RCN) and the medical Royal Colleges, offer accredited leadership training through various external bodies, such as the Institute of Leadership and Management.

24.42 At organisational level, there is similarly a wide variety of practice and commitment to supporting management development. There is no mandated standard requiring a particular level of support to be provided. Similarly, there is no standard requirement for qualifications to attain eligibility for management posts. Dr Lynas considered that the systems adopted at this level were limited compared with what was offered in the private sector. One difficulty faced is that before effective training is offered, an assessment of the individual's needs is required. In the absence of a robust diagnostic tool, this is difficult to provide locally in a cost-effective fashion.

24.43 At regional level, the strategic health authorities (SHAs) are responsible for leadership development strategy. This could involve commissioning external programmes. Much of this work has been led by the NHS Institute for Innovation and Improvement, but run by the SHAs. The Inquiry was told that three SHAs financed and ran leadership academies with membership contributions from other NHS organisations. Other SHAs undertook their own activity in this field. There was a wide variety in the breadth and depth of what was offered.

---

34 Dr Judith Smith and Professor Naomi Chambers *The Regulation and Development of NHS Managers: A discussion paper*, (19 October 2011), paper delivered to the Inquiry Leadership Seminar, p4, www.midstaffspublicinquiry.com/sites/default/files/uploads/Judith_Smith_and_Naomi_Chambers_-_paper_2_0.pdf

35 Dr Judith Smith and Professor Naomi Chambers *The Regulation and Development of NHS Managers: A discussion paper*, (19 October 2011), paper delivered to the Inquiry Leadership Seminar, p3, www.midstaffspublicinquiry.com/sites/default/files/uploads/Judith_Smith_and_Naomi_Chambers_-_paper_2_0.pdf

36 Dr Karen Lynas *The Development and Training of Trust Leaders,* (Paper for the Inquiry seminar on the development of Trust leaders on (18 October 2011), paper delivered to the Inquiry leadership seminar, pp2–3 www.midstaffspublicinquiry.com/sites/default/files/uploads/Karen_Lynas_paper.pdf

24.44 At national level, leadership development work was led mainly by the NHS Institute for Innovation and Improvement and the NLC.

National Leadership Council

24.45 The NLC was set up in April 2009 with the objective of ensuring that the system supported high quality leadership and to challenge where this did not occur. Its activities included:

- Ensuring the delivery of leadership commitments in *High Quality Care of All*;
- Setting out clear, agreed priorities for culture change and leadership across the NHS;
- Producing an annual report featuring examples of inspiring leadership and best practice;
- Ensuring standards of leadership and leadership development, including accreditation.[37]

24.46 In the NLC's first annual report, Sir David Nicholson said:

Leadership does not happen by accident. I have long held the view that developing leadership has been the missing link in the NHS reform story. Unlike other industries and world-class organisations, the NHS has not had a systematic approach to supporting the leaders of today and developing leaders for tomorrow. We have started on a journey to do just that, via the National Leadership Council and the efforts of many people in regions and individual employers.[38]

24.47 He identified the needs of "leadership for quality" as not being:

... about policing the boundaries of individual organisations. It is about putting the interests of patients and the public first, working across boundaries with partners and other organisations, particularly around improving patient pathways.[39]

24.48 Among other actions, the NLC established a clinical leadership framework to identify leadership competences for clinicians and to include leadership training in undergraduate and postgraduate curricula.[40] It promoted clinical leadership fellowships designed to give interested clinicians an opportunity to develop leadership skills. It developed assurance of the quality of senior managers. It commissioned clinical and board leadership development programmes, and the NHS Top Leader programme to develop a supply of people capable of filling leadership roles.

---

37 DN/35 WS0000068431
38 *The Foundation NLC Annual Report – First Year: Executive summary,* National Leadership Council, p3, www.dh.gov.uk/prod_consum_dh/groups/dh_digitalassets/@dh/@en/@abous/documents/digitalasset/dh_117363.pdf
39 *The Foundation NLC Annual Report – First Year: Executive summary,* National Leadership Council, p3, www.dh.gov.uk/prod_consum_dh/groups/dh_digitalassets/@dh/@en/@abous/documents/digitalasset/dh_117363.pdf
40 *Clinical Leadership Competency Framework,* 2011 National Leadership Council, NHS institute for Innovation and Improvement, www.leadershipacademy.nhs.uk/develop-your-leadership-skills/leadership-framework/the-framework-overview

24.49 In 2010, the NLC commissioned the development of a leadership framework:

> *... to create a single over-arching leadership framework for all health staff groups to enable them to understand their progression as a leader and to support fostering and developing talent.*[41]

24.50 The NLC has now been wound up and replaced by the Leadership Academy, which has continued much of its work.

Leadership Academy

24.51 The Leadership Academy is, at the time of writing, still in the early stages of its development. It is led by a programme board which is intended to bring together members of the Academy team and representatives of the NHS Commissioning Board, Health Education England, employers' representatives, the NHS Trust Development Authority, and Public Health England. Currently, the Academy is run by a Managing Director and an Interim Deputy Managing Director/Head of Programmes.[42]

24.52 The Academy declares that it has four key areas of work:

- Developing and embedding a common vision for health leadership;
- Leading the way in leadership development for a new health system;
- Supporting local leadership development;
- Developing and delivering national leadership programmes.[43]

24.53 Among its work programmes are:

- Clinical leadership fellowships, of which 80 have been awarded this year. The programme aims to give fellows the opportunity to develop leadership skills through a learning and experiential programme on a part-time basis in conjunction with their existing clinical roles. The fellows work towards a postgraduate certificate in leadership and service improvement;
- Training for FT governors, the contract of which has been awarded to the Foundation Trust Network;

---

41 www.leadershipacademy.nhs.uk/develop-your-leadership-skills/leadership-framework/the-framework-overview/60-develop-your-leadership-skills/leadership-framework/the-framework/10
42 www.leadershipacademy.nhs.uk/about-us/whos-who
43 www.leadershipacademy.nhs.uk

Chapter 24 Leadership in healthcare

- The NHS Graduate Management Training Scheme, which is open to graduates and current NHS employees, and has specialist courses in general, financial, human resources and health informatics management.[44] The scheme was training 150 graduates in 2012;[45]
- The NHS Top Leaders programme aims to encourage and develop candidates who seek more senior roles in the NHS through a range of development options tailored to meet individual needs. Access to this programme is currently through nomination by the SHAs.[46]

24.54 The Academy has published a Leadership Framework, which is considered below.

Faculty of Medical Leadership and Mangement

24.55 This Faculty is being developed by the Academy of Medical Royal Colleges. The Faculty aims to:

promote the advancement of medical leadership, management and quality improvement at all stages of the medical career for the benefit of patients.[47]

24.56 Professor Sir Bruce Keogh clearly approved of this development and felt it would encourage the growth of medical engagement in leadership roles:

I've been exercised by the fact that there are clearly groups of doctors around the country who are interested in medical management and leadership, but how do we get ordinary doctors to become exposed to that?

So the Academy of Medical Royal Colleges have started to develop a faculty of medical leadership, which is about to become operational, which is currently being led by one of the SHA medical directors, a Dr Peter Lees, and I think that's going to provide a pretty unique opportunity for younger doctors and older ones to be exposed to medical management, if you like.[48]

Leadership framework

24.57 In 2011, the Leadership Academy published the leadership framework that had initially been commissioned by its predecessor, the NLC.[49]

---

44   www.nhsgraduates.co.uk/Default.aspx
45   www.leadershipacademy.nhs.uk/news-and-newsletters/526-sir-david-nicholson-and-nhs-leadership-academy-welcome-2012-cohort-for-the-graduate-management-training-scheme
46   www.leadershipacademy.nhs.uk/areas-of-work/national-programmes/nhs-top-leaders
47   www.fmlm.ac.uk/
48   Keogh T123.185–186
49   *Leadership Framework* (2011), NHS Leadership Academy, www.leadershipacademy.nhs.uk/develop-your-leadership-skills/leadership-framework/supporting-tools-and-documents/documents-to-download

24.58 The framework was the result of widespread consultation within the NHS and representative professional bodies, but not, according to the list of acknowledged contributors in the full framework document, any patient representative groups.[50] It is possible that patients were represented at consultation events.

24.59 It emphasises, as a starting point, the fundamental principles and the core values in the NHS Constitution.[51]

24.60 The framework is designed to be applied at all levels, from individuals working in teams at the front-line to organisational and system leaders. It based itself on a model containing seven domains:

Figure 24.1: The model for the leadership framework

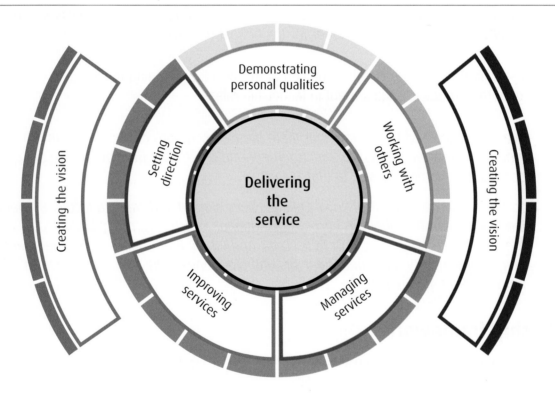

24.61 It was said to represent, "the foundation of leadership behaviour that all staff should aspire to" and to be built on the existing leadership frameworks used by different staff groups.[52]

---

50 See *Leadership Framework* (2011), NHS Leadership Academy, pp55–56 for a full list of acknowledged contributors, www.leadershipacademy.nhs.uk/develop-your-leadership-skills/leadership-framework/supporting-tools-and-documents/documents-to-download

51 *Leadership Framework* (2011), NHS Leadership Academy, p7, www.leadershipacademy.nhs.uk/develop-your-leadership-skills/leadership-framework/supporting-tools-and-documents/documents-to-download

52 *Leadership Framework: A summary* (2011), Leadership Academy, p3, www.leadershipacademy.nhs.uk/areas-of-work/supporting-local-capability/commissioners-and-gps/commissioning/doc_download/9-leadership-framework-a-summary

Chapter 24 Leadership in healthcare

It was considered that, to improve safety and quality of services, it was essential that staff were competent in each of the five core domains in this model.

24.62 Given the events at the Trust, of particular interest in this model are the domains of demonstrating personal quality and improving services. These are set out below.

Demonstrating personal qualities

24.63 Within this domain, effectiveness must be demonstrated in:

- Developing self awareness;
- Managing yourself;
- Continuing personal development;
- Acting with integrity.[53]

24.64 With regard to integrity, competent leaders are said to behave, "in an open, honest and ethical manner," and to:

- *Uphold personal and professional ethics and values, taking into account the values of the organisation and respecting the culture, beliefs and abilities of individuals;*
- *Communicate effectively with individuals appreciating their social, cultural, religious and ethnic backgrounds and their age, gender and abilities;*
- *Value, respect and promote equality and diversity;*
- *Take appropriate action if ethics and values are compromised.*[54]

24.65 The contextual indicators for compliance include acting in an open, honest and inclusive manner; behaviours said to show that an individual is not yet demonstrating achievement in this domain include situations where he or she "Demonstrates behaviours that are counter to core values of openness, inclusiveness, honesty and equality".[55]

Improving services

24.66 The domain for improving services includes the following requirements:

> *Effective leadership requires individuals to make a real difference to people's health by delivering high quality services and by developing improvements to services. To do so, they must demonstrate effectiveness in:*

---

53 *Leadership Framework,* (2011), NHS Leadership Academy, p13, www.leadershipacademy.nhs.uk/develop-your-leadership-skills/leadership-framework/supporting-tools-and-documents/documents-to-download

54 *Leadership Framework* (2011), NHS Leadership Academy, p17, www.leadershipacademy.nhs.uk/develop-your-leadership-skills/leadership-framework/supporting-tools-and-documents/documents-to-download

55 *Leadership Framework* (2011), NHS Leadership Academy, p17–18, www.leadershipacademy.nhs.uk/develop-your-leadership-skills/leadership-framework/supporting-tools-and-documents/documents-to-download

- *Ensuring patient safety;*
- *Critically evaluating;*
- *Encouraging improvement and innovation;*
- *Facilitating transformation.*[56]

24.67   Patient safety is dealt with in the following way:

> *Leaders **ensure patient safety**: assessing and managing the risk to patients associated with service developments, balancing economic considerations with the need for patient safety.*
>
> *Competent leaders:*
>
> - *Identify and quantify the risk to patients using information from a range of sources;*
> - *Use evidence, both positive and negative, to identify options;*
> - *Use systematic ways of assessing and minimising risk;*
> - *Monitor the effects and outcomes of change.*[57]

24.68   The contextual indicators for ensuring patient safety at each organisational level are listed in tabular form:[58]

Table 24.1: The leadership framework's contextual indicators for ensuring patient safety

Element	1 Own Practice/ Immediate Team	2 Whole Service/Across Teams	3 Across Services/ Wider Organisation	4 Whole Organisation/ Wider Healthcare System
4.1 Ensuring Patient Safety	Puts the safety of patients and service users at the heart of their thinking in delivering and improving services. Takes action to report or rectify shortfalls in patient safety.	Reviews practice to improve standards of patient safety and minimise risk. Monitors the impact of service change on patient safety.	Develops and maintains audit and risk management systems which will drive service improvement and patient safety.	Creates a culture that prioritises the health, safety and security of patients and service users. Delivers assurance that patient safety underpins policies, processes and systems.

24.69   It was clearly the intention of this document, prepared and published as it was following the events at the Trust and following the lead of *High Quality Care for All,* the final report of Lord

---

56   *Leadership Framework* (2011), NHS Leadership Academy, p31, www.leadershipacademy.nhs.uk/develop-your-leadership-skills/leadership-framework/supporting-tools-and-documents/documents-to-download

57   *Leadership Framework* (2011), NHS Leadership Academy, p32, www.leadershipacademy.nhs.uk/develop-your-leadership-skills/leadership-framework/supporting-tools-and-documents/documents-to-download

58   *Leadership Framework* (2011), NHS Leadership Academy, p32 and p64, www.leadershipacademy.nhs.uk/develop-your-leadership-skills/leadership-framework/supporting-tools-and-documents/documents-to-download

Darzi's review of the NHS, to stress the importance of patient safety. However, while including it in a domain for improving services may be logical, it appears to make patient safety one of many requirements, rather than the pre-eminent responsibility of all in the service and, in particular, of leaders. Referring to the need to "balance" economic considerations with safety considerations might suggest to some that there is parity between the two.

24.70   Therefore, the framework could be improved by increasing the emphasis given to patient safety in the thinking of all in the health service. There are no doubt many ways this could be done, including by the creation of a separate domain for managing safety, or by defining the service to be delivered as a safe and effective service.

Delivery of training and support

24.71   It will be apparent from the brief descriptions given above that there are many different forms of training and support available and that progressive steps are being taken to offer more uniform standards to be attained through training. This is of necessity an evolutionary process that is, as yet, far from complete. The delivery and uptake of leadership training is variable and, therefore, potentially inconsistent. Dr Smith told the Inquiry, in relation to the training of directors:

> ... training and development of non-executives and of boards I think is broadly accepted to be something that is important, certainly within the health service, and quite a lot of attention has been given to that over the years. I mean, how that actually happens to some extent varies according to the region or indeed the local area, but I think essentially it tends to work out it's, for a particular organisation, the chair, you would expect, usually to take a lead in thinking about the training needs of the particular board and of the non-executives. Indeed, you would expect the chair to carry out appraisal and development conversations, interviews, with certainly their non-executive members.[59]

24.72   She said that training had variously been made available by SHAs, the Appointments Commission and Monitor among others, and that:

> ... in a sense it is quite diverse but I think there's a general acceptance there should be training and development, and there's quite ... a lot available, but it is ultimately going to be the decision of a particular board, particularly through it is [sic] chair, the chair working with chief executive to make a decision as to what it is they actually want to put in place that makes sense for their organisation.[60]

---

59   Smith T6.35–36
60   Smith T6.36–37

Care Quality Commission standards

24.73 The CQC's *Essential standards* and the underlying regulations include some requirements with regard to management. Regulation 5, which applies where a provider is a body other than an individual or a partnership, states that the provider must nominate an individual who is a director, manager or secretary of the body and who is responsible for supervising the management of the carrying on of the regulated activity. The nominated person must be:

> *(a) of good character;*
>
> *(b) physically and mentally fit to supervise the management of the carrying on of the regulated activity and [have] the necessary qualifications, skills and experience to do so; and*
>
> *(c) able to supply to the registered person, or arrange for the availability of, the information specified in Schedule 3.*[61]

24.74 Outcome 23 provides that:

> *People who use services have their needs met because the management is supervised by an appropriate person.*
>
> *This is because providers who comply with the regulations will:*
>
> - *Have a nominated individual who:*
>   - *is of good character*
>   - *is physically and mentally able to perform their role*
>   - *has the necessary qualifications, skills and experience to supervise the management of the regulated activity.*[62]

24.75 The prompts for outcome 23 are:

> - *Has been notified in writing to the CQC.*
> - *Is of good character as they are honest, reliable and trustworthy.*
> - *Is physically and mentally able to do the job, with a plan of support that sets out any reasonable adjustments where necessary. This means they:*
>   - *Do not present a risk to people who use services because of any illness or medical condition they have;*
>   - *Are not placed at risk by the work they will do because of any illness or medical condition they have.*

---

61   Health and Social Care Act 2008 (Regulated Activities) Regulations 2010 [SI 2010/781], Reg 5
62   CQC00110000232, *Essential Standards of Quality and Safety* (March 2010), CQC, p181

- *Has been subject to the necessary checks as described in Schedule 3 of the Health and Social Care Act 2008 (Regulated Activities) Regulations 2010, so that the provider is assured that the nominated individual is suitable for their role.[63]*
- *Has been subject to a check that they are registered with the Independent Safeguarding Authority:*
  - *where they are undertaking a Safeguarding Vulnerable Groups Act 2006 "regulated activity" or "controlled activity"; and*
  - *are required to be registered under the Scheme's phasing-in arrangements;*
- *Has their qualifications, knowledge and skills updated on a regular basis;*
- *Has an awareness and knowledge of diversity and human rights and applies in practice the competencies to support people's diverse needs and human rights;*
- *Is aware of the services' policies, procedures, legislation and standards;*
- *Knows who they are able to contact when expert advice is needed;*
- *Is able to respond to any registered manager requests for resources in order to meet essential standards of quality and safety;*
- *Is able to empower the registered manager, where one is employed, and appropriately delegate authority to them so that they can effectively run the service on a day-to-day basis.[64]*

24.76 This standard does not refer to any director or other leader apart from the nominated individual except for the limited circumstances in which a registered manager is required in an NHS provider. The prompts refer to evidence of qualifications, to updating of knowledge and skills, but not to any requirement for the manager to be running the organisation effectively. There is no outcome relating to the effectiveness of the board as a whole.

Monitor

24.77 Monitor publishes a *Code of Governance*, last updated with effect from April 2010.[65] Although the Code is non-mandatory, FTs are required to disclose how they implement its principles in their annual report and to confirm that they comply with the code, or, if not, provide an explanation for this. The Code also suggests that FTs' annual reports should contain a description of the skills and experience of each director.[66] It advises that care should be taken in the appointment of directors to ensure they have the relevant skills and complement those of existing directors.[67]

---

63 The required information includes a criminal record certificate, documentation of qualifications, evidence of mental and physical fitness, and a full employment history with a satisfactory explanation of any gaps.
64 CQC00110000232–33, *Essential Standards of Quality and Safety* (March 2010), CQC, p181–182
65 MON000500000002, *The NHS Foundation Trust: Code of governance* (March 2010), Monitor. Although the Code appears on Monitor's web site (www.monitor-nhsft.gov.uk/home/news-events-and-publications/our-publications/browse-category/guidance-foundation-trusts/mandat-3) in the "mandatory guidance" category, it is, with the exception of some disclosure requirements, described as non-mandatory guidance.
66 MON000500000013, *The NHS Foundation Trust: Code of governance*, (March 2010), Monitor, para A.3.4
67 MON000500000016, *The NHS Foundation Trust: Code of governance*, (March 2010), Monitor, para C.1

24.78 With regard to personal development, the Code requires directors to receive appropriate induction and regularly to update their knowledge and skills.[68] It is the chairman's responsibility to oversee this. New chief executives and chairs of FTs are required to attend induction seminars run by Monitor (or to justify why their attendance is not required).[69]

24.79 An FT board, and in the case of the non-executives, the board of governors, is encouraged to undertake rigorous appraisal of its performance, collectively and individually, and include in the annual report how this is undertaken. The *Code of Governance* states that:

> *The individual evaluation of directors should aim to show whether each director continues to contribute effectively, to demonstrate commitment and has the relevant skills for the role (including commitment of time for board and committee meetings and any other duties) going forwards. The chairman should act on the results of the performance evaluation by recognising the strengths and addressing the weaknesses of the board, identifying individual and collective development needs and, where appropriate, proposing new members be appointed to the board or seeking the resignation of directors.[70]*

24.80 Monitor assesses the compliance of FTs with the terms of authorisation. It does so through following a compliance framework.[71] Initially it requires information to be provided by FTs on a range of matters in annual and exception reports and in-year submissions. The material through which governance is monitored includes the receipt of third-party reports, information about service performance failures to comply with board statements, and the annual plan.

24.81 An FT board is also required to submit statements to Monitor confirming compliance with governance standards, including annual confirmation that:

> *14. The board is satisfied that all executive and non-executive directors have the appropriate qualifications, experience and skills to discharge their functions effectively, including setting strategy, monitoring and managing performance and risks, and ensuring management capacity and capability.*
>
> *15. The board is satisfied that: the management team has the capacity, capability and experience necessary to deliver the annual plan; and the management structure in place is adequate to deliver the annual plan.[72]*

---

68 MON000500000020, *The NHS Foundation trust: Code of Governance*, (March 2010), Monitor, para D.1
69 *Compliance Framework 2012* (30 March 2012), Monitor, p11 para 30
     www.monitor-nhsft.gov.uk/home/browse-category/guidance-foundation-trusts/mandatory-guidance/compliance-framework-2012/13
70 MON000500000022, *The NHS Foundation Trust: Code of governance* (March 2010), Monitor, para D.2
71 The current version of which is the *Compliance Framework 2012* (30 March 2012), Monitor,
     www.monitor-nhsft.gov.uk/home/browse-category/guidance-foundation-trusts/mandatory-guidance/compliance-framework-2012/13
72 *Compliance Framework 2012* (30 March 2012), Monitor, Appendix C3 page 59 www.monitor-nhsft.gov.uk/home/browse-category/
     guidance-foundation-trusts/mandatory-guidance/compliance-framework-2012/13

24.82   While in the first instance Monitor will rely on board statements made for this purpose, where there is evidence that a board has failed to discharge its functions effectively it reserves the right to "explore the basis" of the statement.[73]

24.83   Thus Monitor's powers of intervention on a finding of a significant breach of the terms of authorisation include powers to remove directors and governors and to appoint interim replacements. It exercises such powers by issuing a direction on the basis of the information in its possession. There is no requirement of any form of due process before such an intervention, which, of course, may need to be undertaken urgently in order to protect patients and the public interest. Monitor's powers in this regard do not extend to lower levels of leader or manager, or, in respect of board directors, to take any action which would lead to their disqualification from obtaining other such roles in an existing FT or elsewhere in the healthcare sector.[74]

24.84   Under the new reforms Monitor will be issuing licences to all providers of NHS-funded care (whether or not they are FTs). It is their stated intention to continue to focus on requiring good leadership and strong financial governance.[75]

24.85   In its formal consultation document on the licensing structure, Monitor has included in the proposed licensing conditions a requirement that directors and governors be fit and proper persons. In the case of those applying for a licence, the applicant will have to confirm that their directors and governors are fit and proper persons.[76]

---

73   *Compliance Framework 2012* (30 March 2012), Monitor, p21 para 70
       www.monitor-nhsft.gov.uk/home/browse-category/guidance-foundation-trusts/mandatory-guidance/compliance-framework-2012/13
74   In authorising an organisation as an FT, Monitor is able to assess the make-up of the board and could refuse an application on the basis of the competence of fitness of proposed directors.
75   Monitor's main role when exercising its new functions will be to "protect and promote the interests of people who use health care services by promoting the provision of services which is economic, efficient and effective, and which maintains or improves the quality of the services". Licences will be issued automatically to FTs. See *Introduction to Monitor's Future Role* (20 June 2012), Monitor, www.monitor-nhsft.gov.uk/monitors-new-role
76   *The new NHS Provider Licence: Consultation document* (31 July 2012), Monitor www.monitor-nhsft.gov.uk/sites/default/files/The%20 new%20NHS%20provider%20licence%20consultation%20document%20final%20-%20310712%20PDF_0.pdf

24.86 The proposed condition is recited in the text box below.[77]

---

1. If the Licensee is an NHS Foundation Trust, the Licensee shall ensure that no person who is an unfit person may become or continue as a Governor.

2. The Licensee shall not appoint as a Director any person who is an unfit person.

3. The Licensee shall ensure that its contracts of service with its Directors contain a provision permitting summary termination in the event of a Director being or becoming an unfit person, and that it enforces those provisions promptly upon discovering any Director to be an unfit person.

4. In this Condition an unfit person is:

   (a) an individual;

      (i) who has been adjudged bankrupt or whose estate has been sequestrated and (in either case) has not been discharged; or

      (ii) who has made a composition or arrangement with, or granted a trust deed for, his creditors and has not been discharged in respect of it; or

      (iii) who within the preceding five years has been convicted in the British Islands of any offence and a sentence of imprisonment (whether suspended or not) for a period of not less than three months (without the option of a fine) was imposed on him; or

      (iv) who is subject to an unexpired disqualification order made under the Company Directors' Disqualification Act 1986; or

   (b) a body corporate, or a body corporate with a parent body corporate:

      (i) where one or more of the Directors of the body corporate or its parent body corporate is an unfit person under the provisions of paragraphs (a) of this paragraph of this Condition, or

      (ii) in relation to which a voluntary arrangement is proposed under section 1 of the Insolvency Act 1986, or

      (iii) which has a receiver (including an administrative receiver within the meaning of section 29(2) of the 1986 Act) appointed for the whole or any material part of its assets or undertaking, or

      (iv) which has an administrator appointed to manage its affairs, business and property in accordance with Schedule B1 to the 1986 Act, or

      (v) which passes any resolution for winding up, or

      (vi) which becomes subject to an order of a Court for winding up.

---

77   *The New NHS Provider Licence: Consultation document* (31 July 2012), Monitor, p78–79, www.monitor-nhsft.gov.uk/sites/default/files/
      The%20new%20NHS%20provider%20licence%20consultation%20document%20final%20-%20310712%20PDF_0.pdf

24.87 The precise scope of the fitness requirement is a matter for the consultation.[78] As currently drafted, the condition is limited to a consideration of formal "fitness" in terms of the absence of criminal convictions, bankruptcy and disqualification as a company director. However, Monitor is considering whether its test should incorporate an obligation to comply with the code of conduct proposed by the Council for Healthcare Regulatory Excellence (CHRE), also subject to consultation, or the code of the Institute of Healthcare Management.[79] One matter of potential concern expressed is the burden such a test might place on organisations not currently subject to similar standards.

Practice in other countries

24.88 At its Leadership seminar Dr Smith and Professor Chambers offered the Inquiry an overview of the position in other countries.[80]

France

24.89 In France, in common with other areas of public administration, to be eligible for a post of hospital director or assistance director a specified rigorous training programme must be completed.

The Netherlands

24.90 The Netherlands has developed training in a similar fashion to the UK.

Canada

24.91 Canada has a College of Health Leaders.[81] It is a member organisation that organises qualifications, support and development for health service leaders of all backgrounds. It offers a qualification as a Certified Health Service Executive, and awards fellowships to distinguished members. It has a Code of Ethics, which includes an obligation to "strive to provide high quality services within the resources available", and to "communicate truthfully and avoid creating misleading expectations."[82]

---

78 *The New NHS Provider Licence: Consultation document* (31 July 2012), Monitor, p3, p14, www.monitor-nhsft.gov.uk/sites/default/files/ The%20new%20NHS%20provider%20licence%20consultation%20document%20final%20-%20310712%20PDF_0.pdf
79 *The New NHS Provider Licence: Consultation document* (31 July 2012), Monitor pp14–16, www.monitor-nhsft.gov.uk/sites/default/files/ The%20new%20NHS%20provider%20licence%20consultation%20document%20final%20-%20310712%20PDF_0.pdf,; for reference to these Codes see *values and standards chapter*
80 Dr Judith Smith and Professor Naomi Chambers *The Regulation and Development of NHS Managers: A discussion paper,* (19 October 2011), paper delivered to the Inquiry Leadership Seminar, pp6–8, www.midstaffspublicinquiry.com/sites/default/files/uploads/Judith_Smith_and_Naomi_Chambers_-_paper_2_0.pdf
81 Previously known as the College of Health Service Executives. www.cchl-ccls.ca
82 *Code of Ethics for Members of the Canadian College of Health Leaders,* Canadian College of Health Leaders, www.cchl-ccls.ca/assets/ethics/CodeEthics.pdf

24.92 Members are expected to report to the College any member they have reasonable grounds to believe has contravened the Code, and to perform an annual self-assessment and attest to compliance with the Code.

Australia

24.93 There is a similar organisation in Australia, the Australasian College of Health Service Management.[83] It too has a Code of Ethics, albeit briefer than the Canadian model. It is worth quoting in full:

> *Members of the Australasian College of Health Service Management shall:*
>
> - *Undertake their duties in the Health Service in an efficient, proper and responsible manner, having special regard for the well being of the consumers of the service.*
> - *Support their colleagues and other health service managers as required and appropriate by providing assistance to other individuals and organisations.*
> - *Contribute to the leadership of the organisation by recognising and developing the inherent skills of all health workers in order to achieve efficient and effective services.*
> - *Seek to improve personal skills, knowledge and experience by undertaking appropriate study and being involved in the College's Continuing Professional Development programme.*
> - *Demonstrate a commitment to the development of other health service managers and interested persons in other health disciplines.*
> - *Ensure that their position is used fairly and appropriately in a manner which must be neither to their personal advantage nor unjustly to the disadvantage of an employee or colleague.*[84]

24.94 Membership entails compliance with certain CPD requirements. The College also runs a national accreditation programme for health management courses.

New Zealand

24.95 New Zealand, on the other hand, has a statutory basis for standards and regulation of the management of healthcare delivery. There is a statutory Code of Health and Disability Services Consumers' Rights.[85] The Code includes rights to:

- Be treated with respect;
- Dignity and independence;

---

83 Previously named the Australian College of Health Service Executives, and before that the Australian College of Health Service Administrators, www.achsm.org.au/about-us/history-of-achsm

84 *Code of Conduct,* Australasian College of Health Service Management, www.achsm.org.au/about-us/code-of-ethics

85 *The Health and Disability Commissioner's Code of Health and Disability Services Consumers' Rights Regulations* (1 July 1996), Health and Disability Commissioner, www.hdc.org.nz/the-act-code/the-code-of-rights

Chapter 24 Leadership in healthcare

- Services of an appropriate standard;
- Effective communication;
- Be fully informed;
- Make an informed choice and give informed consent;
- Complain.

24.96   The right to services of an appropriate standard includes the right to the provision of services with reasonable care and skill, in a manner consistent with the patient's needs, and in a manner minimising the potential harm to the consumer and optimising their quality of life.[86] A breach of the Code found by the Commissioner can result in proceedings brought by or on behalf of the aggrieved person before the Human Rights Review Tribunal, which may award a remedy including a declaration and compensation.[87] There is also a statutory post within the Commissioner's office of Director of Proceedings, who has the power to assist complainants and intervene in relevant proceedings, and to take action before the Human Rights Review Tribunal against healthcare providers (including managers), where there has been a breach of the Code.[88]

24.97   The definition of "healthcare providers" who are obliged to fulfil the rights laid down in the Code, includes those who are "in charge" of providing health services, health practitioners, and any other person providing or holding himself or herself out to provide health services to the public. In at least one case, to which the Inquiry's attention was drawn by Dr Smith and Professor Chambers, findings were made personally against a patient service manager found responsible for breaching the Code in relation to the adequacy of staffing.[89] In the same case, management deficiencies of a clinical director and a nurse team leader were also found to amount to breaches of the Code. The Commissioner ruled that his jurisdiction included non-clinician managers. Recommendations were made that each apologise directly to the complainant, and review their practice. There was also a recommendation that the professional disciplinary body review the competence of the clinical director. The employer was recommended to review and supervise the practice of the patient service manager. The Ministry of Health was recommended to review progress on implementation of recommendations and report to the Commissioner.

86   *The Health and Disability Commissioner's Code of Health and Disability Services Consumers' Rights Regulations* (1 July 1996), Health and Disability Commissioner, Right 4, www.hdc.org.nz/the-act–code/the-code-of-rights
87   *Health and Disability Commissioner Act 1994* [as amended] [New Zealand], Part 4, sections 50–58, www.legislation.govt.nz/act/public/1994/0088/latest/DLM333584.html
88   *Health and Disability Commissioner Act 1994* [as amended] [New Zealand], Part 4, sections 40–49, www.legislation.govt.nz/act/public/1994/0088/latest/DLM333584.html
89   Dr Judith Smith and Professor Naomi Chambers *The Regulation and Development of NHS Managers: A discussion paper,* (19 October 2011), paper delivered to the Inquiry Leadership Seminar, pp6–8, www.midstaffspublicinquiry.com/sites/default/files/uploads/Judith_Smith_and_Naomi_Chambers_-_paper_2_0.pdf *Southland District Health Board Mental Health Services February–March 2001: A report of the Health and Disability Commissioner* (October 2002) Health and Disability Commissioner, www.hdc.org.nz/media/30157/southland%20dhb%20mental%20health%20services.pdf

24.98 Therefore, while many cases considered by the Commissioner appear to involve either the deficiencies of an organisation corporately or individual doctors and nurses, this is not always the case. The powers to bring an individual to account appear to be considerable.

Summary

24.99 This very brief survey of some other countries suggests that there are a variety of approaches that can be divided into four categories:

- Employer supported self-improvement;
- Collegiate professionalisation via supported qualifications and ethical codes;
- Regulatory requirements for qualification;
- Obligations enforced by sanctions.

24.100 These approaches are not, of course, mutually exclusive, and some systems summarised include elements of more than one of them.

Accountability for leaders and managers

The absence of accountability

24.101 The experience of Stafford shows that there is no system of accountability for leaders or managers of healthcare providers that is uniformly fair to the individuals concerned and that satisfies the public. While the compromise arrangements made with Mr Yeates may have satisfied the interest of the Trust in "moving on", neither the individual nor the public were given an opportunity to have it established whether Mr Yeates had acted in a manner rendering him unfit to hold the post of an executive officer. There was nothing to prevent Mr Yeates applying to another healthcare organisation offering him a similar post elsewhere. The same would apply to any executive or non-executive director who was allegedly responsible for a serious systems failure in service.

24.102 In their closing submissions, Action Against Medical Accidents (AvMA) offered a helpful summary of what is required for effective accountability:

> ... establishing accountability should be seen as a process to avoid failings rather than simply ensuring that there is someone to blame when things go wrong. This process consists of five important elements:
>
> - Clear identification of individual responsibility;
> - Provision of training, support and guidance to the individual;
> - Availability of transparent information with respect to fulfilment of that responsibility and established methods of monitoring this information;

- *Providing an appropriate acknowledgement and explanation with respect to failings;*
- *Where necessary and appropriate, pursuit of necessary restrictions or sanctions with respect to that individual, including disciplinary/employment proceedings or regulatory investigation.*[90]

24.103 It is necessary to examine the extent to which the system offers this form of holistic accountability, backed by appropriate support, to leaders and managers.

Professional standards and status of leaders and managers

24.104 As has been seen, NHS leaders are increasingly and properly regarded as professionals: they seek professionally relevant qualifications and there are, or at least have been, professional representative bodies to which they belong. Most importantly, they are responsible for the running of highly complex organisations on which the public rely for their safety. Yet, unless they are registered on a healthcare professional register, they are subject to no compulsory code of conduct or professional disciplinary process.

24.105 In spite of the vital role NHS leaders and managers play in the running of the NHS and in healthcare generally, they are not held in high regard. The King's Fund report gave examples of this.[91]

Manager's Code of Conduct

24.106 As noted in *Chapter 21: Values and standards*, there is a Code of Conduct for NHS Managers, developed in part as a result of the recommendations of the Bristol Inquiry. Although incorporated into at least some managers' contracts of employment, the evidence does not suggest that it is a document much referred to by employers and, in any event, it is not subject to sanction by a separate professional body.

Previous reports

The Bristol Inquiry

24.107 As noted above, the Bristol Inquiry recommended that managers should be subject to professional disciplinary sanction by an independent regulatory body in a manner comparable to doctors and other clinicians. This was not taken forward.

---

90 CLO000000426, *Closing Submissions on behalf of Action Against Medical Accidents*, para 232
91 *The Future of Leadership and Management in the NHS: No more heroes* (2011), King's Fund Commission on Leadership in the NHS, p1–2 www.kingsfund.org.uk/sites/files/kf/future-of-leadership-and-management-nhs-may-2011-kings-fund.pdf

High Quality Care for All

24.108 *High Quality Care for All* accepted that:

> *Whilst the overwhelming majority of NHS managers meet high professional standards every day, a very small number of senior leaders sometimes demonstrate performance or conduct that lets down their staff, their organisations and the patients that they serve.*

24.109 It was not considered that a regulatory body of the type recommended by Professor Sir Ian Kennedy in the Bristol Inquiry was required, but it was stated that the Department of Health (DH) would work with stakeholders:

> *... to ensure that there are fair and effective arrangements to prevent poorly performing leaders from moving on to other NHS organisations inappropriately. While an enhanced Code of Conduct for managers will underpin this, we will consider whether more effective recruitment procedures or a more formal system of assuring suitability for future employment would provide more effective and proportionate safeguards.*[92]

24.110 The report concluded that steps were required to prevent poor performance by managers and to allay public concern about this.

Assuring the quality of senior NHS managers

24.111 The DH commissioned an advisory group chaired by Ian Dalton to consider the issue in relation to senior NHS managers. The group in turn commissioned research from PriceWaterhouseCoopers (PwC) in June 2009. Following extensive contact with stakeholders and research on practice internationally, PwC reported a number of relevant conclusions:

- Generic managers were rarely regulated in their own right, as opposed to by reference to a professional status, as in the case of accountants, lawyers and doctors. No obvious ideal solution had been identified.
- The UK and many other countries had professional organisations which published standards of practice and had development frameworks.
- Many respondents thought there was scope for improving the vetting processes of candidates for senior positions.
- There was thought to be "patchy" adherence to the NHS Code of Conduct.[93]

24.112 Four possible regulatory models were identified:

- Voluntary accreditation and self-regulation, favoured by the majority of respondents;

---

92 DH00960000165, *High Quality Care for All: NHS next stage review final report* (June 2008), Secretary of State for Health, para 28
93 *Assuring the Quality of Senior NHS Managers: final report* (October 2009), PriceWaterhouseCoopers, pp6–10
    www.dh.gov.uk/prod_consum_dh/groups/dh_digitalassets/@dh/@en/@ps/documents/digitalasset/dh_113025.pdf

- Employer-led regulation, supported by a small minority;
- A licensing regime in which a licence would be a prerequisite to holding a senior post, also supported by only a small number of stakeholders;
- Statutory regulation said to have been supported by few stakeholders. It was viewed as disproportionate, costly and unlikely to be accepted by the healthcare sector.[94]

24.113 A patients' focus group asserted that the views and experiences of patients had an important role to play in assisting with the high standards for senior managers. In particular, they thought that patient and staff feedback were needed in appraisals. They sought better due diligence in the recruiting for such posts. Little support was found in the group for statutory regulation.[95]

24.114 The Dalton group's report was published on 23 February 2010.[96] It considered that the research had supported a potential framework of options broadly in line with those described above.

24.115 The group saw the development of standards and ethics as the "bedrock" on which other options might be based. This would involve replacement of the Code of Conduct for NHS Managers with guidance on ethics and standards to be expected of senior managers and non-executive directors, developed in partnership with managers, patients, the public and clinicians. These would include standards of competence.

24.116 The adoption of transparent and robust recruitment and vetting practices, together with improvements in corporate governance, were seen as crucial to ensuring quality in managers. Whilst there was good practice in some parts of the system, the group sought to draw on this to address the issues "systematically".

24.117 It was noted that there was not widespread support for regulation and that the cases for and against it had not been considered widely enough for a consensus to be developed.

24.118 The group recommended that:

- The Code of Conduct should be replaced with a new statement of professional ethics to be used in employment contracts and appraisals;
- Clear standards should be developed by the NLC on the skills and competences expected of good senior NHS managers;
- Guidance on employment contracts should be strengthened;

94 *Assuring the Quality of Senior NHS Managers: Final report* (October 2009), PriceWaterhouseCoopers, pp13–17
    www.dh.gov.uk/prod_consum_dh/groups/dh_digitalassets/@dh/@en/@ps/documents/digitalasset/dh_113025.pdf
95 *Assuring the Quality of Senior NHS Managers: Final report* (October 2009), PriceWaterhouseCoopers, pp18–20
    www.dh.gov.uk/prod_consum_dh/groups/dh_digitalassets/@dh/@en/@ps/documents/digitalasset/dh_113025.pdf
96 *Assuring the Quality of Senior NHS Managers: Report of the Advisory Group on assuring the quality of senior NHS managers,*
    (23 February 2010), DH Workforce/Professional Standards,
    www.dh.gov.uk/prod_consum_dh/groups/dh_digitalassets/@dh/@en/@ps/documents/digitalasset/dh_113026.pdf

- Guidance on recruitment and vetting procedures needed to be improved and uniformly applied;
- Appraisal for senior managers should be strengthened;
- The capability of boards to hold senior managers to account needed to be strengthened;
- The NLC should consult widely on the merits and disadvantages of a more formal regulatory system;
- The NLC should lead and enable the development of a system of professional accreditation for senior managers.[97]

24.119 Dr Smith and Professor Chambers pointed out to the Inquiry that the report recommended a timetable for implementation of these points by December 2010. At the time of the seminars, however, it was unclear what the current status of the report was, given the change of Government, and the subsequent replacement of the NLC with the Leadership Academy.[98]

The Healthy NHS Board: Principles of good governance

24.120 On the same day the Dalton report was published, the NLC published a guide to good governance for NHS boards.[99] This pointed to the need for board members to be appropriately qualified and to have between them the appropriate range of skills. Encouragement was given for boards to use tools such as skills audits, appraisals and to develop a framework of knowledge, skills and competencies required. The guide recommended a systematic approach to board learning and development, not only of board directors but also, in the case of FTs, their governors. Guidance was given on recruitment processes.[100]

The first inquiry report

24.121 The first inquiry report, published the day after the Dalton report, made the following recommendation with regard to trust boards:

> *In light of the findings of this report, the Secretary of State and Monitor should review the arrangements for the training, appointment, support and accountability of executive and non-executive directors of NHS trusts and foundation trusts, with a view to creating and enforcing uniform professional standards for such posts by means of standards formulated and overseen by an independent body given powers of disciplinary sanction.*[101]

---

97   *Assuring the Quality of Senior NHS Managers: Report of the Advisory Group on assuring the quality of senior NHS managers* (23 February 2010), DH Workforce/Professional Standards, pp29–32
      www.dh.gov.uk/prod_consum_dh/groups/dh_digitalassets/@dh/@en/@ps/documents/digitalasset/dh_113026.pdf
98   Dr Judith Smith and Professor Naomi Chambers *The Regulation and Development of NHS Managers: A discussion paper*, (19 October 2011), paper delivered to the Inquiry Leadership Seminar, pp12–13,
      www.midstaffspublicinquiry.com/sites/default/files/uploads/Judith_Smith_and_Naomi_Chambers_-_paper_2_0.pdf
99   *The Healthy NHS Board: Principles of good governance* (23 February 2010), National Leadership Council,
      www.dh.gov.uk/prod_consum_dh/groups/dh_digitalassets/@dh/@en/@abous/documents/digitalasset/dh_117364.pdf
100 *The Healthy NHS Board: Principles of good governance* (23 February 2010), National Leadership Council, pp26–34
      www.dh.gov.uk/prod_consum_dh/groups/dh_digitalassets/@dh/@en/@abous/documents/digitalasset/dh_117364.pdf
101 *Independent Inquiry into care provided by Mid Staffordshire NHS Foundation Trust January 2005–March 2009* (February 2010), Robert Francis QC, page 27, Recommendation 9

24.122 This recommendation was founded on the history surrounding the departure of the Chair and Chief Executive of the Trust, which had resulted in neither of the two being held to account or being offered a fair process by which to respond to the complaints made against them.

24.123 In a letter dated 24 February 2010 to all NHS chairs, drawing the first inquiry's report to their attention, Sir David Nicholson wrote that the Government had accepted all the recommendations from the first inquiry report. It had also accepted a recommendation from the NLC's report for a new system for the accreditation of NHS managers. There would be a consultation on how to take this forward and on whether this should be extended to non-executives.[102]

Quality governance in the NHS: A guide for provider boards

24.124 In March 2011, the National Quality Board (NQB) published a guide for provider boards, *Quality and Governance in the NHS,* largely in the form of checklists or prompts.[103] As the title suggests, it focused on the governance aspects of delivering quality care. The guidance referred to the need for boards to have the necessary leadership, skills and knowledge to ensure delivery of the quality agenda. Boards were prompted to consider whether they had such skills, as well as a systematic process to assess the training needs of board members.[104] It is fair to say, however, that the report did not address the issues raised in the Dalton report, nor was it intended to.

King's Fund Commission report

24.125 In 2011, the King's Fund Commission report, referred to above, acknowledged that there was a need for a more effective mechanism to debar individuals who were clearly culpable in the performance of their duties as healthcare executives. However, the Commission had "reservations" about accreditation or a full-blown disciplinary body.[105] With regard to accreditation, the report argued that the skills needed in various posts were very diverse and that there were risks of creating a new industry in healthcare leadership and management qualifications, and of producing a "bureaucratic barrier" to the recruitment of appropriately talented people. It also argued that creating a "GMC for the managerial profession" would be counterproductive for the same reason, and it was unclear that the benefits would outweigh the costs. They considered that it was the primary responsibility of the board to hold its managers and leaders to account. They raised as a possibility requiring the CQC to consider the effectiveness of senior management as an important determinant of organisational performance and as a factor in the registering and licensing processes.[106]

---

102 DH00000000757–59, Letter from David Nicholson to NHS Chairs (24 February 2010)
103 DH00060000084, *Quality Governance in the NHS: A guide for provider boards* (March 2011), National Quality Board
104 DH00060000098–99, *Quality Governance in the NHS: A guide for provider boards* (March 2011), National Quality Board
105 *The Future of leadership and management in the NHS: no more heroes* 2011, King's Fund Commission on Leadership in the NHS, King's Fund, p ix, www.kingsfund.org.uk/sites/files/kf/future-of-leadership-and-management-nhs-may-2011-kings-fund.pdf
106 *The Future of leadership and management in the NHS: no more heroes* 2011, King's Fund Commission on Leadership in the NHS, King's Fund, pp30–31 www.kingsfund.org.uk/sites/files/kf/future-of-leadership-and-management-nhs-may-2011-kings-fund.pdf

Council for Healthcare Regulatory Excellence review

24.126 In July 2011, in response to the report of the first inquiry and the Dalton review, the DH commissioned the CHRE to develop a set of high level ethical standards for executive and non-executive NHS board members.[107] In October 2011, the CHRE published an interim report consisting of a policy review.

24.127 The review summarised the areas of concern expressed in the literature to be:

- Pre-recruitment training;
- Recruitment and vetting;
- Accountability "on the job" for board members where shortfalls in performance have not been identified and remedied or otherwise addressed;
- Accountability "across the NHS" where failed managers can move on freely to other jobs in the NHS.[108]

24.128 The review noted that the set of ethical standards it had been asked to produce were not to be seen as a solution in themselves, but rather as underpinning for systems of training, recruiting, employing or disciplining senior managers.[109]

24.129 The review referred to existing standards for NHS managers, and standards incidentally applicable to many managers through their membership of a profession (many of which have been described above or in *Chapter 21: Values and standards*). It concluded that although the ethical standards of professionals in many ways reflected those generally expected of NHS managers, namely probity, honesty and integrity, a further necessary quality had been identified:

> *The strength of character to actively challenge decisions, behaviour, or situations that they believe to be wrong, or detrimental to patient welfare.*[110]

24.130 In the report's summary it was asked why, with so many available standards, some board members fail to comply. It also questioned how existing or new standards could address the challenges being brought by the NHS reforms. It noted that the answer to the first question was complex and begged questions of enforcement and competence which the review did not address. It was suggested that part of the answer might relate to the demands of the role:

107 Nicholson T128.75; *Ethical Standards for NHS Board Members: Project brief* (August 2011), CHRE, Appendix A, page 3
www.CHRE.org.uk/_img/pics/library/pdf_1312209783.pdf; Ethical Standards for NHS Board Members in England: Interim report (October 2011), CHRE, paras 1.2, 2.2 www.CHRE.org.uk/_img/pics/library/pdf_1322221113.pdf
108 *Ethical Standards for NHS Board Members in England: Interim report* (October 2011), CHRE, page 7 para 4.14
www.CHRE.org.uk/_img/pics/library/pdf_1322221113.pdf
109 *Ethical Standards for NHS Board Members in England: Interim report* (October 2011), CHRE, pp.7–8 para 4.15–6
www.CHRE.org.uk/_img/pics/library/pdf_1322221113.pdf
110 *Ethical Standards for NHS Board Members in England: Interim report* (October 2011), CHRE, p. 16, para 7.14
www.CHRE.org.uk/_img/pics/library/pdf_1322221113.pdf

Being a senior manager in the NHS is a job that requires a high level of skill and fortitude. Sticking to principles that are, on the face of it, incontrovertible no doubt requires courage in the face of adversity. Furthermore, the application of these principles is most certainly more complex than it seems from the outside, with many decisions being choices between lesser evils, rather than between a right and a wrong.[111]

24.131 As for the second question, the review concluded that, if existing frameworks were not "doing the job now" (as to which the review expressed no opinion), they would be unlikely to do so under the reforms. While considerable training would be required to give doctors and clinicians the competences to manage the new commissioning process:

... Courage and judgement are not qualities that can easily be taught.[112]

24.132 In July 2012 the CHRE published its final advice to the Secretary of State following the consultation and, in November, its final standards. The Secretary of State announced his approval of them at the same time. The detail of the standards as approved is considered in *Chapter 21: Values and standards*.

24.133 As noted in that chapter, the mechanism by which these standards are to be introduced is as yet unclear, but the Chair of the Professional Standards Authority is reported as having made it clear that he does not favour compulsory regulation of managers.[113]

Monitor's proposed "fit and proper person" test

24.134 As mentioned above, under the new licensing regime for which Monitor is to be responsible under the Health and Social Care Act 2012 it is currently proposing that it should be a condition of the licence that directors of a licensed body are "fit and proper" persons. As currently drafted, the proposed condition would require licensed bodies to ensure that no unfit person becomes or continues to be a director or governor. The condition would limit the definition of "unfitness" to formal matters such as bankruptcy, conviction of an offence for which a sentence of not less than three months was imposed, and disqualification under the companies legislation.[114] However, Monitor is also considering whether to include a requirement that governors, directors, or "equivalent people" should adhere to specified standards, such as those recently published by the CHRE and approved by the Secretary of State for members of NHS boards. The options Monitor has put out for consultation are:

111 *Ethical Standards for NHS Board Members in England: Interim report* (October 2011), CHRE, pp.20–21 para 9.3 www.CHRE.org.uk/_img/pics/library/pdf_1322221113.pdf
112 *Ethical Standards for NHS Board Members in England: Interim report* (October 2011), CHRE, p.21 para 9.4 www.CHRE.org.uk/_img/pics/library/pdf_1322221113.pdf
113 www.hsj.co.uk/news/workforce/hunt-backs-new-standards-for-nhs-managers/5051528.article?blocktitle=News&contentID=8805
114 *The New NHS Provider Licence: Consultation document* (July 2012), Monitor. www.monitor-nhsft.gov.uk/sites/default/files/The%20 new%20NHS%20provider%20licence%20consultation%20document%20final%20-%20310712%20PDF_0.pdf

- To specify a set of standards which must be adhered to;
- To require adherence more broadly to generally recognised standards;
- To include a version of such standards in its guidance.

24.135 The purpose of this condition would be to ensure a commitment to the relevant standards, and to prevent someone who had breached those standards becoming or remaining in post. Monitor suggests that a potential disadvantage of such a condition would be that it might impose an additional administrative burden "particularly to licensees not currently obliged to adhere to similar standards".[115]

Summary

24.136 In short, the proposal that managers should be regulated has been met with considerable reservation. While managers and leaders might not be expected to welcome being subjected to regulation, it is fair to acknowledge that these reports evidence little support from patients either. There are clearly a large number of codes of one sort or another offering ethical guidance and standards, and there has been considerable progress in developing a leadership framework for clinicians, and in a number of approaches to individual training. However, no evidence has been seen by the Inquiry suggesting that an accreditation scheme is in the offing.

Views provided to the Inquiry

24.137 Mixed views have been seen by the Inquiry on what professional support needs to be provided for managers and whether some form of professional regulation should be applied to healthcare leadership roles.

24.138 With regard to regulation, although he expressed no view on the regulation of managers, Sir Stephen Moss, former Chair of the Trust, warned of some of the risks of regulation generally:

> *It must be remembered that regulation is a means to an end, not an end in itself. Unfortunately it has developed a life of its own …*

> *In our experience it seems that regulation is full of commentators, some who watch, give opinions and are critical of what they see. Support or help is rarely offered … Antony Sumara surmised that regulators "are not players in the team, they are critics like fans watching a football match" and I would agree.[116]*

---

115 *The New NHS Provider Licence: Consultation document* (July 2012), Monitor, pages 15–16. www.monitor-nhsft.gov.uk/sites/default/files/ The%20new%20NHS%20provider%20licence%20consultation%20document%20final%20-%20310712%20PDF_0.pdf
116 CLO0000001021, *Closing Comments by Sir Stephen Moss on behalf of Mid Staffordshire NHS Foundation Trust*, page 7

24.139 Cynthia Bower, former Chief Executive of the WMSHA and then of the CQC, agreed that there might be a place for a more extensive regime of regulation for managers than the then current powers of Monitor in the case of FTs, and the performance management system in the case of NHS trusts:

> *... my personal belief is that for managers to be subject to some sort of professional regulation or to have to be a part of a professional register, for example, with certain expectations of conduct and training, I think is a good idea, yes. I personally support that.*

> *THE CHAIRMAN: I mean, clearly the regime you have of being able to assess the fitness of the nominated is not really sufficient for that purpose, is it?*

> *A. No, it speaks only to your competence to undertake certain things in relation to our regulated activity. It doesn't speak more broadly about your competence as a manager. We don't have the same ability to, if you like, strike a manager off in a more general sense that a professional body would. So I personally support that*

> *... My personal – this is my personal view, having been a manager for many years, is that it would encourage us to take management more seriously and the skills and the attributes that managers require more seriously than we currently do. So I accept there is a danger of over-regulation. But my personal view is that we should think more deeply and in a more rigorous way about actually what the qualities are that make good managers, particularly good chief executives, and how people are required to go on demonstrating that competence.*[117]

24.140 However, Ms Bower did not consider that regulation of managers would fit in easily with the CQC's current role and responsibilities.[118] This point was emphasised by the CQC in its closing submissions, suggesting instead that it could explore partnership working and information sharing with whatever body was given such a role.[119]

24.141 Sir David Nicholson thought the present position on the regulation of managers was "not sustainable":

> *... if you sit on a board as a chief executive you're sat next to a doctor, a nurse and an accountant, all of whom have regulatory bodies, who have clear national standards about what's expected, both in terms of behaviour and the way that they carry out their jobs and a view about what training and development they would need in order to carry out their jobs. It isn't the same for chief executives and it seems an anomaly, and it needs to be put right.*[120]

---

117 Bower T87.61–62
118 Bower T87.62
119 CLO000000584, *Closing Submissions of the Care Quality Commission,* paras 372–373
120 Nicholson T128.74

24.142 He told the Inquiry that the DH had consulted widely, that there were mixed views and that the concept was "controversial" in management circles. As a result, an evolutionary process was now favoured. Of the CHRE review he said:

We would hope out of that will come a set of standards and behaviours and a code of practice and all of that, and we would want individual organisations to sign up to that, and develop it in that way. It may come in time to a more formal regulatory system, but we think most regulations start off as voluntary and you build up to it, but to use our levers to reinforce and promote it, rather than legislate for it at this moment in time.[121]

24.143 In its closing submissions, the DH recognised that there was strong public and professional concern about instances of senior managers letting people down and avoiding significant consequences for their actions.[122]

24.144 The Healthcare Commission (HCC), in its closing submissions, argued that:

... We can no longer afford ... fracture lines between clinicians and management, or a sense that there is not a shared enterprise, of the delivery of care of the highest possible standards.

... The time has come to ensure that all professions, in each specialty, should define key indicators which measure the essential outcomes of their work, directly or indirectly, and then collect and publish the data which relates to these agreed measures.[123]

24.145 Referring to the responsibilities of trust boards, the HCC contended:

The Board also has to be accountable and demonstrate externally that the necessary standards are being delivered and their handling of the risks within the organisation is accurate and sufficient.

It is our perspective that in UK safety law there is clear responsibility on those providing the service (the duty holder) to assess the risks they face and act on them as reasonably practicable. It is for the regulator to assess whether that is being done, and done adequately ... Given that people's health and safety are threatened by inadequate care, the parallel with the wider approaches to safety law should, we believe, be better recognised.[124]

---

121 Nicholson T128.75
122 As to the CHRE report, see above. CLO000000858, *Closing Statement on Behalf of the Department of Health,* para 144.
123 CLO000001704, *Closing Submissions on behalf of the Healthcare Commission witnesses,* Conclusions, paras 14–15
124 CLO000001705, *Closing Submissions on behalf of the Healthcare Commission witnesses,* Conclusions, paras 21–22

Chapter 24 Leadership in healthcare

24.146 Bearing in mind the potential for personal accountability in health and safety law, this might be seen as an argument in favour of regulatory accountability of senior leaders and managers.

24.147 The South Staffordshire Primary Care Trust (SSPCT) submitted that when recruiting non-executive directors there should be a change in emphasis towards clinical knowledge and patient care, rather than focusing extensively on financial and business experience.[125]

24.148 The Royal College of Physicians (RCP) thought that it was probably impractical and costly to establish a regulated profession of managers in the same way as doctors and lawyers. The backgrounds of managers were more varied and therefore it would be difficult to require prescribed routes of entry. However, they supported the development of national codes of conduct, built into contracts of employment and specifying expectations, particularly with regard to patient care and safety:

> *Health service managers may not constitute a profession in the traditional sense but it is an absolute requirement that they act professionally with the accountability that implies.*[126]

24.149 The RCP observed that there were still barriers or disincentives hindering doctors from taking on formal senior management roles. The hope was expressed that the Faculty of Medical Leadership and Management, referred to above, would assist in reducing these problems.[127]

24.150 AvMA, in its closing submissions, recommended a reinforcement of the Code of Conduct for NHS Managers which, it was suggested, should be made to apply to all NHS managers, including executive and non-executive directors. It was recommended that consideration be given to how breaches of the Code be dealt with, and suggested that to be consistent with healthcare professionals, managers should not only be accountable to their employers, but also to a professional body with whom they were registered and who could withdraw their registration.[128]

24.151 Cure the NHS (CURE) argued that all staff should have a formal accountability for safety and quality written into their contracts and that they should be "audited" reguarly on their activities in this field to include consideration of their contribution to improve safety and quality. They also contended that steps should be taken to prevent managers whose performance had fallen below the required standard from being "moved sideways" to other NHS appointments.[129]

---

125 CLO0000001490, *Written submissions on behalf of South Staffordshire PCT*, para 259
126 CLO0000001511, *Royal College of Physicians' closing statement to the Francis Inquiry*, para 2.1
127 CLO0000001511, *Royal College of Physicians' closing statement to the Francis Inquiry*, para 2.2
128 CLO0000000431, *Closing submissions on behalf of Action Against Medical Accidents*, para 252
129 CLO0000000784, *Written closing submissions of Cure the NHS*, para 14; CLO0000000791 *Written closing submissions of Cure the NHS*, para 50

24.152 The Patients Association (PA) contended that statutory regulation of managers would provide the public with the assurance that there would be a mechanism by which those responsible for serious healthcare failings would be called to account. It considered that the managerial code should be revised and applied to all managers in the NHS and should incorporate a duty to act in the best interests of patients, including a requirement to raise concerns about actual or potential harm to patients. It saw the introduction of statutory regulation for managers as "long overdue" and that given the impact on patient care of poor management it was as important for managers to be regulated as it is for the currently regulated healthcare professionals. It was recognised that regulation would have to include fair process and a screening of complaints. The PA recommended, based on these arguments, that executive and non-executive directors should be subjected to statutory regulation as soon as possible.[130]

Arguments for and against options for reform

Improvements in qualifications, recruitment, development and local accountability

24.153 There seems to be general support for the need, at a minimum, to take steps to make improvements in the areas of training, personal professional development and recruitment practice. It is recognised that today's leaders need to have available to them means of demonstrating their competence and suitability for these roles and to be offered opportunities to develop their abilities through accredited programmes and qualifications. It is accepted that practice in recruitment and vetting procedures is variable and that more uniformity is required. There is support for taking steps to increase the pool of clinicians prepared and qualified to take on senior formal management roles.

24.154 Similarly, the ability of boards to hold their leaders to account is an area considered worthy of further examination. One aspect of this would be either to update the Code of Practice for NHS Managers and ensure it is applied consistently, or to replace it with a code of ethics. The NHS code now produced by the Professional Standards Authority for Health and Social Care (PSA), formerly CHRE, is such a code.

24.155 A nationally applied code of conduct, ethics and professional standards would have the advantage of protecting leaders from undue pressure from whatever source, whether their her own board colleagues, governors, commissioners or others, in relation to matters such as the balance between saving costs and patient safety.

24.156 There has been a great deal of encouraging progress in developing management and leadership training as described above. It is clear that there is a genuine impetus at national level to provide meaningful support through a variety of means. The question remains as to whether this is sufficient to ensure the acceptance and observation of the common positive culture that is so evidently needed throughout the service, but particularly among its leaders,

---

130 CLO000003769–71, *Closing submissions on behalf of the Patients Association* paras 270–278, 27–28

who will have to exemplify it in all they do. While it is necessary and beneficial that the pool from which leaders are chosen contains competent and committed people from many different backgrounds, the increasing diffusion and autonomy of NHS organisations means that entrenching a common leadership culture will become more challenging. A common culture does not require identikit organisations, but it does require a common approach to values and standards. Currently, good work is seemingly being done by the Leadership Academy and similar organisations, but consideration ought to be given to the creation of a physical, as opposed to virtual, leadership or staff college. This would be an institution which could indeed be run by the Leadership Academy and would enable all aspiring leaders to attend training, get to know each other, but above all to go through a common and shared experience. It could provide intensive courses leading to some form of accreditation which could enhance the eligibility of candidates for leadership roles without restricting the sources of recruits. It could also promote excellent practice through research as well as teaching.

Accreditation standards and regulatory sanction

24.157   The principal arguments against imposing a system of accreditation and/or regulation are complexity, administrative burden and cost. There is an argument that such steps would be disproportionate to the goals sought to be achieved and/or addressed. It has been argued that other, lesser measures will suffice, such as improving recruitment and vetting procedures, updating the code of conduct, and strengthening corporate governance and the ability of boards to hold leaders to account.

24.158   Opponents point to the generic nature of management and the difficulty in codifying and testing for competence in such a variable field.

24.159   It is further argued that proceeding to a formal registration system before assessing the benefits in practice of less formal systems would be premature and an unjustified use of scarce health service resources.

24.160   Finally, there is a fear that regulation would make managers defensive and less open, thus defeating the move towards a more open culture.

24.161   Health service leaders and managers occupy positions of considerable responsibility for patient safety and the deployment of public funds. Unlike many other public servants, they can have a direct impact on whether care delivered to vulnerable members of the public is safe, effective and compliant with fundamental standards. Put bluntly, failures on the part of healthcare managers can result in death or harm to patients.

24.162   Their roles are complex and require a high level of skill to perform. Managers are required to work with and oversee highly skilled professionals, many of whom are subject to their own professional codes of conduct, regulatory requirements for training and qualification, and some of whom can be difficult to manage.

24.163 The rationale behind most professional regulatory requirements and sanctions is that they play an important role in protecting the public and maintaining confidence in the profession. The same considerations appear to apply to at least the senior leaders of provider trusts and other healthcare organisations. The public interest is not properly served if persons without the proper competence, training and probity are appointed to these roles. There is currently no clear system by which a consistent set of standards can be applied in the performance of such posts or by which those not possessing the necessary attributes can be prevented from applying for them. There is a risk that persons not possessing the relevant qualities can be appointed and that those found not to be fit for such positions can move from one organisation to another with relative impunity.

24.164 The absence of a system which prevents this means that there is no parity between leaders who are from a general business or administrative background and those who happen to be professionally qualified as doctors, lawyers or accountants and subject to oversight by their own disciplinary bodies. This means that board members theoretically sharing the same organisational authority and responsibility and who should, with regard to patient safety, be adhering to parallel ethical rules, are subject to different regimes in the event of serious non-compliance with necessary standards – or in some cases, to none at all. This is likely to be seen by many as unfair, and may be one of the disincentives preventing clinicians from taking leadership roles observed by the RCP. It produces a potentially unhealthy dynamic in the relationship between a chief executive who, because his background is not subject to any professional regulation, or professional disciplinary consequences from a disregard of patient safety, for example, and a medical director whose ability to work as a registered medical practitioner subsequently is at risk.

24.165 The differences between the traditional professions and managers must be acknowledged. There is currently no common route to qualification for entry to senior managerial status and it might even be undesirable to require one. It would restrict the pool of candidates in an area where diversity is likely to be an advantage. However, that does not mean that an induction in and adherence to common standards and ethics cannot be required of all, whatever their background or formal training. Such a lesser requirement would enhance the spread of the positive common culture that is required throughout the service, and would provide a base from which to develop a regulatory regime, which, in the first instance, could focus on protecting the public by application of a "fit and proper person" test.

A "fit and proper person" test

24.166 Directors of commercial companies require no qualification or statutory demonstration of competence in order to be appointed. However, they are liable to be disqualified by order of the court if found to be unfit for the role. There are other spheres where such a bar can be raised. This could potentially be applied to healthcare leaders with none of the structure required for specifying entry criteria or providing for discipline against a code of conduct, but with merely a responsible body which has access to the court to make the relevant application. In the corporate field the procedure for this is unfortunately lengthy and complex.

24.167 In the case of healthcare leaders, whether within the NHS or the independent sector, Monitor has been granted licensing powers which enable it to include in a "fit and proper person" condition a requirement to observe a code of conduct (see above).

24.168 Taking account of all the arguments that have been presented, and the background of mismanagement at the Trust, it is clear that the public interest in the protection of patients and the maintenance of public confidence in the healthcare service require, as a minimum, a regulator to possess and exercise the power to debar persons from directors' positions who are found unfit to hold such posts. This can be built on the developments being undertaken by Monitor, but must extend beyond a limited test examining only restricted indicators of "unfitness", such as criminal convictions and bankruptcy. It should be made possible under this new regime for a director to be held to account for serious failures of duty and, where appropriate, disqualified from holding such office. This would, it must be recognised, require a greater degree of due process than a restricted test looking only at concluded matters such as convictions, Companies Act disqualifications and bankruptcy, which all rely on determinations of other bodies.

24.169 While in due course it might be desirable for such regulation to be the responsibility of a dedicated statutory body, comparable to the healthcare professional regulators, this is not necessary at this stage. Monitor, assuming it continues to hold the licensing role, could include the relevant requirements in its licensing conditions. These would include obligations:

- For licensed bodies to supply full details of all directors;
- For all directors to comply with a specified code or codes of conduct and standards;
- To require directors as a term of their appointment to abide by these requirements and to submit to the regulatory fitness procedures.

24.170 The regulator would need to arrange for an independent panel to undertake the necessary due process in fitness cases and to set out its procedure.

24.171 It would also be desirable for Monitor and the Secretary of State to arrange for periodic reviews of the applicable codes of conduct and standards to ensure that they meet current needs and expectations.

24.172 While there would be a cost to regulation of this type, there is no reason to believe it would be in any way comparable to that carried by the medical and nursing professions. The numbers of regulated directors are relatively small in comparison, and the number of cases is also likely to be small. Were the system to be extended to other lower level managers then the case for a separate regulatory body would become stronger, but this would not appear to be a proportionate step at the moment.

Standards for boards

24.173 So far in this chapter the focus has been on the status, responsibilities and accountability of individuals. It is clear that there is now considerable guidance available as to what makes an effective board for a healthcare organisation. It is also clear that the absence of effective board leadership was associated at the Trust with appalling care for patients. While the absence of good leadership may possibly be compensated for by the efforts of front-line staff, this will not always be sufficient to protect patients from poor standards of service. Currently the standards by which the CQC regulates provider organisations understandably and properly focus on the outcomes of the service. However, it is arguable that detection of poor leadership could, in some cases, precede detection of poor care outcomes and thereby protect patients earlier. Monitor oversees FT governance. Condition FT4.2 of the proposed licence, which applies only to FTs, states:

> *The Licensee shall apply those principles, systems and standards of good corporate governance which reasonably would be regarded as appropriate for a supplier of health care services to the NHS.*[131]

24.174 Particular requirements are then set out. With regard to organisations which are not FTs the requirements with regard to governance are those set out in the essential standards.

24.175 Anna Walker told the Inquiry that the HCC had considered whether it should assess board capability as part of the annual healthcheck, but had decided not to. This was partly because it was felt to be Monitor's role to oversee boards, partly because of the challenges in formulating standards by which a board could be assessed by a regulator, and partly due to insufficient resources.[132]

24.176 Professor Sir Ian Kennedy said that he had been keen to see a standard to check and test the quality of board leadership included in the healthcheck.[133] He described this as a "missed opportunity", owing to resistance to the concept of accountability at the time among managers.[134]

---

131 *The New NHS Provider Licence: Consultation document* (July 2012), Monitor, p124, para FT4.2 www.monitor-nhsft.gov.uk/sites/default/files/The%20new%20NHS%20provider%20licence%20consultation%20document%20final%20-%20310712%20PDF_0.pdf
132 Anna Walker T83.76–77
133 Kennedy T77.74
134 Kennedy T77.74–75; Kennedy WS0000025878, para 157

24.177 Now a chair of a board, Anna Walker remained unclear as to whether a standard could be created but added:

> *I absolutely think there are some issues about a board and its effectiveness which are really key to an organisation. Whether you can put that into a standard, I'm a little less clear. But an assessment system, which one way or another looks at that, I absolutely agree is very important.*[135]

24.178 Given the work that has already been done, it should be possible to consolidate the common themes of the various codes and standards into an overall code of ethics, standards and conduct applicable to all senior managers and leaders in the NHS. Compliance with the code should be required as part of senior managers' contractual obligations, whether their employer is an FT or a directly controlled NHS organisation. It would need to recognise the variability of requirements relating to different functions, but would need to be informed by the values and principles of the NHS Constitution. It could form the basic point of reference for the "fit and proper person" test to be applied to senior managers by the regulator.

Conclusions

The need for good leadership

24.179 In the foreword to the King's Fund Commission report, Professor Chris Ham made the following valuable statement on leadership in the NHS:

> *The bottom line is that an organisation as large and complex as the NHS cannot be run without high-quality management and leadership. This will happen only through a commitment of time and resources and a willingness to value the role of managers whatever their background.*[136]

24.180 The story of Stafford, as disclosed in the report of the first inquiry, shows what can happen when there is a lack of competent leadership. While it is to be hoped that improvements in regulatory techniques mean that the recurrence of a failure of this magnitude is less likely than it was, no regulatory regime will guarantee that it can detect problems before patients have suffered. The signs of poor leadership may emerge before the decline in an organisation's performance is obvious to external agencies. This means that there is no substitute for strong, ethical and patient-centred leadership in every organisation which is involved in the treatment and care of patients. Its absence increases the risk of harm to them.

---

135 Anna Walker T83.77
136 *The Future of Leadership and Management in the NHS: No more heroes* 2011, King's Fund Commission on Leadership in the NHS, King's Fund, p. vi, www.kingsfund.org.uk/sites/files/kf/future-of-leadership-and-management-nhs-may-2011-kings-fund.pdf

The qualities required of leaders

24.181 Good senior leadership requires all the qualities needed in anyone working in healthcare, but to an outstanding degree. A leader will inspire others to conduct themselves and perform their duties in accordance with the necessary common culture by demonstrating commitment to all its components in everything he or she does. Consideration is given above to what those qualities may be. Others can no doubt be added to the list and it would be helpful for a list to be drawn up of all the qualities generally considered necessary in a good and effective leader. This, in turn, could inform a list of competences a leader would be expected to have.

The leadership pool

24.182 The tenure in office of trust chief executives is shockingly short. The pool of candidates for such posts is often small; that for other director posts can be even smaller. There can be reluctance on the part of suitable clinicians to put themselves forward for consideration. That was certainly the experience in Stafford at one point with regard to the medical director post. Therefore there is an urgent need to encourage clinicians to seek such posts, and indeed others with the potential to do so. It is obvious that the fewer the number of candidates for a post, the greater is the risk of a weak appointment being made.

24.183 Much effort is being put into increasing the availability of management and leadership training at all levels, and this is clearly a positive development to be encouraged. The medical profession is making its contribution with the establishment of the Faculty of Medical Leadership, which is seeking to integrate the development of managerial and leadership skills into the work of its members, and to enhance the professional status of healthcare management.

24.184 The recognition that healthcare management and leadership is, or should be treated as a profession, is important. The concept carries with it a need for members of that profession to commit to a professional code of ethics, conduct and standards relevant to their work, separate from any such commitment they have by reason of other professions. It puts all professionals in the health service on an equal footing. The development of this concept is likely to contribute to the willingness of suitable candidates to come forward, will encourage the integration of a common culture, and offers the possibility of providing assurance to the public about the competence and suitability of those appointed as senior managers and leaders.

Management and leadership training and accreditation

24.185 The recent history of management and leadership training in the NHS has been examined in this chapter. There are numerous initiatives, all of which are positive and encouraging in that they have increased the opportunities and the choices available for the development of individuals at all levels. In a field where there are varying requirements, depending on the type of post being considered, it is not surprising that there have been a multiplicity of approaches. It has been suggested above that, in addition to training of this type, there is a place for providing at least an element of common training, preferably through a staff college which would bring together potential candidates for senior positions and provide an opportunity to offer a common induction into the expectations of leadership. This would reinforce the required culture through shared experience. The college could also assume a role in promoting excellence and good practice in the field. Such a college would preferably require a physical presence rather than being a virtual organisation facilitating events.

24.186 If such a facility could be created, it could provide the route through which an accreditation scheme could be organised. Current thinking appears to be that any accreditation scheme should be voluntary and not a requirement for eligibility. In the first instance, that is probably correct, as it would be prudent to test out the effectiveness of the college and any accreditation scheme. The objective, however, should be to require all leadership posts to be filled by persons who have experienced some shared training and are required to obtain the relevant accreditation.

Standards and a code of conduct

24.187 The reports considered in this chapter make it quite clear that shared standards of management and leadership are not only possible to devise but desirable to implement. Such standards would assist boards to devise means of assessing their own leaders' performance as well as assessment by external agencies. The primary purpose of standards and codes of conduct should be to safeguard the public interest in the protection of patients and the effective running of the health service. The means of implementing such standards and ensuring that they are complied with are now arriving, in particular in the form of Monitor's licensing powers. It is important that there is clarity in any national code for managers and leaders and its relationship with professional codes to which they may also be committed. There should also be scope for organisations to develop their own requirements, providing that they include the relevant national requirements.

24.188 In view of the lack of clarity that has emerged at this Inquiry about precisely who is bound by which codes, the inclusion of any national code devised as a result of this report should be mandatory in the employment contracts of all relevant personnel.

Sanctions for non-compliance with standards by leaders and managers

24.189 Taking into account all the matters considered above, there is a compelling case for introducing a system whereby senior managers and leaders of healthcare organisations can be called to account for serious non-compliance with the standards applying to them. Where appropriate, whatever may be their fate under their contract of employment, they should be disqualified from holding any similar post. The means by which this can be achieved are now potentially available in the licensing scheme for which Monitor will be responsible. As it acknowledges, this scheme would enable it to impose a licensing condition that all board members be "fit and proper persons". A licence could presumably be withdrawn if such a condition were not met. In the case of an FT, Monitor could require the dismissal of a director found to be unfit for the post. A finding that a person was not "fit and proper" would – or could be made to – have the effect that no other healthcare organisation could employ that person as a director.

24.190 The possibility of including a requirement of compliance with a code is being considered by Monitor in this context. A "fit and proper person" test which is confined to the formalities concerning criminal convictions, bankruptcy and the like will not meet the needs of the public interest in protecting patients and maintaining public confidence in the healthcare service. Such a test needs to include requirements of competence and compliance with standards in relation to the post held. Obviously, before a sanction of effective disqualification could be imposed, a form of due process would be required.

24.191 An alternative option, which should be kept under consideration, preferably until after a period in which the licensing solution is followed through, would be to set up an independent professional regulator as was recommended by Sir Ian Kennedy. The need for this, as opposed to the "fit and proper person" solution suggested above, would be greater if it were thought appropriate to extend a regulatory requirement to a wider range of managers and leaders. The proportionality of such a step could be better assessed after reviewing the experience of a licensing provision for directors.

Regulation of boards

24.192 FT boards are subject to extensive scrutiny of their governance arrangements by Monitor. This is intended to be carried through to the new licensing arrangements. However, it is clear from the proposals that these collective requirements are not to be imposed on non-FTs. It is apparent that this area is also not within the remit of the CQC's standards. While account has to be taken of the constitutional differences between FTs and other NHS providers, it is not clear why the oversight of their governance should be any less stringent. Consideration should be given to how this could be brought about.

Summary of recommendations

Recommendation 214

A leadership staff college or training system, whether centralised or regional, should be created to: provide common professional training in management and leadership to potential senior staff; promote healthcare leadership and management as a profession; administer an accreditation scheme to enhance eligibility for consideration for such roles; promote and research best leadership practice in healthcare.

Recommendation 215

A common code of ethics, standards and conduct for senior board-level healthcare leaders and managers should be produced and steps taken to oblige all such staff to comply with the code and their employers to enforce it.

Recommendation 216

The leadership framework should be improved by increasing the emphasis given to patient safety in the thinking of all in the health service. This could be done by, for example, creating a separate domain for managing safety, or by defining the service to be delivered as a safe and effective service.

Recommendation 217

A list should be drawn up of all the qualities generally considered necessary for a good and effective leader. This in turn could inform a list of competences a leader would be expected to have.

Recommendation 218

Serious non-compliance with the code, and in particular, non-compliance leading to actual or potential harm to patients, should render board-level leaders and managers liable to be found not to be fit and proper persons to hold such positions by a fair and proportionate procedure, with the effect of disqualifying them from holding such positions in future.

Recommendation 219

An alternative option to enforcing compliance with a management code of conduct, with the risk of disqualification, would be to set up an independent professional regulator. The need for this would be greater if it were thought appropriate to extend a regulatory requirement to a wider range of managers and leaders. The proportionality of such a step could be better assessed after reviewing the experience of a licensing provision for directors.

Recommendation 220

A training facility could provide the route through which an accreditation scheme could be organised. Although this might be a voluntary scheme, at least initally, the objective should be to require all leadership posts to be filled by persons who experience some shared training and obtain the relevant accreditation, enhancing the spread of the common culture and providing the basis for a regulatory regime.

Recommendation 221

Consideration should be given to ensuring that there is regulatory oversight of the competence and compliance with appropriate standards by the boards of health service bodies which are not foundation trusts, of equivalent rigour to that applied to foundation trusts.

Chapter 25
Common culture applied: the care of the elderly

Key themes

- There should be clear identification of responsibility for each patient's care, led by a named consultant.

- There should be clear nursing responsibilities for each patient's care and a clear dual responsibility at the point of handover.

- The experience of Stafford demonstrates the importance of constantly ensuring patients receive proper food and nutrition.

- Teamwork is vital and the contribution of all individuals in the team needs to be recognised and encouraged.

- There needs to be good communication with and about the patient, with appropriate sharing of information with relatives and supporters.

- The importance of the involvement of patient families and carers should be recognised by those caring for patients.

Introduction

25.1   A common culture supported by evidence-based fundamental standards, a professionalised workforce, informed and inspiring leadership and transparent information systems will all mean nothing unless they result in the practical reality of the safe and effective care received by patients in their homes, on the ward, in a community hospital or in a care home. One true measure of the NHS's effectiveness in delivering hospital care can be found in how well the elderly are looked after. They are a vulnerable group often unable to assert their rights and legitimate expectations for themselves, and have complex needs. It is a measure not just of our health service but also of our civilisation as a society.

25.2   The evidence heard by this Inquiry and the report of the first inquiry include many terrible stories of the experiences undergone by defenceless and vulnerable patients at Stafford Hospital. In contrast, the Inquiry was able to witness many examples of very good practice during visits to various healthcare providers. What follows are some suggestions for what patients and their families might reasonably expect to experience, based on the observations made during those visits and on what has been said elsewhere in this report. It is not intended to be a definition of a care pathway, nor to be entirely inclusive or exclusive.

25.3   While this chapter is titled "Common culture applied: the care of the elderly", the suggestions contained within are not only for them. They reflect what should be good practice for all patients in a healthcare setting, albeit with a slant towards looking after the particularly vulnerable in our society.

Admission

25.4   Arriving in hospital is a worrying and confusing experience for any patient, but is likely to be particularly the case for an elderly patient, who, typically for example, may have fractured a hip or suffered a stroke. In addition to the immediately necessary history taking, investigation, diagnosis and treatment, what else does such a patient need?

- Address by preferred name;
- Accurate history taking and recording;
- Ability to identify staff;
- Allocation of responsibility;
- Induction;
- Reception;
- Involvement of his or her supporters.

Names

25.5   The Inquiry has heard of the understandable importance patients give to being addressed by the name they are happy to be called and not the name which a healthcare professional expects them to use. Therefore, one of the first things that needs to be established is what the patient wishes to be known as. Not everyone wants to be called by their first name, while others will be uncomfortable if addressed formally. Having established the patient's wishes these need to be recorded in a way that all staff approaching the patient know what to call him or her. Compare this to the experience of one patient of the Trust:

... the familiarity was absolutely awful, I thought. They said "What's your name?"
"Mrs Matthews". "What do they call you?" "Mrs Matthews". "Oh, no, we want your
Christian name". I said "Well they call me Kay at home", so they wrote "Kay" up.
And I heard then that everybody was Pam and Lucy.[1]

Accurate history taking and recording

25.6   While there may on occasions be reasons for questions to be repeated, it should not be necessary for every person approaching the patient's bed to seek routine information that has already been obtained previously. It can distress patients to receive the impression they have not been listened to. It should be possible for accurate and accessible records in relation to social and medical history to be digested by staff who are going to interact with particular patients.

Identification of staff

25.7   It should be made easy for all patients to know the names of staff who come to see them, and what their posts are. All too often identity badges are difficult for patients to read or are positioned where they cannot be seen. Hurried and unclear introductions can be difficult for the worried or hard-of-hearing patient to digest. Time may need to be spent explaining to patients who staff are, what they do and why they are there. The range of uniforms or dress codes can be very wide and provide few visual clues to identity. In particular, it can be difficult for patients to distinguish between qualified nursing staff and support workers. Doctors need to take time and care to explain who they are, and what their role is. Patients need to know whether they are talking, for example, to a consultant physician or a trainee anaesthetist.

Allocation of responsibility

25.8   Much of hospital care is by way of teamwork, but patients like to know "their" doctor and "their" nurse. Many hospitals seem to have abandoned the practice of identifying a senior clinician who is in charge of a patient's case. This should be reviewed. A team needs a leader; without identification of one, confusion can creep in, particularly in the mind of the patient. Patients need to know who at any one time is in charge of their case. Most hospital wards have a board at the head of the bed on which that name can and should be written. Lines of responsibility should be clear to all.

---

1   Matthews WS000100604; T11.119

25.9 Mrs Matthews, a retired nurse, was distressed by not being able to find out the name of her consultant:

> *I asked several people who flitted in and out who was the urologist, and no one knew. And I was a bit surprised sister didn't come and have a chat with me, which would have been how it worked in my day. And I kept asking the various staff that came in and out, "Who is the urologist? When does he do his round?" And no one knew ... one morning I came across what I thought was a doctor, she had a stethoscope on and I said "Could you tell me, who is the urologist?" And she said "No". I said "Well, you have a phone, will [you] telephone the department and find out for me?" And she phoned and she said "No one's answering. There's no one there". So I was really back where I started. And so the next day, this would be my fourth day, and nothing had happened ... I saw a doctor leaving a patient in the corner bed, so I asked if he would come and speak to me, and I said "I know you're nothing to do with me but I am very anxious and rather cross. I am taking up a bed. I am here to see a urologist. No one has been to see me. No one knows who it is. And I may as well be at home, because my urine is now a better colour and I am on the antibiotics". So he said, "Right, I'll see what I can do." And still nobody came to talk to me.[2]*

25.10 Elderly patients in particular often have complex nursing needs. It would help coordination of the required care, as well as provide a point of reference for the patient, if a named nurse was nominated for each patient for each shift where this is not done already. Such a step would not exonerate other staff from caring duties, but would help foster a sense of ownership and responsibility among nurses and a professional relationship with patients.

Induction

25.11 Hospital wards are unfamiliar and intimidating places for an anxious and unwell patient. Mrs Matthews' experience described above illustrates the effect of being left without information. Basic information needs to be made readily available about the ward's function, layout, facilities and staffing structure. Hotels manage to do this and it is difficult to see why hospitals cannot do so as well, particularly as it is potentially important for patients' well-being. However, in hospital much of this information may need to be conveyed orally and over a period of time to the patient. And it is not only the patient, but his or her visitors who need this sort of information. It should be available for them in written form and orally on enquiry, with the recognition that – if required – time must be given over to this activity.

Reception

25.12 In order to reassure newly arrived patients, there is no effective substitute for a timely conversation with the ward sister; or, in a ward with a high turnover of patients, another

---

2   Matthews T11.117–118

senior figure who can welcome patients, offer answers to any questions they or their supporters may have, while at the same time assessing and observing their conditions and needs. Patience and care may be required in this exercise, and trying to hurry such occasions can be counterproductive. The Inquiry has seen examples of excellent and dedicated practice by senior nursing staff in this regard. Again, this may be contrasted with the experience of the patient already referred to above:

> *I had to go to ward 10, and a ward secretary or manager came to help me move in a wheelchair. And she pulled [a] bag out of the wardrobe in which my dressing gown and things were hanging, and she said "Is this yours?" I said "No". And I was absolutely appalled to see and smell – it was a bag of very, very dirty washing, and I disclaimed it, of course, [I] said "It isn't mine". And that worried me, that nobody had obviously cleaned the wardrobe out ... the lady escorting me said "Oh, I'll throw that out". And that was the end of it, as far as I was concerned. I was pretty shocked.*[3]

Involvement of patients' supporters

25.13   The social support network available for patients is infinitely variable but will usually consist of close family members, friends and carers. Not all patients and not all supporters will wish for close involvement in the patient's care but some will, and many more will be keen for information about progress to be shared. While patient confidentiality must be rigorously respected and protected, so must the right of patients to ensure that those whom they want to know about their condition are authorised to be informed. Therefore, it is important to establish at the first practicable opportunity what the patient's wishes are in this respect, and to ensure, to the extent appropriate, that supporters are made to feel welcome and advised what they can do to help. Staff need to be briefed on the identities of regular visitors and the extent to which information should be shared with them.

Observations

25.14   A key failing in some of the care at Stafford involved the absence of the required performance or recording of routine observations. A practical problem may be that it is possible for there to be a disconnect between the taking of observations and the opportunity to record them and consider if treatment is required. It would relieve a considerable burden from hard-pressed nursing staff if such recording could be done automatically as observations are taken, with results immediately accessible to all staff electronically in a form that enables progress to be monitored and interpreted. If this cannot be done there needs to be a system whereby ward leaders and named nurses are responsible for ensuring that the observations are carried out and recorded. Naturally, performance of these functions is not sufficient to ensure the patient's well-being; the results must be considered and compared with previous results.

---

3   Matthews T11.116–117

Medicines management

25.15 The benefits of using up-to-date technology to assist in the process of prescribing, administering and recording medication has been discussed in *Chapter 26: Information*. They are particularly clear in the case of the often complex medication needs of the elderly patient or the need for pain relief in others. In the absence of automatic checking and prompting, the process of the administration of medication needs to be overseen by a nurse trained to the correct level, and with appropriate responsibility to do this. A frequent check needs to be done to ensure that all patients have received what they have been prescribed and what they need. This is particularly the case when patients are moved from one ward to another, or returned to the ward after treatment. Incomplete records mean that staff may not be aware of what needs to be administered or whether it has been. Lives can be endangered or even lost by faulty management of medication.

- *A. It was when mum's bed was being wheeled on to the ... ward ... and there was two nurses sort of guiding us into the room, and I just asked if mum could have her teatime medication, because it was now about half past 7. And she said "You're too late for the teatime medication. You should have been here at 4 o'clock".*
  Q. So what happened about that medication?
  A. She didn't get that medication until the night medication, about 11 o'clock.[4]

- *When I arrived Gill was unconscious and on oxygen. There was a doctor and a nurse attending to her and the doctor said "I'm very sorry but Gill's sugar is very high." I said "Oh my gosh ... she is in a hyperglycaemic coma" ... It was apparent Gill had not been given insulin ... As I stood away from the nurses desk ... I heard the doctor ask the nurse "has Mrs Astbury had any insulin today as there is nothing on the chart?" The nurse said "I don't know I have only just come on".*[5]

Nutrition and hydration

25.16 At Stafford some patients were left food and drink and offered inadequate or no assistance in consuming it. Even water or the means to drink it could be hard to come by.

25.17 The experiences at Stafford to which witnesses testified are by no means unique in the NHS in England, as has been shown by the Care Quality Commission dignity and nutrition reports since.

---

4   Bailey T9.61–62
5   Street WS0001000703–704, paras 21–23

- *Swallowing was a problem for Irene and I had to give her Fortisips with a syringe. I was just trying to make sure Irene was eating. However at 5pm you had to go. This was meal time. I could not see whether Irene was eating or not. One time I visited I saw a trolley with a dinner on it at the foot of her bed, out of Irene's reach. I asked the lady next to her whose dinner it was. She told me it was [my wife's]. It had been left uncovered and was stone cold. I found a nurse and asked her whose dinner it was; she told me it was Irene's I said "you're joking, Irene can't eat a dinner". The nursing staff should have known about [her] eating requirements.[6]*

- *They weren't encouraging her. They were putting the glass—you know, a jug of water there. Mum couldn't see the jug of water. She couldn't see the glass to pour the fluids.[7]*

  ... the glasses on the ward, they were flimsy, they were the plastic glasses. And mum's eyesight was really, really bad, and anybody with bad eyesight can't pick the jug up and see where they're pouring into they—by the time you've picked that glass up you've crushed it, you know, its collapsed in your hand.[8]

- *On examining the food and fluid intake chart, mum had only had half a cup of tea over the last 20 plus hours. Some days nothing was marked as being taken, today there were three cups of fluid on the table, all of which were full. She couldn't have drunk them if she tried because all three of the cups were placed way outside her reach.[9]*

- *... some of the people in there can't even get out of bed; they can't fill in their own menu. You would find the food tray was 3 foot away from the bed; they couldn't get a drink. There was just nobody there. I remember a conversation with one of the senior nurses who told me that she was on her own and had 50 meals to serve. I'd have put an apron on myself and gone and helped, that is what you felt you wanted to do.[10]*

- *Q. Did the healthcare assistant who brought her food make any attempt to help her?*

  A. She didn't make any attempt at all. She didn't even speak. There was not a word said when she put the tray down and when she took the tray away.

  Q. So what did you do?

  A. I just said 'She hadn't – she hasn't eaten her food at all'. And she just – she just walked out the door, and as she was going she said 'She never does'.[11]

---

6   Guest WS0000000127, para 27
7   S Whitehouse T13.12–13
8   S Whitehouse T13.12
9   Davies T19.9
10   BH/1 WS0002000014, para 20
11   Bailey T9.61

25.18 Food and drink is important to all patients, but perhaps none more so than the very young and the elderly. Hydration is absolutely vital to maximising their chances of recovery and to stave off deterioration in physical and mental capacity. Dehydration can be insidious with the effects not immediately noticeable to the untrained eye. Lack of food can also lead to deterioration in the patient's condition. Many elderly patients require encouragement to eat and drink sufficiently. On the other hand, well prepared food and drink produced at the time the patient needs it and can enjoy it, accompanied by any necessary assistance, can be a highlight of the patient's day, something to look forward to, and a chance to socialise with other patients and staff. Meal times can offer patients a touch of humanity and normality in otherwise completely unfamiliar surroundings.

25.19 Visits to hospitals indicated that there is a heightened awareness of the need to get systems in place to ensure proper nutrition and hydration for all patients and a variety of local, frequently nurse-inspired, initiatives were seen. As in most other areas of hospital care, imaginative leadership can clearly make an enormous difference to the quality of life and care for elderly patients.

25.20 There are likely to be various approaches which produce the same result. However, the experiences at Stafford suggest that some basic principles require restatement and constant reinforcement in practice and that some relatively easily implemented improvements could also be considered:

- Food and drink that is, so far as is possible, palatable to patients must be made available and delivered to them at a time and in a form they are able to consume.
- Food and drink should, where possible, be delivered to patients in containers and with utensils which enable them to feed themselves, taking account of any physical incapacity.
- Time for meals should be protected in the daily schedule, but, if it is necessary for therapeutic reasons to interrupt mealtimes for a patient, alternatives should be made available when the patient is ready for them.
- If at all practicable, meals should be available to patients when they want them, rather than when it suits the catering service to offer them.
- It is essential that appropriate assistance is made available to patients needing it as and when necessary to consume food or drink.
- No meal or drink should ever be left out of reach of patients able to feed themselves;
- Where patients have not eaten or drunk what is provided at mealtimes this must be noted and the reasons established. Steps should also be taken to remedy the deficit in nutrition and hydration.
- Systems, such as specially marked trays or jugs or other prompts, should be employed to remind staff of those patients who need assistance with eating and drinking.
- For patients capable of eating out of bed, where possible, facilities should be made available on the ward for them to eat at tables, together with other patients if they wish to do so.

Chapter 25 Common culture applied: the care of the elderly

- Mealtimes should be considered as an opportunity for non-intrusive forms of observation and interaction where this is desirable and appropriate.
- Patients' supporters should not be prevented from joining them at mealtimes provided that this does not interfere with the preservation of appropriate levels of nutrition and hydration or with other patients on the ward, and should be encouraged to help with feeding where this is needed and they wish to provide such help.
- For patients who have no willing supporters to assist, but who need help, consideration should be given to engaging volunteers who have had the appropriate level of checks for this purpose.
- Feedback should be obtained preferably in real time but at least regularly from patients, supporters and volunteer helpers on the quality of food and drink and about any necessary adjustments required for individual patients.
- Proper records should be kept of the food and drink supplied to and consumed by elderly patients.

Toileting and washing

25.21   The stories from Stafford of patients not being assisted to get to the toilet in time to prevent accidents and of being left for long periods of time in excrement-stained bedclothes and sheets were particularly shocking to all who heard them. No doubt not all accidents are avoidable. Failure to recognise that one has occurred and to take immediate action is. If the reason for such failures is that there are inadequate staff on the ward then that in itself should be regarded as inexcusable.

25.22   While there has been debate at the Inquiry about the desirability or otherwise of guidance on skill mix and staff-to-patient ratios it should be possible on a daily basis to assess the need for staff on a ward to assist with basic functions such as toileting and bed changing. On hospital visits to busy wards full of elderly, immobile and often confused patients, it seemed possible to undertake sufficient surveillance and intervention to keep patients comfortable, clean and dry. If this is not occurring, something is likely to be wrong either with the ward leadership, staff attitudes, or staff numbers. A hospital that cannot manage such basic patient needs appropriately should be regarded as the cause of serious concern.

- *My mum was left in urine, faeces-ridden sheets, and it would take us so long to find somebody to get my mum the support to be able to change her. And they would take the sheets off and put them in a bin at the end of the bed, but they were left there, and we would constantly move them outside of the room and as soon as we'd gone they would come back into the room again. And we were terrified. My mum's immune system was very low at this time and we didn't want them in the room, but they would change the sheets and just dump them and leave them in there ... My mum had faeces under her nails that I had to clean. I had to clean my mum and provide personal care.*[12]

- *At one stage I noticed that the urine container under the bed was full and needed emptying. When I looked closer I discovered that there was also a dirty nightie under the bed, which had obviously been either concealed or forgotten. I found Irene sitting in her own urine more than once. The bed was wet through. Whenever I asked nurses to come and change Irene, I was upset. I should not have had to press the issue. The staff should have been watching and taking responsibility.*[13]

- *We don't see any reasonable argument why anything like the scale the evidence suggests it does occur, if at all, a patient should be left in their own faeces on a bed, have their call bell repeatedly taken away from them, be told to wet the bed because the nurses don't have time, apparently, to transfer somebody on to a commode. We don't accept that those things should ever happen, and so we feel quite confident in being very firm in our campaigning on those issues.*[14]

Hygiene and cleanliness

25.23 A common theme running through the evidence received at both the first inquiry and the present one was the lack of observance of basic hygiene and appalling standards of cleanliness.

25.24 Everyone is in agreement that very high standards of hygiene and cleanliness are essential in hospitals. While the principal reason is obviously the reduction of the risk of spreading infection, it is not the only one. Visibly clean accommodation and equipment send out a signal about the purpose and commitment of the staff and the organisation, which is likely to reassure patients and visitors and enhance their confidence in the service. It is evidence of a strong positive culture. The opposite is also true. Dirty premises and equipment indicate a badly managed and supervised workforce, which is likely to have low morale and lack the necessary commitment to patients and their well-being.

25.25 In wards caring for the elderly, there is a particular challenge in maintaining cleanliness, but no excuse for not doing so. One of the points observed during the Inquiry's hospital visits was that in well-run wards the cleaning staff, whatever their formal employment arrangements, were regarded as an intrinsic part of the ward team. In areas where cleaners were not personally associated with the ward greater effort had to be expended in maintaining a satisfactory service. It would be a mistake to ever regard cleaning staff as anything other than an essential component of the ward team with a vital contribution to make. This should not be regarded as "menial" or "routine" work. Maintaining that status requires positive leadership

---

12 Hazeldine T11.149–150
13 Guest T12.152
14 Mullan T24.15

by ward managers which both offers encouragement, inclusion and recognition for effective work and zero tolerance for inadequate service.

25.26 Cleanliness is also the responsibility of every member of staff. Everyone from the chairman and chief executive down is capable of picking up and disposing of waste and of alerting staff to spillages, and need to be seen doing so. Patients and visitors should be encouraged to point out any need for cleaning that has been left unattended.

25.27 Likewise hygiene is everyone's business. All staff and visitors need to be reminded to use hand washes and other anti-cross infection measures when they have not done so. Any member of staff, however junior, should be encouraged to remind anyone, however senior, of this requirement.

- *On this occasion I saw evidence of dirt and signs of blood and excretion. There was dust under beds and scum on sinks. Whilst I accept that a residual spot of blood on a sheet which had been properly washed may not present a danger, there were signs here that the situation was more serious. I detected vacant looks on the faces of cleaners, who seemed not to notice the dirt around them.*[15]
- *... when you took the cutlery out [of the packet] ... you could see it but you could feel it a film over the cutlery, and it was dirty and they smelt disgusting. You could look at it and there would be baked on food ... So many meal times, and so often that I thought. Well. There's got to be a fundamental problem here because one person can't be that unfortunate that they keep receiving the only dirty cutlery in the hospital. And I was concerned because at that point I could get out of my bed and go to the toilet and wash my cutlery. But there were people in that hospital, particularly elderly or very unwell vulnerable, if you want to call them that, that couldn't do that.*[16]

Engagement with patients

25.28 The taking of observations, changing the bedclothes and other nursing and caring activities are all opportunities for engagement with patients to establish their well-being, their current needs and simply to provide them with reassurance they are being cared for. It is not an occasion for continuing a conversation with other staff on the ward. The importance of direct engagement with patients was emphasised again by Mrs Matthews in her evidence:

- *Nurses came and went but none seemed to want to look the patients in the eye or have time to do more than strip beds and give prescribed treatments ...*[17]

---

15 Deighton WS0001000204, para 21
16 Monte T18.84–85
17 Matthews WS0001000603, para 4b

Q. You say ... that the nurses came and went, but didn't seem to look anyone in the eye or do more than –

A. No, just one little student sat by me on the first day and chatted about her training and so on. But I never saw her again.[18]

25.29   Hospitals can be very lonely places for patients and human interaction is easy to provide and beneficial. It is something which all staff, not just nurses or healthcare support workers can contribute. Witnesses testified to the fact that it was often a kindly word from a cleaner or a porter which they found particularly helpful. All staff should be encouraged to participate in the care of patients in this way. A certain amount of instruction with regard to the limit of what is appropriate for ancillary staff to do may be helpful, but it would be a mistake to overcomplicate the provision of basic human contact.

25.30   Principally, however, it is the job of nursing staff to engage with patients. Bad care seems often to involve staff who offer perfunctory care while ignoring the humanity of the patient, for example, by continuing a conversation with a colleague about their social lives. It should be possible to communicate clearly with them, reassure patients, observe and offer treatment and care all at the same time. Even better and notable are the nurses who take time to stop by patients for a quick chat. This can be systematised by use of a regular round as suggested by the Prime Minister, the Rt Honourable David Cameron MP.[19]

Interaction with visitors

- *... we were a nuisance. They didn't really want us there. The whole attitude was "Don't bother us, we're busy. Don't ask anything, we haven't got the answers". It was looks and shrugs of the shoulders and things like this if you made a query, you know, as to my mum's health or was anything happening or – you know any query at all ... there were a couple that were very nice, very, very helpful, but the majority, no. It was a lot of the looks and the shrugs and "Yes, we'll do it", you know "when I've got the time", and, you know, you're a pain.*[20]

- *If I wanted to speak to the nurses or raise concerns, they would say "in a minute", and then would finally arrive 20 minutes later or not at all.*[21]

25.31   Different hospitals have different policies about visiting times, the number of visitors allowed at one time and so on. Sometimes these limitations are informed by patient needs and practical constraints of the premises. On other occasions, there may be a suspicion that there are cultural or habitual reasons for them.

---

18   Matthews T11.119–120
19   PM announces new focus on quality and nursing care (6 Jan 2012), Department of Health,
      http://mediacentre.dh.gov.uk/2012/01/06/pm-announces-new-focus-on-quality-and-nursing-care/
20   Cowie T14.17
21   Guest T12.151

25.32   The Inquiry visited a hospice, well known but presumably not atypical. It made a point of designing the premises to give an inclusive feel for visitors and indeed the public in its entrance area, which included a comfortable and spacious cafeteria and sitting area where mobile patients, staff and visitors could mingle freely and in comfort. Visitors were welcome to see patients between 10am and 10pm, and even outside those hours by arrangement.

25.33   Clearly, the therapeutic needs in an acute hospital setting are different from those in a hospice, but an open culture can be better demonstrated by an open welcome to bona fide visitors so long as patients wish to see them, there are no health risks involved and other patients are not disturbed. Visitors should be regarded as a potential contribution to the well-being of the patient who is entitled, particularly if an inpatient stay is protracted, to be protected where possible from the detrimental effects of isolation. Visitors are potential sources of information for hospital staff about patients' needs, potential help in relation to comparative observation (is she looking better/less or more confused … ?), possible advocates for patients and observers of patient treatment. They may want to offer assistance, which, if discussed and agreed, could relieve staff of some tasks which relatives would have carried out at home for the patient.

25.34   For this to work most effectively staff need to be enabled to interact constructively, in a helpful and friendly fashion with visitors. This involves providing them with information when they reasonably seek it and have authority from the patient to receive it. It requires staff to acknowledge the presence of visitors, even when passing them in a courteous and welcoming way. Hospital corridors are full of busy staff, often in a hurry, and they can seem intimidating and remote places. A friendly smile and the occasional offer of directions to those who look lost can go a long way to counteract this.

25.35   It would help if there were areas in wards where more mobile patients and their visitors could meet in relative privacy and comfort without disturbing other patients. In many wards this may not be possible, but even a couple of chairs at the end of a ward can be a help in this regard.

Discharge arrangements

At about 3.30am the phone goes. It was Roy, who said: "Dad, they have told me I have to fetch mum out." "You're joking!" I said. He told me that is how it is at Stafford ... she had Alzheimers ... I had no idea how I was going to get [my wife] home. Fortunately Roy managed to find some mates to help. No attention was given to the fact it was 3.30am in the morning or my situation – I had a quadruple bypass four years ago ... I also did not know how I would get [her] out of the car when Roy arrived with [her] ... We took the commode out to the car and then carried it back to the house with [her] on it. They had at least put a shawl around her shoulders, which is just as well given that she only had a nightie on ... as Roy was settling her in the house ... he discovered that the hospital had left the cannula in her. Fortunately, as he was a paramedic, he knew how to remove this safely.[22]

25.36   The discharge of elderly patients whether from an inpatient ward or A&E, presents many challenges not present with other groups. Frequently arrangements have to be made for their continuing care, rehabilitation and ancillary equipment without which it is not safe to let them go. The required coordination with social services, families and other agencies can be complicated and protracted. This is a principal reason why patients otherwise ready to leave hospital remain, preventing their bed being used for other patients. The resulting delays are wasteful of resources and often distressing for patients and their families.

25.37   In the well-run hospital setting such issues will be addressed by planning for discharge beginning the moment the patient arrives. Many trusts will appoint staff dedicated to gathering the relevant information about patients' needs and making sure the necessary arrangements are in place by the time patients are medically ready for discharge. Some have the capacity to send staff out to fit equipment into patients' homes.

25.38   Many complications can be avoided by close liaison with families, many of whom will have no previous experience at dealing with the relevant agencies. Communications can be an issue and this is an area where the NHS could well develop a greater willingness to communicate by email.

25.39   Two areas of communication which will always require meticulous attention are the prescription and supply of medication to be taken away and the discharge letter to the patient's GP. The provision of medication is often a cause for delay in patients being able to leave the hospital. This should never occur in an efficiently managed ward, where the planning of a discharge includes ensuring in advance that arrangements are in place for the prescription and supply of required medication. The currently common practice of summary discharge letters followed up some time later with more substantive ones should be reconsidered. While this may suffice for simpler cases, many elderly patients have complex

---

22   Guest WS0000000124–125, paras 12–15

needs which could require medical attention at any time. In such cases, the patient's well-being may be prejudiced by the absence of adequate discharge information available to both the GP and, often, staff of the care home, where relevant.

25.40   The timing of discharge is important. It should never be acceptable for patients to be discharged in the middle of the night, still less so at any time without absolute assurance that a patient in need of care will receive it on arrival at the planned destination.

25.41   Discharge from the ward is not always the same as discharge from the hospital, some of which have areas in which patients are asked to wait while transport arrives. These need to be properly staffed and patients must continue to be cared for. Many elderly patients remain unfit to care for themselves, and even those who can do so may become anxious and need reassurance and occasional help. The care offered by a hospital should not end merely because the patient has surrendered a bed.

Teamwork

25.42   Overarching many of the requirements considered in this chapter is the need for effective teamwork between all the different disciplines and services that together provide the collective care often required by an elderly patient. Teams have leaders, but they also consist of members, every one of whom has a contribution to make. They do so more effectively when they are made to feel recognised and respected for that contribution in an atmosphere in which they feel free to voice concerns, clarify uncertainties and make constructive suggestions, even in areas that are not their direct personal responsibility. All should be empowered to speak for the team within the limits of their capability, rather than to assume that absolutely everything is for someone else to do. This requires a flexibility of approach. The team needs clear aims, and a good understanding of the contribution each member can and will make.

Conclusion

25.43   Many of the observations made above could be made about any group of patients, but the particular and complex needs of elderly patients accentuates the need for a service containing these elements to be provided to them. Those special needs would be better catered for if the nursing needs of such patients were recognised as specialist and if the nurses on wards for the elderly, as recommended elsewhere, included some with specialist training and a qualification in caring for the elderly. The work done by healthcare support workers is also particularly important in this area. Not only do they need good supervision and leadership by the qualified staff, they and the public deserve a higher level of recognition for the importance of the work they do. One important way in which this can be achieved, as recommended in *Chapter 23: Nursing*, is by introducing a form of regulation for this grade of worker. Teamwork among all staff responsible for care on the ward, including the doctors, is essential. The contribution of cleaners, maintenance staff and catering staff also needs to be recognised and valued. All have a role to play in offering support to patients and their visitors.

25.44 A ward for the elderly should be a calm, clean and comfortable environment, in which patients receive the help they need, when they need it, with the aim of maximising their prospects of recovery. Information about their condition, progress and care and discharge plans should be available and shared with patients and, where appropriate, their supporters, who must be included in the therapeutic partnership to which all patients are entitled. This is all surely not too much to ask, or expect, in a well-run hospital.

Summary of recommendations

Recommendation 236

Hospitals should review whether to reinstate the practice of identifying a senior clinician who is in charge of a patient's case, so that patients and their supporters are clear who is in overall charge of a patient's care.

Recommendation 237

There needs to be effective teamwork between all the different disciplines and services that together provide the collective care often required by an elderly patient; the contribution of cleaners, maintenance staff, and catering staff also needs to be recognised and valued.

Recommendation 238

Regular interaction and engagement between nurses and patients and those close to them should be systematised through regular ward rounds:

- All staff need to be enabled to interact constructively, in a helpful and friendly fashion, with patients and visitors.
- Where possible, wards should have areas where more mobile patients and their visitors can meet in relative privacy and comfort without disturbing other patients.
- The NHS should develop a greater willingness to communicate by email with relatives.
- The currently common practice of summary discharge letters followed up some time later with more substantive ones should be reconsidered.
- Information about an older patient's condition, progress and care and discharge plans should be available and shared with that patient and, where appropriate, those close to them, who must be included in the therapeutic partnership to which all patients are entitled.

Recommendation 239

The care offered by a hospital should not end merely because the patient has surrendered a bed – it should never be acceptable for patients to be discharged in the middle of the night, still less so at any time without absolute assurance that a patient in need of care will receive it on arrival at the planned destination. Discharge areas in hospital need to be properly staffed and provide continued care to the patient.

Recommendation 240

All staff and visitors need to be reminded to comply with hygiene requirements. Any member of staff, however junior, should be encouraged to remind anyone, however senior, of these.

Recommendation 241

The arrangements and best practice for providing food and drink to elderly patients require constant review, monitoring and implementation.

Recommendation 242

In the absence of automatic checking and prompting, the process of the administration of medication needs to be overseen by the nurse in charge of the ward, or his/her nominated delegate. A frequent check needs to be done to ensure that all patients have received what they have been prescribed and what they need. This is particularly the case when patients are moved from one ward to another, or they are returned to the ward after treatment.

Recommendation 243

The recording of routine observations on the ward should, where possible, be done automatically as they are taken, with results being immediately accessible to all staff electronically in a form enabling progress to be monitored and interpreted. If this cannot be done, there needs to be a system whereby ward leaders and named nurses are responsible for ensuring that the observations are carried out and recorded.

Chapter 26
Information

Key themes

- The effective collection, analysis and dissemination of relevant information is essential for swift identification and prevention of substandard service, facilitating accountability, provision of accessible and relevant information to the public, and supporting patient choice of treatment.

- There is a developed national system of governance of healthcare statistics and information. Consideration needs to be given to systems for accrediting their reliability and rendering them more readily useable by the public.

- Reliable data, enabling comparison of treatment outcomes by reference to individual professionals (where appropriate), provider units and organisations, is an essential element of effective learning for improvement, performance monitoring, and patient choice. Healthcare professionals and organisations, individually and collectively, must commit themselves to identifying with patients and the public, and introducing measures that fairly reflect their performance.

- Real time recording of treatment and medication management can assist decision making, reduce errors and assist performance and quality management.

- Quality accounts provide a vehicle for the audited publication of consistent and comparable information about compliance with standards and other requirements, but there is room for improvement by attention to consistency of presentation, balance in reporting of positive and negative results, and rigorous auditing.

- The Care Quality Commission's (CQC) Quality Risk Profile is an important and developing means of collecting information relevant to the assessment of standards compliance. Consideration needs to be given to how this information can effectively be shared with the public.

- Real time and online means of allowing patients both during and after treatment episodes to feed back their experiences can enhance awareness of issues of concern and accountability.

- It was generally accepted that failure to share relevant information lay at the heart of the failure of the system to detect the scale of the deficiencies at the Trust and that an effective overall system of information is essential.

> - Healthcare information recorded primarily for supporting the safe and effective care of individual patients should also be capable of being used to inform the statistics required for clinical audit, performance data, regulatory oversight and public information. The sharing of good quality information should be a powerful force for promotion of the required common culture. Properly maintained accessible patient records are vital to this process.

Introduction

26.1   In his Bristol Inquiry report Professor Sir Ian Kennedy said:

> *Without information patients and the public will remain disempowered. It is essential that they receive and can gain access to the information they need to participate fully at whatever level their contribution is sought.*[1]

26.2   As can be seen from the relevant recommendations,[2] Sir Ian was in this reference largely focusing on the information given to individual patients about their condition and treatment, but he also recommended the greater use of patient feedback and surveys, a national reporting system and improvements in NHS information systems.[3]

26.3   In 2000, in an article summarising a report drawn to the attention of the Inquiry in Cure the NHS's closing submissions,[4] Dr AC Enthoven remarked:

> *The importance of good information on quality and cost is not limited to market models. It is essential to any properly managed system ...*[5]

26.4   In his introduction to the Department of Health (DH)'s Information Strategy in May 2012, the then Secretary of State for Health, the Rt Hon Andrew Lansley MP, pointed out the importance of information in healthcare:

> *Information can encourage positive changes in the way we live our lives and also the way public resources are used on our behalf. Information also feeds the research that improves care services for us all and will play a key role in creating a public health system that is locally owned, locally led, and able to reflect the needs of the local population.*

---

1   *Learning from Bristol: The report of the public inquiry into children's heart surgery at Bristol Royal Infirmary 1984–1995* (July 2001), Sir Ian Kennedy, p.409, www.bristol-inquiry.org.uk/final_report/index.htm

2   IK/1 WS0000025948, recommendations 4–9

3   IK/1 WS0000025965, recommendations 148–156

4   CLO000000761, *Cure the NHS's closing submissions*

5   *In pursuit of an improving National Health Service*, Enthoven, Health Affairs, 19, no 3 (2000): 102–119, p.107: http://content.healthaffairs.org/content/19/3/102.full.pdf, summarising *In pursuit of an improving National Health Service*, 1999 Nuffield Trust: www.nuffieldtrust.org.uk/sites/files/nuffield/publication/In-pursuit-of-an-improving-NHS.pdf

This is about putting us all in control and enabling a culture of "no decision about me without me".[6]

26.5   The strategy went on to observe:

Information can bring enormous benefits. It is the lifeblood of good health and well-being and is pivotal to good quality care. It allows us to understand how to improve our own and our family's health, to know what our care and treatment choices are and to assess for ourselves the quality of services and support available.

Information can also be used by regulators and by local organisations to head off issues before they become the next major incident.[7]

26.6   It is not within the scope of this report to consider the entire range of issues to which information is vital in the delivery of healthcare services. However, as is clearly recognised by the Government, the effective collection, analysis and dissemination of relevant information is a necessary component of:

- Ensuring, so far as possible, that any shortfall in service standards is brought to light as quickly as possible;
- Ideally, enabling deficiencies to be pre-empted;
- Facilitating accountability for performance;
- Providing the public with a full, accurate and transparent picture of the performance of healthcare providers – both organisations and individuals;
- Informing patients' choice of treatment.

26.7   It is a cardinal feature of the Stafford story that information that would have led to the much earlier appreciation of the problems of the Trust was either not collated, not analysed or not disseminated. The result was that commissioners, performance managers, regulators and the public remained unaware of the extent and significance of the issues for far too long.

26.8   This chapter looks at developments in information handling in the NHS and considers whether the Stafford experience suggests improvements could be made. In doing so, it draws not only from the formal evidence to the Inquiry and material taken into account but the contributions at and arising out of the Inquiry seminars and the hospital visits from.

6   *The Power of Information: Putting all of us in control of the health and care information we need* (21 May 2012), Department of Health, p2, www.dh.gov.uk/en/Publicationsandstatistics/Publications/PublicationsPolicyAndGuidance/DH_134181

7   *The Power of Information: Putting all of us in control of the health and care information we need* (21 May 2012), Department of Health, p.4, www.dh.gov.uk/en/Publicationsandstatistics/Publications/PublicationsPolicyAndGuidance/DH_134181

General considerations

Benefits of effective information management

26.9 There seems to be general agreement that the effective collection, analysis and use of information are essential ingredients of a flourishing health service.

26.10 In a thoughtful paper to the Inquiry for the purpose of the information seminar, Sir Muir Gray identified five main benefits of the use of knowledge in healthcare:

- Improving outcomes;
- Reduction of harm;
- Reduction of waste;
- Mitigation of inequity;
- Prevention of disease and improvement of health.[8]

26.11 In his paper to the same seminar, Professor Martin Elliott stated that:

I have become convinced that data is the most effective way to drive change in an organisation and especially so in healthcare ... data equate with information, and ... healthcare is actually an information economy in which the exchange of valuable data/ information is critical to the well-being of both patient and system ...[9]

Multiplicity of information demands

26.12 Professor Charles Vincent points out that there is a plethora of organisations that require information to be reported by healthcare providers in the NHS:

... reporting systems have mushroomed and, with the new interest in patient safety, no professional speciality or organization is complete without a reporting system. The agencies listed ... have many responsibilities and in most cases receiving information of one kind or another is only a small part of their function. Nevertheless for the NHS to respond, or even remember, the agencies who might require reports is, to say the least, burdensome.[10]

26.13 Professor Vincent listed 24 agencies, including some but not all of those subject to some review by this Inquiry. He also observed that there are a multitude of healthcare databases: approximately 270 at the levels of the UK, England and Wales, and England, and over 1,000

---

8   *Report for the Mid Staffordshire Inquiry led by Robert Francis QC on the Benefits of Knowledge Management* (October 2011), Sir Muir Gray, www.midstaffspublicinquiry.com/inquiry-seminars/information

9   *The Role of Information in Ensuring Quality and Patient Safety* (October 2011), Professor Martin Elliot, www.midstaffspublicinquiry.com/sites/default/files/uploads/Martin_Elliot_paper.pdf

10 Vincent, *Patient Safety*, 2nd edition 2010 pp75–76

if Scotland, Wales and Northern Ireland levels were included, in addition to a further 104 clinical databases.[11]

26.14 Following a commitment in the White Paper *Equity and Excellence: Liberating the NHS*, the DH has attempted to tackle the challenges presented by carrying out a fundamental review of data returns. The resulting consultation on the review's recommendations, published in August 2011, identified 306 data collections of which 197 were commissioned by the DH and 108 by its Arms Length Bodies (ALBs). The review recommended a reduction of 25%. As a result, 58 returns were suspended with immediate effect.[12]

26.15 The Health and Social Care Information Centre conducts a rolling review of data returns, and currently licenses approximately 147 mandatory returns for the DH and its ALBs.[13]

26.16 Clearly, it is important that demands are made only for information that is useful, used and not duplicated elsewhere. This is one of the current tasks of the Health and Social Care Information Centre, formerly called the NHS Information Centre (NHSIC), which succeeded the NHS Information Authority as a special health authority on 1 April 2005 and, following the provisions in the Health and Social Care Act 2012, will be established as an executive non-departmental public body from 1 April 2013.

Standards and verification of information and its interpretation

Hospital Standardised Mortality Ratio and Summary Hospital Level Mortality Indicators

26.17 The first time concerns about Stafford were raised to a level of serious overall concern was when it was perceived to be an outlier in the Hospital Standardised Mortality Ratio (HSMR). As is now well rehearsed, there was considerable debate at the time about the reliability of the methodology, and what was a justifiable interpretation of the results. This debate is in the process of being resolved by the independent consensus group that has produced the modified methodology used for the Summary Hospital Mortality Indicator (SHMI) analysis. In the report of the first inquiry, it was suggested that:

---

11 Vincent, *Patient Safety*, 2nd edition 2010 p106, citing *Potential use of routine databases in health technology assessment*. Raftery et al, *Health Technology Assessment* 2005; Vol. 9: No. 20 www.hta.ac.uk/fullmono/mon920.pdf
12 *Fundamental Review of Data Returns* (August 2011), Department of Health, p.8 www.dh.gov.uk/prod_consum_dh/groups/dh_digitalassets/documents/digitalasset/dh_129740.pdf
13 Information obtained on 10 October 2012 from www.ic.nhs.uk/services/the-review-of-central-returns-rocr; www.ic.nhs.uk/webfiles/Services/ROCR/ROCR_ScheduleV19.xls

... statistics are most respected and relied upon if they are produced by an impeccably independent and transparent source. No adverse inferences with regard to Dr Foster Intelligence are intended at all when I suggest that there may be a case for considering whether a public service should not be tasked with the production of this type of statistic. A public, generally accepted benchmark would surely be a useful resource both for patients and the public.[14]

26.18 An independent working group was set up in response to the recommendation that followed from this observation, and it was this that produced SHMI.[15]

Information Standards Board

26.19 The Information Standards Board was created by the NHS Information Authority and survived the demise of that body in 2005. As developed, the Board, with the support of the Information Standards Management Service which sits within the DH Informatics Directorate, seeks to assure information standards. It does so on a continuous basis using six domains of expertise:

- Clinical;
- Management;
- Technical;
- Social care;
- Information governance;
- Public health and statistics.[16]

26.20 The membership of the Board consists of representatives of a wide range of healthcare stakeholders including the Care Quality Commission (CQC), the professional healthcare regulators, the National Institute for Health and Clinical Excellence (NICE), the National Information Governance Board (NIGB), the NHS Commissioning Board, the Health and Social Care Information Centre and the Review of Central Returns (ROCR). The Board maintains and amends a library of approved data returns.[17] It appears that the Board performs a very useful function in providing the necessary technical support and assurance for healthcare indicators. It does not, however, purport to perform the function of confirming that statistical information is published in a manner that is accurate, reliable and in a form that gives a fair interpretation of the data.

---

14 *Independent Inquiry into care provided by Mid Staffordshire NHS Foundation Trust January 2005 – March 2009* (February 2010), p.370, www.dh.gov.uk/en/Publicationsandstatistics/Publications/PublicationsPolicyAndGuidance/DH_113018

15 *Independent Inquiry into care provided by Mid Staffordshire NHS Foundation Trust January 2005 – March 2009* (February 2010), p.414, recommendation 15, www.dh.gov.uk/en/Publicationsandstatistics/Publications/PublicationsPolicyAndGuidance/DH_113018

16 Information obtained on 19 October 2012 from www.isb.nhs.uk/about/history

17 Information obtained on 19 October 2012 from www.isb.nhs.uk/library/approved

The National Information Governance Board for health and social care

26.21 The NIGB is an independent statutory body established to promote, improve and monitor information governance in health and adult social care. It was set up by the Health and Social Care Act 2008 and given the statutory functions:

> *(a) to monitor the practice followed by relevant bodies in relation to the processing of relevant information,*

> *(b) to keep the Secretary of State, and such bodies as the Secretary of State may designate by direction, informed about the practice being followed by relevant bodies in relation to the processing of relevant information,*

> *(c) to publish guidance on the practice to be followed in relation to the processing of relevant information,*

> *(d) to advise the Secretary of State on particular matters relating to the processing of relevant information by any person, and*

> *(e) to advise persons who process relevant information on such matters relating to the processing of relevant information by them as the Secretary of State may from time to time designate by direction.*[18]

26.22 The information concerned is defined as:

> *(a) patient information,*

> *(b) any other information obtained or generated in the course of the provision of the health service, and*

> *(c) any information obtained or generated in the course of the exercise by a local social services authority in England of its adult social services functions.*[19]

26.23 The Board includes representatives of a variety of healthcare representative bodies including the Royal College of Nursing (RCN) and the Academy of Medical Royal Colleges. Half its membership is drawn from the public.[20]

26.24 The NIGB provides advice on the appropriate use, sharing and protection of patient and service user information. The NIGB also advises on the use of powers under Section 251 of the NHS Act 2006 to permit the duty of confidentiality to be set aside, where other legal routes are not available.

---

18 National Health Service Act 2006, section 250A as inserted by the Health and Social Care Act 2008, section 157, www.legislation.gov.uk/ukpga/2008/14/section/157

19 National Health Service Act 2006, section 250A(4) as inserted by the Health and Social Care Act 2008, section 157, www.legislation.gov.uk/ukpga/2008/14/section/157

20 *NIGB Annual Report 2011* (November 2011), NIGB, p.6: www.nigb.nhs.uk/pubs/Final%20Annual%20Report%202011.pdf

26.25 The NIGB provides this advice to the Secretary of State for Health, but also advises:

- Patients, service users and carers;
- Health and social care organisations and practitioners;
- Researchers and others seeking to use patient and service user information.[21]

26.26 An example of its work is the publication of helpful guidance on the amendment of disputed health records.[22] It has also issued detailed guidance on risk management and governance in respect of information transfer during the transition stage of the latest organisational reforms.[23]

26.27 The NIGB will be abolished on 31 March 2013 and its functions in relation to governance of healthcare information will be transferred to the CQC.[24]

The UK Statistics Authority and the Office of National Statistics

26.28 The UK Statistics Authority (UKSA) is an independent statutory body accountable to Parliament with powers to produce statistics, provide statistical services and promote statistical research.[25] Its principal statutory functions are governance of the Office of National Statistics (ONS) and independent scrutiny of all official statistics produced in the UK, through monitoring and assessment against the Code of Practice for Official Statistics.[26]

26.29 The UKSA aims to ensure that:

- *the right range of statistics are produced;*
- *high and consistent professional standards are maintained; and*
- *official statistics are well explained, including strengths and weaknesses – leading to better decision-making in the public interest.*[27]

---

21   Information obtained on 19 October 2012 from www.nigb.nhs.uk/
22   *Requesting Amendments to Health and Social Care Records: Guidance for patients, service users and professionals* (2010), NIGB 2010, www.nigb.nhs.uk/pubs/amendrecords
23   www.nigb.nhs.uk/pubs/guidance/transguid
24   Health and Social Care Act 2012, section 280, www.legislation.gov.uk/ukpga/2012/7/section/280
25   UKSA was created by the Statistics and Registration Service Act 2007, www.legislation.gov.uk/ukpga/2007/18/contents
26   *UKSA Annual report 2010–11* (July 2011), UKSA, p.12 www.official-documents.gov.uk/document/hc1012/hc09/0998/0998_i.pdf
27   *UKSA Annual report 2010–11* (July 2011), UKSA, p.12, www.official-documents.gov.uk/document/hc1012/hc09/0998/0998_i.pdf

26.30 Part of its work has been the assessment of sets of national statistics against the standards of its Code of Practice. The UKSA has observed that:

Official statistics only fully justify their costs when they are used to the benefit of the public and we have, in effect, challenged the bodies that produce them to do more to help users to get the good out of them. This poses a professional, practical and cultural challenge and one that is likely to take many years to fully deliver its benefits. We are however confident that it will do so.[28]

26.31 The Code of Practice is built round eight principles:[29]

Principle 1: Meeting user needs – The production, management and dissemination of official statistics should meet the requirements of informed decision-making by Government, public services, business, researchers and the public.

Principle 2: Impartiality and objectivity – Official statistics, and information about statistical processes, should be managed impartially and objectively.

Principle 3: Integrity – At all stages in the production, management and dissemination of official statistics, the public interest should prevail over organisational, political or personal interests.

Principle 4: Sound methods and assured quality – Statistical methods should be consistent with scientific principles and internationally recognised best practices, and be fully documented. Quality should be monitored and assured taking account of internationally agreed practices.

Principle 5: Confidentiality – Private information about individual persons (including bodies corporate) compiled in the production of official statistics is confidential, and should be used for statistical purposes only.

Principle 6: Proportionate burden – The cost burden on data suppliers should not be excessive and should be assessed relative to the benefits arising from the use of the statistics.

Principle 7: Resources – The resources made available for statistical activities should be sufficient to meet the requirements of this Code and should be used efficiently and effectively.

Principle 8: Frankness and accessibility – Official statistics, accompanied by full and frank commentary, should be readily accessible to all users.

---

28   *UKSA Annual report 2010–11* (July 2011), UKSA, p.19, www.official-documents.gov.uk/document/hc1012/hc09/0998/0998_i.pdf
29   *Code of Practice for Official Statistics* (January 2009), UK Statistics Authority, www.statisticsauthority.gov.uk/assessment/code-of-practice/code-of-practice-for-official-statistics.pdf

26.32 The Code's practical requirements include:

- Effective engagement with users of statistics to promote trust and maximise public value;
- Equal availability of official statistics to all;
- Protection of statistics producers from political pressures that might influence production or presentation;
- Promotion of comparability within the UK and internationally;
- Dissemination in forms as far as possible accessible to a range of different audiences.

26.33 The UKSA has issued assessments of compliance with the Code of Practice on the DH overall patient experience scores, NHS hospital activity statistics and aspects of the Hospital Episode Statistics (HES).[30] In the latter two assessments, the UKSA confirmed that the statistics either were, or could, be recognised as national statistics but recommended improvements that could be made in their delivery. In both cases it was recommended that the commentary and presentation of statistical releases should be improved to aid user interpretation. In its assessment of patient experience statistics, the UKSA confirmed that they were designated as national statistics subject to certain requirements being met. These included:

- Building on existing activities to increase users' understanding;
- Publication of information about the quality, including strengths and limitations, of patient experience;
- Inclusion of commentary, analysis and charts within the statistics to cover some key points from NHS-trust level results.

26.34 The List of National Statistics issued by the National Statistician includes a number of sets of statistics published by the DH. In addition, those statistics recognised as "official statistics" include a range of other statistics from other healthcare bodies such as the CQC and the NHSIC.[31] The Authority has in the course of 2012 issued assessments of the HES and various other healthcare data collections. It appears that SHMI statistics from June 2012 are recognised as an official statistic but not yet as a national statistic.[32]

26.35 The ONS is the executive arm of the UKSA under the leadership of the National Statistician who is also Chief Executive of the UKSA. The ONS is the "head office" of the Government Statistical Service. It states that it is the UK's largest independent producer of official statistics and the recognised national statistical institute of the UK. It publishes some national statistics relevant to healthcare at a national level. For example, it has published statistical bulletins during the course of 2012 on deaths from MRSA and *C. difficile*.

---

30 *Statistics on Patient Experience in England, Assessment report 91*, (February 2011), UK Statistics Authority; *Statistics on NHS Hospital Activity, Assessment report 228* (June 2012), UK Statistics Authority; *Statistics on Hospital Episodes and Appointments, Assessment report 231* (July 2012), UK Statistics Authority, www.statisticsauthority.gov.uk/assessment/assessment/assessment-reports/index.html
31 *List of National Statistics* (March 2012), www.statisticsauthority.gov.uk/national-statistician/types-of-official-statistics/list-of-national-statistics/index.html
32 www.ic.nhs.uk/webfiles/publications/publications%20calendar/20120614_OfficialStatisticsList.doc

Healthcare information standards

26.36 Under the Health and Social Care Act 2012, when the relevant sections are brought into force, the Secretary of State and the NHS Commissioning Board will have power to set information standards for health services in England.[33] Such standards may relate to any aspect of processing data, including technical data, or information governance standards.[34]

Outcome performance data about organisations and individuals

26.37 Cure the NHS pointed in their closing submissions to the arguments of Dr Enthoven, in the report already quoted above, that:

> *If Clinical Governance means that a hospital Chief E[xecutive] will have to sign an annual statement that s/he personally knows by direct observation and participation that quality monitoring systems are in place (including accurate data reporting) and that corrective action is being taken when quality starts to turn bad, then this is a very important step forward, timely, indeed overdue. However, the CE cannot know how good is the quality in his or her hospital without reference to national data that can support comparisons. So clinical governance can hardly be a meaningful thing without a national high quality clinical database ...[35]*

26.38 Dr Enthoven argued that a high priority should be accorded to making the HES usable for monitoring quality.[36] He commended the wider use of risk-adjusted outcome measures and pointed to examples of US states that collected and published outcome measures not just at provider but at individual professional level. One such state is Pennsylvania, which publishes outcome data for named doctors as well as hospitals for cardiac surgery.[37] Enthoven suggested that the evidence showed that mortality has decreased as a result. He emphasised the importance of healthcare professionals formulating and providing data themselves and the relevance to that of publishing data:

---

33   The powers also extend to adult social care services but these are not within the scope of this Inquiry
34   *Health and Social Care Act 2012,* section 250; *Health and Social Care Act 2012: Explanatory notes,* TSO, 2012, p.227 para 1400, www.legislation.gov.uk/ukpga/2012/7/pdfs/ukpgaen_20120007_en.pdf
35   CLO000000771, *Cure the NHS's closing submissions,* p.190, para 38 and p180, para 38
36   *In pursuit of an improving National Health Service,* Enthoven, Health Affairs, 19, no 3 (2000): 102–119, p.107: http://content.healthaffairs.org/content/19/3/102.full.pdf, summarising *In pursuit of an improving National Health Service,* 1999 Nuffield Trust: www.nuffieldtrust.org.uk/sites/files/nuffield/publication/In-pursuit-of-an-improving-NHS.pdf Enthoven report, p.112
37   *In pursuit of an improving National Health Service,* Enthoven, Health Affairs, 19, no 3 (2000): 102–119, p.107: http://content.healthaffairs.org/content/19/3/102.full.pdf, summarising *In pursuit of an improving National Health Service,* 1999 Nuffield Trust, www.nuffieldtrust.org.uk/sites/files/nuffield/publication/In-pursuit-of-an-improving-NHS.pdf Enthoven report, p.113; *Cardiac Surgery in Pennsylvania 2008–2009* (May 2011) Pennsylvania Health Care Cost Containment Council www.phc4.org/reports/cabg/09/default.htm. Surgeons and hospitals are able to post comments about their results online: www.phc4.org/reports/cabg/09/comments.htm

... what should be clear is that physicians and surgeons ought to be measuring the results of what they do, comparing them on a risk-adjusted basis, examining variations in outcomes and identifying and implementing ways to improve. A society that pays for the care and whose members suffer the consequences of sub-optimal care has a right to expect that such a process is in place and that effective corrective action is being taken in cases of persistent and significant poor performance. Publication is one way of assuring the public on this point.[38]

26.39 He was less enthusiastic about publicly identifying individuals in published data, recognising the need to avoid promoting a negative culture through fear, the need to ensure fully worked through and professionally accepted risk adjustment, and the difficulties of isolating individual performance from that of the team or the surrounding system.[39]

26.40 In the Bristol Inquiry report, Professor Sir Ian Kennedy recommended that:

Patients and the public must be able to obtain information as to the relative performance of the trust and the services and consultant units within the trust.[40]

26.41 His arguments, set out in the report, advocated publication of analysis down to team level:

We recall that our central concern here, as elsewhere, is with the creation of a culture within the hospital and beyond which is patient-centred. If this is the aim, then the question of publication admits of only one answer. The public, who are patients in another guise, should have access to the analysed data. We believe that the data which are put into the public domain should relate not only to the performance of the trust as a whole, but should also describe the performance at the level of a specialty and of the consultant unit. Performance at the level of a specialty or a department is important. It is an intermediate point between the trust as a whole and a consultant unit. Further, it offers an opportunity to address the performance of a service from the patient's perspective, and should include the contribution to care not only of doctors but also a cross-section of healthcare professionals.

38   *In Pursuit of an Improved National Health Service* (1999), Nuffield Trust, p.94, http://content.healthaffairs.org/content/19/3/102.full.pdf
39   *In Pursuit of an Improved National Health Service* (1999), Nuffield Trust, pp.95–96,
      http://content.healthaffairs.org/content/19/3/102.full.pdf
40   IK/1 WS0000025965, recommendation 155

56. It will be objected that audit data is complex and hard to understand. The public will be misled and draw unwarranted conclusions. Healthcare professionals will be unfairly criticised. All of these are, of course, real risks. But they are risks that must be faced and resolved. The alternative, of continued secrecy and anonymity, is no longer a real option. A new compact between the community and its hospitals must be forged in which the public must accept that the price of information is a considered and responsible reaction to it.[41]

26.42   In the UK, such data as exists is generally published at an organisation or higher level of detail. In the case of some specialities, the results of individual practitioners are published. The Society of Cardiothoracic Surgeons (SCTS) has led the field by undertaking a study of outcomes in specified cardiac surgical procedures, continuing the work of Professor Sir Bruce Keogh among others, and publishing the National Adult Cardiac Surgery Database. The latest report was published in June 2012.[42] The SCTS programme includes the publication of named surgeon and hospital mortality rates for the patients and the public.[43] In pursuance of this objective, online information is made available about the mortality rates in specified procedures of its members.[44] The results are also shown on the CQC website, together with detailed explanations.[45]

26.43   The Renal Registry publishes analyses of nephrological treatment outcomes by centre on an interactive website.[46]

26.44   In a paper presented to the Inquiry's information seminar, Professor Elliott observed:

All of us have become familiar with Google, Amazon, the World Wide Web and the iPad. Each day we see outstanding use of graphic design in our public media. We take for granted the ability to search the databases of large organisations to find out more about their products and services, and we expect (and usually get) astonishing levels of services and accuracy. How sad that we have not been able to deliver such quality for users of the NHS.[47]

41   Learning from Bristol: The report of the public inquiry into children's heart surgery at Bristol Royal Infirmary 1984–1995 (July 2001), Sir Ian Kennedy, p.398, paras 55–56, www.bristol-inquiry.org.uk/final_report/index.htm
42   *National Adult Cardiac Surgery Audit Annual Report 2010–2011* (June 2012), NICOR, www.ucl.ac.uk/nicor/audits/Adultcardiacsurgery/publications/pdfs/nacsa_report_2011-2012
43   www.scts.org/professionals/audit_outcomes.aspx
44   www.scts.org/modules/surgeons/default.aspx
45   www.heartsurgery.cqc.org.uk
46   www.renalreg.com/
47   *The Role of Information in Ensuring quality and Safety: Some personal reflections*, (October 2011), Martin Elliott, p. 3 www.midstaffspublicinquiry.com/sites/default/files/uploads/Martin_Elliot_paper.pdf

26.45   He suggested on the basis of a short survey he had conducted that the standards that patients expected to be delivered, and therefore the areas about which they required information, were:

- *Rapid diagnosis and access to experts;*
- *Respect, information and support (good communication);*
- *The right treatment at the right time by the right people;*
- *No complications, no waiting, no delays, no cock ups;*
- *Knowledge of what to expect (the pathway) for life;*
- *Follow up as near home as possible;*
- *Access to innovation and news.*[48]

26.46   In his view, that indicated a need for continuous contact and for real-time current and comparative information. He contended that the system could no longer rely on the commitment of individuals, voluntary work and fundraising to meet the information needs he identified. He considered that data management had to be at the core of future planning and commissioning.

26.47   Professor Elliott, who is Medical Director of Great Ormond Street Hospital for Children NHS Foundation Trust, described the work on comparative outcomes undertaken there. In cardiac care, this combined weekly performance review meetings, with current mortality data, safety performance issues, patient flow complications, analysis of team performance and other measures, all of which contributed to a process of continuous improvement. The Board is supplied with monthly summary reports and it will be possible in due course for the recipient of an exception report to gain access to the underlying relevant data. Data is quality controlled externally via the Central Cardiac Audit Database. This system resulted in the same benchmarked information being used for clinical audit, performance review and comparative outcome statistics.

---

48   *The Role of Information in Ensuring quality and Safety: Some personal reflections* (October 2011), Martin Elliott, p.3
www.midstaffspublicinquiry.com/sites/default/files/uploads/Martin_Elliot_paper.pdf

26.48 Professor Elliott strongly advocated the merits of transparency with regard to this sort of information:

> *We believe that families have a right to know what to expect. They also have a right to know when we don't know. It is our intention to make these outcomes as public as possible in due course, once they are validated. We can understand that this might be perceived as a risk by some clinicians and managers, but we are convinced it is right, simply on the basis that it is what we would want to know for ourselves or on our children's behalf ...*
>
> *We are servants of the people, not guardians of secrets.*[49]

26.49 A different integrated approach to the recording of treatment and measuring performance was described and demonstrated at the same seminar by Dr David Rosser, Medical Director of University Hospitals of Birmingham NHS Foundation Trust (UHB).[50] This Trust uses electronic systems for prescribing and drug administration, requesting results and reporting observation charting. Embedded in these systems, where appropriate, is a decision support facility through a hierarchy of warnings based on over 16,000 rules, many managed by speciality clinicians. Thus, a proposed prescription might be challenged or in extreme cases prevented. The number of challenges varies from month to month, but for example, in April 2010 on over 8,600 occasions, intentions to prescribe were reversed after the issue of a "level 3" warning (issued where a decision is of such potential risk that a password is required to override the system to pursue it). UHB considers that the vast majority of these events represent the prevention of an error by the system. Where an early warning score indicates a psychological deterioration, an automatic email is sent to inform the critical care outreach team. MRSA eradication therapy is automatically prescribed when a positive swab is reported.

26.50 The data collected in this way is also used for quality management. A Quality Outcomes and Research Unit, which is entirely separate from any performance management function, consists of clinicians who formulate quality of care indicators for use within the trust. An informatics team then finds ways of extracting the relevant data. The criteria used by the trust to assess whether such information would be useful are that it should be

- Accurate;
- Relevant to the quality of care delivered to patients;
- Useful to the recipient;
- Timely.

49 *The Role of Information in Ensuring quality and Safety: Some personal reflections,* (October 2011), Martin Elliott, p. 14, 16
    www.midstaffspublicinquiry.com/sites/default/files/uploads/Martin_Elliot_paper.pdf
50 *The Role Of Information In Ensuring Quality And Patient Safety,* (October 2011), David Rosser
    www.midstaffspublicinquiry.com/sites/default/files/uploads/Dr_David_Rosser_paper.pdf

26.51 The results are delivered through an escalating system of automatically generated emails to those who are in a position to make relevant changes, and also used to populate a quality dashboard which displays each area's performance.

26.52 Managers have access to individual level data on, for example, rates of omitted doses by nurse or doctor. This supports a robust performance management system in which, if the automatic emails have no effect, persistent outliers are invited to meetings at which issues are identified and reviewed. Dr Rosser showed the seminar graphs showing a correlation between a dramatic fall in omitted doses and non-charted medications and the introduction of these measures. UHB believes that this focus on error prevention is the reason for a 16.9% reduction in 30-day mortality for emergency inpatients (excluding paediatrics and obstetrics) compared with England acute trusts.

26.53 At the same seminar, the importance was emphasised of clinicians taking the responsibility and lead in the collection of data and acting on the finding to obtain better patient outcomes.[51]

Quality Accounts

26.54 Providers of NHS services are required by law to publish Quality Accounts containing prescribed information relevant to the quality of service provided.[52] The information required to be published in this way includes:[53]

- A statement of the provider's view of the quality of the NHS services provided;
- A description of the areas for quality improvement in the services to be provided in the next two months, including at least three priorities, means for measurement of progress, and how this will be reported;
- Progress made since the previous report;
- Statements by the commissioning Primary Care Trust (PCT) or Strategic Health Authority (SHA), giving their opinion on the accuracy of the provider's statement and any other information relevant to quality of services;
- Statements by Local Involvement Networks (LINks), and overview and scrutiny committees;
- Numerical information about the proportion of national clinical audits and confidential enquiries in which the provider has participated, and the degree of participation (a total of 57 national clinical audits have been listed for inclusion in 2012/13 Quality Accounts);[54]

51 For example in Robin Burgess's paper *How can information be better used within the NHS?*, (October 2011), Robin Burgess (HQIP), p.4
    www.midstaffspublicinquiry.com/sites/default/files/uploads/Robin_Burgess_paper_0.pdf
52 Health Act 2009, section 8, www.legislation.gov.uk/ukpga/2009/21/contents
53 The National health Service (Quality Accounts) Regulations 2010 [SI 2010/279], (as amended), regulations 4,5,7 and schedule 1, para 1,
    www.legislation.gov.uk/uksi/2010/279/contents/made
54 *List of National Clinical Audits for inclusion in Quality Accounts 2012–13* DH, gateway ref 17195
    www.hqip.org.uk/assets/National-Team-Uploads/National-Clinical-Audits-for-Quality-Accounts-2012–13-Feb.pdf

- A description of the action the provider intends to take following review of national clinical audit reports;
- The number of local clinical audit reports reviewed by the provider and the action taken as a result;
- Any conditions imposed by the CQC during registration, and whether the provider was subject to periodic reviews or special reviews. In the latter case, the subject matter and conclusion must be reported;
- Details designed to show the completeness of information submitted for use in the HES.

26.55   The account must be certified to be accurate to the best of the knowledge and belief of the most senior person in the Trust.

26.56   The prescribed information included a number of items from which the actual performance against quality requirements could be gauged. However, in February 2012, the DH and Monitor announced the intention to introduce a mandatory requirement for the accounts for 2012/13 to report against a defined set of quality indicators based on data that trusts already report in one form or another.[55] The requirement will be to report trusts' performance against the indicators, the national average and a supporting commentary explaining any variation from the average and the steps taken to improve quality. The indicators to be reported in this way include:

- SHMI;
- Patient-reported outcome scores for groin hernia surgery, varicose vein surgery, hip replacement surgery and knee replacement surgery;
- Emergency readmission with in 28 days of discharge;
- Responsiveness to inpatients' personal needs;
- Percentage of staff who would recommend the provider to friends or family needing care;
- Percentage of patients risk assessed for venous thrombo-embolism;
- Rate of patient safety incidents and percentage resulting in death or serious harm.[56]

26.57   For the year 2009/10 foundation trusts (FTs) were required to obtain external assurance of their Quality Accounts. 52 FTs used the Audit Commission to undertake this work. Four significant areas for improvement were identified:

- Widespread lack of comprehensive systems and controls for compiling quality accounts, meaning that only limited assurance was likely for many accounts for at least two years;
- Variable arrangements for ensuring data quality;

---

55   *Quality Accounts: Reporting requirements for 2011/2012 and planned changes for 2012/2013* (16 February 2012), Department of Health and Monitor www.dh.gov.uk/prod_consum_dh/groups/dh_digitalassets/@dh/@en/documents/digitalasset/dh_132727.pdf

56   *Quality Accounts: Reporting requirements for 2011/2012 and planned changes for 2012/2013* (16 February 2012), Department of Health and Monitor, Annex e – summary of indicators www.dh.gov.uk/prod_consum_dh/groups/dh_digitalassets/@dh/@en/documents/digitalasset/dh_132727.pdf

- Lack of fully documented or identified key data quality controls;
- Variable interpretation of performance indicator definitions.[57]

26.58   Following a pilot project, from 2011/12 trusts are required to have their Quality Accounts externally audited. NHS acute trusts will have to include a "limited assurance report" from auditors on compliance with the regulations, and new FTs will have to comply with Monitor's requirements for audit assurance.[58] Auditors must also be instructed to test a trust's management on three clinical indicators. Directors are required to sign a statement in the Quality Account that, among other things, it presents a balanced picture of the trust's performance during the reporting period, that the performance information is reliable and accurate, and that there are proper internal controls over the collection and reporting of information.

26.59   For the year 2010/11, the Audit Commission conducted auditors' reviews of 91 NHS acute and mental health trusts, one PCT and 52 out of 136 FTs. For NHS trusts this was a "dry run" exercise because auditors were not required to give an opinion of the accounts. For FTs, auditors were for the first time required to give a limited assurance opinion on the content of the report. The Commission reported that overall it found a positive picture of good and improving performance. Key findings were that:[59]

- 96% of NHS trusts had acceptable arrangements in place to assure themselves that their quality account was fairly stated and 95% complied with the DH requirements. At 15 trusts, auditors suggested improvements in systems and processes such as integrating quality accounts into the trust's wider quality agenda rather than dealing with it as a separate matter;
- Half of NHS trusts did not supply their auditor with a Statement of Director's Responsibilities, in part because the requirement was imposed late in the year;
- Few data quality issues were found on testing MRSA and *C. difficile* performance indicators, but there were problems with the 62-day cancer waiting indicator data;
- Mental health trusts had more issues than acute trusts;
- There was a variation in performance indicators chosen by trusts as a mandatory set of indicators had not been required by the DH;
- With regard to FTs, all received an unqualified limited assurance opinion and complied with Monitor's guidance;
- All Quality Accounts from FTs were consistent with other sources of information and no significant issues were uncovered through indicator testing.

---

57   *Producing Quality Reports – external assurance of foundation trust quality reports 2009/10*, (March 2011), Audit Commission, page 3
www.audit-commission.gov.uk/subwebs/publications/studies/studyPDF/3675.pdf
58   *Quality Accounts: 2011/12 audit guidance* (2 April 2012), Department of Health, page 7
www.dh.gov.uk/prod_consum_dh/groups/dh_digitalassets/@dh/@en/documents/digitalasset/dh_133425.pdf
59   *NHS quality accounts 2010/11, Providing external assurance: findings from auditors' work at NHS trusts and foundation trusts*, (January 2012), Audit Commission, page 3
www.audit-commission.gov.uk/SiteCollectionDocuments/Downloads/nhsqualityaccounts1011.pdf

26.60 Several minor improvements were suggested to the one-third of FTs reviewed.

26.61 As the Patients Association highlighted, Professor Sir Bruce Keogh had concerns about Quality Accounts when he examined early examples:

> *I got sent the best ones to have a look at. And I looked at them, and they looked nice. And then I thought, "Could Mid Staffs have produced a good quality account?" And the answer was "Yes". And I thought, then quality accounts aren't working, if that's possible.*[60]

26.62 In his view, a remedy was to require boards to sign off the Quality Accounts and each relevant "service line" as a means of engaging them in quality assurance and governance. This is now done. He also accepted that standardised reporting requirements would avoid the risk of trusts reporting only indicators where there had been favourable results.[61]

The Care Quality Commission's use of information

Quality Risk Profiles

26.63 The CQC has made a major investment in harnessing information to assist it in identifying registered providers who may be failing to comply with its standards. The most significant part of this work has been the development of the Quality Risk Profile (QRP), replacing the Healthcare Commission (HCC)'s Organisational Risk Profile (ORP). Much evidence has been given to the Inquiry on the operation of the QRP. The Inquiry was also given the opportunity to visit the CQC's headquarters to see the system in operation.

26.64 The intention behind this system is to collate and analyse large quantities of information from multiple sources about registered organisations and to produce, via a scoring system, a risk rating. The risk that is being measured is the potential for non-compliance with the CQC's essential standards for quality and safety. Each item of information is given a weighting by reference to its reliability and relevance as evidence of compliance or non-compliance with the required outcomes. This in turn is reduced to a set of "traffic lights" that will draw to the attention of inspectors organisations that are worthy of closer consideration.[62] Identification of risk by the QRP is not itself a judgement that an organisation is not complying with standards; it is a pointer to assist inspectors to prioritise and target their work.[63] It also provides background information that will assist in their exploration of the performance of particular organisations. It is accepted that there are some outcomes for which there are currently insufficient data sources to assess the risk of non-compliance. The QRP scoring system appears to assume compliance in such cases unless there is evidence of non-compliance, but the

---

60 Keogh T123.123
61 Keogh T123.124–125
62 Hamblin WS0000031025, para 76; T86.35–36
63 Sherlock T85.119–120

expectation is that where the QRP offers insufficient evidence, further evidence would be gathered at reviews to enable a judgement to be made on those outcomes.[64]

26.65 The QRP is not the only available trigger to provoke the CQC's interest in an organisation. This may also occur through, for example, information on outliers and particular information provided by a third party raising concerns.

26.66 The QRP output is shared with providers, commissioners, SHAs and the DH. It is not currently made available to the public, although consideration is being given as to how this might be achieved.[65]

Information collection

26.67 The CQC seeks where possible to use information already obtained by others, and, in particular, that collected as part of routine management and oversight processes. It continually reviews potential new sources of information.[66] Information sources used include contact with local patient groups, LINKs, the public, complaints, and comments left on the NHS Choices website.[67] NHS Choices provides the CQC with between 350 and 600 comments per month about NHS care, albeit that these are filtered to remove potentially defamatory comment.[68]

Complaints

26.68 Unlike the Healthcare Commission (HCC), the CQC has no role in the complaints process and does not consider it should have such a role. Therefore, the information it receives by way of complaints is limited to accounts provided by members of the public who contact the CQC directly, and material supplied by the Parliamentary and Health Service Ombudsman where a complaint made to that body has been upheld. It acknowledges that in spite of these mechanisms there is a loss of useful data in this area.[69]

Whistleblowing

26.69 The CQC has whistleblowing guidance for providers.[70] This draws their attention to the obligations under the essential standards, which support whistleblowing. The guidance states that, on receipt of whistleblowing information, the CQC will do one or more of the following:

---

64 CLO000000535 CQC Closing submissions, para 189
65 Hamblin, T86.144–146
66 Hamblin WS0000031010, paras 18–19
67 Sherlock WS0000032298, paras 52–54
68 Hamblin WS0000031019, para 54
69 CLO000000520 CQC Closing submissions, paras 138–140
70 *Whistleblowing: guidance for providers who are registered with the Care Quality Commission*, (December 2011), Care Quality Commission www.cqc.org.uk/sites/default/files/media/documents/rp_poc_100495_20111206_v2_00_whistleblowing_guidance_for_providers.pdf . The June 2011 version of the document was exhibited to the Inquiry at CJ/8 WS0000076658

- Note the concern and log it, ensuring that the relevant compliance inspector is aware of it and is able to take it into account when assessing the provider's compliance with standards;
- Use the information to assist in decisions about what, if any, form of review to undertake;
- Raise the issue directly with the provider, keeping the identity of the informant confidential;
- Where appropriate, issue a safeguarding alert to the local authority. In such a case, the inspector is expected to monitor the progress and outcome of the authority's investigation;
- Notify the police where the information is about possible illegal activity.[71]

26.70 Providers are discouraged from trying to find out the identities of whistleblowers who have passed information to the CQC, and are advised that:

> ... [the belief that a whistleblower has reported] *is an opportunity to promote your own approach to whistleblowing and reassure your staff that it is safe to raise concerns internally.*[72]

26.71 A guide for workers at registered healthcare providers was published in October 2012.[73] While this encourages employees in the first instance to raise concerns with their employers, it advises them that they may give information directly to the CQC if:

> *You are not confident that the management of the service will deal with your concern properly, or*
>
> *Your concern is very serious, or*
>
> *You are worried that the management may be involved in or associated with the issue of concern.*[74]

26.72 According to the guidance for workers, the CQC has established a dedicated team at its National Contact Centre who log and track the follow-up of these concerns until completion. All such information is forwarded to the relevant compliance inspector. Informants are assured that if they wish their identity to be kept confidential the CQC will seek to respect this, but it is

---

71 *Whistleblowing: guidance for providers who are registered with the Care Quality Commission*, (December 2011), Care Quality Commission, page 8 www.cqc.org.uk/sites/default/files/media/documents/rp_poc_100495_20111206_v2_00_whistleblowing_guidance_for_providers.pdf .

72 *Whistleblowing: guidance for providers who are registered with the Care Quality Commission*, (December 2011), Care Quality Commission, page 9, www.cqc.org.uk/sites/default/files/media/documents/rp_poc_100495_20111206_v2_00_whistleblowing_guidance_for_providers.pdf .

73 *Whistleblowing: Guidance for workers of registered care providers*, (October 2012), CQC www.cqc.org.uk/sites/default/files/media/documents/rp_poc_100494_20120410_v3_00_whistleblowing_guidance_for_employees_of_registered_providers_afte_pcaw_comments_with_changes_tracked_for_publication.pdf

74 *Whistleblowing: Guidance for workers of registered care providers*, (October 2012), CQC, page 4 www.cqc.org.uk/sites/default/files/media/documents/rp_poc_100494_20120410_v3_00_whistleblowing_guidance_for_employees_of_registered_providers_afte_pcaw_comments_with_changes_tracked_for_publication.pdf

made clear that retention of anonymity cannot be guaranteed.[75] The CQC states that it will seek to give feedback to the informant if requested.[76]

26.73   In evidence to the Inquiry, Ms Amanda Sherlock, Director of Operations Delivery at the CQC, explained that following on from initial contact there were four possible handling strategies:

- Noting of the concern for information and consideration in future risk profiling;
- Use of the concern to inform the planned review schedule;
- Use as a trigger for a responsive review;
- "Horizon scanning" by methods including:
    - Reviewing risk information themes and trends for further investigation;
    - Highlighting of similar characteristics between trusts failing to maintain compliance;
    - Widening the scope of current indicators to provide early warning of deviations in performance and the need for intervention;
    - Adjustment of the thematic review schedule in response to emerging issues.[77]

Coroners' Rule 43 reports

26.74   Following the reforms in the handling of the Rule 43 process for coroners, from May 2011 the CQC has had access to Rule 43 reports from the Ministry of Justice.[78] There had previously been thought to be issues concerning confidentiality and information governance that needed to be worked through before the reports could be obtained by the CQC, although it was unclear from the evidence what these were. In any event, such reports suffer from the disadvantage that they will arise after an inquest, which in many cases occurs a significant period after a patient's death and therefore has a limited use as an early warning sign of service failure.

Information from inspectors via engagement forms

26.75   The Inquiry was told that the CQC has devised a method of automatically transferring information from inspectors' assessment records into the QRP, replacing the old engagement forms with a "Share your knowledge" function on the dashboard. This has resulted in a 75% increase in the amount of qualitative information available for analysis, leading to a reduction in the number of outcomes for which the CQC considered it did not have sufficient data, although this had not had an appreciable effect on the risk ratings. However, there did appear to be a correlation between the quantity of negative comments in engagement forms and negative risk ratings.[79]

75   *Whistleblowing: Guidance for workers of registered care providers*, (October 2012), CQC, pages 6–7 www.cqc.org.uk/sites/default/files/media/documents/rp_poc_100494_20120410_v3_00_whistleblowing_guidance_for_employees_of_registered_providers_afte_pcaw_comments_with_changes_tracked_for_publication.pdf
76   *Whistleblowing: Guidance for workers of registered care providers*, (October 2012), CQC, page 9 www.cqc.org.uk/sites/default/files/media/documents/rp_poc_100494_20120410_v3_00_whistleblowing_guidance_for_employees_of_registered_providers_afte_pcaw_comments_with_changes_tracked_for_publication.pdf
77   Sherlock WS0000032319–320, paras 114–115; CLO000000521, Care Quality Commission Closing submissions, para 143
78   Hamblin T86.97
79   Hamblin WS(2) WS0000074470; Hamblin T132.113

Other qualitative information

26.76 In addition to information from the engagement forms, the CQC obtains qualitative information from a variety of sources, including mental health statutory safeguarding interventions, historic information from HCC inspections, the Audit Commission, the Health and Safety Executive (HSE), and healthcare professional regulators. There is also a system for harvesting information from news media.

Quantitative data

26.77 The CQC receives quantitative data relevant to the assessment of risk from a number of sources including:

- Hospital Episode Statistics (HES);
- Mental health minimum dataset;
- Patient surveys;
- Patient-reported outcome measures;
- NHS staff surveys;
- NHS vacancy surveys;
- Compliance with targets;
- Venous thrombo-embolism risk assessments;
- Health Protection Agency (HPA) data about hospital-acquired infections;
- Certain peer review schemes;
- Patient Environment Action Team (PEAT) inspection reports;
- Data underlying NHS Litigation Authority (NHSLA) Clinical Negligence Scheme for Trusts (CNST) scheme assessments.

Incident reports

26.78 The CQC receives statutory incident reports on death, injury abuse and events preventing or likely to prevent the provider's ability to carry on a regulated activity safely. There is no obligation to report near misses but the CQC had received some information about these from the National Patient Safety Agency (NPSA). Incident reports are treated as both quantitative and qualitative data in that local inspectors are expected to follow up local notifications, and Regional Intelligence and Evidence Officers (RIEOs) are expected to look at trends and emerging issues.

Self-declarations

26.79 The CQC guidance requires inspectors to triangulate information submitted by the registered providers themselves, in the shape of compliance assessment forms or self-declarations in any other format, in order to objectively judge compliance. However, the CQC acknowledged that this is not always possible, asserting that this is more of an issue with independent healthcare and adult social care providers than the NHS. Ms Sherlock told the Inquiry that the CQC intended to move away from use of compliance assessment forms as an increasing amount of information became available. She accepted that such forms are only as good as the honesty and rigour with which they are completed.[80]

Developments

26.80 The CQC continues to develop other sources of information that were described by Mr Richard Hamblin in his evidence.[81]

Publication of information

Quality and Risk Profiles

26.81 As indicated above, the CQC is considering how it might put the output of the QRP system into the public domain. Professor Sir Bruce Keogh voiced concern in his evidence that the information was not already public and considered that there were positive benefits in allowing public scrutiny and discussion of the methodology and output:

> … I think the concept is right, but I am already on record for saying my concern about the QRP is it's not in the public domain.
>
> And, you know, the best way of improving these things is to open them to debate and to open them to not just academic debate, but to those people who are users of the service. After all, they have the most significant vested interest.
>
> …
>
> I think having the methodology in the public domain encourages people to take part and to improve it, and I think having the end result of the analysis in the public domain is important. It's important for confidence in the regulator. I think it's important for people's confidence in the NHS.
>
> …
>
> And I think the sooner the better.[82]

26.82 Sir David Nicholson gave evidence to similar effect expressing the belief that, while the QRP was a very powerful tool, it would only really "come of age" when it was open to the public.[83]

26.83 The Patients Association agreed with Sir Bruce's views. It considered that, while continual development of a system such as this was inevitable, that was not a reason for withholding

---

80   Sherlock WS0000032330, paras 137–138; T85.127
81   CLO0000000529 CQC Closing submissions, paras 172–174
82   Keogh T123.71–73
83   Nicholson T128.41–42

publication of current data and methodologies.[84] They pointed to and endorsed the views expressed by Sir Hugh Taylor, former Permanent Secretary of the DH:

> *... the more this information is out there, the better the quality, the better the information gets ... the best way to get the data effective is to get it out there ...*
>
> *... I think consistently policy makers and professionals have underestimated the sophistication of the public in these matters. The public understands that this is a difficult, complex business, and I just think the more information we put in front of them, the better, not least because it will provide an imperative to the professionals and managers in our system to get the data as accurate as possible.[85]*

26.84 Clearly, there are issues to be considered in putting this material into the public domain. Lauren Goodman, a regional intelligence and evidence officer at the CQC, told the Inquiry that there was evidence within the CQC that the QRP did not always reflect as high risk those providers thought by inspectors on the basis of "low level" local information to present a risk.[86] While the system does not prevent inspectors forming their own judgements, this does raise the question of whether the public might inadvertently be misled by the QRP ratings, unless publication includes appropriate explanations and qualifications.

Inspection reports

26.85 The CQC is required to publish reports of inspections undertaken and it does so. It was suggested that the CQC avoided expressing its findings in strong language,[87] but this was not accepted by Ms Sherlock who asserted that strong language was used where it was thought to be appropriate.[88] The first Chair of the CQC, Dame Barbara Young, told the Inquiry that she found the language in some of the HCC's reports, including that on the Trust, "strange":

> *I found it strange at how vivid and detailed the report felt it needed to be. I'm used to a regulatory regime where regulators need to be very, very evidence based and very explicit and very open, but nevertheless not necessarily going for the kind of emotive language that was in some parts of Healthcare Commission reports generally. The same was the case with healthcare acquired infection reports, where every example of poor hygiene would be catalogued in a way that I felt was unnecessary. The important thing is that the regulator is absolutely clear and explicit and open, public about where there is poor performance and what it expects to be done about it, and works very closely with the providers to make sure it happens and is very public about successive reviews of that*

84 CLO000001308–309 Patients Association Closing submissions, para 336
85 Sir Hugh Taylor T126.60–61
86 Goodman T130.123–125
87 Wood WS0000025066, para 159
88 Sherlock WS0000032364, para 248

performance. But the – the degree of I think what I called rather florid language took me aback, from my previous regulatory experience.[89]

26.86　She went on to say that the CQC did not need to rely on such methods to cause their reports to be given proper attention because of the more extensive powers available to it. However, Ms Cynthia Bower made it clear that she did not think that the HCC report into the Trust had been expressed in over-florid language and that it had never been suggested to her at the CQC that reports should be "less hard" on the NHS.[90]

Patient feedback

Patient access to records

26.87　Accuracy of records is obviously vital if safe care is to be delivered to patients. Additionally, retrospective consideration of concerns about treatment is often complicated by factual disputes where patients and their families have a recollection of events that purports to be contradicted by the records. Examples include differences about whether medication has been administered or whether required observations have been undertaken. As correctly stated in the NIGB's guidance to patients on requesting amendments to records:

> *... health and social care organisations that keep records hold that information for a number of people who have a genuine interest in its accuracy and in using it. As the patient or person using the service – in other words, the 'subject' of the record – you have a personal interest in the record being an accurate reflection of your consultation (including your own views and, in a health record, the process of diagnosis).*[91]

26.88　In many cases, the person most likely to detect inaccuracy is the patient, yet currently patients are given limited and, from observation, rarely contemporaneous, access to their records. In a paper-based system, where it is often convenient or even essential that the records be kept at a point remote from the patient, this is inevitable. In an electronic system, there is far less reason why a patient should not have access to his own medical history and treatment record. A patient could then identify inaccuracies in the record, or correct misunderstandings held by those attending him or her. There could be a facility for patients to flag items of information with which they did not agree. There may need to be categories of record to which access should not be permitted for example, where it was desirable for disclosure to be accompanied by an explanation, or where immediate disclosure might inhibit free and candid professional discussions for the benefit of the patient. Such considerations should not be allowed to prevent patients from seeing information about them which they can check for accuracy.

89　Baroness Young T110.42–43
90　Bower T87.95–98
91　*Requesting amendments to health and social care record: guidance for patients, service users and professionals*, NIGB 2010 www.nigb.nhs.uk/pubs/amendrecords page 5

26.89 The technology clearly exists. The NHS is introducing an electronic "Summary Care Record", for those patients who choose not to opt out of its creation. This will include details of medication, allergies and adverse reactions. However, currently, it is intended that direct access will only be accorded to duly authorised healthcare professionals. Patient access will be through an application under the Data Protection Act.[92] In the USA, the Mayo Clinic goes much further, offering patients an app for their smartphone that not only allows them to book appointments online and request repeat prescriptions, but also gives them secure access to their personal health information, including up-to-date results, and enables inquiries and comments to be made by the same route.[93]

Comments in hospital

26.90 Many hospitals seek real-time feedback about services from patients while they are still in hospital receiving treatment. A range of methods is used, including devices allowing patients to input their comments directly, and volunteers seeking information from patients.

26.91 Dr Rosser told the Inquiry's information seminar that one method exploits bedside TV monitors to obtain patient feedback via a survey that patients may complete daily in relation to questions on areas such as food quality, noise and staff attitude. At the Trust utilising the system, some 700 responses are received weekly and swift action can be taken for example, when a cluster of similar concerns arises.[94]

26.92 Feedback of this nature may be useful, but attention needs to be paid to any negative comments or concerns expressed on an individual basis and little if any reassurance taken from the absence of negative feedback or a preponderance of positive comments. The reluctance of many patients and their families to complain, motivated in some cases at least by a fear of adverse repercussions, means that many concerns will not be aired by the use of instant or real-time feedback methods. Consideration should be given to following up patients routinely after discharge as this could provide a wider range of responses as well as being good customer service.

Patient surveys

26.93 The evidence has shown that the results of patient surveys with regard to the Trust disclosed some concerning results. There appear to have been issues about the dissemination and understanding of this type of information. For example, the PCT suggested that surveys had been an under-appreciated resource in the NHS.[95] It described how an increasing focus on such information has developed since 2007.

---

92   www.connectingforhealth.nhs.uk/systemsandservices/scr/staff/faqs/stafffaqs examined 16 October 2012
93   www.mayoclinic.org/mayo-apps/index.html 16 October 2012
94   *The Role Of Information In Ensuring Quality And Patient Safety,* (October 2011), David Rosser, para 2.23
      www.midstaffspublicinquiry.com/sites/default/files/uploads/Dr_David_Rosser_paper.pdf
95   CLO0000001447 South Staffordshire PCT Closing submissions, para 183

26.94   The position of the SHA was that, while some attention had been paid to surveys in 2006–
         2007 they were not perceived as being of much assistance because of limitations in the data.
         In particular, the results became available over a year after being measured.[96]

26.95   The SHA now undertakes a number of initiatives involving feedback from patients and the
         public through its West Midlands Quality Institute and Observatory (West Midlands QI)
         including:

         • An annual telephone survey;
         • Feedback from a residents' panel;
         • An acute hospital/patient safety dashboard. This contains information on a number of
           indicators at provider trust level and is currently published at that level;[97]
         • The results of the inpatient survey are made available online allowing comparison
           between trusts and a choice of comparators;[98]
         • NHS Local: an online service for two-way communication between patients, carers and
           staff that allows comments to be lodged and responses offered. This is linked with NHS
           Choices, a national scheme (see below). This was demonstrated at the Inquiry's
           information seminar. The impression was that usage was variable as was the willingness
           of organisations to post responses.

Web based comment retrieval

26.96   NHS Choices, in addition to a wide range of health and healthcare information resources,
         offers an online facility for the public to record comments, positive and negative, about their
         hospital experience. These are published and the trusts concerned are able to enter their
         responses. This was compared by Professor Keogh to hotel and travel advisory websites,
         which allow customers to register ratings and narrative comments.[99] The overall percentage of
         compliments and criticisms is displayed graphically, with a breakdown of category, and users
         can compare what is said about different hospitals. For example, on a recent examination of
         the entries for Stafford Hospital, 138 comments were available to be viewed, some dating
         back to 2007, and the most recent having been entered in October 2012.[100]

26.97   Patient Opinion is an independently run website that offers a similar facility and exchanges
         comments it receives with the NHS Choices site as well as publishing them on its own. It is
         possible to see if an organisation has looked at a comment and responses are displayed. It is
         funded by subscriptions from health service organisations, which benefit from a range of tools
         made available to subscribers. Patient Opinion gives an analysis of the total comments

96   Shukla T68.31–32
97   www.wmqi.westmidlands.nhs.uk/wmqi-portal/acute-trust-quality-dashboard/ last accessed 23 October 2012;
     www.emqo.eastmidlands.nhs.uk/welcome/quality-indicators/acute-trust-quality-dashboard/?locale=en 22 last accessed 23 October 2012
98   www.wmqi.westmidlands.nhs.uk/news/patient-experience-tracker last accessed 23 October 2012.
99   Keogh T123.182
100 www.nhs.uk/servicedirectories/Pages/HospitalCommentInput.aspx?servicetype=hospital&searchtype=hospitalcommentsearch last
     examined on 17 October 2012

received, the number of responses and the total comments that have resulted in changes. It may choose not to publish very critical complaints if it cannot verify that they are made in good faith. Additionally, potentially defamatory statements are edited. However, the site states it has published over 95% of comments received without change.[101]

26.98   Thus when its site was examined on the same day as the NHS Choices site, it was showing 223 comments about the Trust, 30 staff had been "listening" and 10 comments had resulted in changes. The most recent comment had been posted on the day of examination of the website, and the oldest was four years old.

26.99   Professor Sir Bruce Keogh told the Inquiry that NHS Choices had about 9 million visitors every month, making it one of the most visited healthcare sites in the world, but he suggested that more needed to be done in future to bring the comment facility to the public attention.[102] The difficulty caused by the relatively low numbers of comments registered was echoed by Mr Hamblin of the CQC, who told the Inquiry that the HCC had taken a feed from Patient Opinion but found the numbers "incredibly low". He thought that in retrospect this attempt had been made a little early.[103] However, the feed continues to provide between 350 and 600 comments per month to the CQC, and Mr Hamblin sat on the Clinical Advisory Board of NHS Choices.[104]

Confidentiality

26.100   Much emphasis is rightly placed, both in law and in healthcare practice, on the rights of patients to confidentiality in respect of their healthcare information. The arguments in favour of this have been well rehearsed and require no extensive repetition or analysis here. It is essential that the healthcare system keeps patients' personal and medical information secure from disclosure to unauthorised persons for many reasons, which include:

- Respect for the individual's right to a private life;
- Ensuring patients are free to share all relevant health information with their clinicians;
- Maintenance of public confidence in the healthcare system.

26.101   While the need for confidentiality is clear, there are exceptions to the duty to maintain it. For example, confidential medical information may be disclosed to the extent necessary to prevent serious harm to the patient or another.

26.102   Confidentiality can, however, be claimed to be a barrier to the sharing of information even when this would assist in the management or regulation of healthcare services. Yet, provided

---

101   https://www.patientopinion.org.uk/ last examined on 17 October 2012
102   Keogh T123.182–183
103   Hamblin T86.83
104   Hamblin WS0000031019, para 54

any means of identifying the patient is removed from the information, there is no public interest reason why it should not be used for the purposes of management and regulatory data. Similarly, while security of sensitive personal data is an important duty imposed on the holder of such information, it should not be allowed to prevent its legitimate use.

26.103 The hindrance to the development of an integrated system of access to patient information in the interests of effective care was graphically expressed by Professor Elliott in a paper for the Inquiry's information seminar, describing his experience as a patient:

> The results of [my] tests disappear into a system to which either, but not both, my GP or [consultant] have access and from which I am excluded. I thus have to embark monthly, on a series of visits and phone calls which are completely unnecessary, and which make it very challenging for me to maintain graphical control over my results. This is a waste of everyone's time and must cost a fortune if replicated for other patients. Why don't I own the records, have portal access to see them and allow the GP and [consultant] (and relevant others) access? Security works for my bank, but apparently not easily for the NHS.[105]

26.104 It is important that in designing information-sharing systems that confidentiality and security of personal data are at the forefront of considerations, but it is also important that the appropriate steps are taken to enable properly anonymised data to be used for managerial and regulatory purposes.

The Health and Social Care Information Centre

Organisation and objectives

26.105 The Health and Social Care Information Centre (the Information Centre), formerly called the NHS Information Centre was set up in April 2005. It has some 500 staff and an annual budget of about £50 million. Its declared function is to collect data and information across the whole health and social care system in England, and to process and disseminate it to enable it to be used to deliver high-quality effective care.[106] Since 2007, under the leadership of Mr Tim Straughan as its chief executive, the Information Centre has been changing its focus from the provision of high-level, aggregated figures for "upwards" transmission to the DH and Ministers to a service intended to be useful to and used by the front-line providers and recipients of healthcare. In particular, there has been a change in emphasis from "counting inputs" to collecting information on outcome measures and indicators.[107]

---

105 *The Role of Information in Ensuring Quality and Patient Safety*, Prof Martin Elliott, (October 2011), page 5
   www.midstaffspublicinquiry.com/sites/default/files/uploads/Martin_Elliot_paper.pdf
106 Straughan T99.144
107 Straughan T99.145–148

26.106 Mr Straughan told the Inquiry that the Information Centre had put a lot of effort into:

> ... making sure that we are trusted, credible, reliable, timely[108]

> We have tried to position ourselves as the single authoritative source of health and social care information. Our aim is to stop arguments about whether data is correct and focus more on what the data tells us.[109]

26.107 The Information Centre works within the national code of standards for the statistics it produces, with the aim of ensuring that they are free and seen to be free from political and other interference. As Mr Straughan remarked:

> It's very important to us that we are seen to be independent and operating to the highest possible standards and codes of practice, and that's what we do. We monitor breaches very, very carefully. We report them to the National Statistician. And I'm pleased to say that over the last two or three years there have been very few. It has improved considerably.[110]

26.108 While aiming to be the central repository of all healthcare-related statistical data, the Information Centre only undertakes limited analysis itself, instead providing the raw statistical material to others to undertake this function.

Independence

26.109 Mr Straughan anticipated in his evidence, correctly, that the new legislation (see below) would enable the Information Centre to publish what it thought right to publish. He emphasised the importance of the organisation's independence:

> I think that's why the independence is so very important ... what people want is a credible, independent organization that will transparently provide data, indicators and metrics that people know and trust, and aren't influenced unduly politically or economically or commercially to do otherwise.[111]

26.110 The Information Centre sees its role as being to present the facts and figures in a neutral and objective way, usually through press releases, which are notified to Ministers 24 hours pre release. Any attempts to persuade the Information Centre to express themselves differently are resisted.[112]

---

108 Straughan WS0000043736–37, para 2; T99.149;
109 Straughan WS0000043737, para 4
110 Straughan T99.151
111 Straughan T99.156–157
112 Straughan T99.152–153

26.111 While the Information Centre is therefore independent with regard to the methods used to collect data, analysis and dissemination of results, it is ultimately dependent on the authority of the DH to determine what data is collected. However, to date, it has never been instructed by the DH to stop collecting data it already receives. In fact, Mr Straughan said, the nature of the data collected and the move towards outcomes had never been a political issue so far as he was aware.[113]

Hospital Episode Statistics

26.112 HES lie at the heart of the work of the Information Centre. It receives into the Secondary Uses Service raw data from all hospital providers, including patient identities, gender, age, diagnosis, treatment and so on. The Information Centre then extracts from this material the data as it converts into the HES, having anonymised and otherwise "cleaned" it.

26.113 It had been a feature of HES that the figures were made available some time after the occurrence of the relevant events but, Mr Straughan said, this had now improved. The figures were now released two or three months after the events recorded. They are provided in different ways to a number of NHS and commercial organisations.[114]

26.114 The quality of the data contributed by providers is monitored for coding accuracy by means of a dashboard, and the results are given not only to the providers but also to the CQC.[115] Mr Straughan considered that there should be standards for the quality of data provided written into commissioning contracts.[116]

Complaints data

26.115 The Information Centre publishes national statistics on complaints made by or on behalf of patients to organisations in the NHS. Until 2011–2012, FTs were not obliged to submit this data, although most did so. With effect from 2011–2012 FTs have been obliged to do so.[117]

26.116 The data published include the total number of complaints, and, on an experimental basis from 2011–2012, the total number upheld. The report makes it clear that the number of complaints is not necessarily to be considered an indicator of a provider's performance.[118]

---

113 Straughan T99.153–155
114 Straughan T99.158–159
115 Straughan T99.162
116 Straughan T99.164
117 29 FTs did not do so in 2010–2011: *Data on Written complaints 2011–12*, (August 2012) Health and Social Care Centre, page 4 www.ic.nhs.uk/webfiles/publications/002_Audits/Audits%20and%20performance/complaints1112/Data_on_written_complaints_in_the_NHS_2011_12_Report.pdf
118 *Data on Written complaints 2011–12*, (August 2012) Health and Social Care Centre, page 4 www.ic.nhs.uk/webfiles/publications/002_Audits/Audits%20and%20performance/complaints1112/Data_on_written_complaints_in_the_NHS_2011_12_Report.pdf

26.117 Figures are broken down by service area. In the case of acute hospital complaints, these areas are inpatients, outpatients, and A&E. In 2011–2012, acute hospital inpatient complaints accounted for 31.6% of the total, outpatients 27.6% and A&E 8.7%.[119]

26.118 It is also possible to analyse the professions against whom complaints are made. In 2011–2012, the medical (including surgical) profession accounted for 45.9%, nursing, midwifery and health visiting 21.7%, and trust administrative staff and members 12.7%.[120]

Categories for complaints data

26.119 The subjects of complaints are divided up into very broad categories:

- All aspects of clinical treatment – 46.8% of complaints;
- Attitude of staff – 11.8%;
- Communication/information to patients (written and oral) – 10.1%;
- Appointments, delay/cancellation (outpatients) – 8.3%;
- Admissions, discharge and transfer arrangements – 6.1%;
- Subjects with less than 5% of complaints – 19.0%.[121]

26.120 "All aspects of clinical treatment" is not further broken down in the national statistics and, not surprisingly, is the largest single category of complaint, amounting to 45.8% in 2011–2012. Mr Straughan told the Inquiry that it was the Information Centre's intention to publish more detail in future.[122]

Workforce data

26.121 The Information Centre collates and publishes data on workforce in healthcare organisations, providing breakdowns of numbers, and professions. It has access to data on staffing levels, pay and skill mix, potentially organised by specialty. Trusts are given the facility to compare ther own workforce data with other trusts. There is currently no public access to figures at this level, but Mr Straughan thought there would be no problem in Monitor or the CQC obtaining this information.[123] It would be possible from the available information to benchmark staffing levels in various hospitals.[124]

---

119 *Data on Written complaints 2011–12*, (August 2012) Health and Social Care Centre, page 11
www.ic.nhs.uk/webfiles/publications/002_Audits/Audits%20and%20performance/complaints1112/Data_on_written_complaints_in_the_NHS_2011_12_Report.pdf
120 *Data on Written complaints 2011–12*, (August 2012) Health and Social Care Centre, page 12
www.ic.nhs.uk/webfiles/publications/002_Audits/Audits%20and%20performance/complaints1112/Data_on_written_complaints_in_the_NHS_2011_12_Report.pdf
121 *Data on Written complaints 2011–12*, (August 2012) Health and Social Care Centre, page 14
www.ic.nhs.uk/webfiles/publications/002_Audits/Audits%20and%20performance/complaints1112/Data_on_written_complaints_in_the_NHS_2011_12_Report.pdf
122 Straughan T99.167–168
123 Straughan T99.168–169
124 Straughan T99.170–172

Quality indicators

26.122 The Information Centre has prepared a list of some 273 quality indicators, divided into domains of quality, effectiveness, patient experience and safety.[125] The numbers of indicators in each area are shown in the table below:[126]

Pathway	Quality Dimension		
	Safety	Effectiveness	Experience
Acute care		18	
Children's health		5	
End of life care		3	
Learning disabilities		1	
Long term conditions		46	1
Maternity and newborn		3	
Mental health	3	20	
Other		4	28
Planned care	8	101	29
Staying healthy		3	

26.123 The data for these indicators is available to the public via the Information Centre's website and can be subjected to analysis by commercial organisations such as Dr Foster Intelligence, CHKS and interested individuals. Mr Straughan saw the role of the Information Centre as that of the impartial supplier of data, so that it was for others to undertake whatever detailed analysis was thought to be required.[127] The Information Centre largely limits itself to national and regional level reports. Therefore, he did not consider it part of the Information Centre's role to examine the figures to look for deficiencies such as those that arose at the Trust.[128] Mr Straughan was clear that there is a process by which outside organisations, such as Dr Foster Intelligence and CHKS, can obtain access to the cleaned data to produce analyses of their own.[129]

26.124 The issues surrounding mortality statistics have been examined in *Chapter 5: Mortality statistics*, but the Information Centre has played a coordinating role in obtaining the consensus that has led to SHMI statistics being published as well as the Hospital Standardised Mortality Ratio (HSMR).[130] Mr Straughan agreed that it would be possible to develop SHMI to obtain recognation for it as an official National Statistic.[131]

---

125 Straughan T99.172–173. *Indicators for Quality Improvement* (2009), Health and Social Care Information Centre https://mqi.ic.nhs.uk/IndicatorsList.aspx
126 Table downloaded from http://mqi.ic.nhs.uk/ on 17 October 2012
127 Straughan T99.172–176
128 Straughan T99.198
129 Straughan T99.176
130 Straughan T99.178–179, T99.190–192
131 Straughan T99.206–207

National Patient Safety Agency data

26.125 The National Patient Safety Agency (NPSA) has published statistics on Serious Untoward Incidents (SUIs) on a regular basis. This function has been taken over by the NHS Commissioning Board, following abolition of the NPSA on 1 June 2012 and the figures continue to be published as before.[132] Organisation-level analyses are publicly accessible. Currently this information is not sent to the Information Centre but Mr Straughan thought that any information that potentially had multiple uses for different people or organisations should be provided to it. If provided in a standardised format, this information could be distributed in an open and transparent way.[133]

Future changes under the Health and Social Care Act 2012

26.126 Under the Health and Social Care Act 2012, in provisions due to be implemented in April 2013, the Information Centre will change in status from a special health authority to a non-departmental public body.[134] According to Mr Straughan, this "will ... or may" lead to the accrual of specific additional powers to acquire and access data.[135]

26.127 Under the Act, the Information Centre will be required to have regard to:

- The information standards published by the Secretary of State under section 250 of the Act;
- Guidance issued by the Secretary of State and the NHS Commissioning Board;
- The need to promote the effective, efficient and economic use of resources in the provision of health services and adult social care.

26.128 The Information Centre will be obliged to minimise the burdens it imposes on others, and to exercise its functions effectively, efficiently and economically.[136] It will be obliged to establish and operate a system for the collection or analysis of specified types of information as directed by the Secretary of State or the NHS Commissioning Board.[137] Others may request the Information Centre to establish and operate such systems if it is believed to be necessary or expedient for the exercise of that person's functions in connection with the provision of healthcare or adult social care. Certain types of such request may be mandatory, in particular, requests made by Monitor, the CQC and NICE.[138] The Act appears to make no provision for the Information Centre to collect and analyse information except in compliance with a direction or a request.

---

132 See www.nrls.npsa.nhs.uk/patient-safety-data/ accessed 23 October 2012
133 Straughan T99.200–202
134 *The power of Information: putting all of us in control of the health and care information we need*, (21 May 2012), Department of Health, Page 80, para 5.24 www.dh.gov.uk/prod_consum_dh/groups/dh_digitalassets/@dh/@en/documents/digitalasset/dh_134205.pdf;
135 Straughan T99.155–156
136 Health and Social Care Act 2012, section 253, www.legislation.gov.uk/ukpga/2012/7/section/253
137 Health and Social Care Act 2012, section 254, www.legislation.gov.uk/ukpga/2012/7/section/254
138 Health and Social Care Act 2012. section 255, www.legislation.gov.uk/ukpga/2012/7/section/255

26.129 Subject to certain qualifications, the Information Centre will have a statutory power in pursuance of its functions to require health service bodies to provide it with information, and compliance will not generally be a breach of any obligation of confidence.[139] However, the Act provides no sanction for any body or person who fails to comply with a requirement to provide information. The Information Centre must publish or otherwise disseminate the information it receives pursuant to a direction or a request, again subject to restrictions designed to protect confidentiality.[140] In addition to publication in any form required by a direction or request, the Information Centre may publish information in any other form and manner at such other times as it considers appropriate.[141] In considering the appropriate form, manner and timing of the publication of information, the Information Centre must have regard to:

- The need for the information to be easily accessible;
- The persons whom the Information Centre considers likely to use the information;
- The uses to which the Information Centre considers the information is likely to be put.[142]

26.130 The Act provides a regulatory power to establish an accreditation scheme for information service providers that are not public bodies. Dr Foster intelligence would appear to be an example of a body that could be brought within such a scheme.[143]

26.131 There is also power to confer on the Information Centre the function of establishing, maintaining and publishing a database of quality indicators.[144]

26.132 The position therefore will be that the Information Centre will be restricted in its collection of data by what it is directed or requested to do by the Secretary of State or healthcare organisations, but it will have independence in its analysis and publication of the statistics. It will also, if given the power to do so, become the authority for coordinating the recognition of quality indicators in healthcare. The Information Centre will be able to collect data from the private sector as well as NHS organisations, in relation to the provision of publicly funded health services, but not in relation to independently provided healthcare.[145]

Department of Health Information Strategy

26.133 Professor Sir Brian Jarman suggested to the Inquiry in strong terms that the DH had been reluctant to accept information displaying an adverse statistical outcome.[146] The general

---

139 Health and Social Care Act 2012, section 259, www.legislation.gov.uk/ukpga/2012/7/section/259
140 Health and Social Care Act 2012, sections 260–261, www.legislation.gov.uk/ukpga/2012/7/section/260
141 Health and Social Care Act 2012, section 260(4), (5), www.legislation.gov.uk/ukpga/2012/7/section/260
142 Health and Social Care Act 2012, section 260(6), www.legislation.gov.uk/ukpga/2012/7/section/260
143 Health and Social Care Act 2012, section 267, www.legislation.gov.uk/ukpga/2012/7/section/267
144 Health and Social Care Act 2012, section 268, www.legislation.gov.uk/ukpga/2012/7/section/268
145 Health and Social Care Act 2012, section 259(1)-(2), www.legislation.gov.uk/ukpga/2012/7/section/269
146 Jarman T98.158–159

reaction to HSMR, his principal concern, is addressed in *Chapter 5: Mortality statistics*. The lesson drawn in that chapter was that concerns about methodology, however legitimate, should not overshadow the need to check the real impact services were having on patients. This was a product of the prevailing culture, not of any wilful intent on the part of the DH to hide undesirable news. Whatever may have been the position in the past, the DH is now committed to an ambitious information project. Even Professor Jarman was prepared to accept that there had been a change of attitude since the first inquiry report.[147]

26.134 As mentioned in the introduction to this chapter, in May 2012, the DH published its Information Strategy.[148] The principal ambitions of the strategy relevant to safety and quality standards of information were expressed to be:

> *Information regarded as a health and care service in its own right for us all ... so that information benefits everyone ... ;*
>
> *Information recorded once, at our first contact with professional staff ... supported by consistent use of information standards that enable data to flow (interoperability) between systems whilst keeping our confidential information safe and secure;*
>
> *Our electronic care records progressively become the source for core information used to improve our care, improve services and to inform research etc. – reducing bureaucratic data collections and enabling us to measure quality;*
>
> *A culture of transparency, where access to high quality, evidence based information about services and the quality of care held by Government and health and care services is openly and easily available to us all;*
>
> *An information culture where all health and care professionals ... take responsibility for recording, sharing and using information to improve our care;*
>
> *The widespread use of modern technology to make health and care services more convenient, accessible and efficient;*
>
> *An information system built on innovative and integrated solutions and local decision-making, within a framework of national standards that ensure information can move freely, safely and securely around the system.[149]*

26.135 A central part of the strategy is to aim to connect different information systems, rather than repeat previous attempts at a common system. The aim is to make individual patient records available electronically, to both the patients and their health and care professionals, whilst

---

147 Jarman T98.160–161
148 *The power of information: putting all of us in control of the health and care information we need* (21 May 2012), Department of Health, www.dh.gov.uk/en/Publicationsandstatistics/Publications/PublicationsPolicyAndGuidance/DH_134181
149 *The power of information: putting all of us in control of the health and care information we need* (21 May 2012), Department of Health, pages 5–6 www.dh.gov.uk/en/Publicationsandstatistics/Publications/PublicationsPolicyAndGuidance/DH_134181

allowing the data contained in those records to be available in anonymised form, via the Information Centre, to professionals, commissioners and regulators, as well as the public.

26.136 This is potentially a very important development. If patient records can be used to provide data that directly informs effective safety, quality and performance measures, there is the potential for increasing the accuracy and timeliness of those mechanisms. From the patients' point of view, swift, online access to their records, with a facility to note their own comments, can only serve to enhance their involvement in their own treatment and to improve its accuracy and completeness. It is already recognised that patients should have the facility to have their records amended where this is appropriate.[150]

Submissions at Inquiry

The importance of information

26.137 The DH accepted in its closing submissions that:

> *At a general level, with regard to Mid Staffs, the system clearly failed to work as a system. Organisations did not always work together and information was not always shared appropriately, meaning that opportunities to identify warning signs, and investigate and resolve concerns, were missed ...*[151]

26.138 The HCC made a point about the importance of having the relevant information, and an effective analysis of it, in enabling its investigation team to target the "right" parts of the Trust.[152] This suggests, by implication, that others did not have the benefit of the appropriate information when they undertook visits. The HCC goes on to cite the visits of Ms Cynthia Bower in 2007, Dr Peter Carter in 2008, the Deanery in May 2008, as well as inspections by the SHA and the NHSLA, which, it states, "do not seem to have been successful".[153] This is not in itself a criticism of these individuals, but more a general observation on the importance of information in setting the context of a wide range of interactions between external agencies and a provider trust. The HCC contended that inspections in the healthcare sector were a very useful means of detecting non-compliance with standards, but only when they could be targeted on suspect areas on the basis of effective use of data and analysis. In their view, healthcare provision was too complex to rely on serial overall inspections to uncover failings.[154]

---

150 See *Requesting amendments to health and social care records: guidance for patients, service users and professionals*, (2010), NIGB 2010: www.nigb.nhs.uk/pubs/amendrecords
151 CLO000000807–808 DH Closing submissions, para 16
152 CLO000001598 HCC Closing submissions, para 148
153 CLO000001599 HCC Closing submissions, para 150
154 CLO000001601 HCC Closing submissions para 162

It is our view that data and information should continue to be used as a precursor to and guide for targeted visits. We should not abandon the search to use information – both quantitative and qualitative – in an ever more intelligent way, in favour of "a walk around the wards" – or, even worse, just a few of them. The development of proper Clinical Indicators of good care, and fuller measures of the experience of patients, should provide a proper means of focusing scrutiny on risky areas, and enable judgements to be made on how best to carry out that scrutiny ...[155]

26.139 Foreseeing that resource constraints and the implications of technological advances were likely to make physical inspections more difficult to pursue, they argued that:

The challenge for the future must surely be [to] capture patient and visitor experience in "real time" – i.e. to use the resource which is already available, in the shape of the huge number of visitors to a hospital. Developing and embedding the use of patient-reported outcome measures, particularly in respect of domains which are closely linked to the quality of patient experience, must be an important way forward, together with the development of better measures of clinical outcomes, and reporting of the same.[156]

26.140 Cure the NHS made a number of submissions highlighting the importance of an overall system of information for the NHS, and in particular:

- The need to prevent effective safety and quality initiatives remaining isolated;[157]
- The need to avoid confusion about the purpose of collecting information and its value;[158]
- The need to collect and use data relevant to improving services at the front line and by reference to individual and team performance:

  Individual and team performance measures are the most powerful data for improvement. Such data can be aggregated and used at specialty, division, hospital or NHS level. This is the essential activity which is missing from the NHS. This, together with its associated culture, is what can make the concepts of "right first time" and "zero harm" a reality.[159]

Mortality

26.141 In its submissions on HSMR and its own mortality outliers programme, the HCC made the important point that in the absence of other indicators mortality figures were properly regarded as important, but recognised that it was necessary to work on the development of other indicators that could warn of concerns at an earlier stage.[160]

---

155 CL0000001711 HCC Closing submissions,, para 42
156 CL0000001601 HCC Closing submissions, para 163
157 CL0000000767 Cure the NHS Closing submissions, para 27
158 CL0000000768 Cure the NHS Closing submissions, para 28
159 CL0000000770 Cure the NHS Closing submissions, para 33
160 CL0000001658 HCC Closing submissions, paras 48–50

Serious Untoward Incidents

26.142 The HCC commended SUIs as a useful source of information, but warned against undue reliance on them. This was because SUIs, by definition, depend on something having gone wrong. Further, there is a time lag before a report can percolate through the system, and reports do not pick up many cases of non-diagnosis, or of missed or later diagnosis.[161]

The need for outcome measures and data about healthcare professionals

26.143 In relation to the future, the HCC argued that all professions should define key indicators measuring the essential outcomes of their work, and then collect and publish data relating to those measures. It contends that taking such steps as a matter of urgency will drive up standards:

> *What gets measured gets done.*[162]

26.144 The HCC pointed out that the SCTS had accomplished this and therefore so could others. It was important that the same type of debate as that which surrounded the development of mortality indicators be conducted for other analyses of outcomes, with a view to the profession owning and adopting new measures:

> *Clinicians need to commit to a new drive to develop, agree and then to implement monitoring of those core indicators which they would accept measure the extent to which they are providing a quality service; and publish the results.*[163]

Use of information in and by provider trusts

The need for information to be accessible to all interested parties

26.145 The Patients Association, among others, supported the Government's strategy of moving away from information being held in a relatively inaccessible form to open availability for patients, the public and others interested in it. However, the Association warned that data collection was complicated, and was often given inadequate local priority. It argued that there were huge benefits to be gained from greater transparency to enable better internal and external scrutiny. Provided appropriate explanations were available, and patient confidentiality was preserved, it saw no justification for not publishing the available data.[164]

The need for consistency and comparability

26.146 The Patients Association also emphasised the need for "uniformity and comparability" in any data collection system of the future. It commended the development of core data collection

---

161 CLO000001711–712 HCC Closing submissions, para 43
162 CLO000001704 HCC Closing submissions, paras 15–16
163 CLO000001705 HCC Closing submissions, para 20
164 CLO000003788 Patients Association Closing submissions, paras 333–335

methodologies required of all organisations. It argued that coordination was needed to prevent a "post code lottery" in the availability of information.[165]

Chief Information Officer or Care Monitor

26.147 The HCC and Action Against Medical Accidents (AvMA) supported the suggestion made by Professor Elliott at the Inquiry's information seminar that each trust should have a Chief Information Officer at board level. This officer would be responsible for ensuring that clinicians were fully involved in data collection, and that the organisation's systems incorporated this work.[166] The HCC referred to Professor Sir Ian Kennedy's report on children's services that had made the same recommendation for GP practices.[167] This recommendation was made to facilitate and coordinate the sharing of information between professionals and with families.

26.148 A similar suggestion was made by Professor Sir Muir Gray in his paper for the information seminar. His proposal was that there should be a Chief Knowledge Officer accountable directly to the Chief Executive and responsible for the management of knowledge and its flow into, around and out of the organisation.[168]

26.149 The Patients Association argued that each trust should have a Monitor of Care, independent of it and employed by Local Healthwatch or the CQC. While suggesting that such a post could fulfil the role envisaged by Mr Antony Sumara, former Chief Executive of the Trust, of a figure comparable to Miss Julie Bailey who could feed back a "real perception of what's going on", the functions could include:

- Systematic measurement of patient experience;
- Internal and external audit programmes;
- Assessment of staffing levels;
- Receipt of concerns raised by staff;
- Monitoring of complaints handling;
- Liaison with external agencies;
- Review of coding practices;
- Review of appraisal practices.[169]

26.150 When considering these suggestions, it is as well to bear in mind the evidence of Mr Straughan of the Information Centre as to the importance of having sufficient expertise available for analysing and understanding information:

165 CLO000003788–789 Patients Association Closing submissions, paras 336–337, recommendation 43
166 CLO000001705–706 HCC Closing submissions, para 23; CLO000000469 AvMA Closing submissions, page 115
167 *Getting it right for children and young people: Overcoming cultural barriers in the NHS so as to meet their needs*, (September 2010) Professor Sir Ian Kennedy, pages 68–69, recommendation 17, paras 4.70–4.74 www.dh.gov.uk/prod_consum_dh/groups/dh_digitalassets/@dh/@en/@ps/documents/digitalasset/dh_119446.pdf
168 *Report for the Mid Staffordshire Inquiry on the benefits of knowledge management*, (19 October 2011), Sir Muir Gray, pages 7–8, www.midstaffspublicinquiry.com/inquiry-seminars/information
169 CLO000003791–797 Patients Association Closing submissions, paras 344–370

... What we really need to invest in is ... the analytical expertise and capacity and capability in the system to understand what this data and information is telling them. And that's at all levels of the system from national organisations through commissioners, down to providers of services. We have to invest in analysts and ... train people and clinicians, so that people can start to understand what this data is telling them and when they need to be worried, when they don't need to be worried, and actually what they need to do about it, and that's a huge cultural [shift] and a real challenge for the NHS, and I hope we embrace it but it does need leadership and commitment.

... for me that's a big lesson out of this whole Inquiry is the importance of data and the importance of having standardised data and the importance of people being able to do something with it and make a difference and spot things before they happen.[170]

Self-assessment and quality accounts

26.151 Although self-assessment was frequently questioned during the Inquiry in terms of its effectiveness as a regulatory tool in isolation, the HCC argued that it was a "first, but necessary and essential step in any scrutiny by the regulator". In its view, a formal "account" to the regulator was a proper means of increasing accountability, which could give greater definition to Quality Accounts. The HCC observed that currently there was a variety of practice as to what was included in Quality Accounts and how they were presented, with the result that:

... they are not easily used by the public to compare the performance of one organisation against another, or to see how performance varies over time.[171]

26.152 AvMA suggested that the NHS Commissioning Board should require all NHS bodies to publish a common set of data accessible to the public, including the CNST rating; the state of implementation of action plans in response to patient safety alerts; mortality rates; and data on complaints including outcomes and changes implemented as a result.[172]

26.153 The Patients Association submitted that there should be a greater element of standardisation in Quality Accounts and that the external audit of accounts should be extended to non-FTs. This has now in fact begun (see above). Because of the issues that had been identified, the Association viewed these accounts "with caution" and did not consider they could be an effective means of public accountability without external audit.[173]

170 Straughan T99.199–200
171 CLO000001706–707 HCC Closing submissions, paras 25–26
172 CLO000000470–471 AVMA Closing submissions pages 116–117
173 CLO000003783–784 Patients Association Closing submissions, para 319, recommendation 39

Patient records

26.154 In commendably succinct submissions, the Royal College of Physicians (RCP) recommended that attention be paid to the production of good quality patient records:

> *High quality standardised records are fundamentally important to support the delivery of high quality care and to ensure the provision of data that enables quality to be monitored and emerging issues picked up at an early stage. Patients should have access to their record and be able to write to it as well as read it.*[174]

Patient experience

26.155 It was argued by the HCC that the NHS should redouble its efforts to listen to the voices of patients, their relatives and carers.[175]

26.156 The HCC suggested that as the means now existed for a wide variety of patient and public feedback to be obtained on hospitals' performance against standards, this needed to be more fully integrated into the regulatory process.[176] In particular, it supported the use of patient-reported outcome measures gathered instantaneously for example, through electronic consoles in hospital and the use of social media. However, the HCC warned that it was important to distinguish between those issues on which patients were expert, such as dignity, access to staff and nutrition, and those where they were not necessarily so knowledgeable, such as the quality of clinical treatment.[177]

26.157 The Patients Association recommended that the Nursing and Midwifery Council (NMC)'s revalidation scheme should include an element of mandatory collection of comparable patient experience data.[178]

26.158 The CQC warned that there were concerns nationally about the consistency of patient experience information and therefore counselled caution in considering the extent to which it should use this information in its processes.[179]

26.159 The CQC argued that, although it did not wish to have a role in handling patient complaints, it could benefit from access to more detailed information about complaints. This would include the nature of complaints, the issue raised, the date and the ultimate resolution, in sufficient detail to identify patterns and trends.[180] It was suggested to the Inquiry that there should be a

---

174 CLO000001512 RCP Closing submissions, para 3.1
175 CLO000001714–715 HCC Closing submissions, para 54
176 CLO000001707 HCC Closing submissions, para 27
177 CLO000001715 HCC Closing submissions, paras 59–60
178 CLO000003787 Patients Association Closing submission, recommendation 41
179 CLO000000588 CQC Closing submissions, para 393
180 CLO000000585 CQC Closing submissions, paras 380–381

return to provider organisations submitting this sort of information directly to the CQC.[181] A difficulty mentioned was the danger of overburdening trusts with too detailed an obligation, and the CQC with an excess of information that it could not process, given the large number of complaints made every year. The CQC suggested that "increased prescription" could be sought in relation to the details sought from trusts in the annual reports required under the current regulations.[182] These currently require trusts to provide an annual report that:

- Specifies the number of complaints received;
- Specifies the number of complaints determined to be well founded;
- Specifies the number of complaints referred to the Health Service Commissioner or the Local Commissioner;
- Summarises the subject matter of complaints received, any matters of general importance arising out of those complaints, or the way in which the complaints were handled, and any matters where action has been or is to be taken to improve services as a consequence of those complaints.[183]

26.160 The CQC has the power to ask trusts for any information about compliance with standards, but it appears that it has not exercised this with reference to complaints information.[184]

26.161 Mr Straughan of the Information Centre agreed that much more use could be made of complaints information in terms of detailed classification and that this was potentially a very valuable indicator.[185]

Quality and Risk Profiles

26.162 The Patients Association recommended that the QRP for each organisation be published with any necessary explanation as to its meaning and significance. It was critical of the absence to date of any independent evaluation of the accuracy of information held in the system and pointed to the evidence received by the Inquiry about the potential disconnect between the risk rating in the QRP and concerns about organisations held by CQC staff. It recommended an independent review of the QRP evidence base and rating system.[186]

---

181 Hamblin T83.93–95; Bower T87.75–77; Gordon T88.83
182 CLO000000586 CQC Closing submissions, para 385; Local Authority Social Services and National Health Service Complaints (England) Regulations 2009 [SI 2009/309]
183 Local Authority Social Services and National Health Service Complaints (England) Regulations 2009 [SI 2009/309], Reg 18
184 Bower T87.76
185 Straughan T99.167–168
186 CLO000003748–749 Patients Association Closing submissions, paras 196–198, recommendations 17–18

Conclusions and recommendations

The need for information integration

26.163 Cure the NHS's submissions, that the aggregation and use of individual and team performance measures at the front line is simply "missing", may be an overstatement. There are certainly signs that such information is increasingly available and used. The SCTS reports and the use of information described by Dr Rosser at the information seminar are examples of this. However, Mr Robin Burgess, Chief Executive of the Health Quality Improvement Partnership (HQIP), told the information seminar that:

> *All healthcare information needs to be collected for a purpose; on its own, without incorporation in systems which ensure it is used actively to drive practice, or in the wrong hands, it is often meaningless ... The purposes for which data and information are required, and the needs of its stakeholders, should determine and refine the data that is collected and the way it is analysed and reported. Overall in the NHS too much data is collected which is simply process data which neither drives change nor improves outcomes. It is not embedded in change programmes or systems which enable it to be used meaningfully to drive change activity; it is just data.*[187]

26.164 The DH's Information Strategy recognises the need for such practice to become more widespread, facilitated by the development of a patient information system that becomes the source of performance data used for a range of purposes. This does not require a vast computer system applied throughout the country. Efforts in that direction have not succeeded. However, there is a need for all to accept common information practices, and to feed performance information into shared databases for monitoring purposes.

26.165 An integrated system needs to have:

- A foundation in information collected about individual patients and recorded by those clinically responsible for their care;
- Information and the method of storing it which must have the following characteristics:
  - Immediate availability to those who need to have access to provide safe and effective care for the individual patient;
  - Accessibility to patients as part of the information available to them about their condition and treatment;
  - Responsibility taken by an identifiable professional for the accuracy of each piece of information;
  - A facility to enable corrections to be recorded by both patients and professionals;

---

187 *How can information be better used within the NHS?*, (October 2011), Robin Burgess (HQIP), page 2
www.midstaffspublicinquiry.com/sites/default/files/uploads/Robin_Burgess_paper_0.pdf

- Minimisation of duplication of information and maximisation of its usability for patient care, performance management and regulatory oversight;
- Aggregation of information derived from individual patient care recorded for the purpose of auditing the performance of individuals and teams of healthcare professionals;
- Proportionate availability to patients and public of outcome results at individual, team, provider and national levels, together with full disclosure of the analytical methods;
- Responsibility for implementing and maintaining effective systems of recording, analysis and publication of local performance information to reside with provider boards monitored by the regulator;
- Proportionately reported analysis of results in accordance with independently defined and authoritative statistical standards;
- Verification by external auditing of reported results;
- Regular review to ensure data and statistics produced are the most useful and evidence based available for the purposes for which they are collected;
- Public accessibility via a common user-friendly information gateway;
- Access to raw anonymised data to be made available to any organisation or individual intending in good faith to undertake their own analysis and having the competence to do so.

26.166 The DH Information Strategy appears to contain most if not all of these components, and in the Information Centre the system has the vehicle capable of delivering and coordinating this. The essential point is that healthcare information, serving the primary purpose of supporting safe and effective care to patients, is exploited as a principal source of statistics for professional audit, performance review, regulatory oversight and public information. In an increasingly fragmented system of provision, the sharing of good quality information is a powerful force for driving the necessary common culture and sense of identity throughout the system.

Patient records

26.167 Patient records are, as correctly submitted by the RCP, absolutely vital to the delivery of safe and effective care. Not only do they provide the structure for the immediate care of the patient, they are the repository of the patient's history and the source of nearly all information required to assess the effectiveness of what has been done. The Independent Case Note Review of patient records at the Trust, following the HCC investigation, found many deficiencies in the note keeping in the cases they reviewed. The deficiencies included:

- Notes not completed;
- Gaps in the recording of medication;
- Absence of a chronology;
- Basic observations not recorded;
- Absence of falls assessment;

- Inadequate evidence of Do Not Resuscitate (DNR) decisions;
- Many different types of poorly designed forms;
- Patient movements between wards not recorded;
- Missing or illegible notes and chaotic files;
- Dates and times commonly missing;
- Identities of authors of notes often absent;
- Lack of documented management plans.[188]

26.168 The Astbury case described in other chapters exemplifies the issues that can arise from inadequate note keeping.

26.169 Nothing in the evidence to this Inquiry challenged the findings of the first inquiry that there were deficiencies in note keeping at the Trust sufficient to require a review of its procedures to be undertaken.[189]

26.170 Any form of record is only as effective as the accuracy and thoroughness of the entries made, and the care with which it is stored. A visit to any hospital ward will show the observer the burden on staff of keeping records up to date while under the inevitable pressures of caring for patients. The effort required to ensure that paper records are available for outpatient appointments must be considerable. Every litigator of clinical cases will have experience of lost notes, disordered files and illegible entries. In the age of portable media devices and instant internet access, conventional means of record keeping look increasingly outmoded and inefficient. This issue is clearly recognised in the DH's Information Strategy (see above) and the move towards a common electronic health record, and the wise acceptance after past failed attempts that a universal IT system is not the way forward.

26.171 Visits to hospitals have shown up a number of applications of electronic note keeping, from A&E to drug prescribing and charting. The NHS Summary Care Record is intended to provide an easily accessible set of basic patient information to healthcare professionals but, apparently, more limited access to patients. It appears that at least one institution in the USA has developed real-time online access for patients and professionals to their health records. In a world in which most adults are now accustomed to operating bank accounts remotely, and dealing with other aspects of their daily lives in this way, the time has surely come for similar facilities to be developed for patients. Such developments must be encouraged, and providers required to adopt best practice in the field.

---

188 Laker WS0000002495, para 119; ML/13 WS0000002587 PCT0011000016; TRUST00030007983–985 *Themes arising from the review of case notes for a sample of patients treated by Mid Staffordshire NHS Foundation Trust January 2005 to March 2009* (June 2010); Laker T44.80–87

189 *Independent Inquiry into care provided by Mid Staffordshire NHS Foundation Trust January 2005–March 2009* (February 2010), Chapter 8 pages 115–117 paras 223–234; page 413, para 48, recommendation 12, www.dh.gov.uk/en/Publicationsandstatistics/Publications/PublicationsPolicyAndGuidance/DH_113018

26.172 The approaches described by Professor Elliott and Dr Rosser (see above) provide a very strong argument for the introduction of electronic based note keeping and clinical communication systems in hospitals. They are able to combine better accuracy with significant error reduction and the basis for a wide range of performance and outcome monitoring. Clearly, the cost of such systems has to be considered carefully, but so does the evidence suggesting that errors and mortality rates will be reduced.

26.173 It is suggested that the following principles should be applied in considering the introduction of electronic patient information systems:

- Patients need to be granted user-friendly, real-time and retrospective access to read their records, and a facility to enter comments. They should be enabled to have a copy of records in a form usable by them, if they wish to have one. If possible, the NHS Summary Care Record should be made accessible in this way;
- Systems should be designed to include prompts and defaults where these will contribute to safe and effective care and to accurate recording of information on first entry;
- Systems should include a facility to alert supervisors where actions that might be expected have not occurred, or where likely inaccuracies have been entered;
- Systems should, where practicable and proportionate, be capable of collecting performance management and audit information automatically, appropriately anonymised direct from entries, to avoid unnecessary duplication of input;
- Systems must be designed by healthcare professionals in partnership with patient groups to secure maximum professional and patient engagement in ensuring accuracy, utility and relevance both to the needs of individual patients and to collective professional, managerial and regulatory requirements;
- Systems must be capable of reflecting changing needs and local supplements over and above nationally required fundamental standards.

26.174 Systems that achieve these characteristics will at the same time:

- Promote a real partnership between patients and their clinicians;
- Improve the accuracy of record keeping;
- Reduce the risk of error in prescription of treatment, and of harm to patients;
- Provide the basis for less duplication of effort in performance and regulatory monitoring.

26.175 Such an approach would have the potential of accelerating the arrival of relevant data in the HES: it currently takes around three months from the time a patient is seen for the event to be registered with HES, because of the time taken to "clean" records.[190]

---

190 Straughan WS0000043741–742, paras 17, 20

Chapter 26 Information

Provider board responsibility for information

26.176 Boards must remain responsible for ensuring the effective management of information in their organisations. This responsibility includes the obligation to:

- Ensure that proper patient record keeping systems are in place;
- Require appropriate clinical and other audits to be conducted and that the information necessary to do so is made available by and to all relevant staff;
- Prepare and publish accurate and reliable performance statistics in accordance with best practice, and the requirements of their commissioners and regulators;
- Supply the required information for collective statistical analyses of performance.

26.177 There may be no single way in which such obligations can be fulfilled and any general information requirements should not inhibit providers from supplying more than the minimum information to patients, staff and the public: therefore innovation and development in the information field should be encouraged.

26.178 The responsibility of directors with regard to the management of information is likely to be onerous and incapable of being met without significant technical support. The suggestion that each organisation should have a board level Chief Information Officer has merit. The position ensures that information matters are given their proper importance and that there is a focus of accountability and line management for this function. Such an officer could have many if not all of the responsibilities the Patients Association suggest should be given to an independent Monitor of Care. However, while the recommendation to create an independent Monitor of Care is worthy of consideration, it appears to suffer the disadvantage of combining the role of an independent monitor with internal responsibilities. Such a person does not effectively compare with the figure envisaged by Mr Sumara and would require considerable technical support. A Board member with responsibility for information would not supplant the role of the CQC local inspector or Local Healthwatch organisation in monitoring compliance with information standards.

26.179 A principal means of disseminating information about performance is through Quality Accounts. This is considered below.

Quality Accounts

26.180 Quality Accounts, which were one of the innovations arising out of the work of Lord Darzi and *High Quality Care for All: NHS next stage review final report,* have huge potential for furthering the required common culture, transparency and openness regarding the quality of a provider's services, as well as being a vehicle for reinforcing the accountability of the board. Clearly, such a new concept takes time to develop and it is no criticism of what has been done to date to suggest a direction of travel in relation to improving what is being done in this respect. A number of points appear to require attention.

Consistency

26.181 The regulations and other requirements that govern the content of the accounts should result in a degree of consistency in the nature of the statements submitted, allowing comparisons to be made between organisations. Attention needs to be paid to ensure that the reports as a whole are presented in a format and order that allows easy access to information that the public are likely to want to have. There is a natural temptation to allow less encouraging results to be overshadowed by positive news by making the former more difficult to find than the latter. At the same time, over-prescriptive requirements can result in a document that is difficult to read and therefore of reduced utility to the public. The key points that should be kept under review are the need to present the report in a form that facilitates comparison with the organisation's own previous performance and with national comparators. One way in which this could be done is to require that such results be highlighted.

26.182 Quality Accounts provide NHS and foundation trusts with an opportunity to inform the public as well as regulators of what they have achieved and of their future plans.

Balance

26.183 As has been remarked elsewhere, there is a tendency among NHS organisations to focus on their "good" news and to give less emphasis to the "bad". It can therefore be difficult on occasions to locate matters of concern in some Quality Accounts. One of the lessons of Stafford is that organisations in difficulty can succumb to the temptation of emphasising apparent achievements at the expense of recognising adequately the need for substantial improvements. If a common culture of transparency and openness is to be fully embraced, equal – if not more – prominence should be given to recognition of things that need to be put right than to areas where standards are being complied with. At the same time, organisations need to be able to inform the public fully and fairly of their achievements and the areas in which they justifiably regard their performance as excellent.

26.184 The CQC and/or Monitor should keep the accuracy, fairness and balance of Quality Accounts under review and be enabled to require corrections to be issued where appropriate. In the event of an organisation failing to take that action, the regulator should be able to issue their own statement of correction.

Audit

26.185 The recent moves towards external auditing of accounts are very welcome. At Stafford, it is clear that the internal auditor was able to detect deficiencies in the process of self-declaration for the Annual Health Check. The expertise is therefore available to enable auditing of declarations against standards in much the same way as it is available for financial accounts.

Chapter 26 Information

26.186 Clearly, requirements for auditing should be proportionate and not unnecessarily burdensome. However, while the requirement for examination of three clinical indicators is a start, this may in reality not be sufficient to enable a reliable assurance of the accuracy of the accounts to be given. Auditors should be given a wider remit enabling them to use their professional judgement in examining the reliability of all statements in the accounts.

Accountability and sanction

26.187 The requirement that directors personally authenticate the accounts is one that reinforces the board's responsibility, not only for internal governance but the accuracy of its public statements about its performance. In *Chapter 22: Openness, transparency and candour*, it is recommended that for extreme cases of misleading statements a criminal sanction should be available. A director who is knowingly party to a deliberately misleading statement in a Quality Account should be subject to such a sanction and also to accountability under the regulatory procedure for senior managers which has also been recommended.

Quality and Risk Profiles

26.188 The development of the QRP is described briefly above. It has the potential to be a highly valuable tool in assisting CQC staff to identify organisations that may require a closer look at their compliance. It is still in the course of development and will require constant review of the quality of the information contributing to it, and to the scoring and weighting systems. The CQC rightly acknowledge that it is not a system that produces a judgement about compliance, but merely a tool pointing towards potential areas of concern in a systematic way. To the extent that it is useful as an indicator for inspectors, it would also be useful for the public. In the common culture of transparency that it is necessary to foster, the information behind the QRP – as well as the ratings and methodology – should be placed in the public domain, together with appropriate explanations to enable the public to understand the limitations of this tool. Sharing it with the public in this way is likely to assist in its development.

26.189 The Patients Association's recommendation for an urgent independent evaluation of the QRP and its methodology is something for the CQC to consider, but care needs to be taken not to overburden an already challenged organisation with processes that may in fact hinder or delay improvements. The important point for all to remember is that the QRP does not produce an end result in itself, but is merely a potential aid to focus inspectors on areas requiring their attention. If at the same time it is recognised that the absence of a possible cause for concern in the QRP does not signify that an organisation is compliant, then reviews and development of this system should be left to the CQC to decide upon, aided by the contribution from public disclosure of the results and methods.

Patient feedback

26.190 It is recognised that effective patient feedback is a powerful means of scrutinising the performance of providers in terms of safety and quality. It is encouraging to see a widening range of options being made available to the public to register their observations about the quality of care provided and to share those with others. In a society that increasingly relies on internet and social media based applications for its information, the days when it might have been justifiable to rely on a periodic conventional survey have now passed. Such a method suffers from a number of disadvantages, not least of which is that its results tend to arrive too late to be currently relevant. A consideration of the experience of Stafford, and also the positive developments in obtaining feedback that have occurred, suggest a number of principles that should be applied in this area in future:

- Obtaining feedback from patients and others during an outpatient appointment or a course of inpatient treatment is desirable to offer but not a sufficient means of obtaining a true account of patient and public opinion of a service. It is quite clear that patients and their supporters can be very reluctant to raise concerns or make critical comments at a time when they feel vulnerable. That is not a reason for providers not to concern themselves in seeking out responses while patients are in hospital: to do so can demonstrate a caring attitude and foster confidence among patients and supporters to raise matters that are worrying them.
- Follow-up contact with patients after the conclusion of their treatment may be productive. It appears from responses on resources such as NHS Choices that helpful comments about providers are often made shortly after the treatment episode. While patient-initiated comments are always useful and should be considered with care, a proactive system for following up patients shortly after discharge would not only be good "customer service" – it would probably provide a wider range of responses.
- Publication of comments online, good and bad, is a powerful tool for patient choice and in forcing providers to address, in public, criticisms made. While making a response is not mandatory, failure to do so is likely to cause the public to draw adverse inferences.
- While there are likely to be many different gateways offered through which patient and public comments can be made, it would be helpful for there to be consistency across the country in methods of access to avoid confusion, and for the output to be published in a manner allowing fair and informed comparison between organisations. This is not intended to suggest that anything other than encouragement should be offered to impressive contributions made in this field by organisations such as Patient Opinion. The NHS should be commended for its willingness to cooperate with Patient Opinion, exchange information with it and make use of its facilities. As was recognised by Professor Sir Bruce Keogh, however, it would be helpful if the profile of this sort of feedback facility was raised and kept in the public eye.
- Results and analysis of patient feedback need to be made available to all stakeholders as near "real time" as possible, even if later adjustments have to be made.

- The Information Centre, in consultation with the the DH, the NHS Commissioning Board and the Parliamentary and Health Service Ombudsman, should develop a means of publishing more detailed breakdowns of clinically related complaints.

Publication of regulatory inspection reports

26.191 It is clearly desirable in the public interest that the results of inspections by regulators are in the public domain. Such findings, positive or negative, are part of the information the public is entitled to have to assist it in, among other things, forming judgements about which provider to choose for treatment, and in holding both providers and commissioners to account. Reports are currently made available to the public via the CQC's website and each provider trust carries a link to those that concern it. This appears to be sufficient to generate public interest where appropriate.

26.192 As the findings of such reports form the basis on which regulatory intervention may be taken, it is important that they include the facts on which they are based, and that conclusions are rational and clearly expressed. Quite what language is used is a matter of style rather than of substance. What may strike Dame Barbara Young as "emotive" may be to others a proper way of describing the impact of poor care on patients. The style of CQC reports is different from that adopted at least in the HCC report on the Trust, but they have not shied away from explicit descriptions of findings in, for example, the series of reports on dignity and nutrition. Neither style can be in itself a matter for criticism. What is important is whether the extent of the findings made is sufficiently described to be understood by a member of the public.

Development of published outcome performance measures

26.193 It is no easy task to identify methodologies that fairly and reliably analyse the comparative performance of units and individual healthcare professionals in all fields. The difficulties to be faced include the proper reflection of case mix and complicating collateral conditions, and the relative contributions of individuals, teams and the systems in which they work. Major steps have been taken in overcoming such hurdles when measuring performance in heart surgery, but little progress appears to have been made in other fields. The demand, however, for such information will not recede. Not only is it increasingly likely to be expected by the public, but it will be required for revalidation purposes for doctors.

26.194 The time has come when a greater effort is required by professionals, and the healthcare system generally, to identify and introduce measures that fairly reflect the effectiveness of the treatment offered in individual organisations, the units within them and, where possible, the individual treating doctors. In many cases, if not all, mortality may be an inappropriate measure or an inadequate one. Where this is the case, the search for comparative measures must extend to other less "blunt" indicators. It is important to guard against the perceived risk of units or individuals seeking to "massage" their results – for example, by offering treatment to the less challenging cases – by including measures that would detect such a reaction. Consideration also needs to be given to the different needs of professionals, regulators and the public in terms of the presentation and content of the information published. Merely granting open access to raw statistical data is unlikely to be sufficient to assist the public in comparing one organisation with another. This is not a reason for withholding publication of and access to the data for those who want it, but is a reason for working carefully to provide unbiased and fair explanations of the significance that can be attached to the results. It is unlikely that it will be possible or appropriate to extract individual specific performance data in all cases. Much work in healthcare is the result of team rather than individual efforts and it may not always be possible to identify the contributions of particular team members. So far as the public is concerned, they are likely to be most interested in information from which they might draw conclusions about the relative efficacy of one source of treatment against another. In some cases, their focus will be the individual surgeon who performs an operation; in others, it will be the ward, unit or even the hospital as a whole.

26.195　How is it that this need for information, apparent since at least the Bristol Inquiry but only partly addressed since, is to be better met?

- The DH, the Information Centre and the CQC should engage with each representative specialty organisation in order to consider how best to develop comparative statistics on the efficacy of treatment in that specialty, for publication and use in performance oversight, revalidation, and the promotion of patient knowledge and choice. Professor Jarman, for one, saw it as necessary for each specialty to be involved.[191]
- It must be recognised to be the professional duty of all healthcare professionals to collaborate in the provision of information required for such statistics.
- In designing the methodology for such statistics and their presentation, the DH, the Information Centre, the CQC and the specialty organisations should seek and have regard to the views of patient groups and the public about the information needed by them.
- In the case of each specialty, a programme of development should be prepared, published, and subjected to regular review.
- All such statistics should be made available online and accessible through provider websites, as well as other gateways such as the CQC.
- Resources must be allocated to and by provider organisations to enable the relevant data to be collected and forwarded to the relevant central registry.

26.196　The strategy published by the NHS Commissioning Board on 18 December 2012 developing comparative outcome information for surgeons is a welcome development and complements the recommendations made on this issue as set out above. To ensure synergy in this vitally important piece of work, the NHS Commissioning Board should take these recommendations forward as part of the work it has now set in train.

191　Jarman T98.176–177

Serious Untoward Incidents

26.197 Information about incidents is clearly important to any assessment of the safety of a provider organisation. The standards applied to statistical information about SUIs should be the same as for any other healthcare information and in particular the principles around transparency and accessibility. It would therefore be desirable for the data to be supplied to and processed by the Information Centre and through the Centre made publicly available in the same way as other quality related information.

Authentication of healthcare statistical information

26.198 Although this was not a subject of examination during the formal evidence before the Inquiry, it appears that there is an impressive system in the UK for the setting of standards for national and recognised official statistics, and for the assessment of compliance with those standards. This has been applied to various healthcare statistics. Clearly this should continue. Given their importance to the public there is a need for a review by the DH, the Information Centre and the UKSA of patient outcome statistics, including hospital mortality and other outcome indicators. In particular, there could be benefit from consideration of the extent to which these statistics can be published in a form more readily usable by the public.

26.199 To the extent that that they are not already recognised as national or official statistics, the DH and the Information Centre should work towards establishing such status for SHMI or any successor hospital mortality figures, and other patient outcome statistics, including reports showing provider-level detail.

26.200 The story described in the first inquiry report, and here, of the reaction to the HSMR figures, the debate about methodology and the painstaking steps taken since to achieve consensus in the development of the SHMI suggests that there is a demonstrable need for an accreditation system to be available for healthcare-relevant statistical methodologies. It is necessary to enable the public to have confidence in the output of statistics and to provide trust managers and others with guidance as to which methodology to adopt. The lay member of the public, or the senior manager, is unlikely to be able to make useful judgements in this highly technical area, complicated by the strong opinions held by experts. Another reason why accreditation would be useful would be to address the suggestion made by Professor Jarman that managers would tend to choose statistics that gave them the answer they wanted.[192] The power to create an accreditation scheme has been included in the Health and Social Care Act 2012: it should be used as soon as practicable.

26.201 It is clear from the evidence before the Inquiry relating to the coding issues arising in the Trust that there is potential for providers' data from which healthcare statistics are produced to be inaccurate to an extent that undermines the reliability of subsequent analysis. The only

---

192 Jarman T98.145–146

practical way of ensuring reasonable accuracy is vigilant auditing at local level of the data put into the system. This is important work that must be continued and where possible improved.

The role of the Health and Social Care Information Centre

26.202 As noted above, the remit of the Information Centre will expand when the relevant statutory provisions are brought into force and the underlying regulations are produced. The regulations should ensure that the Information Centre can play its full part in the direction of travel indicated earlier. In addition, the Centre should be enabled to undertake more detailed statistical analysis of its own than currently appears to be the case. That is not to suggest that other organisations inside and outside the system should cease doing so, but the Information Centre can undoubtedly add value by the production and review of performance and standards-related statistics, exploiting the vast amount of data in its possession.

Summary of recommendations

Recommendation 244

There is a need for all to accept common information practices, and to feed performance information into shared databases for monitoring purposes. The following principles should be applied in considering the introduction of electronic patient information systems:

- Patients need to be granted user friendly, real time and retrospective access to read their records, and a facility to enter comments. They should be enabled to have a copy of records in a form useable by them, if they wish to have one. If possible, the summary care record should be made accessible in this way.
- Systems should be designed to include prompts and defaults where these will contribute to safe and effective care, and to accurate recording of information on first entry.
- Systems should include a facility to alert supervisors where actions which might be expected have not occurred, or where likely inaccuracies have been entered.
- Systems should, where practicable and proportionate, be capable of collecting performance management and audit information automatically, appropriately anonymised direct from entries, to avoid unnecessary duplication of input.
- Systems must be designed by healthcare professionals in partnership with patient groups to secure maximum professional and patient engagement in ensuring accuracy, utility and relevance, both to the needs of the individual patients and collective professional, managerial and regulatory requirements.

Systems must be capable of reflecting changing needs and local requirements over and above nationally required minimum standards.

Recommendation 245

Each provider organisation should have a board level member with responsibility for information.

Recommendation 246

Department of Health/the NHS Commissioning Board/regulators should ensure that provider organisations publish in their annual quality accounts information in a common form to enable comparisons to be made between organisations, to include a minimum of prescribed information about their compliance with fundamental and other standards, their proposals for the rectification of any non-compliance and statistics on mortality and other outcomes. Quality accounts should be required to contain the observations of commissioners, overview and scrutiny committees, and Local Healthwatch.

Recommendation 247

Healthcare providers should be required to lodge their quality accounts with all organisations commissioning services from them, Local HealthWatch, and all systems regulators.

Recommendation 248

Healthcare providers should be required to have their quality accounts independently audited. Auditors should be given a wider remit enabling them to use their professional judgement in examining the reliability of all statements in the accounts.

Recommendation 249

Each quality account should be accompanied by a declaration signed by all directors in office at the date of the account certifying that they believe the contents of the account to be true, or alternatively a statement of explanation as to the reason any such director is unable or has refused to sign such a declaration.

Recommendation 250

It should be a criminal offence for a director to sign a declaration of belief that the contents of a quality account are true if it contains a misstatement of fact concerning an item of prescribed information which he/she does not have reason to believe is true at the time of making the declaration.

Recommendation 251

The Care Quality Commission and/or Monitor should keep the accuracy, fairness and balance of quality accounts under review and should be enabled to require corrections to be issued where appropriate. In the event of an organisation failing to take that action, the regulator should be able to issue its own statement of correction.

Recommendation 252

It is important that the appropriate steps are taken to enable properly anonymised data to be used for managerial and regulatory purposes.

Recommendation 253

The information behind the quality and risk profile – as well as the ratings and methodology – should be placed in the public domain, as far as is consistent with maintaining any legitimate confidentiality of such information, together with appropriate explanations to enable the public to understand the limitations of this tool.

Recommendation 254

While there are likely to be many different gateways offered through which patient and public comments can be made, to avoid confusion, it would be helpful for there to be consistency across the country in methods of access, and for the output to be published in a manner allowing fair and informed comparison between organisations.

Recommendation 255

Results and analysis of patient feedback including qualitative information need to be made available to all stakeholders in as near "real time" as possible, even if later adjustments have to be made.

Recommendation 256

A proactive system for following up patients shortly after discharge would not only be good "customer service", it would probably provide a wider range of responses and feedback on their care.

Recommendation 257

The Information Centre should be tasked with the independent collection, analysis, publication and oversight of healthcare information in England, or, with the agreement of the devolved governments, the United Kingdom. The information functions previously held by the National Patient Safety Agency should be transferred to the NHS Information Centre if made independent.

Recommendation 258

The Information Centre should continue to develop and maintain learning, standards and consensus with regard to information methodologies, with particular reference to comparative performance statistics.

Recommendation 259

The Information Centre, in consultation with the Department of Health, the NHS Commissioning Board and the Parliamentary and Health Service Ombudsman, should develop a means of publishing more detailed breakdowns of clinically related complaints.

Recommendation 260

The standards applied to statistical information about serious untoward incidents should be the same as for any other healthcare information and in particular the principles around transparency and accessibility. It would, therefore, be desirable for the data to be supplied to, and processed by, the Information Centre and, through them, made publicly available in the same way as other quality related information.

Recommendation 261

The Information Centre should be enabled to undertake more detailed statistical analysis of its own than currently appears to be the case.

Recommendation 262

All healthcare provider organisations, in conjunction with their healthcare professionals, should develop and maintain systems which give them:

- Effective real-time information on the performance of each of their services against patient safety and minimum quality standards;
- Effective real-time information of the performance of each of their consultants and specialist teams in relation to mortality, morbidity, outcome and patient satisfaction.

In doing so, they should have regard, in relation to each service, to best practice for information management of that service as evidenced by recommendations of the Information Centre, and recommendations of specialist organisations such as the medical Royal Colleges.

The information derived from such systems should, to the extent practicable, be published and in any event made available in full to commissioners and regulators, on request, and with appropriate explanation, and to the extent that is relevant to individual patients, to assist in choice of treatment.

Recommendation 263

It must be recognised to be the professional duty of all healthcare professionals to collaborate in the provision of information required for such statistics on the efficacy of treatment in specialties.

Recommendation 264

In the case of each specialty, a programme of development for statistics on the efficacy of treatment should be prepared, published, and subjected to regular review.

Recommendation 265

The Department of Health, the Information Centre and the Care Quality Commission should engage with each representative specialty organisation in order to consider how best to develop comparative statistics on the efficacy of treatment in that specialty, for publication and use in performance oversight, revalidation, and the promotion of patient knowledge and choice.

Recommendation 266

In designing the methodology for such statistics and their presentation, the Department of Health, the Information Centre, the Care Quality Commission and the specialty organisations should seek and have regard to the views of patient groups and the public about the information needed by them.

Recommendation 267

All such statistics should be made available online and accessible through provider websites, as well as other gateways such as the Care Quality Commission.

Recommendation 268

Resources must be allocated to and by provider organisations to enable the relevant data to be collected and forwarded to the relevant central registry.

Recommendation 269

The only practical way of ensuring reasonable accuracy is vigilant auditing at local level of the data put into the system. This is important work, which must be continued and where possible improved.

Recommendation 270

There is a need for a review by the Department of Health, the Information Centre and the UK Statistics Authority of the patient outcome statistics, including hospital mortality and other outcome indicators. In particular, there could be benefit from consideration of the extent to which these statistics can be published in a form more readily useable by the public.

Recommendation 271

To the extent that summary hospital-level mortality indicators are not already recognised as national or official statistics, the Department of Health and the Health and Social Care Information Centre should work towards establishing such status for them or any successor hospital mortality figures, and other patient outcome statistics, including reports showing provider-level detail.

Recommendation 272

There is a demonstrable need for an accreditation system to be available for healthcare-relevant statistical methodologies. The power to create an accreditation scheme has been included in the Health and Social Care Act 2012, it should be used as soon as practicable.

Chapter 27
Table of recommendations

Rec. no.	Theme	Recommendation	Chapter
	Accountability for implementation of the recommendations		
		These recommendations require every single person serving patients to contribute to a safer, committed and compassionate and caring service.	
1	Implementing the recommendations	It is recommended that: • All commissioning, service provision regulatory and ancillary organisations in healthcare should consider the findings and recommendations of this report and decide how to apply them to their own work; • Each such organisation should announce at the earliest practicable time its decision on the extent to which it accepts the recommendations and what it intends to do to implement those accepted, and thereafter, on a regular basis but not less than once a year, publish in a report information regarding its progress in relation to its planned actions; • In addition to taking such steps for itself, the Department of Health should collate information about the decisions and actions generally and publish on a regular basis but not less than once a year the progress reported by other organisations; • The House of Commons Select Committee on Health should be invited to consider incorporating into its reviews of the performance of organisations accountable to Parliament a review of the decisions and actions they have taken with regard to the recommendations in this report.	Introduction
2		The NHS and all who work for it must adopt and demonstrate a shared culture in which the patient is the priority in everything done. This requires: • A common set of core values and standards shared throughout the system; • Leadership at all levels from ward to the top of the Department of Health, committed to and capable of involving all staff with those values and standards; • A system which recognises and applies the values of transparency, honesty and candour; • Freely available, useful, reliable and full information on attainment of the values and standards; • A tool or methodology such as a cultural barometer to measure the cultural health of all parts of the system.	20
	Putting the patient first		
		The patients must be the first priority in all of what the NHS does. Within available resources, they must receive effective services from caring, compassionate and committed staff, working within a common culture, and they must be protected from avoidable harm and any deprivation of their basic rights.	
3	Clarity of values and principles	The NHS Constitution should be the first reference point for all NHS patients and staff and should set out the system's common values, as well as the respective rights, legitimate expectations and obligations of patients.	21

Rec. no.	Theme	Recommendation	Chapter
4		The core values expressed in the NHS Constitution should be given priority of place and the overriding value should be that patients are put first, and everything done by the NHS and everyone associated with it should be informed by this ethos.	21
5		In reaching out to patients, consideration should be given to including expectations in the NHS Constitution that: • Staff put patients before themselves; • They will do everything in their power to protect patients from avoidable harm; • They will be honest and open with patients regardless of the consequences for themselves; • Where they are unable to provide the assistance a patient needs, they will direct them where possible to those who can do so; • They will apply the NHS values in all their work.	21
6		The handbook to the NHS Constitution should be revised to include a much more prominent reference to the NHS values and their significance.	21
7		All NHS staff should be required to enter into an express commitment to abide by the NHS values and the Constitution, both of which should be incorporated into the contracts of employment.	21
8		Contractors providing outsourced services should also be required to abide by these requirements and to ensure that staff employed by them for these purposes do so as well. These requirements could be included in the terms on which providers are commissioned to provide services.	21
	Fundamental standards of behaviour	Enshrined in the NHS Constitution should be the commitment to fundamental standards which need to be applied by all those who work and serve in the healthcare system. Behaviour at all levels needs to be in accordance with at least these fundamental standards.	
9		The NHS Constitution should include reference to all the relevant professional and managerial codes by which NHS staff are bound, including the Code of Conduct for NHS Managers.	21
10		The NHS Constitution should incorporate an expectation that staff will follow guidance and comply with standards relevant to their work, such as those produced by the National Institute for Health and Clinical Excellence and, where relevant, the Care Quality Commission, subject to any more specific requirements of their employers.	21
11		Healthcare professionals should be prepared to contribute to the development of, and comply with, standard procedures in the areas in which they work. Their managers need to ensure that their employees comply with these requirements. Staff members affected by professional disagreements about procedures must be required to take the necessary corrective action, working with their medical or nursing director or line manager within the trust, with external support where necessary. Professional bodies should work on devising evidence-based standard procedures for as many interventions and pathways as possible.	20
12		Reporting of incidents of concern relevant to patient safety, compliance with fundamental standards or some higher requirement of the employer needs to be not only encouraged but insisted upon. Staff are entitled to receive feedback in relation to any report they make, including information about any action taken or reasons for not acting.	2

Rec. no.	Theme	Recommendation	Chapter
	A common culture made real throughout the system – an integrated hierarchy of standards of service		
		No provider should provide, and there must be zero tolerance of, any service that does not comply with fundamental standards of service. Standards need to be formulated to promote the likelihood of the service being delivered safely and effectively, to be clear about what has to be done to comply, to be informed by an evidence base and to be effectively measurable.	
13	The nature of standards	Standards should be divided into: • Fundamental standards of minimum safety and quality – in respect of which non-compliance should not be tolerated. Failures leading to death or serious harm should remain offences for which prosecutions can be brought against organisations. There should be a defined set of duties to maintain and operate an effective system to ensure compliance; • Enhanced quality standards – such standards could set requirements higher than the fundamental standards but be discretionary matters for commissioning and subject to availability of resources; • Developmental standards which set out longer term goals for providers – these would focus on improvements in effectiveness and are more likely to be the focus of commissioners and progressive provider leadership than the regulator. All such standards would require regular review and modification.	21
14		In addition to the fundamental standards of service, the regulations should include generic requirements for a governance system designed to ensure compliance with fundamental standards, and the provision and publication of accurate information about compliance with the fundamental and enhanced standards.	9
15		All the required elements of governance should be brought together into one comprehensive standard. This should require not only evidence of a working system but also a demonstration that it is being used to good effect.	11
16	Responsibility for setting standards	The Government, through regulation, but after so far as possible achieving consensus between the public and professional representatives, should provide for the fundamental standards which should define outcomes for patients that must be avoided. These should be limited to those matters that it is universally accepted should be avoided for individual patients who are accepted for treatment by a healthcare provider.	21
17		The NHS Commissioning Board together with Clinical Commissioning Groups should devise enhanced quality standards designed to drive improvement in the health service. Failure to comply with such standards should be a matter for performance management by commissioners rather than the regulator, although the latter should be charged with enforcing the provision by providers of accurate information about compliance to the public.	21
18		It is essential that professional bodies in which doctors and nurses have confidence are fully involved in the formulation of standards and in the means of measuring compliance.	21
	Responsibility for, and effectiveness of, healthcare standards		
19	Gaps between the understood functions of separate regulators	There should be a single regulator dealing both with corporate governance, financial competence, viability and compliance with patient safety and quality standards for all trusts.	10

Rec. no.	Theme	Recommendation	Chapter
20	Responsibility for regulating and monitoring compliance	The Care Quality Commission should be responsible for policing the fundamental standards, through the development of its core outcomes, by specifying the indicators by which it intends to monitor compliance with those standards. It should be responsible not for directly policing compliance with any enhanced standards but for regulating the accuracy of information about compliance with them.	21
21		The regulator should have a duty to monitor the accuracy of information disseminated by providers and commissioners on compliance with standards and their compliance with the requirement of honest disclosure. The regulator must be willing to consider individual cases of gross failure as well as systemic causes for concern.	21
22		The National Institute for Health and Clinical Excellence should be commissioned to formulate standard procedures and practice designed to provide the practical means of compliance, and indicators by which compliance with both fundamental and enhanced standards can be measured. These measures should include both outcome and process based measures, and should as far as possible build on information already available within the system or on readily observable behaviour.	21
23		The measures formulated by the National Institute for Health and Clinical Excellence should include measures not only of clinical outcomes, but of the suitability and competence of staff, and the culture of organisations. The standard procedures and practice should include evidence-based tools for establishing what each service is likely to require as a minimum in terms of staff numbers and skill mix. This should include nursing staff on wards, as well as clinical staff. These tools should be created after appropriate input from specialties, professional organisations, and patient and public representatives, and consideration of the benefits and value for money of possible staff: patient ratios.	21
24		Compliance with regulatory fundamental standards must be capable so far as possible of being assessed by measures which are understood and accepted by the public and healthcare professionals.	21
25		It should be considered the duty of all specialty professional bodies, ideally together with the National Institute for Health and Clinical Excellence, to develop measures of outcome in relation to their work and to assist in the development of measures of standards compliance.	21
26		In policing compliance with standards, direct observation of practice, direct interaction with patients, carers and staff, and audit of records should take priority over monitoring and audit of policies and protocols. The regulatory system should retain the capacity to undertake in-depth investigations where these appear to be required.	9
27		The healthcare systems regulator should promote effective enforcement by: use of a low threshold of suspicion; no tolerance of non-compliance with fundamental standards; and allowing no place for favourable assumptions, unless there is evidence showing that suspicions are ill-founded or that deficiencies have been remedied. It requires a focus on identifying what is wrong, not on praising what is right.	9
28	Sanctions and interventions for non-compliance	Zero tolerance: A service incapable of meeting fundamental standards should not be permitted to continue. Breach should result in regulatory consequences attributable to an organisation in the case of a system failure and to individual accountability where individual professionals are responsible. Where serious harm or death has resulted to a patient as a result of a breach of the fundamental standards, criminal liability should follow and failure to disclose breaches of these standards to the affected patient (or concerned relative) and a regulator should also attract regulatory consequences. Breaches not resulting in actual harm but which have exposed patients to a continuing risk of harm to which they would not otherwise have been exposed should also be regarded as unacceptable.	21

Rec. no.	Theme	Recommendation	Chapter
29		It should be an offence for death or serious injury to be caused to a patient by a breach of these regulatory requirements, or, in any other case of breach, where a warning notice in respect of the breach has been served and the notice has not been complied with. It should be a defence for the provider to prove that all reasonably practicable steps have been taken to prevent a breach, including having in place a prescribed system to prevent such a breach.	21
30	Interim measures	The healthcare regulator must be free to require or recommend immediate protective steps where there is reasonable cause to suspect a breach of fundamental standards, even if it has yet to reach a concluded view or acquire all the evidence. The test should be whether it has reasonable grounds in the public interest to make the interim requirement or recommendation.	9
31		Where aware of concerns that patient safety is at risk, Monitor and all other regulators of healthcare providers must have in place policies which ensure that they constantly review whether the need to protect patients requires use of their own powers of intervention to inform a decision whether or not to intervene, taking account of, but not being bound by, the views or actions of other regulators.	10
32		Where patient safety is believed on reasonable grounds to be at risk, Monitor and any other regulator should be obliged to take whatever action within their powers is necessary to protect patient safety. Such action should include, where necessary, temporary measures to ensure such protection while any investigation required to make a final determination is undertaken.	10
33		Insofar as healthcare regulators consider they do not possess any necessary interim powers, the Department of Health should consider introduction of the necessary amendments to legislation to provide such powers.	10
34		Where a provider is under regulatory investigation, there should be some form of external performance management involvement to oversee any necessary interim arrangements for protecting the public.	9
35	Need to share information between regulators	Sharing of intelligence between regulators needs to go further than sharing of existing concerns identified as risks. It should extend to all intelligence which when pieced together with that possessed by partner organisations may raise the level of concern. Work should be done on a template of the sort of information each organisation would find helpful.	9
36	Use of information for effective regulation	A coordinated collection of accurate information about the performance of organisations must be available to providers, commissioners, regulators and the public, in as near real time as possible, and should be capable of use by regulators in assessing the risk of non-compliance. It must not only include statistics about outcomes, but must take advantage of all safety related information, including that capable of being derived from incidents, complaints and investigations.	9
37	Use of information about compliance by regulator from: • Quality accounts	Trust Boards should provide, through quality accounts, and in a nationally consistent format, full and accurate information about their compliance with each standard which applies to them. To the extent that it is not practical in a written report to set out detail, this should be made available via each trust's website. Reports should no longer be confined to reports on achievements as opposed to a fair representation of areas where compliance has not been achieved. A full account should be given as to the methods used to produce the information. To make or be party to a wilfully or recklessly false statement as to compliance with safety or essential standards in the required quality account should be made a criminal offence.	11

Rec. no.	Theme	Recommendation	Chapter
38	• Complaints	The Care Quality Commission should ensure as a matter of urgency that it has reliable access to all useful complaints information relevant to assessment of compliance with fundamental standards, and should actively seek this information out, probably via its local relationship managers. Any bureaucratic or legal obstacles to this should be removed.	11
39		The Care Quality Commission should introduce a mandated return from providers about patterns of complaints, how they were dealt with and outcomes.	11
40		It is important that greater attention is paid to the narrative contained in, for instance, complaints data, as well as to the numbers.	11
41	• Patient safety alerts	The Care Quality Commission should have a clear responsibility to review decisions not to comply with patient safety alerts and to oversee the effectiveness of any action required to implement them. Information-sharing with the Care Quality Commission regarding patient safety alerts should continue following the transfer of the National Patient Safety Agency's functions in June 2012 to the NHS Commissioning Board.	11
42	• Serious untoward incidents	Strategic Health Authorities/their successors should, as a matter of routine, share information on serious untoward incidents with the Care Quality Commission.	11
43	• Media	Those charged with oversight and regulatory roles in healthcare should monitor media reports about the organisations for which they have responsibility.	6
44		Any example of a serious incident or avoidable harm should trigger an examination by the Care Quality Commission of how that was addressed by the provider and a requirement for the trust concerned to demonstrate that the learning to be derived has been successfully implemented.	11
45	• Inquests	The Care Quality Commission should be notified directly of upcoming healthcare-related inquests, either by trusts or perhaps more usefully by coroners.	11
46	• Quality and risk profiles	The Quality and Risk Profile should not be regarded as a potential substitute for active regulatory oversight by inspectors. It is important that this is explained carefully and clearly as and when the public are given access to the information.	11
47	• Foundation trust governors, scrutiny committees	The Care Quality Commission should expand its work with overview and scrutiny committees and foundation trust governors as a valuable information resource. For example, it should further develop its current 'sounding board events'.	11
48		The Care Quality Commission should send a personal letter, via each registered body, to each foundation trust governor on appointment, inviting them to submit relevant information about any concerns to the Care Quality Commission.	11
49	Enhancement of monitoring and the importance of inspection	Routine and risk-related monitoring, as opposed to acceptance of self-declarations of compliance, is essential. The Care Quality Commission should consider its monitoring in relation to the value to be obtained from: • The Quality and Risk Profile; • Quality Accounts; • Reports from Local Healthwatch; • New or existing peer review schemes; • Themed inspections.	11
50		The Care Quality Commission should retain an emphasis on inspection as a central method of monitoring non-compliance.	11

Rec. no.	Theme	Recommendation	Chapter
51		The Care Quality Commission should develop a specialist cadre of inspectors by thorough training in the principles of hospital care. Inspections of NHS hospital care providers should be led by such inspectors who should have the support of a team, including service user representatives, clinicians and any other specialism necessary because of particular concerns. Consideration should be given to applying the same principle to the independent sector, as well as to the NHS.	11
52		The Care Quality Commission should consider whether inspections could be conducted in collaboration with other agencies, or whether they can take advantage of any peer review arrangements available.	11
53	Care Quality Commission independence, strategy and culture	Any change to the Care Quality Commission's role should be by evolution – any temptation to abolish this organisation and create a new one must be avoided.	11
54		Where issues relating to regulatory action are discussed between the Care Quality Commission and other agencies, these should be properly recorded to avoid any suggestion of inappropriate interference in the Care Quality Commission's statutory role.	11
55		The Care Quality Commission should review its processes as a whole to ensure that it is capable of delivering regulatory oversight and enforcement effectively, in accordance with the principles outlined in this report.	11
56		The leadership of the Care Quality Commission should communicate clearly and persuasively its strategic direction to the public and to its staff, with a degree of clarity that may have been missing to date.	11
57		The Care Quality Commission should undertake a formal evaluation of how it would detect and take action on the warning signs and other events giving cause for concern at the Trust described in this report, and in the report of the first inquiry, and open that evaluation for public scrutiny.	11
58		Patients, through their user group representatives, should be integrated into the structure of the Care Quality Commission. It should consider whether there is a place for a patients' consultative council with which issues could be discussed to obtain a patient perspective directly.	11
59		Consideration should be given to the introduction of a category of nominated board members from representatives of the professions, for example, the Academy of Medical Royal Colleges, a representative of nursing and allied healthcare professionals, and patient representative groups.	11
Responsibility for, and effectiveness of, regulating healthcare systems governance – Monitor's healthcare systems regulatory functions			
60	Consolidation of regulatory functions	The Secretary of State should consider transferring the functions of regulating governance of healthcare providers and the fitness of persons to be directors, governors or equivalent persons from Monitor to the Care Quality Commission.	11 10
61		A merger of system regulatory functions between Monitor and the Care Quality Commission should be undertaken incrementally and after thorough planning. Such a move should not be used as a justification for reduction of the resources allocated to this area of regulatory activity. It would be vital to retain the corporate memory of both organisations.	11 10
62	Improved patient focus	For as long as it retains responsibility for the regulation of foundation trusts, Monitor should incorporate greater patient and public involvement into its own structures, to ensure this focus is always at the forefront of its work.	11 10
63	Improved transparency	Monitor should publish all side letters and any rating issued to trusts as part of their authorisation or licence.	10

Rec. no.	Theme	Recommendation	Chapter
64	Authorisation of foundation trusts	The authorisation process should be conducted by one regulator, which should be equipped with the relevant powers and expertise to undertake this effectively. With due regard to protecting the public from the adverse consequences inherent to any reorganisation, the regulation of the authorisation process and compliance with foundation trust standards should be transferred to the Care Quality Commission, which should incorporate the relevant departments of Monitor.	4
65	Quality of care as a pre-condition for foundation trust applications	The NHS Trust Development Authority should develop a clear policy requiring proof of fitness for purpose in delivering the appropriate quality of care as a pre-condition to consideration for support for a foundation trust application.	4
66	Improving contribution of stakeholder opinions	The Department of Health, the NHS Trust Development Authority and Monitor should jointly review the stakeholder consultation process with a view to ensuring that: • Local stakeholder and public opinion is sought on the fitness of a potential applicant NHS trust for foundation trust status and in particular on whether a potential applicant is delivering a sustainable service compliant with fundamental standards; • An accessible record of responses received is maintained; • The responses are made available for analysis on behalf of the Secretary of State, and, where an application is assessed by it, Monitor.	4
67	Focus on compliance with fundamental standards	The NHS Trust Development Authority should develop a rigorous process for the assessment as well as the support of potential applicants for foundation trust status. The assessment must include as a priority focus a review of the standard of service delivered to patients, and the sustainability of a service at the required standard.	4
68		No NHS trust should be given support to make an application to Monitor unless, in addition to other criteria, the performance manager (the Strategic Health Authority cluster, the Department of Health team, or the NHS Trust Development Authority) is satisfied that the organisation currently meets Monitor's criteria for authorisation and that it is delivering a sustainable service which is, and will remain, safe for patients, and is compliant with at least fundamental standards.	4
69		The assessment criteria for authorisation should include a requirement that applicants demonstrate their ability to consistently meet fundamental patient safety and quality standards at the same time as complying with the financial and corporate governance requirements of a foundation trust.	4
70	Duty of utmost good faith	A duty of utmost good faith should be imposed on applicants for foundation trust status to disclose to the regulator any significant information material to the application and to ensure that any information is complete and accurate. This duty should continue throughout the application process, and thereafter in relation to the monitoring of compliance.	4
71	Role of Secretary of State	The Secretary of State's support for an application should not be given unless he is satisfied that the proposed applicant provides a service to patients which is, at the time of his consideration, safe, effective and compliant with all relevant standards, and that in his opinion it is reasonable to conclude that the proposed applicant will continue to be able to do so for the foreseeable future. In deciding whether he can be so satisfied, the Secretary of State should have regard to the required public consultation and should consult with the healthcare regulator.	4
72	Assessment process for authorisation	The assessment for an authorisation of applicant for foundation trust status should include a full physical inspection of its primary clinical areas as well as all wards to determine whether it is compliant with fundamental safety and quality standards.	4

Rec. no.	Theme	Recommendation	Chapter
73	Need for constructive working with other parts of the system	The Department of Health's regular performance reviews of Monitor (and the Care Quality Commission) should include an examination of its relationship with the Department of Health and whether the appropriate degree of clarity of understanding of the scope of their respective responsibilities has been maintained.	10
74	Enhancement of role of governors	Monitor and the Care Quality Commission should publish guidance for governors suggesting principles they expect them to follow in recognising their obligation to account to the public, and in particular in arranging for communication with the public served by the foundation trust and to be informed of the public's views about the services offered.	10
75		The Council of Governors and the board of each foundation trust should together consider how best to enhance the ability of the council to assist in maintaining compliance with its obligations and to represent the public interest. They should produce an agreed published description of the role of the governors and how it is planned that they perform it. Monitor and the Care Quality Commission should review these descriptions and promote what they regard as best practice.	10
76		Arrangements must be made to ensure that governors are accountable not just to the immediate membership but to the public at large – it is important that regular and constructive contact between governors and the public is maintained.	10
77		Monitor and the NHS Commissioning Board should review the resources and facilities made available for the training and development of governors to enhance their independence and ability to expose and challenge deficiencies in the quality of the foundation trust's services.	10
78		The Care Quality Commission and Monitor should consider how best to enable governors to have access to a similar advisory facility in relation to compliance with healthcare standards as will be available for compliance issues in relation to breach of a licence (pursuant to section 39A of the National Health Service Act 2006 as amended), or other ready access to external assistance.	10
79	Accountability of providers' directors	There should be a requirement that all directors of all bodies registered by the Care Quality Commission as well as Monitor for foundation trusts are, and remain, fit and proper persons for the role. Such a test should include a requirement to comply with a prescribed code of conduct for directors.	10
80		A finding that a person is not a fit and proper person on the grounds of serious misconduct or incompetence should be a circumstance added to the list of disqualifications in the standard terms of a foundation trust's constitution.	11
81		Consideration should be given to including in the criteria for fitness a minimum level of experience and/or training, while giving appropriate latitude for recognition of equivalence.	11
82		Provision should be made for regulatory intervention to require the removal or suspension from office after due process of a person whom the regulator is satisfied is not or is no longer a fit and proper person, regardless of whether the trust is in significant breach of its authorisation or licence.	10
83		If a "fit and proper person test" is introduced as recommended, Monitor should issue guidance on the principles on which it would exercise its power to require the removal or suspension or disqualification of directors who did not fulfil it, and the procedure it would follow to ensure due process.	10

Rec. no.	Theme	Recommendation	Chapter
84		Where the contract of employment or appointment of an executive or non-executive director is terminated in circumstances in which there are reasonable grounds for believing that he or she is not a fit and proper person to hold such a post, licensed bodies should be obliged by the terms of their licence to report the matter to Monitor, the Care Quality Commission and the NHS Trust Development Authority.	10
85		Monitor and the Care Quality Commission should produce guidance to NHS and foundation trusts on procedures to be followed in the event of an executive or non-executive director being found to have been guilty of serious failure in the performance of his or her office, and in particular with regard to the need to have regard to the public interest in protection of patients and maintenance of confidence in the NHS and the healthcare system.	10
86	Requirement of training of directors	A requirement should be imposed on foundation trusts to have in place an adequate programme for the training and continued development of directors.	10
Responsibility for, and effectiveness of, regulating healthcare systems governance – Health and Safety Executive functions in healthcare settings			
87	Ensuring the utility of a health and safety function in a clinical setting	The Health and Safety Executive is clearly not the right organisation to be focusing on healthcare. Either the Care Quality Commission should be given power to prosecute 1974 Act offences or a new offence containing comparable provisions should be created under which the Care Quality Commission has power to launch a prosecution.	13
88	Information sharing	The information contained in reports for the Reporting of Injuries, Diseases and Dangerous Occurrences Regulations should be made available to healthcare regulators through the serious untoward incident system in order to provide a check on the consistency of trusts' practice in reporting fatalities and other serious incidents.	13
89		Reports on serious untoward incidents involving death of or serious injury to patients or employees should be shared with the Health and Safety Executive.	13
90	Assistance in deciding on prosecutions	In order to determine whether a case is so serious, either in terms of the breach of safety requirements or the consequences for any victims, that the public interest requires individuals or organisations to be brought to account for their failings, the Health and Safety Executive should obtain expert advice, as is done in the field of healthcare litigation and fitness to practise proceedings.	13
Enhancement of the role of supportive agencies			
91	**NHS Litigation Authority** Improvement of risk management	The Department of Health and NHS Commissioning Board should consider what steps are necessary to require all NHS providers, whether or not they remain members of the NHS Litigation Authority scheme, to have and to comply with risk management standards at least as rigorous as those required by the NHS Litigation Authority.	15
92		The financial incentives at levels below level 3 should be adjusted to maximise the motivation to reach 3.	15
93		The NHS Litigation Authority should introduce requirements with regard to observance of the guidance to be produced in relation to staffing levels, and require trusts to have regard to evidence-based guidance and benchmarks where these exist and to demonstrate that effective risk assessments take place when changes to the numbers or skills of staff are under consideration. It should also consider how more outcome based standards could be designed to enhance the prospect of exploring deficiencies in risk management, such as occurred at the Trust.	15

Rec. no.	Theme	Recommendation	Chapter
94	Evidence-based assessment	As some form of running record of the evidence reviewed must be retained on each claim in order for these reports to be produced, the NHS Litigation Authority should consider development of a relatively simple database containing the same information.	15
95	Information sharing	As the interests of patient safety should prevail over the narrow litigation interest under which confidentiality or even privilege might be claimed over risk reports, consideration should also be given to allowing the Care Quality Commission access to these reports.	15
96		The NHS Litigation Authority should make more prominent in its publicity an explanation comprehensible to the general public of the limitations of its standards assessments and of the reliance which can be placed on them.	15
97	**National Patient Safety Agency functions**	The National Patient Safety Agency's resources need to be well protected and defined. Consideration should be given to the transfer of this valuable function to a systems regulator.	17
98		Reporting to the National Reporting and Learning System of all significant adverse incidents not amounting to serious untoward incidents but involving harm to patients should be mandatory on the part of trusts.	17
99		The reporting system should be developed to make more information available from this source. Such reports are likely to be more informative than the corporate version where an incident has been properly reported, and invaluable where it has not been.	17
100		Individual reports of serious incidents which have not been otherwise reported should be shared with a regulator for investigation, as the receipt of such a report may be evidence that the mandatory system has not been complied with.	17
101		While it may be impracticable for the National Patient Safety Agency or its successor to have its own team of inspectors, it should be possible to organise for mutual peer review inspections or the inclusion in Patient Environment Action Team representatives from outside the organisation. Consideration could also be given to involvement from time to time of a representative of the Care Quality Commission.	17
102	Transparency, use and sharing of information	Data held by the National Patient Safety Agency or its successor should be open to analysis for a particular purpose, or others facilitated in that task.	17
103		The National Patient Safety Agency or its successor should regularly share information with Monitor.	17
104		The Care Quality Commission should be enabled to exploit the potential of the safety information obtained by the National Patient Safety Agency or its successor to assist it in identifying areas for focusing its attention. There needs to be a better dialogue between the two organisations as to how they can assist each other.	17
105		Consideration should be given to whether information from incident reports involving deaths in hospital could enhance consideration of the hospital standardised mortality ratio.	17
106	**Health Protection Agency** Coordination and publication of providers' information on healthcare associated infections	The Health Protection Agency and its successor, should coordinate the collection, analysis and publication of information on each provider's performance in relation to healthcare associated infections, working with the Health and Social Care Information Centre.	16

Rec. no.	Theme	Recommendation	Chapter
107	Sharing concerns	If the Health Protection Agency or its successor, or the relevant local director of public health or equivalent official, becomes concerned that a provider's management of healthcare associated infections is or may be inadequate to provide sufficient protection of patients or public safety, they should immediately inform all responsible commissioners, including the relevant regional office of the NHS Commissioning Board, the Care Quality Commission and, where relevant, Monitor, of those concerns. Sharing of such information should not be regarded as an action of last resort. It should review its procedures to ensure clarity of responsibility for taking this action.	16
108	Support for other agencies	Public Health England should review the support and training that health protection staff can offer to local authorities and other agencies in relation to local oversight of healthcare providers' infection control arrangements.	16
Effective complaints handling			
		Patients raising concerns about their care are entitled to: have the matter dealt with as a complaint unless they do not wish it; identification of their expectations; prompt and thorough processing; sensitive, responsive and accurate communication; effective and implemented learning; and proper and effective communication of the complaint to those responsible for providing the care.	
109		Methods of registering a comment or complaint must be readily accessible and easily understood. Multiple gateways need to be provided to patients, both during their treatment and after its conclusion, although all such methods should trigger a uniform process, generally led by the provider trust.	3
110	Lowering barriers	Actual or intended litigation should not be a barrier to the processing or investigation of a complaint at any level. It may be prudent for parties in actual or potential litigation to agree to a stay of proceedings pending the outcome of the complaint, but the duties of the system to respond to complaints should be regarded as entirely separate from the considerations of litigation.	3
111		Provider organisations must constantly promote to the public their desire to receive and learn from comments and complaints; constant encouragement should be given to patients and other service users, individually and collectively, to share their comments and criticisms with the organisation.	3
112		Patient feedback which is not in the form of a complaint but which suggests cause for concern should be the subject of investigation and response of the same quality as a formal complaint, whether or not the informant has indicated a desire to have the matter dealt with as such.	3
113	Complaints handling	The recommendations and standards suggested in the Patients Association's peer review into complaints at the Mid Staffordshire NHS Foundation Trust should be reviewed and implemented in the NHS.	3
114		Comments or complaints which describe events amounting to an adverse or serious untoward incident should trigger an investigation.	3
115	Investigations	Arms-length independent investigation of a complaint should be initiated by the provider trust where any one of the following apply: • A complaint amounts to an allegation of a serious untoward incident; • Subject matter involving clinically related issues is not capable of resolution without an expert clinical opinion; • A complaint raises substantive issues of professional misconduct or the performance of senior managers; • A complaint involves issues about the nature and extent of the services commissioned.	3

Rec. no.	Theme	Recommendation	Chapter
116	Support for complainants	Where meetings are held between complainants and trust representatives or investigators as part of the complaints process, advocates and advice should be readily available to all complainants who want those forms of support.	3
117		A facility should be available to Independent Complaints Advocacy Services advocates and their clients for access to expert advice in complicated cases.	3
118	Learning and information from complaints	Subject to anonymisation, a summary of each upheld complaint relating to patient care, in terms agreed with the complainant, and the trust's response should be published on its website. In any case where the complainant or, if different, the patient, refuses to agree, or for some other reason publication of an upheld, clinically related complaint is not possible, the summary should be shared confidentially with the Commissioner and the Care Quality Commission.	3
119		Overview and scrutiny committees and Local Healthwatch should have access to detailed information about complaints, although respect needs to be paid in this instance to the requirement of patient confidentiality.	3
120		Commissioners should require access to all complaints information as and when complaints are made, and should receive complaints and their outcomes on as near a real-time basis as possible. This means commissioners should be required by the NHS Commissioning Board to undertake the support and oversight role of GPs in this area, and be given the resources to do so.	3
121		The Care Quality Commission should have a means of ready access to information about the most serious complaints. Their local inspectors should be charged with informing themselves of such complaints and the detail underlying them.	3
122	Handling large-scale complaints	Large-scale failures of clinical service are likely to have in common a need for: • Provision of prompt advice, counselling and support to very distressed and anxious members of the public; • Swift identification of persons of independence, authority and expertise to lead investigations and reviews; • A procedure for the recruitment of clinical and other experts to review cases; • A communications strategy to inform and reassure the public of the processes being adopted; • Clear lines of responsibility and accountability for the setting up and oversight of such reviews. Such events are of sufficient rarity and importance, and requiring of coordination of the activities of multiple organisations, that the primary responsibility should reside in the National Quality Board.	3
Commissioning for standards			
123	Responsibility for monitoring delivery of standards and quality	GPs need to undertake a monitoring role on behalf of their patients who receive acute hospital and other specialist services. They should be an independent, professionally qualified check on the quality of service, in particular in relation to an assessment of outcomes. They need to have internal systems enabling them to be aware of patterns of concern, so that they do not merely treat each case on its individual merits. They have a responsibility to all their patients to keep themselves informed of the standard of service available at various providers in order to make patients' choice reality. A GP's duty to a patient does not end on referral to hospital, but is a continuing relationship. They will need to take this continuing partnership with their patients seriously if they are to be successful commissioners.	7

Rec. no.	Theme	Recommendation	Chapter
124	Duty to require and monitor delivery of fundamental standards	The commissioner is entitled to and should, wherever it is possible to do so, apply a fundamental safety and quality standard in respect of each item of service it is commissioning. In relation to each such standard, it should agree a method of measuring compliance and redress for non-compliance. Commissioners should consider whether it would incentivise compliance by requiring redress for individual patients who have received sub-standard service to be offered by the provider. These must be consistent with fundamental standards enforceable by the Care Quality Commission.	7
125	Responsibility for requiring and monitoring delivery of enhanced standards	In addition to their duties with regard to the fundamental standards, commissioners should be enabled to promote improvement by requiring compliance with enhanced standards or development towards higher standards. They can incentivise such improvements either financially or by other means designed to enhance the reputation and standing of clinicians and the organisations for which they work.	7
126	Preserving corporate memory	The NHS Commissioning Board and local commissioners should develop and oversee a code of practice for managing organisational transitions, to ensure the information conveyed is both candid and comprehensive. This code should cover both transitions between commissioners, for example as new clinical commissioning groups are formed, and guidance for commissioners on what they should expect to see in any organisational transitions amongst their providers.	7
127	Resources for scrutiny	The NHS Commissioning Board and local commissioners must be provided with the infrastructure and the support necessary to enable a proper scrutiny of its providers' services, based on sound commissioning contracts, while ensuring providers remain responsible and accountable for the services they provide.	7
128	Expert support	Commissioners must have access to the wide range of experience and resources necessary to undertake a highly complex and technical task, including specialist clinical advice and procurement expertise. When groups are too small to acquire such support, they should collaborate with others to do so.	7
129	Ensuring assessment and enforcement of fundamental standards through contracts	In selecting indicators and means of measuring compliance, the principal focus of commissioners should be on what is reasonably necessary to safeguard patients and to ensure that at least fundamental safety and quality standards are maintained. This requires close engagement with patients, past, present and potential, to ensure that their expectations and concerns are addressed.	7
130	Relative position of commissioner and provider	Commissioners – not providers – should decide what they want to be provided. They need to take into account what can be provided, and for that purpose will have to consult clinicians both from potential providers and elsewhere, and to be willing to receive proposals, but in the end it is the commissioner whose decision must prevail.	7
131	Development of alternative sources of provision	Commissioners need, wherever possible, to identify and make available alternative sources of provision. This may mean that commissioning has to be undertaken on behalf of consortia of commissioning groups to provide the negotiating weight necessary to achieve a negotiating balance of power with providers.	7

Rec. no.	Theme	Recommendation	Chapter
132	Monitoring tools	Commissioners must have the capacity to monitor the performance of every commissioning contract on a continuing basis during the contract period: • Such monitoring may include requiring quality information generated by the provider. • Commissioners must also have the capacity to undertake their own (or independent) audits, inspections, and investigations. These should, where appropriate, include investigation of individual cases and reviews of groups of cases. • The possession of accurate, relevant, and useable information from which the safety and quality of a service can be ascertained is the vital key to effective commissioning, as it is to effective regulation. • Monitoring needs to embrace both compliance with the fundamental standards and with any enhanced standards adopted. In the case of the latter, they will be the only source of monitoring, leaving the healthcare regulator to focus on fundamental standards.	7
133	Role of commissioners in complaints	Commissioners should be entitled to intervene in the management of an individual complaint on behalf of the patient where it appears to them it is not being dealt with satisfactorily, while respecting the principle that it is the provider who has primary responsibility to process and respond to complaints about its services.	7
134	Role of commissioners in provision of support for complainants	Consideration should be given to whether commissioners should be given responsibility for commissioning patients' advocates and support services for complaints against providers.	7
135	Public accountability of commissioners and public engagement	Commissioners should be accountable to their public for the scope and quality of services they commission. Acting on behalf of the public requires their full involvement and engagement: • There should be a membership system whereby eligible members of the public can be involved in and contribute to the work of the commissioners. • There should be lay members of the commissioner's board. • Commissioners should create and consult with patient forums and local representative groups. Individual members of the public (whether or not members) must have access to a consultative process so their views can be taken into account. • There should be regular surveys of patients and the public more generally. • Decision-making processes should be transparent: decision-making bodies should hold public meetings. Commissioners need to create and maintain a recognisable identity which becomes a familiar point of reference for the community.	7
136		Commissioners need to be recognisable public bodies, visibly acting on behalf of the public they serve and with a sufficient infrastructure of technical support. Effective local commissioning can only work with effective local monitoring, and that cannot be done without knowledgeable and skilled local personnel engaging with an informed public.	7
137	Intervention and sanctions for substandard or unsafe services	Commissioners should have powers of intervention where substandard or unsafe services are being provided, including requiring the substitution of staff or other measures necessary to protect patients from the risk of harm. In the provision of the commissioned services, such powers should be aligned with similar powers of the regulators so that both commissioners and regulators can act jointly, but with the proviso that either can act alone if the other declines to do so. The powers should include the ability to order a provider to stop provision of a service.	7

Rec. no.	Theme	Recommendation	Chapter
Local scrutiny			
138		Commissioners should have contingency plans with regard to the protection of patients from harm, where it is found that they are at risk from substandard or unsafe services.	7
Performance management and strategic oversight			
139	The need to put patients first at all times	The first priority for any organisation charged with responsibility for performance management of a healthcare provider should be ensuring that fundamental patient safety and quality standards are being met. Such an organisation must require convincing evidence to be available before accepting that such standards are being complied with.	8
140	Performance managers working constructively with regulators	Where concerns are raised that such standards are not being complied with, a performance management organisation should share, wherever possible, all relevant information with the relevant regulator, including information about its judgement as to the safety of patients of the healthcare provider.	8
141	Taking responsibility for quality	Any differences of judgement as to immediate safety concerns between a performance manager and a regulator should be discussed between them and resolved where possible, but each should recognise its retained individual responsibility to take whatever action within its power is necessary in the interests of patient safety.	8
142	Clear lines of responsibility supported by good information flows	For an organisation to be effective in performance management, there must exist unambiguous lines of referral and information flows, so that the performance manager is not in ignorance of the reality.	8
143	Clear metrics on quality	Metrics need to be established which are relevant to the quality of care and patient safety across the service, to allow norms to be established so that outliers or progression to poor performance can be identified and accepted as needing to be fixed.	8
144	Need for ownership of quality metrics at a strategic level	The NHS Commissioning Board should ensure the development of metrics on quality and outcomes of care for use by commissioners in managing the performance of providers, and retain oversight of these through its regional offices, if appropriate.	8
Patient, public and local scrutiny			
145	Structure of Local Healthwatch	There should be a consistent basic structure for Local Healthwatch throughout the country, in accordance with the principles set out in *Chapter 6: Patient and public local involvement and scrutiny.*	6
146	Finance and oversight of Local Healthwatch	Local authorities should be required to pass over the centrally provided funds allocated to its Local Healthwatch, while requiring the latter to account to it for its stewardship of the money. Transparent respect for the independence of Local Healthwatch should not be allowed to inhibit a responsible local authority – or Healthwatch England as appropriate – intervening.	6
147	Coordination of local public scrutiny bodies	Guidance should be given to promote the coordination and cooperation between Local Healthwatch, Health and Wellbeing Boards, and local government scrutiny committees.	6
148	Training	The complexities of the health service are such that proper training must be available to the leadership of Local Healthwatch as well as, when the occasion arises, expert advice.	6
149	Expert assistance	Scrutiny committees should be provided with appropriate support to enable them to carry out their scrutiny role, including easily accessible guidance and benchmarks.	6

Rec. no.	Theme	Recommendation	Chapter
150	Inspection powers	Scrutiny committees should have powers to inspect providers, rather than relying on local patient involvement structures to carry out this role, or should actively work with those structures to trigger and follow up inspections where appropriate, rather than receiving reports without comment or suggestions for action.	6
151	Complaints to MPs	MPs are advised to consider adopting some simple system for identifying trends in the complaints and information they received from constituents. They should also consider whether individual complaints imply concerns of wider significance than the impact on one individual patient.	6
Medical training and education			
152	Medical training	Any organisation which in the course of a review, inspection or other performance of its duties, identifies concerns potentially relevant to the acceptability of training provided by a healthcare provider, must be required to inform the relevant training regulator of those concerns.	18
153		The Secretary of State should by statutory instrument specify all medical education and training regulators as relevant bodies for the purpose of their statutory duty to cooperate. Information sharing between the deanery, commissioners, the General Medical Council, the Care Quality Commission and Monitor with regard to patient safety issues must be reviewed to ensure that each organisation is made aware of matters of concern relevant to their responsibilities.	18
154		The Care Quality Commission and Monitor should develop practices and procedures with training regulators and bodies responsible for the commissioning and oversight of medical training to coordinate their oversight of healthcare organisations which provide regulated training.	18
155		The General Medical Council should set out a standard requirement for routine visits to each local education provider, and programme in accordance with the following principles: • The Postgraduate Dean should be responsible for managing the process at the level of the Local Educational Training Board, as part of overall deanery functions. • The Royal Colleges should be enlisted to support such visits and to provide the relevant specialist expertise where required. • There should be lay or patient representation on visits to ensure that patient interests are maintained as the priority. • Such visits should be informed by all other sources of information and, if relevant, coordinated with the work of the Care Quality Commission and other forms of review. The Department of Health should provide appropriate resources to ensure that an effective programme of monitoring training by visits can be carried out. All healthcare organisations must be required to release healthcare professionals to support the visits programme. It should also be recognised that the benefits in professional development and dissemination of good practice are of significant value.	18
156		The system for approving and accrediting training placement providers and programmes should be configured to apply the principles set out above.	18

Rec. no.	Theme	Recommendation	Chapter
157	Matters to be reported to the General Medical Council	The General Medical Council should set out a clear statement of what matters; deaneries are required to report to the General Medical Council either routinely or as they arise. Reports should include a description of all relevant activity and findings and not be limited to exceptional matters of perceived non-compliance with standards. Without a compelling and recorded reason, no professional in a training organisation interviewed by a regulator in the course of an investigation should be bound by a requirement of confidentiality not to report the existence of an investigation, and the concerns raised by or to the investigation with his own organisation.	18
158	Training and training establishments as a source of safety information	The General Medical Council should amend its standards for undergraduate medical education to include a requirement that providers actively seek feedback from students and tutors on compliance by placement providers with minimum standards of patient safety and quality of care, and should generally place the highest priority on the safety of patients.	18
159		Surveys of medical students and trainees should be developed to optimise them as a source of feedback of perceptions of the standards of care provided to patients. The General Medical Council should consult the Care Quality Commission in developing the survey and routinely share information obtained with healthcare regulators.	18
160		Proactive steps need to be taken to encourage openness on the part of trainees and to protect them from any adverse consequences in relation to raising concerns.	18
161		Training visits should make an important contribution to the protection of patients: • Obtaining information directly from trainees should remain a valuable source of information – but it should not be the only method used. • Visits to, and observation of, the actual training environment would enable visitors to detect poor practice from which both patients and trainees should be sheltered. • The opportunity can be taken to share and disseminate good practice with trainers and management. Visits of this nature will encourage the transparency that is so vital to the preservation of minimum standards.	18
162		The General Medical Council should in the course of its review of its standards and regulatory process ensure that the system of medical training and education maintains as its first priority the safety of patients. It should also ensure that providers of clinical placements are unable to take on students or trainees in areas which do not comply with fundamental patient safety and quality standards. Regulators and deaneries should exercise their own independent judgement as to whether such standards have been achieved and if at any stage concerns relating to patient safety are raised to the, must take appropriate action to ensure these concerns are properly addressed.	18
163	Safe staff numbers and skills	The General Medical Council's system of reviewing the acceptability of the provision of training by healthcare providers must include a review of the sufficiency of the numbers and skills of available staff for the provision of training and to ensure patient safety in the course of training.	18
164	Approved Practice Settings	The Department of Health and the General Medical Council should review whether the resources available for regulating Approved Practice Setting are adequate and, if not, make arrangements for the provision of the same. Consideration should be given to empowering the General Medical Council to charge organisations a fee for approval.	18
165		The General Medical Council should immediately review its approved practice settings criteria with a view to recognition of the priority to be given to protecting patients and the public.	18

Rec. no.	Theme	Recommendation	Chapter
166		The General Medical Council should in consultation with patient interest groups and the public immediately review its procedures for assuring compliance with its approved practice settings criteria with a view in particular to provision for active exchange of relevant information with the healthcare systems regulator, coordination of monitoring processes with others required for medical education and training, and receipt of relevant information from registered practitioners of their current experience in approved practice settings approved establishments.	18
167		The Department of Health and the General Medical Council should review the powers available to the General Medical Council in support of assessment and monitoring of approved practice settings establishments with a view to ensuring that the General Medical Council (or if considered to be more appropriate, the healthcare systems regulator) has the power to inspect establishments, either itself or by an appointed entity on its behalf, and to require the production of relevant information.	18
168		The Department of Health and the General Medical Council should consider making the necessary statutory (and regulatory changes) to incorporate the approved practice settings scheme into the regulatory framework for post graduate training.	18
169	Role of the Department of Health and the National Quality Board	The Department of Health, through the National Quality Board, should ensure that procedures are put in place for facilitating the identification of patient safety issues by training regulators and cooperation between them and healthcare systems regulators.	18
170	Health Education England	Health Education England should have a medically qualified director of medical education and a lay patient representative on its board.	18
171	Deans	All Local Education and Training Boards should have a post of medically qualified postgraduate dean responsible for all aspects of postgraduate medical education.	18
172	Proficiency in the English language	The Government should consider urgently the introduction of a common requirement of proficiency in communication in the English language with patients and other persons providing healthcare to the standard required for a registered medical practitioner to assume professional responsibility for medical treatment of an English-speaking patient.	18
Openness, transparency and candour			
	Openness – enabling concerns and complaints to be raised freely without fear and questions asked to be answered.		
	Transparency – allowing information about the truth about performance and outcomes to be shared with staff, patients, the public and regulators.		
	Candour – any patient harmed by the provision of a healthcare service is informed of the fact and an appropriate remedy offered, regardless of whether a complaint has been made or a question asked about it.		
173	**Principles of openness, transparency and candour**	Every healthcare organisation and everyone working for them must be honest, open and truthful in all their dealings with patients and the public, and organisational and personal interests must never be allowed to outweigh the duty to be honest, open and truthful.	22
174	Candour about harm	Where death or serious harm has been or may have been caused to a patient by an act or omission of the organisation or its staff, the patient (or any lawfully entitled personal representative or other authorised person) should be informed of the incident, given full disclosure of the surrounding circumstances and be offered an appropriate level of support, whether or not the patient or representative has asked for this information.	22

Rec. no.	Theme	Recommendation	Chapter
175		Full and truthful answers must be given to any question reasonably asked about his or her past or intended treatment by a patient (or, if deceased, to any lawfully entitled personal representative).	22
176	Openness with regulators	Any statement made to a regulator or a commissioner in the course of its statutory duties must be completely truthful and not misleading by omission.	22
177	Openness in public statements	Any public statement made by a healthcare organisation about its performance must be truthful and not misleading by omission.	22
178	**Implementation of the duty** Ensuring consistency of obligations under the duty of openness, transparency and candour	The NHS Constitution should be revised to reflect the changes recommended with regard to a duty of openness, transparency and candour, and all organisations should review their contracts of employment, policies and guidance to ensure that, where relevant, they expressly include and are consistent with above principles and these recommendations.	22
179	Restrictive contractual clauses	"Gagging clauses" or non disparagement clauses should be prohibited in the policies and contracts of all healthcare organisations, regulators and commissioners; insofar as they seek, or appear, to limit bona fide disclosure in relation to public interest issues of patient safety and care.	22
180	Candour about incidents	Guidance and policies should be reviewed to ensure that they will lead to compliance with *Being Open*, the guidance published by the National Patient Safety Agency.	22
181	**Enforcement of the duty** Statutory duties of candour in relation to harm to patients	A statutory obligation should be imposed to observe a duty of candour: • On healthcare providers who believe or suspect that treatment or care provided by it to a patient has caused death or serious injury to a patient to inform that patient or other duly authorised person as soon as is practicable of that fact and thereafter to provide such information and explanation as the patient reasonably may request; • On registered medical practitioners and registered nurses and other registered professionals who believe or suspect that treatment or care provided to a patient by or on behalf of any healthcare provider by which they are employed has caused death or serious injury to the patient to report their belief or suspicion to their employer as soon as is reasonably practicable. The provision of information in compliance with this requirement should not of itself be evidence or an admission of any civil or criminal liability, but non-compliance with the statutory duty should entitle the patient to a remedy.	22
182	Statutory duty of openness and transparency	There should be a statutory duty on all directors of healthcare organisations to be truthful in any information given to a healthcare regulator or commissioner, either personally or on behalf of the organisation, where given in compliance with a statutory obligation on the organisation to provide it.	22
183	Criminal liability	It should be made a criminal offence for any registered medical practitioner, or nurse, or allied health professional or director of an authorised or registered healthcare organisation: • Knowingly to obstruct another in the performance of these statutory duties; • To provide information to a patient or nearest relative intending to mislead them about such an incident; • Dishonestly to make an untruthful statement to a commissioner or regulator knowing or believing that they are likely to rely on the statement in the performance of their duties.	22

Rec. no.	Theme	Recommendation	Chapter
184	Enforcement by the Care Quality Commission	Observance of the duty should be policed by the Care Quality Commission, which should have powers in the last resort to prosecute in cases of serial non-compliance or serious and wilful deception. The Care Quality Commission should be supported by monitoring undertaken by commissioners and others.	22
	Nursing		

185	Focus on culture of caring	There should be an increased focus in nurse training, education and professional development on the practical requirements of delivering compassionate care in addition to the theory. A system which ensures the delivery of proper standards of nursing requires:
		• Selection of recruits to the profession who evidence the:
		  – Possession of the appropriate values, attitudes and behaviours;
		  – Ability and motivation to enable them to put the welfare of others above their own interests;
		  – Drive to maintain, develop and improve their own standards and abilities;
		  – Intellectual achievements to enable them to acquire through training the necessary technical skills;
		• Training and experience in delivery of compassionate care;
		• Leadership which constantly reinforces values and standards of compassionate care;
		• Involvement in, and responsibility for, the planning and delivery of compassionate care;
		• Constant support and incentivisation which values nurses and the work they do through:
		  – Recognition of achievement;
		  – Regular, comprehensive feedback on performance and concerns;
		  – Encouraging them to report concerns and to give priority to patient well-being.
			23

186	Practical hands-on training and experience	Nursing training should be reviewed so that sufficient practical elements are incorporated to ensure that a consistent standard is achieved by all trainees throughout the country. This requires national standards.	23
187		There should be a national entry-level requirement that student nurses spend a minimum period of time, at least three months, working on the direct care of patients under the supervision of a registered nurse. Such experience should include direct care of patients, ideally including the elderly, and involve hands-on physical care. Satisfactory completion of this direct care experience should be a pre-condition to continuation in nurse training. Supervised work of this type as a healthcare support worker should be allowed to count as an equivalent. An alternative would be to require candidates for qualification for registration to undertake a minimum period of work in an approved healthcare support worker post involving the delivery of such care.	23
188	Aptitude test for compassion and caring	The Nursing and Midwifery Council, working with universities, should consider the introduction of an aptitude test to be undertaken by aspirant registered nurses at entry into the profession, exploring, in particular, candidates' attitudes towards caring, compassion and other necessary professional values.	23
189	Consistent training	The Nursing and Midwifery Council and other professional and academic bodies should work towards a common qualification assessment/examination.	23
190	National standards	There should be national training standards for qualification as a registered nurse to ensure that newly qualified nurses are competent to deliver a consistent standard of the fundamental aspects of compassionate care.	23
191	Recruitment for values and commitment	Healthcare employers recruiting nursing staff, whether qualified or unqualified, should assess candidates' values, attitudes and behaviours towards the well-being of patients and their basic care needs, and care providers should be required to do so by commissioning and regulatory requirements.	23
192	Strong nursing voice	The Department of Health and Nursing and Midwifery Council should introduce the concept of a Responsible Officer for nursing, appointed by and accountable to, the Nursing and Midwifery Council.	23

Rec. no.	Theme	Recommendation	Chapter
193	Standards for appraisal and support	Without introducing a revalidation scheme immediately, the Nursing and Midwifery Council should introduce common minimum standards for appraisal and support with which responsible officers would be obliged to comply. They could be required to report to the Nursing and Midwifery Council on their performance on a regular basis.	23
194		As part of a mandatory annual performance appraisal, each Nurse, regardless of workplace setting, should be required to demonstrate in their annual learning portfolio an up-to-date knowledge of nursing practice and its implementation. Alongside developmental requirements, this should contain documented evidence of recognised training undertaken, including wider relevant learning. It should also demonstrate commitment, compassion and caring for patients, evidenced by feedback from patients and families on the care provided by the nurse. This portfolio and each annual appraisal should be made available to the Nursing and Midwifery Council, if requested, as part of a nurse's revalidation process.

At the end of each annual assessment, the appraisal and portfolio should be signed by the nurse as being an accurate and true reflection and be countersigned by their appraising manager as being such. | 23 |
195	Nurse leadership	Ward nurse managers should operate in a supervisory capacity, and not be office-bound or expected to double up, except in emergencies as part of the nursing provision on the ward. They should know about the care plans relating to every patient on his or her ward. They should make themselves visible to patients and staff alike, and be available to discuss concerns with all, including relatives. Critically, they should work alongside staff as a role model and mentor, developing clinical competencies and leadership skills within the team. As a corollary, they would monitor performance and deliver training and/or feedback as appropriate, including a robust annual appraisal.	23
196		The Knowledge and Skills Framework should be reviewed with a view to giving explicit recognition to nurses' demonstrations of commitment to patient care and, in particular, to the priority to be accorded to dignity and respect, and their acquisition of leadership skills.	23
197		Training and continuing professional development for nurses should include leadership training at every level from student to director. A resource for nurse leadership training should be made available for all NHS healthcare provider organisations that should be required under commissioning arrangements by those buying healthcare services to arrange such training for appropriate staff.	23
198	Measuring cultural health	Healthcare providers should be encouraged by incentives to develop and deploy reliable and transparent measures of the cultural health of front-line nursing workplaces and teams, which build on the experience and feedback of nursing staff using a robust methodology, such as the "cultural barometer".	23
199	Key nurses	Each patient should be allocated for each shift a named key nurse responsible for coordinating the provision of the care needs for each allocated patient. The named key nurse on duty should, whenever possible, be present at every interaction between a doctor and an allocated patient.	23
200		Consideration should be given to the creation of a status of Registered Older Person's Nurse.	23
201	Strengthening the nursing professional voice	The Royal College of Nursing should consider whether it should formally divide its "Royal College" functions and its employee representative/trade union functions between two bodies rather than behind internal "Chinese walls".	23
202		Recognition of the importance of nursing representation at provider level should be given by ensuring that adequate time is allowed for staff to undertake this role, and employers and unions must regularly review the adequacy of the arrangements in this regard.	23

Rec. no.	Theme	Recommendation	Chapter
203		A forum for all directors of nursing from both NHS and independent sector organisations should be formed to provide a means of coordinating the leadership of the nursing profession.	23
204		All healthcare providers and commissioning organisations should be required to have at least one executive director who is a registered nurse, and should be encouraged to consider recruiting nurses as non-executive directors.	23
205		Commissioning arrangements should require the boards of provider organisations to seek and record the advice of its nursing director on the impact on the quality of care and patient safety of any proposed major change to nurse staffing arrangements or provision facilities, and to record whether they accepted or rejected the advice, in the latter case recording its reasons for doing so.	23
206		The effectiveness of the newly positioned office of Chief Nursing Officer should be kept under review to ensure the maintenance of a recognised leading representative of the nursing profession as a whole, able and empowered to give independent professional advice to the Government on nursing issues of equivalent authority to that provided by the Chief Medical Officer.	23
207	Strengthening identification of healthcare support workers and nurses	There should be a uniform description of healthcare support workers, with the relationship with currently registered nurses made clear by the title.	23
208		Commissioning arrangements should require provider organisations to ensure by means of identity labels and uniforms that a healthcare support worker is easily distinguishable from that of a registered nurse.	23
209	Registration of healthcare support workers	A registration system should be created under which no unregistered person should be permitted to provide for reward direct physical care to patients currently under the care and treatment of a registered nurse or a registered doctor (or who are dependent on such care by reason of disability and/or infirmity) in a hospital or care home setting. The system should apply to healthcare support workers, whether they are working for the NHS or independent healthcare providers, in the community, for agencies or as independent agents. (Exemptions should be made for persons caring for members of their own family or those with whom they have a genuine social relationship.)	
210	Code of conduct for healthcare support workers	There should be a national code of conduct for healthcare support workers.	23
211	Training standards for healthcare support workers	There should be a common set of national standards for the education and training of healthcare support workers.	23
212		The code of conduct, education and training standards and requirements for registration for healthcare support workers should be prepared and maintained by the Nursing and Midwifery Council after due consultation with all relevant stakeholders, including the Department of Health, other regulators, professional representative organisations and the public.	23

Rec. no.	Theme	Recommendation	Chapter
213		Until such time as the Nursing and Midwifery Council is charged with the recommended regulatory responsibilities, the Department of Health should institute a nationwide system to protect patients and care receivers from harm. This system should be supported by fair due process in relation to employees in this grade who have been dismissed by employers on the grounds of a serious breach of the code of conduct or otherwise being unfit for such a post.	23
	Leadership		
214	Shared training	A leadership staff college or training system, whether centralised or regional, should be created to: provide common professional training in management and leadership to potential senior staff; promote healthcare leadership and management as a profession; administer an accreditation scheme to enhance eligibility for consideration for such roles; promote and research best leadership practice in healthcare.	24
215	Shared code of ethics	A common code of ethics, standards and conduct for senior board-level healthcare leaders and managers should be produced and steps taken to oblige all such staff to comply with the code and their employers to enforce it.	24
216	Leadership framework	The leadership framework should be improved by increasing the emphasis given to patient safety in the thinking of all in the health service. This could be done by, for example, creating a separate domain for managing safety, or by defining the service to be delivered as a safe and effective service.	24
217	Common selection criteria	A list should be drawn up of all the qualities generally considered necessary for a good and effective leader. This in turn could inform a list of competences a leader would be expected to have.	24
218	Enforcement of standards and accountability	Serious non-compliance with the code, and in particular, non-compliance leading to actual or potential harm to patients, should render board-level leaders and managers liable to be found not to be fit and proper persons to hold such positions by a fair and proportionate procedure, with the effect of disqualifying them from holding such positions in future.	24
219	A regulator as an alternative	An alternative option to enforcing compliance with a management code of conduct, with the risk of disqualification, would be to set up an independent professional regulator. The need for this would be greater if it were thought appropriate to extend a regulatory requirement to a wider range of managers and leaders. The proportionality of such a step could be better assessed after reviewing the experience of a licensing provision for directors.	24
220	Accreditation	A training facility could provide the route through which an accreditation scheme could be organised. Although this might be a voluntary scheme, at least initially, the objective should be to require all leadership posts to be filled by persons who experience some shared training and obtain the relevant accreditation, enhancing the spread of the common culture and providing the basis for a regulatory regime.	24
221	Ensuring common standards of competence and compliance	Consideration should be given to ensuring that there is regulatory oversight of the competence and compliance with appropriate standards by the boards of health service bodies which are not foundation trusts, of equivalent rigour to that applied to foundation trusts.	24
	Professional regulation of fitness to practise		
222	**General Medical Council** Systemic investigation where needed	The General Medical Council should have a clear policy about the circumstances in which a generic complaint or report ought to be made to it, enabling a more proactive approach to monitoring fitness to practise.	12

Rec. no.	Theme	Recommendation	Chapter
223	Enhanced resources	If the General Medical Council is to be effective in looking into generic complaints and information it will probably need either greater resources, or better cooperation with the Care Quality Commission and other organisations such as the Royal Colleges to ensure that it is provided with the appropriate information.	12
224	Information sharing	Steps must be taken to systematise the exchange of information between the Royal Colleges and the General Medical Council, and to issue guidance for use by employers of doctors to the same effect.	12
225	Peer reviews	The General Medical Council should have regard to the possibility of commissioning peer reviews pursuant to section 35 of the Medical Act 1983 where concerns are raised in a generic way, in order to be advised whether there are individual concerns. Such reviews could be jointly commissioned with the Care Quality Commission in appropriate cases.	12
226	**Nursing and Midwifery Council** Investigation of systemic concerns	To act as an effective regulator of nurse managers and leaders, as well as more front-line nurses, the Nursing and Midwifery Council needs to be equipped to look at systemic concerns as well as individual ones. It must be enabled to work closely with the systems regulators and to share their information and analyses on the working of systems in organisations in which nurses are active. It should not have to wait until a disaster has occurred to intervene with its fitness to practise procedures. Full access to the Care Quality Commission information in particular is vital.	12
227		The Nursing and Midwifery Council needs to have its own internal capacity to assess systems and launch its own proactive investigations where it becomes aware of concerns which may give rise to nursing fitness to practise issues. It may decide to seek the cooperation of the Care Quality Commission, but as an independent regulator it must be empowered to act on its own if it considers it necessary in the public interest. This will require resources in terms of appropriately expert staff, data systems and finance. Given the power of the registrar to refer cases without a formal third party complaint, it would not appear that a change of regulation is necessary, but this should be reviewed.	12
228	Administrative reform	It is of concern that the administration of the Nursing and Midwifery Council, which has not been examined by this Inquiry, is still found by other reviews to be wanting. It is imperative in the public interest that this is remedied urgently. Without doing so, there is a danger that the regulatory gap between the Nursing and Midwifery Council and the Care Quality Commission will widen rather than narrow.	12
229	Revalidation	It is highly desirable that the Nursing and Midwifery Council introduces a system of revalidation similar to that of the General Medical Council, as a means of reinforcing the status and competence of registered nurses, as well as providing additional protection to the public. It is essential that the Nursing and Midwifery Council has the resources and the administrative and leadership skills to ensure that this does not detract from its existing core function of regulating fitness to practise of registered nurses.	12
230	Profile	The profile of the Nursing and Midwifery Council needs to be raised with the public, who are the prime and most valuable source of information about the conduct of nurses. All patients should be informed, by those providing treatment or care, of the existence and role of the Nursing and Midwifery Council, together with contact details. The Nursing and Midwifery Council itself needs to undertake more by way of public promotion of its functions.	12
231	Coordination with internal procedures	It is essential that, so far as practicable, Nursing and Midwifery Council procedures do not obstruct the progress of internal disciplinary action in providers. In most cases it should be possible, through cooperation, to allow both to proceed in parallel. This may require a review of employment disciplinary procedures, to make it clear that the employer is entitled to proceed even if there are pending Nursing and Midwifery Council proceedings.	12

Rec. no.	Theme	Recommendation	Chapter
232	Employment liaison officers	The Nursing and Midwifery Council could consider a concept of employment liaison officers, similar to that of the General Medical Council, to provide support to directors of nursing. If this is impractical, a support network of senior nurse leaders will have to be engaged in filling this gap.	12
233	**For joint action** Profile	While both the General Medical Council and the Nursing and Midwifery Council have highly informative internet sites, both need to ensure that patients and other service users are made aware at the point of service provision of their existence, their role and their contact details.	12
234	Cooperation with the Care Quality Commission	Both the General Medical Council and Nursing and Midwifery Council must develop closer working relationships with the Care Quality Commission – in many cases there should be joint working to minimise the time taken to resolve issues and maximise the protection afforded to the public.	12
235	Joint proceedings	The Professional Standards Authority for Health and Social Care (PSA) (formerly the Council for Healthcare Regulatory Excellence), together with the regulators under its supervision, should seek to devise procedures for dealing consistently and in the public interest with cases arising out of the same event or series of events but involving professionals regulated by more than one body. While it would require new regulations, consideration should be given to the possibility of moving towards a common independent tribunal to determine fitness to practise issues and sanctions across the healthcare professional field.	12
Caring for the elderly			
Approaches applicable to all patients but requiring special attention for the elderly			
236	Identification of who is responsible for the patient	Hospitals should review whether to reinstate the practice of identifying a senior clinician who is in charge of a patient's case, so that patients and their supporters are clear who is in overall charge of a patient's care.	25
237	Teamwork	There needs to be effective teamwork between all the different disciplines and services that together provide the collective care often required by an elderly patient; the contribution of cleaners, maintenance staff, and catering staff also needs to be recognised and valued.	25
238	Communication with and about patients	Regular interaction and engagement between nurses and patients and those close to them should be systematised through regular ward rounds: • All staff need to be enabled to interact constructively, in a helpful and friendly fashion, with patients and visitors. • Where possible, wards should have areas where more mobile patients and their visitors can meet in relative privacy and comfort without disturbing other patients. • The NHS should develop a greater willingness to communicate by email with relatives. • The currently common practice of summary discharge letters followed up some time later with more substantive ones should be reconsidered. • Information about an older patient's condition, progress and care and discharge plans should be available and shared with that patient and, where appropriate, those close to them, who must be included in the therapeutic partnership to which all patients are entitled.	25
239	Continuing responsibility for care	The care offered by a hospital should not end merely because the patient has surrendered a bed – it should never be acceptable for patients to be discharged in the middle of the night, still less so at any time without absolute assurance that a patient in need of care will receive it on arrival at the planned destination. Discharge areas in hospital need to be properly staffed and provide continued care to the patient.	25

Rec. no.	Theme	Recommendation	Chapter
240	Hygiene	All staff and visitors need to be reminded to comply with hygiene requirements. Any member of staff, however junior, should be encouraged to remind anyone, however senior, of these.	25
241	Provision of food and drink	The arrangements and best practice for providing food and drink to elderly patients require constant review, monitoring and implementation.	25
242	Medicines administration	In the absence of automatic checking and prompting, the process of the administration of medication needs to be overseen by the nurse in charge of the ward, or his/her nominated delegate. A frequent check needs to be done to ensure that all patients have received what they have been prescribed and what they need. This is particularly the case when patients are moved from one ward to another, or they are returned to the ward after treatment.	25
243	Recording of routine observations	The recording of routine observations on the ward should, where possible, be done automatically as they are taken, with results being immediately accessible to all staff electronically in a form enabling progress to be monitored and interpreted. If this cannot be done, there needs to be a system whereby ward leaders and named nurses are responsible for ensuring that the observations are carried out and recorded.	25
Information			
244	Common information practices, shared data and electronic records	There is a need for all to accept common information practices, and to feed performance information into shared databases for monitoring purposes. The following principles should be applied in considering the introduction of electronic patient information systems: • Patients need to be granted user friendly, real time and retrospective access to read their records, and a facility to enter comments. They should be enabled to have a copy of records in a form useable by them, if they wish to have one. If possible, the summary care record should be made accessible in this way. • Systems should be designed to include prompts and defaults where these will contribute to safe and effective care, and to accurate recording of information on first entry. • Systems should include a facility to alert supervisors where actions which might be expected have not occurred, or where likely inaccuracies have been entered. • Systems should, where practicable and proportionate, be capable of collecting performance management and audit information automatically, appropriately anonymised direct from entries, to avoid unnecessary duplication of input. • Systems must be designed by healthcare professionals in partnership with patient groups to secure maximum professional and patient engagement in ensuring accuracy, utility and relevance, both to the needs of the individual patients and collective professional, managerial and regulatory requirements. Systems must be capable of reflecting changing needs and local requirements over and above nationally required minimum standards.	26
245	Board accountability	Each provider organisation should have a board level member with responsibility for information.	26
246	Comparable quality accounts	Department of Health/the NHS Commissioning Board/regulators should ensure that provider organisations publish in their annual quality accounts information in a common form to enable comparisons to be made between organisations, to include a minimum of prescribed information about their compliance with fundamental and other standards, their proposals for the rectification of any non-compliance and statistics on mortality and other outcomes. Quality accounts should be required to contain the observations of commissioners, overview and scrutiny committees, and Local Healthwatch.	26
247	Accountability for quality accounts	Healthcare providers should be required to lodge their quality accounts with all organisations commissioning services from them, Local Healthwatch, and all systems regulators.	26

Rec. no.	Theme	Recommendation	Chapter
248		Healthcare providers should be required to have their quality accounts independently audited. Auditors should be given a wider remit enabling them to use their professional judgement in examining the reliability of all statements in the accounts.	26
249		Each quality account should be accompanied by a declaration signed by all directors in office at the date of the account certifying that they believe the contents of the account to be true, or alternatively a statement of explanation as to the reason any such director is unable or has refused to sign such a declaration.	26
250		It should be a criminal offence for a director to sign a declaration of belief that the contents of a quality account are true if it contains a misstatement of fact concerning an item of prescribed information which he/she does not have reason to believe is true at the time of making the declaration.	26
251	Regulatory oversight of quality accounts	The Care Quality Commission and/or Monitor should keep the accuracy, fairness and balance of quality accounts under review and should be enabled to require corrections to be issued where appropriate. In the event of an organisation failing to take that action, the regulator should be able to issue its own statement of correction.	26
252	Access to data	It is important that the appropriate steps are taken to enable properly anonymised data to be used for managerial and regulatory purposes.	26
253	Access to quality and risk profile	The information behind the quality and risk profile – as well as the ratings and methodology – should be placed in the public domain, as far as is consistent with maintaining any legitimate confidentiality of such information, together with appropriate explanations to enable the public to understand the limitations of this tool.	26
254	Access for public and patient comments	While there are likely to be many different gateways offered through which patient and public comments can be made, to avoid confusion, it would be helpful for there to be consistency across the country in methods of access, and for the output to be published in a manner allowing fair and informed comparison between organisations.	26
255	Using patient feedback	Results and analysis of patient feedback including qualitative information need to be made available to all stakeholders in as near "real time" as possible, even if later adjustments have to be made.	26
256	Follow up of patients	A proactive system for following up patients shortly after discharge would not only be good "customer service", it would probably provide a wider range of responses and feedback on their care.	26
257	Role of the Health and Social Care Information Centre	The Information Centre should be tasked with the independent collection, analysis, publication and oversight of healthcare information in England, or, with the agreement of the devolved governments, the United Kingdom. The information functions previously held by the National Patient Safety Agency should be transferred to the NHS Information Centre if made independent.	26
258		The Information Centre should continue to develop and maintain learning, standards and consensus with regard to information methodologies, with particular reference to comparative performance statistics.	26
259		The Information Centre, in consultation with the Department of Health, the NHS Commissioning Board and the Parliamentary and Health Service Ombudsman, should develop a means of publishing more detailed breakdowns of clinically related complaints.	26
260	Information standards	The standards applied to statistical information about serious untoward incidents should be the same as for any other healthcare information and in particular the principles around transparency and accessibility. It would, therefore, be desirable for the data to be supplied to, and processed by, the Information Centre and, through them, made publicly available in the same way as other quality related information.	26

Rec. no.	Theme	Recommendation	Chapter
261		The Information Centre should be enabled to undertake more detailed statistical analysis of its own than currently appears to be the case.	26
262	Enhancing the use, analysis and dissemination of healthcare information	All healthcare provider organisations, in conjunction with their healthcare professionals, should develop and maintain systems which give them: • Effective real-time information on the performance of each of their services against patient safety and minimum quality standards; • Effective real-time information of the performance of each of their consultants and specialist teams in relation to mortality, morbidity, outcome and patient satisfaction. In doing so, they should have regard, in relation to each service, to best practice for information management of that service as evidenced by recommendations of the Information Centre, and recommendations of specialist organisations such as the medical Royal Colleges. The information derived from such systems should, to the extent practicable, be published and in any event made available in full to commissioners and regulators, on request, and with appropriate explanation, and to the extent that is relevant to individual patients, to assist in choice of treatment.	26
263		It must be recognised to be the professional duty of all healthcare professionals to collaborate in the provision of information required for such statistics on the efficacy of treatment in specialties.	26
264		In the case of each specialty, a programme of development for statistics on the efficacy of treatment should be prepared, published, and subjected to regular review.	26
265		The Department of Health, the Information Centre and the Care Quality Commission should engage with each representative specialty organisation in order to consider how best to develop comparative statistics on the efficacy of treatment in that specialty, for publication and use in performance oversight, revalidation, and the promotion of patient knowledge and choice.	26
266		In designing the methodology for such statistics and their presentation, the Department of Health, the Information Centre, the Care Quality Commission and the specialty organisations should seek and have regard to the views of patient groups and the public about the information needed by them.	26
267		All such statistics should be made available online and accessible through provider websites, as well as other gateways such as the Care Quality Commission.	26
268	Resources	Resources must be allocated to and by provider organisations to enable the relevant data to be collected and forwarded to the relevant central registry.	26
269	Improving and assuring accuracy	The only practical way of ensuring reasonable accuracy is vigilant auditing at local level of the data put into the system. This is important work, which must be continued and where possible improved.	26
270		There is a need for a review by the Department of Health, the Information Centre and the UK Statistics Authority of the patient outcome statistics, including hospital mortality and other outcome indicators. In particular, there could be benefit from consideration of the extent to which these statistics can be published in a form more readily useable by the public.	26
271		To the extent that summary hospital-level mortality indicators are not already recognised as national or official statistics, the Department of Health and the Health and Social Care Information Centre should work towards establishing such status for them or any successor hospital mortality figures, and other patient outcome statistics, including reports showing provider-level detail.	26

Rec. no.	Theme	Recommendation	Chapter
272		There is a demonstrable need for an accreditation system to be available for healthcare-relevant statistical methodologies. The power to create an accreditation scheme has been included in the Health and Social Care Act 2012, it should be used as soon as practicable.	26
Coroners and inquests			
Making more of the coronial process in healthcare-related deaths			
273	Information to coroners	The terms of authorisation, licensing and registration and any relevant guidance should oblige healthcare providers to provide all relevant information to enable the coroner to perform his function, unless a director is personally satisfied that withholding the information is justified in the public interest.	14 / 22
274		There is an urgent need for unequivocal guidance to be given to trusts and their legal advisers and those handling disclosure of information to coroners, patients and families, as to the priority to be given to openness over any perceived material interest.	2
275	Independent medical examiners	It is of considerable importance that independent medical examiners are independent of the organisation whose patients' deaths are being scrutinised.	14
276		Sufficient numbers of independent medical examiners need to be appointed and resourced to ensure that they can give proper attention to the workload.	14
277	Death certification	National guidance should set out standard methodologies for approaching the certification of the cause of death to ensure, so far as is possible, that similar approaches are universal.	14
278		It should be a routine part of an independent medical examiners's role to seek out and consider any serious untoward incidents or adverse incident reports relating to the deceased, to ensure that all circumstances are taken into account whether or not referred to in the medical records.	14
279		So far as is practicable, the responsibility for certifying the cause of death should be undertaken and fulfilled by the consultant, or another senior and fully qualified clinician in charge of a patient's case or treatment.	14
280	Appropriate and sensitive contact with bereaved families	Both the bereaved family and the certifying doctor should be asked whether they have any concerns about the death or the circumstances surrounding it, and guidance should be given to hospital staff encouraging them to raise any concerns they may have with the independent medical examiner.	14
281		It is important that independent medical examiners and any others having to approach families for this purpose have careful training in how to undertake this sensitive task in a manner least likely to cause additional and unnecessary distress.	14
282	Information for, and from, inquests	Coroners should send copies of relevant Rule 43 reports to the Care Quality Commission.	14
283		Guidance should be developed for coroners' offices about whom to approach in gathering information about whether to hold an inquest into the death of a patient. This should include contact with the patient's family.	14
284	Appointment of assistant deputy coroners	The Lord Chancellor should issue guidance as to the criteria to be adopted in the appointment of assistant deputy coroners.	14
285	Appointment of assistant deputy coroners	The Chief Coroner should issue guidance on how to avoid the appearance of bias when assistant deputy coroners are associated with a party in a case.	14

Rec. no.	Theme	Recommendation	Chapter
Department of Health leadership			
286	Impact assessments before structural change	Impact and risk assessments should be made public, and debated publicly, before a proposal for any major structural change to the healthcare system is accepted. Such assessments should cover at least the following issues: • What is the precise issue or concern in respect of which change is necessary? • Can the policy objective identified be achieved by modifications within the existing structure? • How are the successful aspects of the existing system to be incorporated and continued in the new system? • How are the existing skills which are relevant to the new system to be transferred to it? • How is the existing corporate and individual knowledge base to be preserved, transferred and exploited? • How is flexibility to meet new circumstances and to respond to experience built into the new system to avoid the need for further structural change? • How are necessary functions to be performed effectively during any transitional period? • What are the respective risks and benefits to service users and the public and, in particular, are there any risks to safety or welfare?	19
287		The Department of Health should together with healthcare systems regulators take the lead in developing through obtaining consensus between the public and healthcare professionals, a coherent, and easily accessible structure for the development and implementation of values, fundamental, enhanced and developmental standards as recommended in this report.	19
289	Clinical input	The Department of Health should ensure that there is senior clinical involvement in all policy decisions which may impact on patient safety and well-being.	19
289	Experience on the front line	Department of Health officials need to connect more to the NHS by visits, and most importantly by personal contact with those who have suffered poor experiences. The Department of Health could also be assisted in its work by involving patient/service user representatives through some form of consultative forum within the Department.	19
290		The Department of Health should promote a shared positive culture by setting an example in its statements by being open about deficiencies, ensuring those harmed have a remedy, and making information publicly available about performance at the most detailed level possible.	19

Annex A
Inquiry Terms of Reference

Terms of Reference

Inquiry into the operation of the commissioning, supervisory and regulatory bodies in relation to their monitoring role at Mid Staffordshire NHS Foundation Trust

Robert Francis QC recommended that the Department should consider an independent examination of the role of the commissioning, supervisory and regulatory bodies in the monitoring of Mid-Staffordshire NHS Foundation Trust.

Following that recommendation, he has been invited to build on the work of the Inquiry into the care provided by Mid Staffordshire NHS Foundation Trust between January 2005 and March 2009, by undertaking an investigation into the role of the commissioning, supervisory and regulatory bodies and systems in detecting and correcting deficiencies in service provision of the type he has identified.

The systems in place are now different from those in place at the time of the events he has reviewed. The Inquiry will take into account these developments as identified by, among others, the National Quality Board's *Review of Early Warning systems in the NHS*, in looking for the lessons to be learned.

The Inquiry will be conducted under the Inquiries Act 2005.

Comments were sought from interested parties on the draft Terms of Reference and we have considered these views in setting the Terms of Reference for this further independent Inquiry.

The Terms of Reference for this further Inquiry are:

- To examine the operation of the commissioning, supervisory and regulatory organisations and other agencies, including the culture and systems of those organisations in relation to their monitoring role at Mid Staffordshire NHS Foundation Trust between January 2005 and March 2009 and to examine why problems at the Trust were not identified sooner; and appropriate action taken. This includes, but is not limited to, examining, the actions of the Department of Health, the local Strategic Health Authority, the local Primary Care Trust(s), the Independent Regulator of NHS Foundation Trusts (Monitor), the Care Quality

Commission, the Health and Safety Executive, local scrutiny and public engagement bodies and the local Coroner.[1]

- Where appropriate to build on the evidence given to the first inquiry and its conclusions, without duplicating the investigation already carried out, and to conduct the inquiry in a manner which minimises interference with the Mid-Staffordshire NHS Foundation Trust's work in improving its service to patients.
- To identify the lessons to be drawn from that examination as to how in the future the NHS and the bodies which regulate it can ensure that failing and potentially failing hospitals or their services are identified as soon as is practicable.
- In identifying the relevant lessons, to have regard to the fact that the commissioning, supervisory and regulatory systems differ significantly from those in place previously and the need to consider the situation both then and now.
- To make recommendations to the Secretary of State for Health based on the lessons learned from the events at Mid Staffordshire; and to use best endeavours to issue a Report to him by March 2011.

The Chair will decide the precise scope of the Inquiry and details of how, and where, the Inquiry will be conducted.

The Chair will be able to appoint an expert panel with expertise in regulatory systems and NHS management to support the Inquiry's work, including non-NHS experts, with expertise in regulatory, business and management structures.

---

1   This list should also include predecessor bodies of these organisations where relevant in accordance with the time period the Inquiry is examining.

Annex B
The Inquiry team

Name	Role
Robert Francis QC	Inquiry Chairman
Tom Kark QC	Counsel to the Inquiry
Ben Fitzgerald	Junior Counsel
Tom Baker	Junior Counsel
Joanna Hughes	Junior Counsel
Alan Robson	Secretary to the Inquiry
Catherine Pearson	Deputy Secretary
Joanna Edwards	Senior Administrative Officer
Suzanne How	Business and Office Manager
James Buckley	Communications Lead from November 2012
Anthony Aston	Inquiry Press Officer from September 2010 to February 2012
Alice Oliver	Inquiry Press Officer from September 2010 to February 2012
Gaby Insley	Inquiry Press Officer from September 2010 to February 2012
Kara Bradley	Inquiry Press Officer from September 2010 to February 2012
David Sims	TSOL Inquiry Solicitor – June to September 2010
Susie Riches-Kapur	TSOL Inquiry Solicitor – June to September 2010
Steven Grigg	TSOL Inquiry Solicitor – June to September 2010
Duncan Henderson	TSOL Inquiry Solicitor – June to September 2010
Jennifer Lund	TSOL Inquiry Solicitor – June to September 2010
Jackie Wright	TSOL Costs Draughtsman
Peter Watkin-Jones	Solicitor to the Inquiry
Sarah Garner	Associate Solicitor
Luisa Gibbons	Associate Solicitor
Catherine Henney	Associate Solicitor
Peter Shervington	Solicitor
Tom Henderson	Solicitor
Chloe Jones	Solicitor
Tina Wing	Paralegal
Stacey Knifton	Secretary
Marie Wood	Secretary
Christopher Jones	Solicitor
Robert Ryder	Associate Solicitor

Andrew Bennett	Solicitor
Louise Gaughan	Solicitor
Isabelle Makeham	Associate Solicitor
Gina Margaroni	Solicitor
Glenn Newberry	Inquiry Costs Draughtsman
Richard Cressall	Solicitor
Amanda Jenner	Solicitor
Sarah Bromley	Trial Director
Annette Orzel	Court Reporter
Sarah Hogan	Court Reporter
Barbara Aston	Security – Legion Security
Dr Robin Loof	Pupil Barrister
Morag Ofili	Pupil Barrister
Fallon Alexis	Pupil Barrister
Tom Stevens	Pupil Barrister
Tim Naylor	Pupil Barrister
Abby Bright	Pupil Barrister
Rhys Meggy	Pupil Barrister
Polly Dyer	Pupil Barrister
Tom Coke-Smyth	Pupil Barrister
Abimbola Johnson	Pupil Barrister
Tom Doble	Pupil Barrister
Katherine Buckle	Pupil Barrister

Annex C
Core participant teams

Name of core participant	Solicitors' names	Counsel
Action against Medical Accidents (AvMA) and the Patients Association (PA)	Adam Chapman	Peter Skelton
Care Quality Commission (CQC) (Includes Healthcare Commission)	Carlton Sadler Katrina McCrory	Eleanor Grey QC (HCC) Debra Powell (CQC)
Cure the NHS	Derek Miller	Jeremy Hyam Kate Beattie
Department of Health (DH)	Sue Pickering Philip Elvy	Gerard Clarke
Health Protection Agency (HPA)	Stirling Harcus	Paul Spencer
Mid Staffordshire NHS Foundation Trust	Andrew Vernon	Katie Price Nick Mullany
Monitor	Richard Caird	Karon Monaghan Amelia Walker
National Patient Safety Agency (NPSA)	Janice Barber	N/A
NHS Litigation Authority	John Riddell	N/A
South Staffordshire Primary Care Trust (PCT)	Nick Parsons	Rachel Langdale QC Rob Harland
The Royal College of Physicians (RCP)	N/A	N/A
West Midlands Strategic Health Authority (SHA)	Allan Mowat	Sally Smith QC Christopher Mellor

Annex D
Inquiry assessors and Independent expert witnesses

Table 1: Inquiry assessors

Name	Job title	Organisation
Professor David Black MA MBA FRCP FAcadMed	Consultant Physician in Geriatric Medicine and Honorary Chair in Medical Education	Queen Mary's Hospital, Sidcup; Brighton and Sussex Medical School
Sir Cyril Chantler	Chairman	University College London Partners
Nigel Edwards	Senior Fellow and Director	The King's Fund, KPMG LLP
Professor Tricia Hart MA MHSM DipHSM RGN RM RHV CPT FPCert	Chief Executive	South Tees Hospitals NHS Foundation Trust
Professor Peter Homa CBE	Chief Executive	Nottingham University Hospital NHS Trust
Professor Peter Hutton PhD FRCA FRCP FIMechE	Consultant Anaesthetist and Honorary Professor	University Hospital Birmingham NHS Foundation Trust
Sir Adrian Montague CBE	Non-executive Chairman and Non-executive Director	3i, Michael Page International plc, Anglian Water Group Ltd and CellMark Investments AB of Gothenburg Skanksa AB of Stockholm
Dr Judith Smith	Head of Policy	Nuffield Trust for research and policy studies in Healthcare services

Table 2: Inquiry independent expert witnesses

Name	Job title	Organisation
Professor Christopher Newdick	Professor of Medical and Contract Law, Careers Officer	University of Reading, School of Law
Dr Judith Smith	Head of Policy	Nuffield Trust for research and policy studies in Healthcare services
Professor Charles Vincent	Professor of Clinical Safety Research	Imperial College London, Department of Surgery and Cancer
Professor Kieran Walshe	Professor of Health Policy and Management	University of Manchester, Business School

Annex E
Healthcare provider visits

Between December 2011 and February 2012, I was fortunate enough to be able to visit a number of healthcare providers to discuss some of the themes brought out during the course of the seminars and in evidence.

The opportunity to hear the views of a whole range of providers at every level was enormously helpful.

Due to the nature of the difficulties in Mid Staffordshire NHS Foundation Trust, in the six hospitals and one hospice that I visited, the agenda for the day was largely designed around following the elderly care pathway. I also visited other wards, including A&E deparments. I was also able to speak to individuals from the boards at each of the care provider sites.

I would like to thank:

St Christopher's Hospice. Dame Barbara Monroe and all those who took the time to talk to me and the team about training and end of life care.

Newcastle upon Tyne Hospitals NHS Foundation Trust. Sir Leonard Fenwick, Kingsley Smith, the governors and non-executive directors (NEDs) that took time to speak to us, as well as those on the wards visited and in the Melville Day Hospital.

Gateshead Health NHS Foundation Trust. Ian Renwick and his staff we met through our visit, in particular those on Jubilee Wing.

Nottingham University Hospital NHS Trust. Professor Peter Homa, Dr Peter Barrett and the team who took time out to talk to me.

University Hospitals Birmingham NHS Foundation Trust. Dame Julie Moore, Sir Albert Bore, Dr David Rosser, those nurses from the military ward who took time out to give me a different perspective on care, as well as everyone else who spent time talking to me and the team.

Royal Surrey County Hospital NHS Foundation Trust. Nick Moberly, Peter Dunt and all those who came to speak to me during lunch. Those working on the wards, Forget Me Not Bay and in A&E who took time out of their day.

University College London Hospitals NHS Foundation Trust. Sir Robert Naylor, Richard Murley, Professor Katherine Fenton, the Elderly Care team, those in A&E and all those non-executive directors and governors that spent time talking to me.

Annex F
Witnesses called to give oral evidence

Witness	Role	Organisation	Date called to give evidence
Chairman, Inquiry Counsel and core participants	Opening submissions		8 to 11 November 2010
Professor Chris Newdick	Expert evidence	University of Reading, School of Law	15 and 16 November 2010
Professor Judith Smith		Nuffield Trust for research and policy studies in Healthcare services	15 and 16 November 2010
Professor Charles Vincent		Imperial College London, Department of Surgery and Cancer	17 November 2010
Professor Kieran Walshe		University of Manchester, Business School	18 November 2010
Julie Bailey	Evidence from patients and their families		22 and 23 November 2010
Janet Robinson			23 November 2010
Christine Dalziel			24 November 2010
Catherine Matthews			24 November 2010
Debra Hazeldine			24 November 2010
Ron Street			25 November 2010
Sandra Whitehouse			29 November 2010
Dr Marc Whitehouse			29 November 2010
Beverley Howell			29 November 2010
Elizabeth Cowie			30 November 2010
June Locke			30 November 2010
Roger Dobbing			6 and 7 December 2010
Nicola Monte			7 December 2010
Terence Deighton	Evidence on patient and public involvement		1 December 2010
Robin Bastin			2 and 6 December 2010
Ken Lownds			8 and 9 December 2010
Chris Welch	Former Manager	Patient and Public Involvement Forum	13 December 2010
Caroline Lingard	Senior Service Manager	Age UK South Staffordshire	14 December 2010

Witness	Role	Organisation	Date called to give evidence
Rod Hammerton	Former Chair	Patient and Public Involvement Forum	14 December 2010
Peter Walsh	Chief Executive	Action against Medical Accidents	15 December 2010
Dr Kieran Mullan	Head of Engagement and Strategy	Patients Association	16 December 2010
Nick Maslen	Chief Executive	Age UK	10 January 2011
Matt Snowden	Director for Business Development and Resources	Faculty of Health at Staffordshire University	10 January 2011
Linda Seru	Former Director of the Hosting Service	Staffordshire County LINK	11 January 2011
Jackie Owen	Interim Director	Stafford LINk	12 January 2011
Valerie Harrison	Chief Executive	POhWER	13 January 2011
Sharon Llewellyn	Former Complaints Manager	Mid Staffordshire NHS Foundation Trust	17 and 18 January 2011
Dr Ian Wilson	GP and Former Chair	Stafford GP group	18 January 2011
Dr Mike Rawle	GP	Mill Bank Surgery	18 January 2011
Steve Powell	Chair	Practice-based commissioning consortium (Stafford and surrounds)	19 January 2011
Dr Ian Greaves	GP and Director	Gnosall Health Centre	20 January 2011
Dr Janet Eames	GP	Mansion House Surgery	20 January 2011
Dr Malcolm MacKinnon	GP	Cumberland House Practice	24 January 2011
Dr Peter Glennon	GP	Browning Street Surgery	24 January 2011
Matthew Ellis	Councillor with Cabinet responsibility for Social Care And Health	Stafford County Council	25 January 2011
Ian Thompson	Chief Executive	Stafford Borough Council	26 January 2011
Councillor Philip Jones	Former Chair of Health Overview and Scrutiny Committee	Stafford Borough Council	27 January 2011
Councillor Ann Edgeller	Chair of Health Overview and Scrutiny Committee	Stafford Borough Council	27 and 31 January 2011
Dr Alan Fletcher	Principal Medical Examiner (Sheffield pilot)	Sheffield teaching hospitals NHS Foundation Trust	31 January 2011
Christine Shelton-Baron	Member of Health Overview and Scrutiny Committee; former Mayor	Stafford Borough Council	31 January 2011
Dr Tony Wright	Former MP for Cannock Chase		1 February 2011
David Kidney	Former MP for Stafford		3 February 2011
Jeremy Lefroy MP	MP for Stafford		4 February 2011
Bill Cash MP	MP for Stone		4 February 2011

Witness	Role	Organisation	Date called to give evidence
Janet Eagland	Chair of Health Overview and Scrutiny Committee	Stafford County Council	8 February 2011
Mark Young	Officer with responsibility for Mid Staffordshire NHS Foundation Trust until October 2009	Unite	8 February 2011
Denise Breeze	Former RCN union representative at Mid Staffordshire NHS Foundation Trust and Trust Outpatients department manager	Royal College of Nursing	9 February 2011
Adrian Legan	Assistant Officer	Royal College of Nursing	9 February 2011
Karen Jennings	National Secretary	Unison	10 February 2011
Kath Fox	Branch Officer at Mid Staffordshire NHS Foundation Trust until also Bereavement Officer at the Trust	Unison	10 February 2011
Dr Mike Laker	Independent Case Notes Reviewer		14 February 2011
Christine Woodward	Former Patient and Public Involvement Forum Member and Trust Governor	Patient and Public Involvement Forum	15 February 2011
Dr Peter Daggett	Former Consultant Physician	Mid Staffordshire NHS Foundation Trust	16 February 2011
Dr Pradip Singh	Consultant Gastroenterologist	Mid Staffordshire NHS Foundation Trust	16 February 2011
Sandra Barrington	Nurse and Staff Governor	Mid Staffordshire NHS Foundation Trust	17 February 2011
Andrew Haigh	Coroner for South Staffordshire		28 February 2011
Dr Shaun Nakash	Clinical Director for Emergency Care and Clinical Lead for Acute Medicine	Mid Staffordshire NHS Foundation Trust	1 March 2011
Derek Thomas	Project Manager for Medical Staffing	Mid Staffordshire NHS Foundation Trust	1 March 2011
Dr Chris Turner	Former Clinical Lead for Emergency Medicine	Mid Staffordshire NHS Foundation Trust	2 March 2011
Dr Philip Coates	Former Consultant and Clinical Governance Lead	Mid Staffordshire NHS Foundation Trust	2 March 2011
Sue Adams	Nurse and Royal College of Nursing Steward	Mid Staffordshire NHS Foundation Trust	3 March 2011
Dr David Durrans	Consultant Surgeon and Former Acting Medical Director	Mid Staffordshire NHS Foundation Trust	3 and 10 March 2011
Dr Peter Carter	Chief Executive and General Secretary	Royal College of Nursing	7 March 2011
Julie Hendry	Director of Quality and Patient Experience	Mid Staffordshire NHS Foundation Trust	7 and 8 March 2011
Peter Bell	Former Non-executive Director	Mid Staffordshire NHS Foundation Trust	8 March 2011

Annex F Witnesses called to give oral evidence

Witness	Role	Organisation	Date called to give evidence
David Stone	Former Interim Chair	Mid Staffordshire NHS Foundation Trust	9 March 2011
Dr Manjit Obhrai	Medical Director	Mid Staffordshire NHS Foundation Trust	10 March 2011
Mike Gill	Former Finance Director and Deputy Chief Executive	Mid Staffordshire NHS Foundation Trust	14 and 15 March 2011
Eric Morton	Former Interim Chief Executive	Mid Staffordshire NHS Foundation Trust	15 March 2011
Antony Sumara	Former Chief Executive	Mid Staffordshire NHS Foundation Trust	16 March 2011
Sir Stephen Moss	Former Chair	Mid Staffordshire NHS Foundation Trust	16 March 2011
Dr Val Suarez	Former Medical Director	Mid Staffordshire NHS Foundation Trust	22 March 2011
John Newsham	Former Finance Director and Deputy Chief Executive	Mid Staffordshire NHS Foundation Trust	23 March 2011
Karen Morrey	Former Director of Operations	Mid Staffordshire NHS Foundation Trust	24 March 2011
Dr Helen Moss	Former Director of Nursing	Mid Staffordshire NHS Foundation Trust	28 March 2011
Geraint Griffiths	Former Locality Director	South Staffordshire Primary Care Trust	29 March 2011
Yvonne Sawbridge	Director of Quality and Nursing	South Staffordshire Primary Care Trust	30 and 31 March 2011
Stuart Poynor	Chief Executive	South Staffordshire Primary Care Trust	31 March 2011
Alex Fox	Chair	South Staffordshire Primary Care Trust	1 April 2011
Ian Cumming	Chief Executive	West Midlands Strategic Health Authority	6 April 2011
Dr Rashmi Shukla	Regional Director of Public Health	West Midlands Strategic Health Authority	7 April 2011
Peter Blythin	Director of Nursing and Workforce	West Midlands Strategic Health Authority	11 and 12 April 2011
Steve Allen	Former Director of Planning and Information, and then Director of Performance and Information	West Midlands Strategic Health Authority	12 and 13 April 2011
Phil Taylor	Former Director of Finance and Performance	Shropshire and Staffordshire Strategic Health Authority	13 and 14 April 2011
Peter Shanahan	Former Finance Director and Former Acting Chief Executive	West Midlands Strategic Health Authority	14 and 21 April 2011
Cynthia Bower	Former Chief Executive	West Midlands Strategic Health Authority	18 and 19 April 2011
Elizabeth Buggins	Chair	West Midlands Strategic Health Authority	19 April 2011
Eamon Kelly	Former Director of Commissioning and Performance	West Midlands Strategic Health Authority	20 April 2011
Professor Sir Ian Kennedy	Former Chair	Healthcare Commission	4 May 2011
Shelagh Hawking	Former Senior Assessment Manager	Healthcare Commission	5 May 2011
Dr Andrea Gordon	Former Area Manager	Healthcare Commission	5 May 2011

Witness	Role	Organisation	Date called to give evidence
Marcia Fry	Former Head of Operational Development	Healthcare Commission	6 May 2011
Nigel Ellis	Former Head of Investigations	Healthcare Commission	9 May 2011
Dr Heather Wood	Former Investigation Manager	Healthcare Commission	10 May 2011
Martin Bardsley	Former Head of Screening and Surveillance	Healthcare Commission	11 May 2011
Anna Walker	Former Chief Executive	Healthcare Commission	12 May 2011
Roger Davidson	Former Head of External Affairs	Healthcare Commission	16 May 2011
Dame Jo Williams	Chair	Care Quality Commission	16 May 2011
Amanda Sherlock	Director of Operations Delivery	Care Quality Commission	17 May 2011
Richard Hamblin	Director of Intelligence	Care Quality Commission	18 May 2011
Cynthia Bower	Chief Executive	Care Quality Commission	19 May 2011
Dr Andrea Gordon	Regional Manager	Care Quality Commission	23 May 2011
Miranda Carter	Assessment Director	Monitor	23 May 2011
David Hill	Senior Assessment Manager	Monitor	24 May 2011
Adrian Masters	Director of Strategy	Monitor	25 May 2011
Edward Lavelle	Former Regulatory Operations Director	Monitor	26 May 2011
Stephen Hay	Chief Operating Officer	Monitor	31 May 2011
Dr William Moyes	Former Executive Chairman	Monitor	31 May and 1 June 2011
William Price	Former Chief Executive	South Western Staffordshire Primary Care Trust	2 June 2011
Robert Cleary	Former Head of Standards Based Assessment	Healthcare Commission	7 June 2011
Susan Fisher	Former Finance Director	South Western Staffordshire Primary Care Trust	8 June 2011
Jane Eminson	Former Consultant	West Midlands Specialised Commissioning team	8 June 2011
Mike Brereton	Former Chair	Shropshire and Staffordshire Strategic Health Authority	9 June 2011
Professor Sir Brian Jarman	Director of Dr Foster Unit	Imperial College London	13 June 2011
Roger Taylor	Director of Research and Public Affairs	Dr Foster Intelligence	14 June 2011
Tim Straughan	Chief Executive	NHS Information Centre	14 June 2011
Dr Paulette Myers	Former Deputy Director of Health Strategy and Head of Clinical Governance	Shropshire and Staffordshire Strategic Health Authority	15 June 2011
Justin McCracken	Chief Executive	Health Protection Agency	16 June 2011

Witness	Role	Organisation	Date called to give evidence
Dr Musarrat Afza	Consultant in Communicable Disease Control	Health Protection Agency	16 June 2011
Dr Suzette Woodward	Director of Patient Safety	National Patient Safety Agency	20 June 2011
Professor Alistair Scotland	Director of National Clinical Assessment Service	National Patient Safety Agency	20 June 2011
Professor Calum Paton	Professor of Health Policy	Keele University	21 June 2011
Sir Andrew Dillon	Chief Executive	National Institute for Health and Clinical Excellence	22 June 2011
Niall Dickson	Chief Executive and Registrar	General Medical Council	23 June 2011
Professor Dickon Weir-Hughes	Chief Executive and Registrar	Nursing and Midwifery Council	27 June 2011
John Black	President	Royal College of Surgeons	27 June 2011
Paul Streets	Former Chief Executive	Postgraduate Medical Education and Training Board	28 June 2011
Professor Andy Garner	Dean of The Faculty of Health	Keele University	28 June 2011
Ann Abraham	Parliamentary and Health Service Ombudsman		29 June 2011
Clive Brookes	Principal Inspector	Health and Safety Executive	30 June 2011
Baroness Barbara Young	Former Chair	Care Quality Commission	4 July 2011
Geoffrey Podger	Chief Executive	Health and Safety Executive	5 July 2011
Steve Walker	Chief Executive	NHS Litigation Authority	6 July 2011
Alison Bartholomew	Risk Management Director	NHS Litigation Authority	7 July 2011
John Heyworth	President	College of Emergency Medicine	7 July 2011
Dr Elizabeth Hughes	Postgraduate Medical Dean	West Midlands Strategic Health Authority	5 September 2011
Hilary Jones	Dean of Faculty of Health	Staffordshire University	5 September 2011
The Rt Hon Andy Burnham MP	Former Minister of State and Secretary of State for Health		6 September 2011
The Rt Hon Ben Bradshaw MP	Former Minister of Health		7 September 2011
Dame Christine Beasley	Chief Nursing Officer for England	Department of Health	8 September 2011
Warren Brown	Former Head of Foundation Trust Team	Department of Health	12 September 2011
Sir Andrew Cash	Former Director-General of Provider Development	Department of Health	13 September 2011
John Holden	Current Director of System Regulation; Former Head of Foundation Trust Team	Department of Health	14 September 2011

Witness	Role	Organisation	Date called to give evidence
David Flory	Director-General of NHS Finance, Performance and Operations; NHS Deputy Chief Executive	Department of Health	15 September 2011
Professor Sir Liam Donaldson	Former Chief Medical Officer; current Chair of the National Patient Safety Agency	Department of Health	19 September 2011
Professor Sir Bruce Keogh	NHS Medical Director	Department of Health	20 September 2011
Gary Belfield	Former Director-General of Commissioning	Department of Health	21 September 2011
Dame Una O'Brien	Permanent Secretary; former Director-General of Policy and Strategy	Department of Health	22 September 2011
Sir Hugh Taylor	Former Permanent Secretary	Department of Health	26 September 2011
Sir David Nicholson	NHS Chief Executive; Former Interim Chief Executive of Shropshire and Staffordshire Strategic Health Authority	Department of Health	27 and 28 September 2011
Toni Brisby	Former Chair	Mid Staffordshire NHS Foundation Trust	3 October 2011
Lauren Goodman	Regional Intelligence and Evidence Officer	Care Quality Commission	4 October 2011
Rona Bryce	Senior Operations Analyst	Care Quality Commission	4 October 2011
Stuart Knowles	Former Trust Solicitor	Mid Staffordshire NHS Foundation Trust	5 October 2011
Kate Levy	Former Trust Board Secretary and Head of Legal Services	Mid Staffordshire NHS Foundation Trust	5 October 2011
Sampana Banga	Head of Operational Intelligence	Care Quality Commission	6 October 2011
Richard Hamblin	Director of Intelligence	Care Quality Commission	6 October 2011
Trudi Williams	Former Deputy Director of Clinical Standards	Mid Staffordshire NHS Foundation Trust	7 October 2011
Helene Donnelly	Former Nurse	Mid Staffordshire NHS Foundation Trust	7 October 2011
Closing submissions	Core participants		21 to 23 November, and 29 November 2011
Amanda Pollard	Inspector	Care Quality Commission	28 November 2011
Kay Sheldon	Non-executive Board member	Care Quality Commission	28 November 2011
Closing submissions	Counsel to the Inquiry and Inquiry Chairman		1 December 2011

Annex G
Witness statements read into the record

Witness	Role	Organisation	Date statement read into the record
Jeff Guest	Evidence from patients and their families		25 November 2010
Patient relative B			25 November 2010
Patient relative A			30 November 2010
John James			30 November 2010
Gillian Peacham			2 December 2010
Graham Harvey			7 December 2010
Castell Davis			8 December 2010
Patricia Meadon			9 December 2010
Thomas Bentham			9 December 2010
June Chell			9 December 2010
William Hudson			13 December 2010
Patient relative C			13 December 2010
Wendy Wintle	Evidence on patient and public involvement		13 December 2010
Dr Subhas Chandra Dey	GP	Armitage Surgery, Staffordshire	19 January 2011
Dr Bhupinder Cooner	Former Patient and Public Involvement Forum Manager	Age UK South Staffordshire	19 January 2011
Martin Yeates	Former Chief Executive	Mid Staffordshire NHS Foundation Trust	3 October 2011
Malcolm Alexander – first and second statements	Chair	National Association of LINk Members	2 December 2011
Steve Allen – second statement	Former Director of Planning and Information, then of Performance and Information	West Midlands Strategic Health Authority	2 December 2011
Dr Philip Ballard	Chair of Professional Executive Committee and Former Medical Director; GP	South Staffordshire Primary Care Trust	2 December 2011
David Bawden	Former Head of Provider Methods	Care Quality Commission	2 December 2011

Witness	Role	Organisation	Date statement read into the record
Dr Roger Beal	Former Chair of Professional Executive Committee; GP	South Western Staffordshire Primary Care Trust	2 December 2011
Dame Christine Beasley – second statement	Chief Nursing Officer	Department of Health	2 December 2011
Gill Bellord	Director of Core Services	NHS Employers	2 December 2011
Dr David Bennett	Interim Chief Executive	Monitor	2 December 2011
Francis Blunden	Senior Policy Manager	NHS Confederation	2 December 2011
Chris Bostock		Department of Health	2 December 2011
Cynthia Bower – third statement	Chief Executive	Care Quality Commission	2 December 2011
Christine Bowers	Governor	Mid Staffordshire NHS Foundation Trust	2 December 2011
Rona Bryce – second statement	Senior Operations Analyst	Care Quality Commission	2 December 2011
Dr Verghese Cheeran David	Ear, Nose and Throat Consultant	Mid Staffordshire NHS Foundation Trust	2 December 2011
Sandra Chittenden	Former Head of Central Region	Healthcare Commission	2 December 2011
Dr Philip Coates – second statement	Former Consultant and Clinical Governance Lead	Mid Staffordshire NHS Foundation Trust	2 December 2011
Stephanie Coffey	Senior Compliance Manager	Monitor	2 December 2011
Steve Coneys	Former Director of Communications and Public Affairs	West Midlands Strategic Health Authority	2 December 2011
CQC commissioners – statement	John Harwood, Professor Deirdre Kelly and Martin Marshall	Care Quality Commission	2 December 2011
Professor Bernard Crump	Former Chief Executive	Shropshire and Staffordshire Strategic Health Authority	2 December 2011
Roger Davidson – second statement	Former Head of External Affairs	Healthcare Commission	2 December 2011
Dr Kenneth Deacon	Medical Director	South Staffordshire Primary Care Trust	2 December 2011
Murray Devine	Former Head of Patient Safety Policy and Investigations Team	Department of Health	2 December 2011
Lorraine Foley	Former Director of Informatics	Healthcare Commission	2 December 2011
Mike Gill – second statement	Former Finance Director and Deputy Chief Executive	Mid Staffordshire NHS Foundation Trust	2 December 2011
Andrew Haigh – second statement	Coroner	Ministry of Justice	2 December 2011
Alan Hall	Director of Performance	Department of Health	2 December 2011
Michael Harper	Patient relative		2 December 2011

Witness	Role	Organisation	Date statement read into the record
Julie Hendry – third statement	Director of Quality and Patient Experience	Mid Staffordshire NHS Foundation Trust	2 December 2011
Dr Paul Hiley	Head of Department of Histopathology	Mid Staffordshire NHS Foundation Trust	2 December 2011
David Hill – second statement	Senior Assessment Manager	Monitor	2 December 2011
Lyn Hill-Tout	Chief Executive	Mid Staffordshire NHS Foundation Trust	2 December 2011
Andrew Hodge	Legal Representative of Martin Yeates		2 December 2011
Ray Horseman	Application Support Analyst	Department of Health	2 December 2011
Dr Elizabeth Hughes – second statement	Postgraduate Medical Dean	West Midlands Strategic Health Authority	2 December 2011
David Johnstone	Former Director of Operations	Care Quality Commission	2 December 2011
Professor Sir Ian Kennedy – second statement	Former Chair	Healthcare Commission	2 December 2011
Sandra Haynes-Kirkbright – first and second statements	Clinical Coding Service and Data Quality Manager	Mid Staffordshire NHS Foundation Trust	2 December 2011
Professor Sir Brian Jarman – second, third and fourth statements	Director	Dr Foster Unit at Imperial College London	2 December 2011
Shaun Lintern	Journalist	Former Stafford *Express and Star* health correspondent	2 December 2011
Jonathan Lloyd	Former Director of Performance	West Midlands Strategic Health Authority	2 December 2011
Christine Lloyd-Jennings	Director of Human Resources	Mid Staffordshire NHS Foundation Trust	2 December 2011
Kate Lobley	Former Director of Operations	Healthcare Commission	2 December 2011
John Lotz	Former Medical Director	Mid Staffordshire NHS Foundation Trust	2 December 2011
Janice Lyons	Regional Business Manager	Dr Foster Intelligence	2 December 2011
Hugo Mascie-Taylor	Medical Director	NHS Confederation	2 December 2011
Dr Hamish Meldrum	Chairman	British Medical Association	2 December 2011
Sir Stephen Moss – second statement	Chair	Mid Staffordshire NHS Foundation Trust	2 December 2011
Yvonne Mowlds	Portfolio Director	Monitor	2 December 2011
Dr William Moyes – third statement	Former Executive Chairman	Monitor	2 December 2011
Jim Muir	Former Chair of Health Overview and Scrutiny Committee	Stafford County Council	2 December 2011
Dr Manjit Obhrai – second and third statements	Former Medical Director	Mid Staffordshire NHS Foundation Trust	2 December 2011

Witness	Role	Organisation	Date statement read into the record
Colin Ovington – first and second statements	Director of Nursing	Mid Staffordshire NHS Foundation Trust	2 December 2011
Jean-Pierre Parsons	Former Chief Executive	Cannock Chase Primary Care Trust	2 December 2011
Chris Plant	Head of HR Operations	Mid Staffordshire NHS Foundation Trust	2 December 2011
Mark Powell	Former Associate Director for Performance	South Staffordshire Primary Care Trust	2 December 2011
Stuart Poynor – second and third statements	Chief Executive	South Staffordshire Primary Care Trust	2 December 2011
Jonathan Pugh – first and second statements	Information Services Manager	Mid Staffordshire NHS Foundation Trust	2 December 2011
Andre Rebello	Honorary Secretary and Executive Officer	Coroners Society of England and Wales	2 December 2011
Paul Robinson	Head of Market Intelligence	CHKS	2 December 2011
Peter Shanahan – second statement	Former Finance Director and Former Acting Chief Executive	West Midlands Strategic Health Authority	2 December 2011
Amanda Sherlock – second, third, fourth and fifth statements	Director of Operations Delivery	Care Quality Commission	2 December 2011
Dr Rashmi Shukla – second statement	Regional Director of Public Health	West Midlands Strategic Health Authority	2 December 2011
Professor David Spiegelhalter	Former Statistical Consultant	Healthcare Commission	2 December 2011
Peter Spilsbury	Director of Qipp Delivery	West Midlands Strategic Health Authority	2 December 2011
Christine Stewart	Patient relative		2 December 2011
David Stone – second statement	Former Interim Chair	Mid Staffordshire NHS Foundation Trust	2 December 2011
Antony Sumara – third and fourth statements	Former Chief Executive	Mid Staffordshire NHS Foundation Trust	2 December 2011
Phil Taylor – first and second statements	Former Director of Performance and Finance and Deputy Chief Executive	Shropshire and Staffordshire Strategic Health Authority	2 December 2011
David Tomlinson	Patient relative		2 December 2011
Giles Wilmore	Director of Quality Framework and Qipp	Department of Health	2 December 2011
Dr Heather Wood – second, third and fourth statements	Former Investigation Manager	Healthcare Commission	2 December 2011

Annex H
Trust senior post holders

Senior team during the period relevant to the Inquiry's Terms of Reference

Post	Name	Appointed	Ended
Chief Executive	David O'Neill	1998	June 2005
Acting Chief Executive	John Newsham	June 2005	August 2005
Chief Executive	Martin Yeates	December 2005 (interim from September to December 2005)	March 2009
Chief Operating Officer	Karen Morrey	May 2006	September 2009
Finance Director and Deputy CEO	John Newsham	1992 (Deputy CEO pre 1998)	June 2008
Finance Director and Deputy CEO	Michael Gill	July 2008	April 2010
Medical Director	Dr John Gibson	2003	March 2006
Medical Director	Dr Val Suarez	September 2006	March 2009
Medical Director	Dr Manjit Obhrai	April 2009	July 2012
Director of Nursing and Quality	Jan Harry	February 1998	2002
Director of Clinical Standards and Chief Nurse	Jan Harry	2002 (Chief Nurse in 2006)	July 2006
Director of Nursing and Governance	Dr Helen Moss	December 2006	October 2009
Director of Human Resources	Norma Sadler	May 2000	July 2006

Non-executive Directors during the period relevant to the Inquiry's Terms of Reference

Name	Appointed	Ended
Joan Fox (Non-executive)	1999	October 2006 (completed term of office)
Gerry Hindley (Vice-Chair)	April 2000 (January to July 2006 seconded to North Staffordshire Trust)	January 2009 (completed term of office)
David Denny (Non-executive)	October 2000	February 2009 (completed term of office)
Toni Brisby (Chair)	October 2004	March 2009
Peter Bell (Non-executive)	November 2005	March 2009
Mike Wall (Non-executive)	November 2005	March 2009
Roger Carder (Non-executive)	April 2007	In post
Sir Stephen Moss (Non-executive)	February 2009	Chair since July 2009
Dennis Heywood (Non-executive)	February 2009	In post
David Stone (Interim Chair)	March 2009	July 2009

Annex I
Serious untoward incident data on Trust nurse staffing levels 2005–2009

The following tables show the number of serious untoward incidents by year and ward in which nursing levels were recorded as a factor.

2005

Ward	January	February	March	April	May	June	July	August	September	October	November	December	Totals
Ward 3	1				2			4		1		1	9
Littleton	2		3				1	6	8	13	7	3	43
Ward 11	3	11	7	5	2	10	10	1	4	1	5	7	66
Unknown	1	1						1					3
EAU	8	3							1			1	13
Ward 7	2				4				2			6	14
Ward 10	1	2	7	3		2	2	5	2	1			25
TOD	4					2		1	1				8
Hollybank	1			4		2					1		8
Ward 12	3		1	2	2	3	5	1	3	1		4	25
Gastroenterology		1			1	1		2	2				7
Stafford Clinic		3				1	1			1			6
Ward 1		2			4	1		1	1	1		1	11
Delivery Unit		1	2			2		1		2	4	4	16
Obstetrics		1											1
SGH Outpatients			1		2		1		1		2	2	9
Ward 6			4		6	9	10	1	4	6	1	5	46
Ward 14			1				2		1				4

Ward	January	February	March	April	May	June	July	August	September	October	November	December	Totals
Leehall Ward Elderly Care			2			1							3
Ward 9			1		1	1	1	2	2	1	1	2	12
Ward 8				1								1	2
Nuclear Medicine				1				1					2
Critical Care Unit				3	1							3	7
SGH Theatre				4									4
Ward 2				1			3						4
Fairoak					1			1				2	4
Cardiac Care					1								1
Elective Orthopaedic Centre						1	1	1					3
CCH Outpatients						1						2	3
Hilton Main Ward							1		1	2			4
PAC Unit							1						1
A&E								1	1				2
Acute Cardiac Care								1	1				2
SGH Dental									1				1
PDU									1				1
SCBU										2			2
CCH Theatre										1			1
Paediatrics										1			1
General Surgery										3			3
Obstetrics and Gynaecology											1		1
Shugborough Ward											1		1
Thoracic Medicine											1		1
Metabolic Department											1		1
	26	25	29	24	27	37	39	31	37	37	25	44	381

2006

Ward	January	February	March	April	May	June	July	August	September	October	November	December	Totals
Littleton	4	2					1	7	6	4	11	2	**37**
Ward 7	4	7			1						3	1	**16**
Ward 11	7	5	7	1			2	2	3	5	10	3	**45**
Ward 12	6		6				1	1	1		2		**17**
Ward 8	1												**1**
Ward 1	1				1		1	1	1				**5**
Delivery Suite	2	2	1	1							2		**8**
Hollybank	6	1	4	6	1			10	5	5	1	1	**40**
Ward 6	5	9	1			2			1		4	2	**24**
SCBU	2		1										**3**
Ward 9	1					2							**3**
Fairbank	1	1							1		1		**4**
Ward 3	2												**2**
A&E	1	1	2				1	3	1		1	1	**11**
Stafford Clinic	1	7											**8**
Obstetric Day Ward		1											**1**
Gastroenterology		1	1	5		1				1	1		**10**
SGH Theatre		1	1		3						2	1	**8**
PDU		1		1	2			1	1	1			**7**
Cardiac Unit		1											**1**
Eye Centre				1									**1**
Ward 2			1					1			2	1	**5**
SGH Outpatient			1		1								**2**
CCH Outpatient			1										**1**
EAU			1		1		1				1		**4**
Ward 10				1	1			4	2	2	1	3	**14**
Acute Cardiac Care					3	1			2			2	**8**
CCH Theatre						1					4		**5**

Annex I Serious untoward incident data on Trust nurse staffing levels 2005–2009

Ward	January	February	March	April	May	June	July	August	September	October	November	December	Totals
SGH Physiotherapy						12	13						25
SGH Occupational Therapy							1			4			5
CCH Physiotherapy								5					5
SGH Portering and Security								1					1
SGH Phlebotomy								2					2
SGH EEG									1				1
SGH X-ray Department										1			1
Nuclear Medicine										1	1	1	3
Hilton Main Ward										1	1		2
	44	40	28	16	14	19	21	38	25	25	48	18	336

Annex I Serious untoward incident data on Trust nurse staffing levels 2005–2009

2007

Ward	January	February	March	April	May	June	July	August	September	October	November	December	Totals
A&E	3	1				1		1		4	4	1	**15**
Ward 6	2	7	1	1				1		1	1		**14**
Ward 7	8	1	2	1			1	3	5		4	3	**28**
General Surgical Department	1								1				**2**
Fairoak	10								2			1	**13**
SGH Theatre	1		4	2			3	4	13		4	1	**32**
Ward 2	2	1	1					2					**6**
Ward 1	1						1		1				**3**
Ward 14	1												**1**
Short Stay Unit	1	3											**4**
Ward 11	1	1		1	2	1	2		1				**9**
Littleton	2	3							2		4	3	**14**
Delivery Suite	1	2	1	1	2			2	1			2	**12**
Acute Cardiac Unit	1		2		4						1		**8**
Nuclear Medicine		1	2		2		1		4		1	1	**12**
Ward 9		3	1		2		3	8	1				**18**
SGH Breast Care Unit		3									1		**4**
Surgery		2											**2**
Hilton Main Ward		1					1		2	1		1	**6**
Critical Care Unit		2							3			1	**6**
PDU			1										**1**
Ward 10			2			1		1		1	1	3	**9**
Obstrtrics			1										**1**
CCH Outpatients			1	4									**5**
Hollybank			2	1		1	6	6	3	4	1	2	**26**
Short Stay Unit			1					1					**2**
CCH Theatre				1					1				**2**

Ward	January	February	March	April	May	June	July	August	September	October	November	December	Totals
SCBU						3	1		1			1	6
Ward 12						1			1		1		3
Shugborough Ward						2		5	5		1		13
Haematology Department							1						1
Gastroenterology							2	1	1				4
SGH Cardiology							1		2	1	1		5
Cardiac Catheterisation Lab							1			1			2
EAU							1	1		1		1	4
SGH Outpatient								2					2
SGH X-ray								1		1	1		3
SGH Dietrics Department								4	8	5	1		18
Trauma and Orthopaedic Ward									2	1	3	1	7
Community Midwifery – Central									1				1
Lea Hall Day Unit									1				1
Lung Function										1			1
CCH Day Ward										1			1
CCH Anaesthetic											1		1
CCH X-ray											1		1
Bradbury House												1	1
Diagnostic Unit												1	1
Ophthalmology												1	1
	35	31	22	12	12	10	25	43	62	23	32	25	332

2008

Ward	January	February	March	April	May	June	July	August	September	October	November	December	Totals
Hollybank	1			3	2							1	**7**
Nuclear Medicine	1					1							**2**
Delivery suite	2			1	1				1			2	**7**
Ward 7	2	7	5	1	1	3	3	5	5		5	2	**39**
EAU	2	1	2		1	1	1	1	2	5			**16**
SGH Breast Care Unit	1												**1**
A&E	2	1	1			1	2	1		2	4	6	**20**
Littleton Ward	1		1			1	1						**4**
SGH Theatre	4				1		1	1	1	1	2	2	**13**
Ward 10	3	4	2	1		1	1			1	2	3	**18**
SCBU	1	6	5				2		1			2	**17**
CCH Physiotherapy		1											**1**
Ward 12		2	1		1		1	2				1	**8**
Ward 6		2			2	1				1	1		**7**
Ward 2		1										1	**2**
Trauma and Orthopaedic		1	1		1	1	1	1	3	4	7	1	**21**
SGH Physiotherapy		1											**1**
SGH Anaesthetic		1	1										**2**
Cardiac Catheterisation Labs		1											**1**
CCH Theatres		1				1			1				**3**
SGH Catering			1										**1**
Day Ward			1										**1**
Ward 8			1					1		1	1	2	**6**
SGH Portering and Security			3					1					**4**
EPR			1										**1**

Annex I Serious untoward incident data on Trust nurse staffing levels 2005–2009

Ward	January	February	March	April	May	June	July	August	September	October	November	December	Totals
Davy Unit			1										1
All			1				2	1					4
Acute Cardiac Care			1		1		1				1		4
Obstetrics			1										1
Ward 14				1							1		2
Hilton Main Ward				1				1	2				4
SGH Outpatients				1	1				1				3
Ward 9					1		2					1	4
Ward 11						1		1					2
Medical Staffing							1			1			2
Ward 1							1						1
Minor Injuries Unit							1						1
Critical Care Unit							1	11	8		1	3	24
Paediatrics Assessment Unit							1						1
CDU								1	1	1			3
Fairoak Ward								1	1	1			2
Shugborough Ward									3	1			4
Paediatrics										2			2
Short Stay Unit											1		1
Obstetric Theatre											1		1
SGH Occupational Therapy												1	1
Community Midwife – Chase												1	1
	20	30	30	9	13	13	22	29	29	21	27	29	272

Ward	January	February	March	April	May	June	July	August	September	October	November	December	Totals
Ward 7	14	5	5	7	9	3	4	3	3	4	1	3	61
Ward 10	4		3	7	5	4	1	8	4	5	2	1	44
Hilton Main Ward	4		4	2		1				1			12
Trauma and Orthopaedics	2			1		1	3	3		2		3	15
Delivery Suite		1		1	1	7	1	8					19
Surgery	1	1	2										3
EAU	4	2	4	4	2	9	2	1	1	5	1	2	37
Ward 8	1	1		5	1		5	1					14
Acute Cardiac Unit	1		1	1			2					1	6
Ward 11	1	1	5	7	2	3	1			2			22
Ward 6	1								1				2
CCH Theatres	1	1			1						1		4
A&E	2	2			3	2		2	7	4	1	13	36
Nuclear Medicine	1												1
CDU		3	1	3			1		1				9
SGH Physiotherapy		1	2	2				1		1			5
Ward 12		1	2	4	3		1	2			1		14
Short Stay Unit		1				1			1		1		5
Ward 14		3											3
CCH Portering and Security		1		1									1
Ambuline		1											1
ESA			1										1
SCBU			4	2		1				2			9
SGH Car Park			1							1			2
Human Resources			1										1
SGH Occupational Therapy			1						2				2
SGH Outpatients			2	2			1		2		2		7
Ward 9			3	3	4	9	1				1	2	20

Annex I Serious untoward incident data on Trust nurse staffing levels 2005-2009

Ward	January	February	March	April	May	June	July	August	September	October	November	December	Totals
SGH Theatres				2	4		1	1	1			1	10
Fairoak				2		1			1		1		5
Ward 1				1			3	2	2	2	3	2	15
Ophthalmology				1									1
Littleton				1		1			1				3
Obs and Gynae				1									1
Bradbury House				1									1
Hollybank					1					1			2
Critical Care Unit					1		1		1			1	4
Urology					1								1
Ward 2					1	2	5	3	2	2			15
Rheumatology					1								1
Facilities						2							2
Medical Electronics						1							1
SGH Phlebotomy						1							1
CCH Public Areas (external)							1						1
Community Midwife – Central								1					1
Endoscopy Unit								1	1				2
CCH Physiotherapy									1				1
CCH Main Reception									1				1
CCH Car Park											3		3
Speech and Langugae Therapy											1		1
ENT											2		2
SGH Breast Care Unit											1		1
Medical Staffing											1		1
Metabolic Department												1	1
AMU												1	1
	38	23	35	61	40	49	34	37	31	33	23	31	435

Annex J
An overview of the NHS[1]

Introduction

The findings detailed in this report, specifically the failures of the relevant regulatory and commissioning bodies to detect the nature and scale of the problems at the Trust, cannot properly be understood without an appreciation of the perpetual changes, the result of (near-constant) fluctuations in political policy, to which the NHS has been subject. This overview aims to provide what will inevitably be a very high level and brief history of the provision and regulation of healthcare, focusing on the changes that have been made to how healthcare has been provided and the development of quality regulation. For these purposes, "quality regulation" can be defined as follows: the arrangements put in place to oversee or scrutinise (as distinct from those managing or directing) health services, with a particular focus on the institutions, organisations, structures and processes managing the delivery of healthcare.[2] The expert reports commissioned by the Inquiry from Dr Judith Smith, Professor Christopher Newdick and Professor Kieran Walshe provide assistance in relation to these issues and form the basis for this section.[3] This overview will proceed chronologically, but not every policy initiative or Department of Health (DH) publication will be mentioned. It will not summarise all of the many views or seek to reach any conclusion on the merit of governmental policies and the changes effected. Rather, this overview is designed to assist the reader in understanding the nature and history of the healthcare bodies which were in existence at the time of the Inquiry's Terms of Reference, thereby providing some context for the events that took place in Stafford.

1948–1979

The NHS was established in 1948 by the National Health Service Act 1946 and began operating on 5 July 1948. Prior to this date, healthcare had been delivered in a rather piecemeal fashion through voluntary hospitals and hospitals owned by local authorities.

From establishment to 1974, the organisation's structure enjoyed relative stability, primarily because little policy attention was paid to it: hospitals, which were nationalised, were managed either by hospital management committees, which were responsible to regional health boards, or, in respect of teaching hospitals, by boards of governors.[4] Funding travelled directly from the Ministry of Health to the board of governors or to regional health boards (which in turn passed it to the hospital

---

1   Authored by pupil barristers at QEB Holis Whiteman
2   EXP0000000081–82 Walshe, Professor Kieran, "The Development of Healthcare Regulation in England: A Background paper for the Mid-Staffordshire Public Inquiry"
3   EXP0000000081 *et seq.* Newdick, Christopher & Smith, Dr Judith, "The Structure and Organisation of the NHS: A report for the independent inquiry into care provided by Mid Staffordshire NHS Foundation Trust January 2005–March 2009", EXP0000000001 *et seq.*; Walshe, "The Development of Healthcare Regulation in England"
4   EXP0000000002, para 3; Newdick & Smith, "The Structure and Organisation of the NHS"

management committees). General practice and other primary care services were administered by local executive councils, whilst community and public health services were the responsibility of local government.

However, by the end of the 1960s a consensus was already developing that this tripartite division was a source of problems. A series of reviews proposed a more integrated system of management, culminating in the National Health Service Reorganisation Act 1973, which introduced changes to the hierarchical structure with effect from 1 April 1974. Under this Act, 14 regional health authorities (RHAs) were created in England, which were responsible for planning local health services. Members were appointed by the Secretary of State for Social Services. Beneath that strata, 90 area health authorities (AHAs) were established in England, with chairs appointed by the Secretary of State and non-executive members appointed by the RHAs and local authorities. These bodies were expected to liaise with local authorities. Most areas were further divided into health districts, administered by district management teams. The aim was to unify health services by bringing under one authority all the services which had previously been administered by regional hospital boards, hospital management committees, executive councils and local health authorities. Primary care contractors (eg doctors, dentists, pharmacists) came to be managed by family practitioner committees, rather than local executive councils. The intention was to create better coordination between health and local authorities. To foster this, the boundaries of the AHAs were designed to match those of the local authorities providing social services. "This reorganisation set the overall framework for the organisational arrangements that remain[ed] in place in the NHS in 2010."[5]

The 1974 reorganisation was subject to criticism for creating too many administrative tiers, which resulted in additional bureaucracy and unnecessary delays. There were also clashes between AHAs and district management teams on matters of strategic direction. In response, the Royal Commission, chaired by Sir Alec Merrison, was established in 1976. It reported in 1979, recommending a streamlined structure with only one level of administrative authority below RHAs.[6] The consultative paper published in December 1979 and entitled *Patients First* proposed removing the area tier and establishing district health authorities (DHAs) to combine the functions, which would strengthen management at a local level. Such recommendations led to the enacting of the Health Services Act 1980. AHAs were disbanded and 192 new DHAs were created in England, which came into operation on 1 April 1982. This Act also gave family practitioner committees independent status as employing authorities.

1990 onwards: the purchaser–provider split

By the late 1980s, a range of pressures were facing the NHS including funding constraints, long waiting times for treatment, and criticisms about the lack of patient choice. This led the Conservative Government of the day to conclude that, despite the number of measures introduced in an attempt to improve efficiency (eg general management, annual performance reviews (re-named cost

---

5   EXP0000000002, para 3; Newdick & Smith, "The Structure and Organisation of the NHS"
6   Royal Commission on the NHS, *Report of the Royal Commission on the NHS*, Cm 7615 (1979), London: HMSO

improvement programmes in 1984) and resource management initiatives), there was a need for a wide-ranging review of the NHS.

Working for Patients

This review, conducted in 1988, resulted in the publication of the White Paper *Working for Patients* in 1989. The main focus of this White Paper was on the creation of a competitive environment.[7] The proposed reforms were enacted by the National Health Service and Community Care Act 1990, which came into force on 1 April 1991. It introduced major changes to the management of the NHS, creating a separation between the roles of the "purchasers" of healthcare (DHAs and GP fundholders (see below)) and the "providers" of care (hospitals, community services and ambulance services). Hospitals were also encouraged to apply for self-governing status as NHS trusts, giving them managerial independence from DHAs.

The concept of an NHS trust was as follows: it was self-governing, headed by a Trust Board whose chairman was appointed by the Secretary of State. The board was responsible for the management of the hospital, and staff contracts would be held directly by the trust rather than by RHAs. A trust would derive its income from contracts with purchasers. However, whilst self-governing, the Secretary of State retained ultimate control; for example, the Trust Board was required to submit an annual financial report to the Minister.

DHAs had previously been responsible for deciding what services to provide in their district and for directly managing the same. The new system involved what was termed an "internal market", in which purchasers and providers contracted with each other for services, with purchasers at liberty to change providers if they could find better services elsewhere. The term "commissioning" was used to describe the process. Such "contracts" were not legally binding and were commonly termed "service level agreements". The logic underpinning the reforms was that money would no longer flow automatically from purchaser to provider; rather, providers would have to compete for business, and in doing so improve efficiency and quality of care, and purchasers could concentrate on assessing needs, planning services and ensuring that an appropriate mix of services was available for their specific population.

The concept of "GP fundholders" was also introduced, allowing doctors' practices to hold budgets for buying a limited range of health services (eg outpatient visits and some common operations) and, consequently, have considerable independence when deciding which services to purchase for their patients. It was envisaged that this system would lead to more attention being paid to the services that patients wanted.

There was a generally cautious approach to implementation: self-governing trusts and GP fundholding were phased in in annual "waves" between 1991 and the mid-1990s. The first wave

---

7 Secretaries of State for Health, Wales, Northern Ireland and Scotland, *Working for Patients,* Cm 555 (1989) London: HMSO

introduced 57 NHS trusts and 306 GP fundholders.[8] The second wave started operating on
1 April 1992, and another 139 NHS trusts were introduced in April 1993. By 1 April 1994, there
were 419 NHS trusts and some 9,000 GP fundholders.[9] Around 50% of GPs became GP fundholders
over the seven years of the scheme.[10] Purchasers (or commissioners), then DHAs, proceeded with
caution, using unsophisticated block contracts to buy services from providers.[11]

Managing the New NHS

In *Managing the New NHS*, published in October 1993, the Government proposed a further
restructuring, which included the abolishment of RHAs in order for them to be replaced by eight
regional offices and the merger of DHAs and family health service authorities.[12] RHAs were reduced
from 14 to eight before their abolishment in the Health Authorities Act 1995, which came into force
on 1 April 1996. This Act also merged DHAs and family health service authorities into a single tier of
100 health authorities, which then existed until 2002.

The New NHS. Modern. Dependable

Following its election in 1997, the Labour Government set out its health policy framework in a White
Paper in December of that year entitled *The New NHS. Modern. Dependable*.[13] This formalised a
number of promises Labour had made in its 1997 election manifesto. The White Paper committed
the Labour Government to maintaining the "purchaser–provider" split but abolished the so-called
"internal market", which was viewed by the new Government as costly, and a creator of distortion in
clinical priorities. Labour placed emphasis on planning and collaboration rather than competition. This
resulted in major changes being made to the functions of NHS bodies and the relationships between
them.

The reforms, enacted through the Health Act 1999, which inserted a section 16A into the NHS Act
1977, transferred the primary responsibility for purchasing (or "commissioning") healthcare to 481
new local commissioning bodies called primary care groups (PCGs). PCGs were collectives of GP
practices and community nurses in the area.

> *These PCGs were to operate initially as sub-committees of Health Authorities and then,
> over time (a period of 10 years was mooted), assume additional commissioning and
> funding responsibilities as Primary Care Trusts (PCTs) – "freestanding bodies accountable to*

8   The Public Inquiry into Children's Heart Surgery at the Bristol Royal Infirmary, *Learning From Bristol: The report of the public inquiry into
     children's heart surgery at the Bristol Royal Infirmary 1984–1995*, Cm 5207, Annex A, Chapter 2, para 57, http://webarchive.
     nationalarchives.gov.uk/20090811143745/www.bristol-inquiry.org.uk/final_report/annex_a/chapter_2_6.htm
9   The Public Inquiry into Children's Heart Surgery at the Bristol Royal Infirmary, *Learning From Bristol*, Annex A, Chapter 2, para 57,
     http://webarchive.nationalarchives.gov.uk/20090811143745/www.bristol-inquiry.org.uk/final_report/annex_a/chapter_2_6.htm
10   EXP0000000035, para 83; Newdick & Smith, "The Structure and Organisation of the NHS"
11   EXP0000000007, para 17; Newdick & Smith, "The Structure and Organisation of the NHS"
12   Department of Health, *Managing the New NHS*, Cm 555 (1993) London: HMSO
13   Department of Health, *The New NHS. Modern. Dependable.*, Cm 3807 (1997) London: HMSO

the Health Authority for commissioning care" also taking responsibility for the provision of community health services.[14]

The role of health authorities consequently changed significantly, with it becoming one of "strategic leadership". This involved a greater focus on assessing and formulating strategies to address community needs and overseeing the commissioning activities of PCGs. The previous contracting system was replaced with longer-term service level agreements, which had to last at least three years, thereby reducing the number of times contracts were switched between providers. GP fundholding was eradicated, a product of Labour's view that decision-making had become fragmented and administrative costs had grown, with existing fundholders becoming part of PCGs.

The Commission for Health Improvement

The Health Act 1999 also established the Commission for Health Improvement (CHI) (later the Healthcare Commission, subsequently replaced by the Care Quality Commission (see below)). For many years, the NHS had made relatively little use of statutory regulation, relying instead upon central direction from the Department of Health (DH). By the end of the 1990s, a mosaic of regulatory organisations existed, each with its own statutory responsibilities and spheres of influence. It was made up of, amongst other things, the professional regulatory bodies, Royal Colleges, the Health Services Ombudsman and the NHS Litigation Authority (NHSLA), as well as organisations of a more general nature, such as the Health and Safety Executive (HSE) and the National Audit Office (NAO). However, it could not be said that a coherent, systematic or effective system was in place for the inspection or regulation of the NHS.[15]

CHI was established in 1999 in response to a perceived crisis in NHS services, which followed a series of public failures in the quality of care provided. In particular, the coming to light of grave deficiencies in the paediatric care provided at Bristol Royal Infirmary during the 1990s dealt serious damage to the reputation of the NHS.[16] This was the first time that there was independent regulation of clinical performance.

CHI was established as a non-departmental public body, responsible to the Secretary of State for Health, who exercised considerable influence over the organisation, and to whom reports were addressed. The Secretary of State appointed the Board of Commissioners, set the annual budget and could direct the areas or issues to be examined. CHI had four main statutory functions:

- To undertake a rolling programme of four-yearly clinical governance reviews of NHS organisations;
- To investigate serious failures in the NHS when requested to do so by the Secretary of State or when asked to do so by others;

---

14 EXP0000000007, para 18; EXP00000000036, para 85; Newdick & Smith, "The Structure and Organisation of the NHS"
15 EXP0000000084 Walshe, "The Development of Healthcare Regulation in England"
16 EXP0000000085 Walshe, "The Development of Healthcare Regulation in England"

- To conduct national service reviews, monitoring progress in the implementation of standards set by the National Institute for Health and Clinical Excellence (NICE), national service frameworks and, where required, other priorities;
- To provide advice and guidance to the NHS on clinical governance.[17]

Anna Walker, former Chief Executive of the Healthcare Commission (HCC) (which would come to replace CHI), told the Inquiry that CHI's chief role was to improve clinical governance within individual trusts.[18] Clinical governance was defined by the DH as a "framework through which NHS organisations are accountable for continuously improving the quality of their services and safeguarding high standards of care by creating an environment in which excellence in clinical care will flourish". However, CHI did not set regulatory requirements, explicit criteria, standards or targets by which clinical governance was to be measured or judged.[19]

CHI's preferred methodology for assessing clinical governance was to conduct five-day visits (clinical governance reviews), carried out by a multidisciplinary team, to around a quarter of trusts each year. This was preceded by a long period of preparation where trusts would submit a large body of requested information.[20] A report would then be produced containing a descriptive narrative and explicit performance ratings, along with key areas for action. The relevant trust would be required to work with CHI to produce an action plan in response to the report. Responsibility for monitoring subsequent improvement and compliance with the action plan fell to the trust itself and the DH.[21]

CHI also assumed responsibility for the performance star rating system previously operated by the DH. Trusts were assessed by reference to strategic priorities, key targets and indicators set by the Government and awarded a rating of zero to three stars depending on levels of performance.[22] During its existence, CHI broadened the scope of the star rating system beyond the achievement of specific, government-set targets, to take account of other indicators of performance such as the results of patient and staff surveys.[23]

The introduction of CHI clearly represented progress as a single, statutory body responsible for quality and safety replacing the complex, *ad hoc* mosaic that preceded it. However, it was felt in some quarters that the system of inspections placed too great a burden on Trust Boards and was too bureaucratic.[24]

---

17 EXP0000000085 Walshe, "The Development of Healthcare Regulation in England"
18 Walker WS0000028540, para 13
19 EXP0000000085 Walshe, "The Development of Healthcare Regulation in England"
20 Walker WS000028540-1, para 15
21 EXP0000000086 Walshe, "The Development of Healthcare Regulation in England"
22 Walker WS0000028540, para 14
23 Walker WS000028540, para 15
24 Donaldson WS0000070216, para 72; Kennedy WS0000025845, para 35

The NHS Plan: A plan for investment, a plan for reform

The Labour Government had promised to honour the previous Government's health spending plans.[25] This proved untenable and, in March 2000, to quell the criticisms about "underfunding and lack of service capacity", the Chancellor's budget committed the Government to sustained investment in the NHS so that it would grow by a third in real terms over five years.[26]

In July 2000, the Government published *The NHS Plan: A plan for investment, a plan for reform*.[27] As well as historic underinvestment, it described the NHS as being a "1940s system operating in a 21st century world", with a lack of uniform standards, performance-inducing incentives and patient focus.[28] *The NHS Plan* committed to targeted investment and introduced a number of reforms to modernise the health service – these reforms were, as characterised by Newdick and Smith, the "strings" with which the money came attached.[29] "There was a strong focus on improving access to services for individual patients, especially in relation to waiting lists and times and expanding the choice of provider."[30] It stated, for example, that "by the end of 2004, no one will wait more than 4 hours in an A&E Department from arrival to transfer, discharge or admission to a bed in the hospital" (this became an operational standard in 2005).[31] There was also reinforcement of a Government commitment to the principle of earned autonomy for high-performing organisations, "which would be allowed greater spending freedoms and be subject to less close performance managing".[32]

Shifting the Balance of Power within the NHS: Securing delivery

In his evidence to the Inquiry, Sir David Nicholson characterised the early years of last decade as being "a period of rapid capacity building and expansion, target setting and some modernisation and system reforms", driven by the intention to devolve responsibility for planning and delivering health services to the local level and to focus on the interests of the service user.[33] It had been envisaged that the structural changes outlined in *The New NHS* would take a period of 10 years to be implemented. The first PCGs were established in 1999, the first primary care trusts (PCTs) in 2000 and by 2001 it had become apparent that the original 10-year timescale for establishing PCTs was to become a much more condensed three-year trajectory.[34]

The re-elected Labour Government embarked on the largest reorganisation of the NHS for two decades with the DH consultation document *Shifting the Balance of Power Within the NHS: Securing delivery*, published in July 2001.[35] It signalled that all PCGs were to become PCTs in 2002, establishing

---

25   EXP0000000007–9, para 19; Newdick & Smith, "The Structure and Organisation of the NHS"
26   EXP0000000007–9, para 19; Newdick & Smith, "The Structure and Organisation of the NHS"; Nicholson WS0000067635, para 15
27   DH00000003210 *et seq.* Department of Health, *The NHS Plan*, Cm 4818 (2000)
28   Nicholson WS0000067635, para 16
29   EXP0000000008, para 20; Newdick & Smith, "The Structure and Organisation of the NHS"
30   EXP0000000008, para 20; Newdick & Smith, "The Structure and Organisation of the NHS"
31   Nicholson WS0000067635, para 17
32   EXP0000000008, para 21; Newdick & Smith, "The Structure and Organisation of the NHS"
33   Nicholson WS0000067634, paras 13–14
34   EXP0000000036, paras 85–6; Newdick & Smith, "The Structure and Organisation of the NHS"
35   DH00000001404 *et seq.* Department of Health, *Shifting the Balance of Power Within the NHS: Securing delivery* (DH, 2001)

them as statutory commissioning organisations.[36] Further, health authorities were to be replaced by much larger strategic health authorities (SHAs) (thus leading to the abolishment of over two-thirds of the health authorities). Prior to publication there had been 95 health authorities, overseen by eight regional offices of the NHS Executive within the DH. *Shifting the Balance of Power* paved the way for the establishment, from April 2002, of 303 locally based PCTs, which reported to 28 new SHAs.[37] These reforms were intended to be the means by which to enable the NHS to achieve the aims and targets set out in *The NHS Plan* of 2000. They were referred to, in an article by Smith, Walshe and Hunter in the *British Medical Journal*, as "the redisorganisation of the NHS" – as this major reorganisation came just three years after the abolition of fundholding and the setting up of PCGs.[38]

The roles of these new bodies were described in *Shifting the Balance of Power*: SHAs were to "step back from service planning and commissioning to lead the strategic development of the local health service and performance manage PCTs and NHS trusts on the basis of local accountability agreements" and PCTs were to take on a greater role in the provision of services, becoming "the cornerstone of the local NHS; devolving power and responsibility to PCTs offers real opportunities to engage local communities in decisions that affect their local health services".[39]

The functions of PCTs were (and still are) defined by the National Health Service (Functions of Strategic Health Authorities and Primary Care Trusts and Administration Arrangements) (England) Regulations 2002 (for a full list of functions please see Annex A of the 2008 DH publication *The Role of the Primary Care Trust Board in World Class Commissioning*).[40] Regulation 3 provides that certain key functions of the Secretary of State under the NHS Act 1977 (and, subsequently, the NHS Act 2006) are to be exercisable by PCTs. These functions included the duty under section 3 of the NHS Act 1977 (now section 3 of the 2006 Act) to provide, to such an extent as the PCT considers necessary to meet all reasonable requirements:

- Hospital accommodation (s.3(1)(a));
- Medical, dental, nursing and ambulance services (s.3(1)(c));
- Facilities for the care of expectant and nursing mothers and young children (s.3(1)(d));
- Facilities for the prevention of illness, the care of persons suffering from illness and the aftercare of persons who have suffered illness (s.3(1)(e));
- Other services required for the diagnosis and treatment of illness (s.3(1)(f)).

Regulation 3(2)(b) made clear that, from 2002, in general it is the PCT that exercises the functions under section 3 and that SHAs are to act in this regard "only to the extent necessary to support and manage the performance of Primary Care Trusts in the exercise of those functions".

---

36 EXP0000000037, para 86; Newdick & Smith, "The Structure and Organisation of the NHS"
37 EXP0000000037, para 89; Nicholson WS0000067636, para 19; Newdick & Smith, "The Structure and Organisation of the NHS"
38 Smith, Walshe and Hunter, The "redisorganisation" of the NHS, *British Medical Journal*, 1 December 2001, Vol 323 pp1263–4, www.bmj.com/content/323/7324/1262
39 DH00000001410 & DH00000001417 Department of Health, *Shifting the Balance of Power Within the NHS: Securing delivery* (2001); Newdick & Smith, "The Structure and Organisation of the NHS", EXP0000000037, paras 89–90
40 TRU00010007149 *et seq.* Department of Health, *The Role of the Primary Care Trust Board in World Class Commissioning* (2008)

Shifting the Balance of Power: The next steps

The DH document *Shifting the Balance of Power: The next steps*, published in January 2002, set out the DH's policy in relation to the new SHAs. It defined the functions of the SHA as follows:

> 2.2.3   The three key functions of a Strategic Health Authority are:
>
> - *creating a coherent strategic framework;*
> - *agreeing annual performance agreements and performance management;*
> - *building capacity and supporting performance improvement.*[41]

Under the heading "Organisation and Operation", the document listed "specific activity" of the new SHAs and included "ensuring the delivery of safe, quality services through effective clinical governance arrangements in PCTs and in NHS Trusts".[42] It placed emphasis on the performance management role of SHAs, stating that "they will in effect be responsible for managing NHS locally on behalf of the Department". However, it went on to state:

> 3.8.3   *Increasingly performance assessment will rely on external and publicly available information and assessment provided, for example, through the performance rating (star) system or CHI inspections.*
>
> 3.8.4   *In future it will be StHAs which will take on the main performance management function. They will negotiate Trust and PCT annual performance agreements; monitor in-year performance; address under performance; oversee the development of recovery plans and monitor their implementation, providing support to the local NHS to assist under performing organisations; and, assess the adequacy of local operational plans.*
>
> ...
>
> 3.8.6   *The way performance management is undertaken will also need to change to reflect the following principles:*
>
> - *organisations will be assessed on the basis of performance against a small group of priorities and progress towards the longer term vision of the NHS.*
> - *performance management of StHAs, PCTs and NHS Trusts will adopt the principles of earned autonomy to allow high performing organisations the greatest level of operational freedom. Such organisations will be subject to lighter touch financial, operational and monitoring requirements.*
> - *performance management will give more attention to health outcomes and patient impact. In particular PCTs will be performance managed on the outcomes of the care that they provide (including preventive health*

---

41   DH00060000011 Department of Health, *Shifting the Balance of Power: The next steps* (2002)
42   DH00060000013 Department of Health, *Shifting the Balance of Power: The next steps* (2002)

improvement work and the commissioning of acute services). Process indicators that currently stand as proxies for outcomes will increasingly be phased out, giving PCTs much more operational freedom in the way their services are configured and run.

- *the new performance management system will place maximum responsibility on organisations to manage their own performance. They should report on information which they need for themselves."*[43]

Therefore, whilst the SHA's role in performance management of PCTs and NHS trusts was to be central, it was to be narrowly defined: the SHA was to rely on data returns by organisations and the assessments of others rather than carry out its own inspections.

SHAs were created by the Health Authorities (Establishment and Abolition) (England) Order 2002. The powers of SHAs have been set out in successive versions of the National Health Service (Functions of Strategic Health Authorities and Primary Care Trusts and Administration Arrangements) (England) Regulations 2002. The regulations delegate to SHAs (and to PCTs) many of the Secretary of State's functions in relation to the NHS under the National Health Service Acts (1977 and 2006), including the duty to promote a comprehensive health service and the power to give directions to NHS trusts about their exercise of any functions (limited to those trusts within the particular SHA's area).[44] This was a power explicitly not delegated to PCTs.[45]

The Secretary of State's core functions under the NHS Acts for the provision of NHS services, including "medical services" and hospital accommodation, were delegated by the regulations to PCTs. The same functions were delegated to the SHAs for the purpose of performance management of the PCTs only.[46] Under Regulation 3(5), "every Strategic Health Authority shall exercise the [delegated] functions ... for the benefit of its area or to secure the effective provision of services by Primary Care Trusts and NHS Trusts for which they are the appropriate Strategic Health Authority". The overall scheme has remained consistent through successive versions of the legislation. PCTs were to ensure the practical provision of services at a local level while SHAs were to ensure the comprehensiveness of the service at a regional level by performance-managing PCTs and directing trusts where necessary.

---

43 DH00060000023–4 Department of Health, *Shifting the Balance of Power: The next steps*
44 SI 2002/2375 Regulation 3(3) & Schedule 2
45 SI 2002/2375 Regulation 5(2)
46 SI 2002/2375 Regulation 3(2) & Schedule 1, Part 2

1   The SHAs were to differ significantly from the old RHAs: Professor Ian Cumming said in his evidence to the Inquiry:

> [T]he name "strategic health authority" was deliberately chosen to differentiate from the regional health authorities ... [which] used to employ somewhere in the region of 2,000 members of staff and ... were expected to manage the health service and the delivery of healthcare in their area ... Shifting the Balance of Power ... makes it clear that the size of a strategic health authority should be 75 people ... covering 5,000 square miles, looking after GBP 10 billion of money a year and with responsibility for more than 50 NHS organisations ... These are very small organisations, with an emphasis on the S in SHA, strategic.[47]

Delivering the NHS Plan

The Government's commitment to earned autonomy was furthered in 2002 with the publication of *Delivering the NHS Plan*, which proposed the establishment of NHS foundation trusts (FTs).[48] FTs were to be directly accountable to Parliament and to their board of governors, rather than SHAs, and were not subject to the Secretary of State's directions. "This policy was a recognition by ministers that the NHS should not be seen as a nationalised industry and that it was important to give real operational autonomy to providers in the system."[49] Furthermore, the independence that trusts would obtain was seen as a powerful incentive to drive up clinical quality and financial performance.

FTs and their independent regulator, Monitor, were established by the Health and Social Care (Community Health and Standards) Act 2003.[50] "The Act was passed in November 2003 and the DH encouraged the first applications in December 2003"; indeed, the Secretary of State for Health declared an expectation that all NHS trusts should be in a position to apply for FT status within five years.[51] The first 10 FTs were established in April 2004. They became subject to another of the new reforms, Payment by Results, a tariff-based payment system.

Monitor was designed to be the economic regulator of FTs and the assessor of trusts applying to become FTs. It was established as an independent regulator, with FTs fully under its control and no longer under the direction of the Secretary of State (as recognised by a Memorandum of Understanding between the DH and Monitor).[52] Its role, detailed initially in the Health and Social Care (Community Health and Standards) Act 2003, became (from 1 March 2007) prescribed by the provisions of the NHS Act 2006. Section 31 of the Act provides that there "continues to be" a body corporate known as the independent regulator of FTs. Section 33 provides that a trust may make an application to the regulator (Monitor) to become an FT if the application is supported by the Secretary

---

47   Cumming T67.14
48   DH00000003898 *et seq*. Department of Health, *Delivering the NHS Plan: Next steps on investment, next steps on reform* (DH, 2002)
49   Taylor WS0000061928, para 11
50   DH00000003946 Health and Social Care (Community Health and Standards) Act 2003
51   Cash WS0000061513, para 5
52   AM/6 WS0000035723

of State for Health (this section replaced section 4 of the 2003 Act). It follows that the ultimate decision as to whether or not to grant FT status lies in the hands of Monitor, but Monitor may not grant that status unless prior approval has been sought and obtained from the Secretary of State for Health.

Section 52 of the Act (previously section 23 of the 2003 Act) empowers Monitor to take action in relation to any failing FT that is found to be in significant breach of its authorisation. Monitor has power under the Act to require a trust to do or not to do specified things within a specified time limit and/or remove any or all of the trust's board of directors or board of governors. That action did not and does not include a power to de-authorise an FT once one has been created, because the provision allowing such action is not yet in force. There appeared to be considerable confusion among a number of witnesses who were under the impression that not only was this provision on the statute book but it had been brought into force. Section 53(6) provided that the HCC could make recommendations to Monitor if it was of the view that there were significant failings in the provision of healthcare provided by an FT or significant failings in the running of an FT. Some of the failings in the legislation were described by Professor Kieran Walshe who told the Inquiry:

> ... one thing I would note is that Monitor's powers of enforcement over FTs were not particularly well graduated. It clearly had the opportunity for low level informal action ... but its next step up I think was to intervene and remove the board of the FT which is a fairly nuclear sanction.[53]

A number of measures were taken to encourage NHS trusts to become FTs: in 2005 a "whole health community diagnostic" was developed as a joint project between the DH, SHAs and Monitor.[54] All NHS trusts were required to complete it, with the support of their SHAs, to determine whether they were ready to apply to become an FT. Furthermore, on 7 November 2005 the decision was taken by the then Secretary of State for Heath (Rt Hon Patricia Hewitt MP) to widen the entry pool to two-star-rated organisations (previously only three-star-rated trusts had been permitted to apply).

The Healthcare Commission

The Health and Social Care (Community Health and Standards) Act 2003 also replaced CHI with the Commission for Healthcare Audit and Inspection, otherwise known as the HCC. This change had been proposed in April 2002, when the DH published proposals for the creation of two "super-regulators": the Commission for Healthcare Audit and Inspection, to regulate all healthcare provision, and the Commission for Social Care Inspection, to regulate all social care. The reforms came against the backdrop of the wider health policy, which sought a move towards greater diversity and plurality in healthcare provision, the introduction of greater choice for patients and the development of a "self-improving" healthcare system. This was to be brought about by limiting the role played by central government and the DH to policy development and oversight, whilst the responsibility for

---

53   Walshe T8.85
54   Cash WS0000061518, para 24

healthcare system management and the actual delivery of the service would be delegated to others.[55]

The HCC was established with the general responsibility of "encouraging improvement in the provision of healthcare by and for NHS bodies".[56] It was to assume all of the duties performed by CHI, the private healthcare regulation function of the National Care Standards Commission, the value-for-money audit function for the NHS of the Audit Commission, and some regulatory functions previously performed by the DH.[57] The role of the HCC was therefore broader in scope than that assumed by CHI, with a different focus and a "lighter touch" in its methodology.[58]

Like the CHI, the HCC was a non-departmental public body funded largely by the DH (although some funding was obtained by levies on private service providers). However, its board was appointed by the NHS Appointments Commission on behalf of the DH. The HCC was responsible for the regulation of around 582 NHS trusts and 1,400 healthcare providers in the independent sector. It was a sizeable body, employing 600 staff, 1,400 associates and exhibiting an annual turnover of £62 million.[59]

The role, function and effectiveness of the HCC is dealt with elsewhere in the main body of the Inquiry report as is the HCC's annual health check.

Creating and commissioning a patient-led NHS

In March 2005, the Government published *Creating a Patient-led NHS: Delivering the NHS Improvement plan*, which focused on making the health service more patient centred.[60] This was followed in July of the same year by *Commissioning a Patient-led NHS*, which signalled a further reorganisation by the DH.[61] Its proposed reforms aimed to strengthen commissioning and reduce the costs associated with SHAs and PCTs; for example, the aim was reduce PCT management costs by 15%, and more closely align NHS organisational boundaries with those of local government.[62] This vision combined with a commitment to make savings of £250 million in overhead costs.

The Government believed that such aims could be furthered by creating fewer and larger PCTs, so that managerial talent and leadership were concentrated in fewer organisations. In order to strengthen the role of PCTs, SHAs were given a more strategic role and were to be reconfigured to match regional government boundaries. The culmination of the proposals led to, in July 2006, the disestablishment of the 28 existing SHAs and the statutory establishment of 10 new larger ones. This was followed, in October 2006, by a reduction in the number of PCTs: 303 PCTs were reduced to 152

55 EXP0000000089 Walshe, "The Development of Healthcare Regulation in England"
56 Walker AW/4 WS0000028831
57 EXP0000000089 Walshe, "The Development of Healthcare Regulation in England"
58 Donaldson WS0000070216, para 72
59 EXP0000000090 Walshe, "The Development of Healthcare Regulation in England"
60 DH00000004140 *et seq.* Department of Health, *Creating a Patient-led NHS: Delivering the NHS improvement plan* (2005); Nicholson WS0000067638, para 29
61 DH00000004179 *et seq.* Department of Health, *Commissioning a Patient-led NHS,* Cm 6268 (2005)
62 EXP0000000038, para 91; Newdick & Smith, "The Structure and Organisation of the NHS"

through a series of mergers (except in London, where no mergers took place).[63] The result was that at a time of great change for the PCTs, the organisations tasked with overseeing their activities were also in transition.

Practice Based Commissioning

Practice Based Commissioning (PBC) was also introduced in 2005, having been announced in the October 2004 publication *Practice Based Commissioning: Engaging practices in commissioning*.[64] The concept had been suggested in *The New NHS*, which stated "over time the Government expects that ... PCTs will extend indicative budgets to individual practices for the full range of services" and in the proposal detailed in *The NHS Improvement Plan*, which stated "from April 2005, GP practices that wish to do so will be given indicative commissioning budgets".

PBC enabled PCTs to allocate to certain GP practices an "indicative budget" to commission treatment for their patients.[65] They were to take responsibility for a budget covering acute, community and emergency care. PCTs would be responsible for placing and managing contracts with providers on their behalf.[66] The GP practices could also be awarded incentive monies, to be spent on behalf of their patients, if they achieved specified savings and service objectives. It was introduced as the logical extension to reforms that sought to devolve more power to the front line; as stated in *Commissioning a Patient-led NHS,* the Government was committed to PBC as a way of devolving power to local doctors and nurses to improve patient care. The logic behind it was that it would provide greater and more relevant choices for patients, improving the quality of service offered, reduce hospital waiting times, and respond to patient preferences.

Financial pressures

This period of structural change and organisational reform resulted in financial difficulties for some NHS organisations; indeed, a number of organisations were said to have "got ahead of themselves and recruited too many staff".[67] "The NHS closed 2005/06 with a net deficit of £547m. The gross deficit was over £1.3bn and 179 NHS organisations finished the year in deficit."[68] HM Treasury introduced more stringent financial controls on DH expenditure, which, in turn, led to stricter monitoring and performance management further down the organisational hierarchy; for example, an external assessment was commissioned by the DH in December 2005 of 100 PCTs and NHS trusts that were forecasting significant deficits or aware of underlying financial problems. In February 2006, a National Programme Office for Turnaround was implemented, which worked with those bodies that were subject to particular financial difficulties in developing recovery plans. The NHS ended with a

---

63 Nicholson WS0000067640, para 38; EXP0000000038, para 91; Newdick & Smith, "The Structure and Organisation of the NHS"
64 Department of Health, *Practice Based Commissioning: Engaging practices in commissioning* (2004), www.dh.gov.uk/en/Publicationsandstatistics/Publications/PublicationsPolicyAndGuidance/DH_4090357; www.dh.gov.uk/prod_consum_dh/groups/dh_digitalassets/@dh/@en/documents/digitalasset/dh_4090359.pdf
65 EXP0000000018, para 46; Newdick & Smith, "The Structure and Organisation of the NHS"
66 DH00000001179 Department of Health, *Commissioning a Patient-led NHS*
67 Nicholson WS0000067660, para 101
68 Nicholson WS0000067638, para 31

net surplus of £515 million in 2006/07, with the gross deficit reduced to £917 million, and the number of NHS organisations in deficit reduced to 82.[69]

World Class Commissioning

World Class Commissioning was a DH initiative launched in December 2007 to improve the quality of commissioning across England. The DH published guidance documentation entitled *World Class Commissioning: Vision* and *World Class Commissioning: Competencies*, which set out in greater detail than before the core skills expected of commissioners and objectives to be achieved. Such competencies included engaging with the public and patients, working collaboratively with clinicians, promoting improvement and innovation, and managing the local health system.[70] The publications were followed up by a process of assessment of PCTs against the competencies that had been set out. Gary Belfield, who in 2007 became Director of Commissioning at the DH, with particular responsibility for World Class Commissioning, explained to the Inquiry that "the introduction of WCC in 2007/08 was the first comprehensive approach to the development of commissioning competencies and defining the important role of commissioners in the NHS in England ... Previously no one had really defined what commissioning was in any detailed way".[71] Stuart Poynor, in his evidence to the Inquiry, agreed that World Class Commissioning was a positive step in setting out the key competencies of commissioners for the first time and being backed up by an assessment process. He said: "I think that WCC took the commissioning standards to a different level. It addressed engagement and governance and set out standards that could be attained. My view is that it gave real focus to the commissioning process".[72]

High Quality Care for All: NHS next stage final review

In June 2007, Lord Darzi of Denam was appointed a Parliamentary Under Secretary at the DH and given the responsibility of leading the NHS Next Stage Review. Around 60,000 people contributed to the review locally and nationally.[73] On 1 June 2008, the review's report, *High Quality Care for All: NHS next stage final review* (also known as the "Darzi Report") was published.[74] It introduced a particular focus on quality: its stated aim was to "put quality at the heart of the NHS". It proposed that all NHS organisations should be required by statute to publish quality accounts (along with financial ones) – a proposal intended to increase transparency, which would promote quality and expose poor performance. It emphasised the role of PCTs to "challenge providers to achieve high quality care". It referred back to the World Class Commissioning programme as the route by which improvements in commissioning and care would be driven.[75]

---

69   Nicholson WS0000067639, para 35
70   SSPCT WS (Provisional) PCT00000000016–7, paras 40–42
71   Belfield WS0000058366, para 41
72   Poynor WS0000014349–50, paras 290–291. SSPCT was first assessed pursuant to WCC in December 2008 (ranked 74 out of 152 PCTs), and for a second time in 2010 (ranked 24 out of 152 PCTs). The initiative was discontinued in 2010.
73   Nicholson WS0000067643, para 47
74   DH00000004226 Department of Health, *High Quality Care for All: NHS next stage final review*, Cm 7432 (2008)
75   SSPCT WS (Provisional) PCT00000000017, para 43

A National Quality Board (NQB) was also established under the chairmanship of Sir David Nicholson, in order to align all key management and regulatory bodies around quality as the organising principle.

The Care Quality Commission

The Health and Social Care Act 2008 merged the HCC, the Mental Health Act Commission (MHAC) and the Commission for Social Care Inspection (CSCI, previously responsible for social care) and formed the new Care Quality Commission (CQC).[76] The CQC came into existence on 1 April 2009 and continues to operate today. The formation of the CQC was part of a general shift in the approach to public sector regulation set out in the 2005 Budget statement, which provided the blueprint for regulatory reform over the following years:

> *But it is also right to lessen the burden of regulation and enhance our flexibility while still ensuring high standards. So instead of a one size fits all approach which can mean that unnecessary inspections are carried out while necessary ones are not carried out, the best practice risk-based regulation now means more inspection only where there is more risk and a light and limited touch where there is less risk ...*

> *... And in addition to reducing inspection bodies from 35 to just nine I can also announce a further reduction. We are today bringing forward proposals for a reduction in public sector inspectorates from 11 to four – with single inspectorates for criminal justice, for education and children's services, for social care and health, and for local services ...*[77]

Una O'Brien, former Director General for Policy and Strategy at the DH during the establishment of the CQC, identified four policy objectives behind the Government's desire for reform, and in particular the establishment of a single regulator for health and social care:

- The need and opportunity to make efficiencies in the number of regulators;
- The policy objective to streamline the regulatory impact on provider organisations;
- The opportunity to improve and align the approach to regulation across health and social care;
- The opportunity to give the new regulator a wider, potentially tougher, range of sanctions and enforcement powers it could use, independently of Government, on behalf of patients and the public, to help tackle failures and to deliver essential standards of safety and quality.[78]

The CQC, as an amalgamation of three previously separate bodies, consequently has a far broader remit than the HCC. It is responsible for monitoring an increasingly wide range of services, including

---

76   DH00000004318 Health and Social Care Act 2008
77   O'Brien WS0000059311, para 14
78   O'Brien WS0000059316, para 32

NHS trusts, adult social care providers, independent ambulance providers and, from April 2012, general practices.[79] It does so with an annual budget "one quarter lower than the sum of those provided to its predecessor bodies and with a workforce of 2,100, a reduction of 800 on the combined predecessor workforce of 2,900".[80]

The role and functioning of the CQC is dealt with elsewhere in the main body of the Inquiry report.

The CQC approach is put into practice through a two-stage process. All providers of regulated services must apply for and be granted registration, which requires an assessment of compliance with the Essential Standards and an ongoing commitment to continue to abide by them. This ongoing compliance is then monitored by a process of continuous review and, where necessary, inspection.

During a window in January 2010, all NHS service providers were required to apply for registration by completing an online form declaring compliance (or otherwise) with the 16 Essential Standards. The declaration would be analysed against information held by the CQC about the provider in order to determine whether further scrutiny, which may have included an inspection visit, would be required. The providers were then given access to the information held relating to them, as the CQC wanted to "engender a culture of honesty". Where non-compliance was declared, the provider had to provide an action plan to remedy the situation, the credibility of which was assessed by the CQC. Providers could be authorised despite non-compliance with the attachment of conditions mandating remedial action within a set time frame. In the first year, 378 NHS trusts were registered, of which 22 carried conditions, including the Trust itself.[81] All new providers of a service must apply for registration (even if registered for other services).

Once registered, a service provider need not re-register for the same service. Instead, its compliance is monitored continuously by the CQC, which focuses on the patient care outcomes set out in the Essential Standards.

The Health and Social Care Act 2012 and beyond

"The coalition government elected in May 2010 moved rapidly to develop its health policy plans and published a white paper, Equality and Excellence – Liberating the NHS in July 2010."[82] It sought to take the principle of devolving commissioning power closer to the patient a stage further, proposing the abolition of both SHAs and PCTs and the passing of commissioning power to groups of GP practices, termed GP Consortia, which would have a budget with which to commission care.[83] This proposal responded to the dissatisfaction expressed by some GPs that they had not been given the degree of responsibility they sought through PBC, and in particular their desire for real budgets.

---

79   Williams WS0000032065, para 12
80   Bower WS/2 WS0000037363, para 6
81   Bower WS/2 WS0000037372–75, paras. 27–35; Williams WS0000032067–68, paras 20–21
82   Newdick & Smith, "The Structure and Organisation of the NHS", EXP0000000008, para 23; *Equality and Excellence: Liberating the NHS*, Cm 7881 (2010), www.dh.gov.uk/prod_consum_dh/groups/dh_digitalassets/@dh/@en/@ps/documents/digitalasset/dh_117794.pdf
83   EXP0000000018–9 Newdick & Smith, "The Structure and Organisation of the NHS"

It was proposed that a new NHS Commissioning Board would be introduced, which would undertake the commissioning of specialised services, primary care, material care and prison health services. This board would oversee and regulate GP Consortia. Responsibility for public health would be transferred to local authorities, and local health and well-being boards would be established within local authorities, whose role will be to oversee commissioning. Performance targets would be abolished and replaced with an NHS outcomes framework, against which the performance of GP Consortia would be measured. Monitor's role would be expanded, becoming an economic regulator of all NHS providers (not just FTs), and a national Healthwatch body is to be established within the CQC. It was proposed that all NHS trusts would become autonomous FTs. The CQC's role is to be strengthened, to ensure that it is an "effective quality inspectorate across both health and social care".[84] It was envisaged that such reforms would reduce NHS management costs by 45%.[85] A period of consultation on such proposals closed in October 2010.

In April 2011, the then Secretary of State for Health (Rt Hon Andrew Lansley MP) announced that an exercise would be undertaken to consider the Government's proposals for modernising the NHS, halting the Health and Social Care Bill's (the Bill that would give effect to the Government's reforms) progress through Parliament. This exercise was led by the independent NHS Future Forum (a group of 45 senior professionals from across health and social care, chaired by Professor Steve Field), which published its report on 13 June 2011. In the Government response, whilst the fundamental principles as set out in *Equality and Excellence* remained, a number of changes were made to the initial proposals to take account of conclusions reached by the Forum, for example, GP Consortia will be called "clinical commissioning groups" (CCGs) and will have governing bodies, with at least one nurse and one specialist doctor. [86]These groups will be established by April 2013. The Health and Social Care Bill gained royal assent to become the Health and Social Care Act 2012 on 27 March 2012.[87] The DH press release ended: "... the implementation of the Act will now enable clinical leaders, patients' representatives and local government to all take new and leading roles in shaping more effective services".[88]

Conclusion

The mechanism by which the quality of healthcare is regulated remains, therefore, in a state of flux. There has been a consistent process of amalgamation as regulation becomes concentrated in the hands of fewer bodies with ever-broader spheres of influence and responsibilities, motivated both by a policy shift towards the "light touch" devolved management of healthcare in general, and by a desire to garner efficiency savings. Moreover, no consensus has emerged as to the best approach to assessing and ensuring compliance with fundamental standards of quality set by the centre.

---

84   Department of Health; 2010 *Equality and Excellence*, para 6t,
     www.dh.gov.uk/prod_consum_dh/groups/dh_digitalassets/@dh/@en/@ps/documents/digitalasset/dh_117794.pdf
85   *Equality and Excellence*, para 7w,
     www.dh.gov.uk/prod_consum_dh/groups/dh_digitalassets/@dh/@en/@ps/documents/digitalasset/dh_117794.pdf
86   Department of Health, *Government Response to NHS Future Forum Report*, Cm 8113 (2001),
     www.dh.gov.uk/prod_consum_dh/groups/dh_digitalassets/documents/digitalasset/dh_127719.pdf
87   http://mediacentre.dh.gov.uk/2012/03/27/health-and-social-care-bill-gains-royal-assent/
88   http://mediacentre.dh.gov.uk/2012/03/27/health-and-social-care-bill-gains-royal-assent/

The Health and Social Care Act 2012 is the fruition of the Government's policy to devolve commissioning power and responsibility to the local level, with the aim to eradicate bureaucracy (and reduce costs) and put patients at the heart of the NHS. In doing so, profound organisational changes have been made – change, as this background chapter has illustrated, is not new to the NHS. But with repeated reorganisations does come the need for caution. Whilst proposed with the best of intentions, the practical effect of such changes on the organisations themselves must be considered.

Professor Kieran Walshe, who provided an expert report to the Inquiry entitled *The Development of Healthcare Regulation in England: A background paper for the Mid Staffordshire Public Inquiry,* made the point that the constant reorganisation within the NHS (with particular reference to regulatory bodies) itself made it extremely difficult to evaluate whether it had had a positive impact on services to patients. Professor Walshe said this:

> *While the rapid pace of reform in regulation in some ways simply reflects the rate of change in the National Health Service and the wider healthcare system, it also means that there is a fragmented and complex history from which it is not straightforward to draw clear and coherent conclusions. It has been almost impossible to undertake the crucial task of evaluating the work of regulatory agencies, understanding their impact on the performance of healthcare organisations and the quality of service provided to patients, and using that knowledge both to learn about the business of inspection and regulation and to improve the regulatory regime in healthcare.*

He went on to state that constant reorganisation made the achievement of improvement harder: "An obvious but important lesson is that establishing an effective set of regulatory arrangements takes time, and repeated revisions of the policy objectives, purposes and mechanisms make effective regulation more difficult and less likely".[89] This logic does not only apply to regulatory bodies. It is imperative that organisational memory and learning is not repeatedly eroded and that there is time provided for organisations to learn, focus and improve on their day-to-day roles and responsibilities to ensure that quality care is being provided for patients.

This overview has sought to provide the briefest of sketches of the changes that the NHS underwent from its inception up to the present day. It is hoped that it will provide a context in which to place the events that occurred at Mid Staffordshire.

---

89   EXP0000000097 Walshe, "The Development of Healthcare Regulation in England"

Annex K
Are foundation trusts legally bound by the NHS Constitution?[1]

Issue

1   We have been asked to examine a potential loophole in the NHS that means foundation trusts (FTs) may not be bound by the terms of the NHS Constitution and the patient guarantees contained within the Constitution. The issue arose in an article published in the *Health Service Journal* on 2 November 2011, a copy of which is attached at Appendix 1. This paper examines that issue.

The NHS Constitution and the duty of have regard to it

2   The NHS Constitution brings together in one place details of what staff, patients and the public can expect from the NHS and sets out the rights of an NHS patient. These rights cover how patients access health services, the quality of care they will receive, the treatments and programmes available, confidentiality, information and the right to complain if things go wrong.[2] The Health Act 2009 introduced the NHS Constitution, and section 2 of the Act introduced a duty for a number of NHS bodies (this includes FTs, NHS trusts, special health authorities, the Care Quality Commission (CQC) and Monitor), that in performing their duties, they must "have regard to the NHS Constitution".[3] Therefore, whilst there is a legal duty to consider the NHS Constitution there is no mandatory obligation to comply with or implement the Constitution. The words "have regard" infers an obligation to consider the Constitution, but no more. Neither the Health Act nor the NHS Constitution state that there are any sanctions where an NHS body fails in this duty. Consequently, the NHS Constitution appears to be a set of guiding principles to be considered rather than being a set of propositions to which organisations will be legally bound.

3   This may not be a concern. As set out on page 4 of the *Handbook to the NHS Constitution* (published on 8 March 2012):

---

1   Authored by Eversheds LLB
2   The most recent update to the NHS Constitution was on 8 March 2012.
3   Section 3 of the Health and Social Care Act 2012 inserted Section 1B into the Health Act 2009, which provides that the Secretary of State must also have regard to the NHS Constitution when exercising his/her functions.

The Constitution sets out a number of rights, which include rights conferred explicitly by law and rights derived from legal obligations imposed on NHS bodies and other healthcare providers. The Constitution brings together these rights in one place but it does not create or replace them.

The NHS Constitution handbook also recognises as follows: "This Constitution also contains pledges which the NHS is committed to achieve, supported by its management and regulatory systems. The pledges are not legally binding and cannot be guaranteed for everyone all of the time, because they express an ambition to improve, going above and beyond legal rights. This Handbook explains in detail what each of the pledges means and current actions to meet them. Some of the pledges, such as those relating to waiting times for treatment, are long-standing commitments on which the NHS already has a track record of success and strong mechanisms in place to ensure delivery. In other areas, the pledges refer to relatively new commitments that the NHS is working towards achieving.

4   Therefore, it is clear that the NHS Constitution itself is not legally binding. Notwithstanding this, the issue as to whether FTs are bound to national standards and targets in the same way as other organisations is still an issue and is examined further below.

Statement of NHS accountability

5   The NHS Constitution commits the Government to providing a statement of NHS accountability which describes the system of responsibility and accountability for taking decisions in the NHS. The statement of NHS accountability also provides a summary of the current structure and functions of the NHS in England. The NHS Constitution (version dated March 2012) at page 4 states:

The NHS is a national service funded through national taxation, and it is the Government which sets the framework for the NHS and which is accountable to Parliament for its operation. However, most decisions in the NHS, especially those about the treatment of individuals and the detailed organisation of services, are rightly taken by the local NHS and by patients with their clinicians. The system of responsibility and accountability for taking decisions in the NHS should be transparent and clear to the public, patients and staff. The Government will ensure that there is always a clear and up-to-date statement of NHS accountability for this purpose.

6   The Statement of NHS Accountability (dated 21 January 2009) then provides a summary of the structure of the NHS and the roles and responsibilities of each of its parts. On page 8 it does state that:

national standards and the legal framework for the NHS are the responsibility of ministers and apply to NHS foundation trusts just as they do to other parts of the NHS.

7   This suggests that national standards apply to FTs in the same way that they do to other NHS bodies. However, the NHS's Operating Framework and Monitor's Compliance Framework (which applies to the current regime) suggest contrary to this, as set out below. It seems that FTs may not be strictly subject to all national standards as is envisaged by the Statement of NHS Accountability.

The Operating Framework and Monitor's Compliance Framework

8   The current set of standards issued by the Secretary of State is the NHS Operating Framework 2012/13. The Operating Framework outlines the business and planning arrangements for the NHS. The Operating Framework for 2012/13 states that:

It describes the national priorities, system levers and enablers for NHS organisations to maintain and improve the quality of services provided, while delivering transformational change and maintaining financial stability.

9   The Operating Framework and its accompanying technical guidance sets out the indicators and performance measures against which providers are monitored, for example, waiting times and other indicators, financial and business rules and specified levels of service quality. At page 45, paragraph 5.3 of the NHS Operating Framework for 2012/13 it states as follows:

The accountability arrangements described in this NHS Operating Framework sit within an overall context of the NHS system during 2012/13, key to which continue to be:

- *the current statutory framework, where PCTs and SHAs continue to be the statutory units of accountability;*
- *the NHS Constitution, which secures patient and staff rights;*
- *contracts, which form the means of doing business between commissioners and providers;*
- *the Care Quality Commission, who carry out inspections and other activity to regulate NHS providers against essential standards of safety and quality; and*
- *Monitor, who ensure NHS Foundation Trusts are meeting their terms of authorisation, including their contribution to delivery against the national priorities set out in this NHS Operating Framework.*

10   Therefore, it seems that FTs' accountability at the present time is determined in a number of ways:

- It is a condition of each FT's authorisation (as granted by Monitor) that it meets national clinical and quality standards;
- FTs' service/commissioning agreements with PCTs will usually specify that the services provided must comply with national quality and safety standards;
- Like all other NHS bodies, NHS FTs are inspected against national standards by the healthcare regulator (CQC, and formerly the Healthcare Commission). Monitor would receive copies of inspection reports and decide what, if any, action is needed in the event of failings.

11   However, what is clear is that FTs operate under a different system of accountability than that of NHS trusts, and FTs are not required to comply with Department of Health management and operational guidance. They are also exempt from some current management targets (as was envisaged by the legislation, which saw an increased level of independence and autonomy with FTs).

12   It is Monitor who is responsible for holding FTs to account for their performance, and the system of accountability is different to that of other NHS trusts. The explanatory notes for section 2 of the Health and Social Care (Community Health and Standards) Act 2003 state as follows:

> *The Independent Regulator is responsible for setting the terms of, and granting authorisation to, NHS foundation trusts, and monitoring their compliance with the terms of authorisation and the requirements set out in Part 1.*

13   Schedule 2 section 6(1) of the 2003 Act provides that Monitor is responsible for regulating its own procedure and making any arrangements it considers appropriate for the discharge of its functions, and section 8(1) gives Monitor general powers to do anything that is necessary or desirable in relation to its functions. In the exercise of these powers, Monitor published its first Compliance Framework on 31 March 2005. This has since been updated, the most recent version being dated 30 March 2012. Monitor's Compliance Framework sets out [the]:

> *approach Monitor will take to assess the compliance of NHS foundation trusts with their terms of Authorisation ("the Authorisation") and to intervene where necessary." The introduction of the framework goes on to state that "while NHS foundation trusts remain public institutions, they are neither subject to direction by the Secretary of State for Health nor the performance management requirements of the Department of Health.*

14   Turning to Monitor's Compliance Framework, the provisions of note are on pages 7 and 8 and state as follows:

> *NHS foundation trusts are therefore required to provide board statements certifying ongoing compliance with their Authorisation and other legal requirements, including, but not limited to:*
>
> *...*
>
> - *Delivering healthcare services to specified standards under agreed contracts with their commissioners;*
> - *Maintaining registration with the Care Quality Commission and addressing conditions associated with registration;*
>
> *...*
>
> *Complying with healthcare targets and indicators these targets and indicators are set out in Appendix B of Monitor's Compliance Framework and they are the set of measures compiled by Monitor and used to assess the quality of governance at FTs, rather than being national standards or targets;*
>
> *...*
>
> *Complying with statutory requirements, their Authorisation, their constitution, their contracts with commissioners and guidance issued by Monitor;*
>
> *...*
>
> - *Having regard to the NHS Constitution."*

15   Further, page 55 of Monitor's Compliance Framework states that:

> *the board is required to confirm that: the board will ensure that the NHS foundation trust will, at all times, have regard to the NHS constitution.*

16   Therefore, Monitor's Compliance Framework also makes it clear that FTs are not bound by the NHS Constitution but rather that it is a requirement for FTs to take the NHS Constitution into account and no more. This is as envisaged by the Health Act 2009. Perhaps more importantly, the framework makes it clear that FTs are required to meet the targets and indicators set by Monitor and in commissioning contracts but not necessarily as set out under the NHS Operating Framework.

Terms of authorisation and relevant legislation

17   Under section 6 of the Health & Social Care (Community Health and Standards) Act 2003, Monitor is given the power to authorise applicants to be FTs where Monitor is satisfied that they have met the necessary criteria, as well as any other requirements that Monitor considers appropriate. Further, at section 6(4) of the Act it states: "The authorisation may be given on any terms the regulator considers appropriate".

18   In preparing this note, we have considered and reviewed a copy of Mid Staffordshire NHS Foundation Trust's Terms of Authorisation and its Constitution. For comparison purposes we have also reviewed the Birmingham Children's Hospital Foundation Trust's Terms of Authorisation and Constitution. The relevant provisions in the two sets of documents are identical and the following is of note:

The Terms of Authorisation

19   Part 3 of the Terms of Authorisation deals with compliance and enforcement and the healthcare standards that the FT must follow. The relevant provisions are as follows:

> 4. *Compliance and enforcement*
>
> (1) *The Trust shall comply with:*
>
> *Any requirement imposed on it under the Act or any other enactment;*
>
> *The requirement to have regard to the NHS Constitution in performing its NHS functions in accordance with section 2 of the Health Act 2009*
>
> *The Conditions of this Authorisation;*
>
> *The terms of its constitution;*
>
> ...
>
> *The terms of its contract with bodies which commission the Trust to provide goods and service (including education and training, accommodation and other facilities) for the purposes of the health service in England."*
>
> ...
>
> 6. *Health care and other standards*
>
> ...
>
> (2) *The Trust shall comply with the healthcare targets and indicators set out in the Compliance Framework (as may be amended from time to time).*

20   In fact, Condition 6(2) of the Terms of Authorisation (as set out above) was amended in April 2010. Previously the provision had stated:

> *The Trust shall comply with statements of standards in relation to the provision of health care published by the Secretary of State under section 46 of the Health and Social Care (Community Health and Standards) Act 2003, as currently set out in the Department of Health publication Health and Social Care Standards and Planning Framework (July 2004) as may be amended from time to time. This being the annual operating framework (the context of the NHS Operating Framework and its applicability to FTs is already set out at paragraphs 8 to 10 above).*

21   Therefore, FTs' Terms of Authorisation also make it clear that FTs are subject to Monitor's targets and standards rather than the national standards set out in the NHS Operating Framework.

Relevant legislation

22   The National Health Service Act 2006 (the "Act") does not help to shed any light on this issue. Section 35 of the Act determines the authorisation of FTs and Section 35(4) goes on to state that "The authorisation may be given on any terms the regulator considers appropriate". The Act does not specify the legal framework for FTs or the standards to which they must adhere.

Reform – the impact of the Health and Social Care Act 2012

23   The Health and Social Care Act 2012 (HSCA) received royal assent in 2012. The legislation makes vast changes to the structure and regulation of the NHS.

24   In particular, the legislation has created a number of new healthcare bodies. They have been formed to improve efficiency within the healthcare sector and generally improve healthcare service outcomes for patients. Consequently, under sections 33 and 34 of the HSCA, from 1 April 2013 PCTs and SHAs shall be abolished. Some of the new healthcare bodies introduced under the HSCA include the NHS Commissioning Board and Clinical Commissioning Groups, which are responsible for the commissioning and delivery of medical and healthcare services.

25   Another such change is the role of Monitor. Under the legislation Monitor becomes the healthcare sector regulator for the entire NHS, an extension of its existing role as the independent regulator for FTs only. Section 62 of the HSCA defines Monitor's main duty to be:

> *... to protect and promote the interests of people who use health care services by promoting the provision of services which is economic, efficient and effective, and maintains or improves the quality of services.*

26   Section 61(b) also states that Monitor will continue to be the independent regulator of FTs.

27   One important change that will be introduced regarding regulation is the requirement of a licence for providers of NHS services (section of the 81 HSCA). The licence will set out a range of conditions that providers must meet and is the key tool that Monitor will use to ensure that FTs, as well as other NHS service providers, are carrying out their functions to the requisite standard.

28   Monitor will develop a version of the licence for FTs that contains extra conditions relating to governance so that Monitor can continue to carry out its oversight role. It is important to note that the licence will replace the current Terms of Authorisation for FTs as previously detailed in this section at paragraphs 13 to 20.

29   With regard to the current status of these reforms, Monitor is in the process of drafting the first set of standard conditions which will be used in the licensing framework. The Department of Health has issued a consultation paper entitled *Protecting and Promoting Patients' Interests – Licensing Providers for NHS Services,* which solicits views on the parameters of the proposed licensing framework. Responses to the consultation were due by 22 October 2012.

30   Monitor and the Department of Health are working to enable Monitor to bring the new licensing regime into force for FTs from April 2013 and for other providers of NHS services from April 2014. The new licensing regime will replace Monitor's current Compliance Framework as detailed previously in paragraphs 8 and 9.

31   Overall, the potential effect of the reforms on the regulation and governance of FTs may not be hugely different from the current regulation as specifically performed by Monitor; Monitor will continue to regulate FTs in the same way as before. However, the full extent and detail of the conditions that will be used in the new licensing regime for FTs are not known at this time and their effect will have to be carefully considered.

32   With regard to the NHS Constitution, the reforms do not place a legal duty on any NHS service provider, including FTs, that makes the NHS Constitution obligatory. Indeed, section 3(1) of the HSCA has the effect of inserting the wording below into section 1A of the National Health Service Act 2006, "In exercising functions in relation to the health service, the Secretary of State must have regard to the NHS Constitution."

33   Once again, the language used relating to the NHS Constitution is to "have regard to," which reaffirms the viewpoint that there is no binding legal obligation to follow the NHS Constitution.

Conclusion

34 From a review of the legislative framework around FTs, it is clear that FTs are not legally bound by the NHS Constitution but only have a legal duty to consider the NHS Constitution. However, as this also appears to be the case for other NHS organisations, this is perhaps not surprising. Further, FTs are not legally bound by the national standards set out in the NHS Operating Framework. Rather, FTs are required to adhere to the current standards and targets set by Monitor under their Compliance Framework, and to the terms of any commissioning contracts with PCTs and terms of registration with the CQC. In the future, the standards and targets will be set out in the licensing regime also under the regulation and oversight of Monitor.

35 Currently, FTs can still be brought to account when failing to meet standards, by virtue of their contractual relationship with the commissioners. Under FTs' Terms of Authorisation and Monitor's Compliance Framework, FTs are required to comply with the terms of their contracts with commissioning bodies. Arguably, the commissioning contracts should be designed with the national priorities and the NHS Constitution in mind; indeed PCTs, as commissioning bodies, have to "have regard" to the NHS Constitution and "take account" of the NHS Operating Framework when carrying out their duties. Therefore, these contracts will act as a legal lever to enforce these standards against FTs.

36 As previously stated, the introduction of the HSCA will make considerable changes to the commissioning structure and delivery of healthcare and medical services. However, the key point to note is that the new commissioning bodies as well as the other healthcare bodies introduced by the HSCA must still "have regard" to the NHS Constitution. This is stated in sections 2(1) and (2) of the Health Act 2009, as amended by the HSCA. Therefore, the new regime under the HSCA will not implement or enforce any stricter interpretation or level of compliance with the NHS Constitution than the previous regime.

Comparison against the *Health Service Journal* article

37 Referring back to the HSJ's article upon which this paper was based (which appears Appendix 1 to this section), there appears to be some misunderstanding within the article as to the issue at hand.

38 Paragraph 1 of the article states that there is a "potential loophole that could allow foundation trusts to escape the patient guarantees laid out in the NHS constitution". Further, at paragraph it states: "According to the [Monitor's] minutes: 'Whilst foundation trusts were required to 'have regard' to the constitution in their decision making, a decision not to adhere to it would not necessarily mean a breach of their terms authorisation.'"

39   It is correct that failing to adhere to the NHS Constitution would not render FTs in breach of their Terms of Authorisation. However, the article does not address the fact that all NHS bodies are only required to "have regard" to the NHS Constitution. It is not the case that "FTs escape the patient guarantees" that others are subject to. If paragraph 2 of the article is correct in that the Prime Minister did give an "assurance that trusts would continue to be held to the NHS constitution" then this assurance was misplaced.

40   The final paragraph of the article raises a concern that "although boards would find it difficult to disregard the constitution, economic pressure could result in 'slippage' against its provisions". This may indeed be a concern, but one that applies to other NHS bodies, and not just FTs.

Appendix 1 to the paper "Are FTs legally bound by the NHS Constitution?"

Health Service Journal (HSJ)

2 November 2011, Wednesday

LENGTH: 356 words

HEADLINE: Monitor examines FTs' patient guarantees loophole

BODY:

Monitor has revealed it is examining a potential loophole that could allow foundation trusts to escape the patient guarantees laid out in the NHS constitution.

The loophole has the potential to undermine the prime minister's assurance that trusts would continue to be held to the NHS constitution, including waiting times pledges, which he gave after the NHS Future Forum reported in June.

The regulator's board minutes revealed that directors considered "the ethical approach to decision making expected from the boards of foundation trusts, particularly regarding their duties in respect of the NHS constitution".

According to the minutes: "Whilst foundation trusts were required to 'have regard' to the constitution in their decision making, a decision not to adhere to it would not necessarily mean a breach of their terms of authorisation."

They added the issue would become "increasingly important" as trusts faced a harsher operating environment.

The meeting decided further work was required, to help Monitor make a "clear decision on the lines of accountability in such cases".

The Foundation Trust Network said the annual operating framework set out how trusts should observe the constitution.

A spokeswoman said: "Not complying with the operating framework might be a breach of the terms of authorisation, but might not be. So Monitor is right to look at this on a case by case basis. I doubt any foundation trust would deliberately set out to ignore the provisions of the constitution."

An acute foundation trust chief executive said the 18 week deadline within which patients had to start consultant-led treatment could be affected. "We are seeing primary care trusts really squeeze trusts on the amount they will spend on elective care – in effect putting a cap on it – which will inevitably result in 18 week breaches," he said.

Another acute trust chief executive added that although boards would find it difficult to disregard the constitution, economic pressures could result in "slippage" against its provisions. "If reflected in commissioner contracts [any slippage could] be addressed through the contractual process," he said.

LOAD-DATE: November 2, 2011

Annex L
Care Quality Commission report comparison table

This table is a comparison of the key points arising from the recent Department of Health (DH) Performance and capability review of the Care Quality Commission (CQC)[1] against the evidence given to the Inquiry.

Both witness statements and transcripts have been used from: Cynthia Bower, Dame Jo Williams, Amanda Sherlock, Amanda Pollard and Kay Sheldon.

Largely, the evidence that the Inquiry received agrees with the DH findings from the review. Where there are gaps, these relate in general to the relationship between the DH and the CQC, and the future of the CQC. The evidence given to the Inquiry gave limited detail on these points.

Comparison of findings from the DH's Performance and Capability Review of the CQC against the evidence given to the Inquiry

Key points from the DH review	Evidence to the Inquiry
Page 5, paragraph 7 – CQC has faced operational and strategic difficulties, as previously documented.	Reflected in evidence of: • Kay Sheldon WS paras 1, 7, 12, 36 • Cynthia Bower T87.6 • Amanda Sherlock T85.46
Page 5, paragraph 7 – Both the Department and CQC underestimated the scale of the task establishing a new regulator	Reflected in evidence of: • Kay Sheldon WS paras 7, 8 • Dame Jo Williams T84.98–104
Page 6, paragraph 9 , bullet 1 – Current limitations in strategic direction can make CQC too responsive to events and lead to uncertainty both within CQC and externally about its role in the wider health and care system	Reflected in evidence of: • Kay Sheldon WS paras 62, 74 • Amanda Pollard WS paras 57, 92, 93 • Dame Jo Williams WS para 49 • Amanda Sherlock T85.82
Page 17, paragraph 2.19, bullet 2 – Accountabilities are unclear. There is a blurring of the boundary between the Board and the executive team	Reflected in evidence of: • Kay Sheldon WS paras 13, 23, 25, 27, 32

---

1   Department of Health, 23 February 2012, *Performance and Capability Review: Care Quality Commission*, www.dh.gov.uk/prod_consum_dh/groups/dh_digitalassets/@dh/@en/documents/digitalasset/dh_132791.pdf

Key points from the DH review	Evidence to the Inquiry
Page 22, paragraph 3.15 – The Board raised concerns that while data was available it was difficult to contextualise. Management information systems are improving but are still not strong enough to inform strategic decisions	Reflected in evidence of: • Kay Sheldon WS para 75
Page 23, paragraph 3.17 – The early years of transition have been a challenging time for the CQC Board and the executive team, but there are signs of stability	Not entirely consistent with evidence: • Kay Sheldon WS para 35: "lack of clarity around the role of the Board still persists. We have recently had two Board development days and, as a result ... but there is still little understanding and/or acknowledgement around our role on the Board"
Page 23, paragraph 3.18 – The CQC leadership has been more visible and is demonstrating greater confidence. The Board has begun to move from a position of supporting the executive team to one of being more challenging	Evidence of Kay Sheldon WS para 27: • "There has always been a pressure for us to agree and support everything the executive does. Dame Jo Williams' overriding view is that the Board should be supportive and encouraging of the executive as much a possible and that the executive are working in a very stressful and difficult environment."
Page 23, paragraph 3.18 – Board members have more recently been involved in setting strategy	Evidence of Kay Sheldon WS para 67: • "My concerns about the proposed changes [to the current regulatory model] are that they have not been appropriately considered in a clear strategic context. The Board did not receive full and necessary information to support the proposed changes and potential implications. In my view we should have had a full discussion about the strategic context and directions."
Page 23, paragraph 3.19 – The relationship with the Department is generally effective, with regular contacts at working level and regular exchange of information	Reflected in evidence of: • Dame Jo Willams WS para 55 • Amanda Sherlock WS para 94 • Cyntha Bower WS paras 86–87
Page 24, paragraph 3.22 – ...Relationships on the CQC Board have become fractured	Reflected in evidence of: • Kay Sheldon WS paras 77, 78, 85
Page 24, paragraph 3.25 – More work is needed to enable members of the Board to carry out their roles effectively and operate more clearly as a team, including recognising issues of equality and diversity	Reflected in evidence of: • Kay Sheldon WS paras 83, 84, 86, 87
Page 25, paragraph 3.28 – However, no one the Panel met advocated for a complete reorganisation	No evidence to the Inquiry
Page 25, paragraph 3.31 – Similarly, staff morale following transition is improving	Reflected in evidence of: • Kay Sheldon WS paras 36, 38, 40 • Amanda Pollard WS paras 25, 28 • Dame Jo Williams WS para 59 • Cynthia Bower WS para 105
Page 25–25, paragraph 3.32 – The responsibilities of CQC are not always understood. Many provider organisations that the review panel met, although sympathetic to the scale of the CQC task, expressed discontent about CQC's record on engagement. For example, they indicated that key decisions on fees and role in quality improvement had not been sufficiently well explained	Reflected in evidence of: • Amanda Sherlock WS paras 83, 85
Page 26, paragraph 3.36 – On a specific point, concerns have been raised about how far the former Mental Health Act Commission functions have integrated	Reflected in evidence of: • Kay Sheldon WS para 76

Key points from the DH review	Evidence to the Inquiry
Page 27, paragraph 3.41 – More practically there remains risks that registration is seen as purely an administrative exercise both by CQC and by providers	Not supported in evidence of: • Amanda Pollard WS para 22 • Amanda Sherlock WS paras 29, 50 • Cynthia Bower T87.20
Page 28, paragraph – 3.42 Similarly, feedback from providers and the frontline indicates that increasing numbers of inspections may not be the more effective way of minimising risks	Reflected in evidence of: • Amanda Sherlock WS paras 44, 145
Page 30, paragraph 3.53 – As with other regulators, ensuring consistency in decision making across different sectors and locations remains a continuing tension for CQC	Reflected in evidence of: • Amanda Pollard WS para 70 • Dame Jo Williams T84.126 Not reflected in evidence of: • Cynthia Bower T87.32 • Amanda Sherlock T85.122
Page 30, paragraph 3.55 – A key finding of the Health Select committee and NAO reports was that growing inspector caseloads should be addressed	Concerns as to caseload reflected in evidence of: • Amanda Pollard WS paras 50, 54 • Cynthia Bower T87.4
Page 30, paragraph 3.56 – On a related point, there is more training in place for inspectors and ongoing support	Concerns as to training in evidence of: • Kay Sheldon WS paras 36, 56 • Amanda Pollard WS paras 31, 43, 62, 67 Evidence of more training and support: • Amanda Sherlock WS paras 155, 156, 161, 170, 217 • Dame Jo Williams T84.161 • Cynthia Bower T87.27, WS paras 28, 151, 152

Annex M
Example of National Institute for Health and Clinical Excellence (NICE) Quality Standard

National Institute for Health and Clinical Excellence (NICE) published a quality standard for the treatment of dementia in 2010. This consists of 10 quality statements. The first concerns appropriately trained staff:

People with dementia receive care from staff appropriately trained in dementia care.

This is accompanied by a quality measure:

Structure: Evidence of local arrangements to provide and maintain up to date dementia training for staff.

The measure required is of the proportion of staff working with people with dementia who have dementia care training.

The method of measuring this is contained in a NICE guideline for audit support (NICE CG42 criterion 9), first issued in November 2006 and updated in October 2012:

Criterion no.	Criterion	Exceptions	Definition of terms and/ or general guideline	Data source
9	Dementia-care training is available for all staff working with older people in the health, social care and voluntary sectors, appropriate to their different roles and responsibilities. *(Primary and acute health care, voluntary care services and social care services)*	None	A range of training should be offered from short information courses to in-depth professional training. Subjects covered should include: • training in the use of the NICE dementia guideline • the early signs of symptoms of dementia, and it major subtypes • progression/prognosis of dementia and consequences for the person with dementia their carers, family and their social network • applying the principles of patient-centred care • the importance and use of communication skills for working with people with dementia and their carers • assessment and pharmacological treatment of dementia. This criterion would be useful for providing evidence for the Quality Standard on Dementia, statement 1: appropriately trained staff.	Published training programme available to staff through paper or electronic circulation. Audit of training records for a range of staff working with older people to demonstrate attendance at training courses appropriate to their role and responsibilities for care. This may be included in the electronic staff record register of training.

It will be noted that this measure suggests that appropriate training should be available for *all* staff working with older people in the health sector, not limited to those with dementia. It does not require all staff treating dementia patients to have undergone such training, or suggest a proportion of the staff who should have done. The standard itself is similarly broad: a requirement that patients receive care does not in itself require all care to be given by such staff.

Some quality standards are more demanding. Quality statement 4 requires:

> *People with dementia have an assessment and an ongoing personalised care plan, agreed across health and social care, that identifies a named care coordinator and addresses their individual needs.*

The quality measure is:

> *Evidence of local arrangements to ensure services are tailored to an individual's needs.*

Two processes are described for auditing this measure:

Proportion of people with dementia whose individual needs are assessed and whose care plan states how those needs will be addressed.

Proportion of people with a named health or social care coordinator.

The tools offered for this are:

NICE CG42 criterion 6:

Criterion no.	Criterion	Exceptions	Definition of terms and/ or general guideline	Data source
6	Percentage of people with dementia who are service users with a documented combined care plan where there is evidence that: • the care plan has been agreed and, as appropriate, reviewed at an agreed frequency, to take account of any changing needs for the person with dementia or their carers • there is a named health and/ or social care worker assigned to operate the plan • the care plan has been endorsed by the person with dementia and/or their carers. *(Primary health care and social care services)*	None	Combined care plans should cover: • activities of daily life (ADLs) and the current level of ability of the person with dementia • advice given about ADLs, including toileting skills • environmental modifications to aid independent living • physical exercise • structured group cognitive stimulation programme • pharmacological interventions • assessment and monitoring for depression and/or anxiety. The care plan should be agreed between care providers and with the person with dementia and their carer, as appropriate. This criterion could be useful for providing evidence for the Quality Standard on Dementia, statement 4: assessment and personalised care plan. (Standard = 100%)	Results of regular audits of a sample of combined care plans in operation across the local dementia services provided by health and social care agencies.

This measure appears to require 100% compliance

The Royal College of Psychiatrists National Audit section 2 contains a long list of requirements to be included in the case notes of patients with dementia [see Figure 1]. The audit has been demonstrated in the first national report to be effective in that it showed a significant and concerning disconnect between hospital policies and practice:

Annex M Example of National Institute for Health and Clinical Excellence (NICE) Quality Standard **1771**

Figure 1: Requirements to be included in the case notes of people with dementia

Information collected at hospital level around multidisciplinary assessment for people with dementia shows that:

- *84% of hospital assessment guidelines/procedures included assessment of functioning (this includes basic activities of daily living, instrumental activities of daily living, activity/ exercise status, gait and balance). However, only 26% of casenotes showed that an assessment of functioning had been carried out.*
- *96% of hospital assessment procedures included assessment of nutritional status. However, only 70% of casenotes showed that an assessment of nutritional status had been carried out.*
- *75% of hospital assessment procedures included assessment of mental state. However, only 43% of casenotes showed that a standardised mental status test had been carried out.*
- *96% of hospital assessment procedures included social assessment and 91% reported that assessment includes environmental assessment. However, 72% of casenotes showed a formal care provision assessment, and 65% of casenotes showed a home safety assessment had been carried out.*
- *13% of casenotes showed no formal pressure sore risk assessment.*
- *19% of casenotes did not show that the patient was asked about any continence needs as part of the assessment.*
- *24% of casenotes did not show that the patient was asked about the presence of any pain as part of the assessment.*

The findings demonstrate a gap between policy and practice. Adherence to multidisciplinary assessment procedures should be clarified and reinforced.

Report of the National Audit of Dementia Care in General Hospitals 2011 (2011), Royal College of Psychiatrists, Executive summary page 13

www.rcpsych.ac.uk/pdf/NATIONAL%20REPORT%20-%20Full%20Report%201201122.pdf

2	Problem list		1.9	**BGS 2005** Comprehensive Assessment for the Older Frail patient in hospital
2a	Co-morbid conditions	Answer **'N/A'** if it is recorded that there are no co-morbid conditions	1.9	**BGS 2005** Comprehensive Assessment for the Older Frail patient in hospital
2b	Record of current medication for physical condition	Answer **'N/A'** if it is recorded that there are no co-morbid conditions	1.9	**BGS 2005** Comprehensive Assessment for the Older Frail patient in hospital
2c	Record of current medications for mental health conditions	Answer **'N/A'** if it is recorded that no medications were being taken on admission		**GBS 2005** Comprehensive Assessment for the Older Frail patient in hospital
2d	Mobility	Assessment of gait, balance, mobility Answer **'N/A'** if this cannot be assessed for recorded reasons	1.9	**GBS 2005** Comprehensive Assessment for the Older Frail patient in hospital
2e	Nutritional status	Answering **'Yes'** to 2e will prompt question 2e1–2e5		**GBS 2005** Comprehensive Assessment for the Older Frail patient in hospital
2e1 and 2e2		Answer **'Yes'** for recording of weight and height if BMI (body mass index) is recorded Answer **'N/A'** if this cannot be assessed for recorded reasons	1.9	**GBS 2005** Comprehensive Assessment for the Older Frail patient in hospital
2e3	Referral for specialist input	This can be referral to a dietician or to a Speech and Language Therapist if there is difficulty swallowing Answer **'Yes'** if referral has taken place or if it is noted that no referral is needed Answer **'No'** if there is no recorded assessment of whether such a referral is needed	1.9	**GBS 2005** Comprehensive Assessment for the Older Frail patient in hospital
2e4	Identification of help needed with eating and drinking	This could be prompts, assistance or aids required to ensure intake of food and fluids, need for particular foods (eg soft textured or puréed, etc) Answer **'Yes'** if it is noted that help is needed, or if it is noted that no help is needed Answer **'No'** if there is no recorded assessment of whether help is needed	1.9	**NICE/SCIE Clinical Guideline 42 (2006)** Supporting people with dementia and their carers in health and social care
2e5	If identification of help needed with eating/drinking is identified is this recorded in the care or management plan?	This question is only applicable if **'Yes'** is answered to 2e4	1.9	
2f	Management plan for medical condition	This is the management plan for the primary medical condition	1.20	**NICE/SCIE Clinical Guideline 42 (2006)** Supporting people with dementia and their carers in health and social care

2g	Nursing management plan for the dementia or symptoms of dementia or 'confusional state'	This should be the management plan, or elements of the management plan, relating to specific needs arising from dementia or memory problems. It may also be contained within the management plan for the medical condition	**NICE/SCIE Clinical Guideline 42 (2006)** Supporting people with dementia and their carers in health and social care
		This could include ability to take medication without assistance or reminder, ability to make relevant responses to enquiries about progress, ability to indicate pain or distress, notes regarding risk of agitiation or distress, risk of delirium, and other risk factors or needs rleating to the dementia likely to affect care, treatment and outcome	
		These examples are illustrative and not exhaustive	

Annex N
Expenditure of the Mid Staffordshire NHS Foundation Trust Public Inquiry April 2010 to November 2012

Expenditure type	1 April 2010 to 31 March 2011	1 April 2011 to 31 March 2012	1 April 2012 to 30 November 2012
Legal services (Note 4)	£4,592,800	£3,893,950	£558,550
General staffing	£650,550	£856,850	£561,650
Running costs	£104,900	£137,500	£12,550
IT and managed services	£396,750	£390,750	£36,750
Inquiry venue and offices	£249,800	£243,050	–
Communications	£131,700	£121,550	£2,100
Experts and assessors	£49,700	£34,300	£8,550
TOTAL	£6,176,200	£5,677,950	£1,180,150

These are full provisional accounts up to the end of November 2012. Final accounts will be prepared in due course and published on the Inquiry website.

Notes:

1   The financial year runs from 1 April to 31 March.

2   Only expenditure authorised through or on behalf of the Inquiry Secretariat is included in these figures.

3   Figures have been rounded to the nearest £50 and are inclusive of VAT where applicable.

4   Legal services includes costs for the Solicitor to the Inquiry and team, Counsel to the Inquiry and team and those organisations/individuals in receipt of an award for legal costs by the chairman under Section 40 of the Inquiries Act 2005.

5   Other organisations involved in the Inquiry will have costs that are met internally and are not included within the Inquiry's figures.

Annex O
Acronyms and abbreviations

Acronym Explanation

A

A&E	Accident and Emergency Department
ACAS	Advisory, Conciliation and Arbitration Service
ADL	Activities of Daily Life
AHA	Area Health Authority
AHC	Annual Health Check
ALB	Arms Length Body
APS	Approved Practice Setting
AvMA	Action against Medical Accidents

B

BBCSHA	Birmingham and Black Country Strategic Health Authority
BLTPCT	Burntwood, Lichfield and Tamworth Primary Care Trust
BMA	British Medical Association
BMJ	British Medical Journal

C

C. difficile	Clostridium difficile, a serious bacterial infection capable of causing severe gastrointestinal symptoms, frequently acquired in hospital
CCDC	Consultant in Communicable Disease Control
CCG	Clincial Commissioning Group
CCH	Cannock Chase Hospital
CCPCT	Cannock Chase Primary Care Trust
CDU	Clinical Decisions Unit
CEO	Chief Executive Officer
CfHCC	Connecting for Health Coding Clinic
CGG	Clinical Governance Groups
CHAI	Commission for Healthcare, Audit and Inspection
CHC	Community Health Council
CHI	Commission for Health Improvement
CHKS	A provider of comparative information and quality improvement services for healthcare professionals
CHRE	Council or Healthcare Regulatory Excellence (see also PSA)

CIP	Cost Improvement Plan
CNO	Chief Nursing Officer
CNST	Clinical Negligence Scheme for Trusts
CP	Core Participant
CPD	Continuing Professional Development
CQC	Care Quality Commission (from April 2009)
CQUIN	Commissioning for Quality and Innovation
CSCI	Commission for Social Inspection
CURE	Cure the NHS

D

DFI	Dr Foster Intelligence
DFU	Dr Foster Unit
DGH	District General Hospital
DH	Department of Health
DHA	District Health Authority
DNR	Do Not Resusitate

E

EAU	Emergency Assessment Unit
ED	Emergency Department
EGG	Executive Governance Group
ESPCT	East Staffordshire Primary Care Trust
EWTD	European Working Time Directive

F

FT	NHS Foundation Trust

G

GMC	General Medical Committee
GP	General Practitioner
GRE	Glycopeptide Resistant Enterococci

H

HA	Health Authority
HCAI	Healthcare Associated Infection
HCC	Healthcare Commission
HCPC	Health and Care Professions Council
HDD	Historical due diligence
HEE	Health Education England

HES	Hospital Episode Statistics
HPA	Health Protection Agency
HPU	Helath Protection Unit
HQIP	Health Select Committee
HSCA	Health and Social Care Act
HSCIC	Health and Social Care Information Centre
HSE	Health and Safety Executive
HSJ	Health Service Journal
HSMR	Hospital Standardised Mortality Ratio

I

IBP	Integrated Business Plan
ICAS	Independent Complaints Advocacy Services
IHI	Institute of Healthcare Improvement
ICU	Intensive Care Unit

J

JCI	Joint Commission International

K

KPI	Key Performance Indicator

L

LaRS	Local and Regional Services
LETB	Local Education and Training Board
LINk	Local Involvement Networks
LMC	Local Medical Committee
LREC	Local Research Ethics Committee
LTFM	Long Term Financial Model

M

MHAC	Mental Health Act Commission
MCCD	Medical Certificate of Cause of Death
MEE	Medical Education England
MoU	Memorandum of Understanding
MP	Member of Parliament
MRSA	Methicillin-resistant *Staphylococcus aureus*
MSSA	Methicillin-sensitive *Staphylococcus aureus*

N

NALM	National Association of LINks Members
NAO	National Audit Office
NCAS	National Clinical Assessment Service
NCEPOD	National Confidential Enquiry into Patient Outcome and Death
NED	Non-Executive Director
NHS	National Health Service
NHSFT	National Health Service Foundation Trust
NHSIC	NHS Information Centre
NHSLA	NHS Litigation Authority
NHST	NHS Trust
NICE	National Institute for Health and Clinical Excellence (from April 2005)
NIGB	National Information Governance Board
NLC	National Leadership Council
NMC	Nursing and Midwifery Council
NPSA	National Patient Safety Agency
NQB	National Quality Board
NRLS	National Reporting and Learning System
NSF	National Service Framework
NSR	Next Stage Review

O

OHPA	Office of the Health Professions Adjudicator
ONS	Office of National Statistics
ORP	Organsational Risk Profile (HCC)
OSC	Overview and Scrutiny Committee

P

PA	Patients Association
PALS	Patient Advice and Liaison Service
PBC	Practice Based Commissioning
PbR	Payment by Results
PCG	Primary Care Group
PCT	Primary Care Trust
PEAT	Patient Environment Action Team
PEC	Professional Executive Committee
PHLS	Public Health Laboratory Service
PIAG	Patient Information Advisory Group
PMETB	Postgraduate Medical Education and Training Board
POhWER	Advocacy Service provider
PPIF	Public and Patient Involvement Forum

PROMS	Patient Reported Outcome Measures
PSA	The Professional Standards Authority for Health and Social Care (formerly the CHRE)
PSF	Patient Safety Forum
PWC	Price Waterhouse Coopers

Q

QA	Quality Account
QI	Quality Information
QIPP	Quality, Innovation, Productivity and Prevention (A DH programme of work)
QRP	Quality and Risk Profile

R

RCN	Royal College of Nursing
RCP	Royal College of Physicians
RCS	Royal College of Surgeons
RHA	Regional Health Authority
RIDDOR	Reporting of Injuries, Diseases and Dangerous Occurrences Regulations
RIEO	Regional Intelligence and Evidence Officer (CQC)
RO	Responsible Officer
ROCR	Review of Central Returns

S

SaSSHA	Shropshire and Staffordshire SHA
SCTS	Society for Cardiothoracic Surgery
SGH	Stafford General Hospital
SHA	Strategic Health Authority
SHMI	Summary Hospital-Level Mortality Indicator
SMR	Standardised Mortality Rate
SSI	Surgical Site Infection
SSISS	Surgical Site Infection Surveillance Service
SSPCT	South Staffordshire PCT
SUI	Serious Untoward Incident
SWSPCT	South West Staffordhire PCT

T

the Board	The Trust Board
the Hospital	Stafford Hospital
the Inquiry	This inquiry
the Trust	Mid-Staffordshire NHS Foundation Trust, formerly the Mid-Staffordshire NHS Trust